Spanish
DeMYSTiFieD®

14 292

DeMYSTiFieD® Series

Accounting Demystified
Advanced Calculus Demystified
Advanced Physics Demystified
Advanced Statistics Demystified
Algebra Demystified
Alternative Energy Demystified
Anatomy Demystified
asp.net 2.0 Demystified
Astronomy Demystified
Audio Demystified
Biology Demystified
Biotechnology Demystified
Business Calculus Demystified
Business Math Demystified
Business Statistics Demystified
C++ Demystified
Calculus Demystified
Chemistry Demystified
Circuit Analysis Demystified
College Algebra Demystified
Corporate Finance Demystified
Databases Demystified
Data Structures Demystified
Differential Equations Demystified
Digital Electronics Demystified
Earth Science Demystified
Electricity Demystified
Electronics Demystified
Engineering Statistics Demystified
Environmental Science Demystified
Everyday Math Demystified
Fertility Demystified
Financial Planning Demystified
Forensics Demystified
French Demystified
Genetics Demystified
Geometry Demystified
German Demystified
Home Networking Demystified
Investing Demystified
Italian Demystified
Java Demystified
JavaScript Demystified
Lean Six Sigma Demystified
Linear Algebra Demystified

Logic Demystified
Macroeconomics Demystified
Management Accounting Demystified
Math Proofs Demystified
Math Word Problems Demystified
MATLAB® Demystified
Medical Billing and Coding Demystified
Medical Terminology Demystified
Meteorology Demystified
Microbiology Demystified
Microeconomics Demystified
Nanotechnology Demystified
Nurse Management Demystified
OOP Demystified
Options Demystified
Organic Chemistry Demystified
Personal Computing Demystified
Philosophy Demsytified
Pharmacology Demystified
Physics Demystified
Physiology Demystified
Pre-Algebra Demystified
Precalculus Demystified
Probability Demystified
Project Management Demystified
Psychology Demystified
Quality Management Demystified
Quantum Mechanics Demystified
Real Estate Math Demystified
Relativity Demystified
Robotics Demystified
Sales Management Demystified
Signals and Systems Demystified
Six Sigma Demystified
sql Demystified
Statics and Dynamics Demystified
Statistics Demystified
Technical Analysis Demystified
Technical Math Demystified
Trigonometry Demystified
uml Demystified
Visual Basic 2005 Demystified
Visual C# 2005 Demystified
xml Demystified

Spanish
DeMYSTiFieD®

Premium 3rd Edition

Jenny Petrow

New York   Chicago   San Francisco   Athens   London   Madrid
Mexico City   Milan   New Delhi   Singapore   Sydney   Toronto

3 4 5 6 7 8 9   QFR   21 20 19 18

ISBN   978-1-259-83685-5
MHID   1-259-83685-1

e-ISBN   978-1-259-83686-2
e-MHID   1-259-83686-X

Trademarks: McGraw-Hill Education, the McGraw-Hill Education logo, Demystified, and related trade dress are trademarks or registered trademarks of McGraw-Hill Education and/or its affiliates in the United States and other countries and may not be used without written permission. All other trademarks are the property of their respective owners. McGraw-Hill Education is not associated with any product or vendor mentioned in this book.

Maps created by Douglas Norgord, Geographic Techniques.

McGraw-Hill Education products are available at special quantity discounts to use as premiums and sales promotions or for use in corporate training programs. To contact a representative, please visit the Contact Us pages at www.mhprofessional.com.

McGraw-Hill Education Language Lab App
Audio recordings, vocabulary flashcards, and an auto-fill glossary are available to support your study of this book. Go to www.mhlanguagelab.com to access the online version of the application, or to locate links to the mobile app for iOS and Android devices. (Note Internet access is required to access audio via the app). More details about the features of the app are available on the inside front cover.

Contents

Acknowledgments

Thank you, Saskia, for your careful eye, helpful input, and constant cheerleading. Thanks, Gorky, for saving the day with your invaluable comments. Thanks to Adam for feeding me and watching over me, and to Camille, for putting up with me. Final thanks to everyone who offered encouragement and suggestions (there are too many to count), especially Mom, Dad, Eliza, Jonathan, Karen, Juan Manuel, Jeff, and Ellen.

Introduction

Welcome to *Spanish Demystified*. You've probably picked up this book because you're learning Spanish, thinking of learning it, or trying to reawaken some long dormant Spanish skills. Whatever your motivation, this book will present a clear and useful way to learn and practice Spanish.

Learning a language can be one of the most enjoyable and rewarding tasks you will ever undertake. And this is not propaganda from an enthusiastic language teacher. My own Spanish learning experience has taken a non-traditional path and came somewhat late in life. In 1997 I packed up my things and moved to Spain with little more than *hola* and *gracias* under my belt. Since then I have unearthed Central American Spanish and Andean Spanish, Spanish from the Southern Cone and from the Caribbean. I have worked with Guatemalans, Peruvians, Colombians, Bolivians, Dominicans, and Chileans in their native tongue and I continue to discover new subtleties and variations of one of the world's most-spoken languages.

For many, learning a foreign language can be an intimidating undertaking. This book tries to make the task more accessible by starting with the Spanish you already know—and there's more than you think. As the Latino population in the United States continues to grow, many of us hear Spanish every day. Furthermore, Spanish already imbues our own popular culture. Imagine how many sentences you can already make simply by using the *Yo quiero…* construction from the old Taco Bell commercial! Because so many people in the world speak Spanish (more than 400 million), Spanish language media are ubiquitous, even in non-Spanish-speaking countries. Take advantage of the presence of Spanish-language television, newspapers, radio, and magazines to put what you learn to use, and to familiarize yourself with Latin cultures.

As you are learning, it's important to remember that there is no universal Spanish. Every region has its own slang, its own sayings, its own vocabulary—even its own verb conjugations. Spanish usage in Spain and the Americas especially can differ significantly. As such, I have done my best to present what I consider to be a representative Latin American Spanish. You might not learn the local *modismos* (expressions) but you should be understood wherever you go. For instance, while you may hear *guagua*, *camioneta*, or *camión* depending on whether you are in Cuba, Guatemala, or Mexico, the word *autobús* should get you on a bus in any of these countries. And for those of you learning continental (or Iberian) Spanish—don't fret. I have noted the most important differences between the Spanish spoken in Spain and Latin America. In addition, I have presented the Spanish *vosotros* form for all verbs, although you will not be "tested" on it.

I have tried to infuse *Spanish Demystified* with my own love for the language and the excitement I feel every time I speak or hear it. I hope this excitement comes through on the page and motivates you to take what you learn in this book and immerse yourself as much as possible in the world of Spanish.

How to Use This Book

You can use this book in two ways. You can move sequentially, from beginning to end, building up your Spanish knowledge chapter by chapter. Or, you can jump around, using the Table of Contents to pick and choose the grammar points you most need *demystified* for you. This book may be used as a self-study guide or as a complement to a course. Because *Spanish Demystified* uses a grammar-focused approach, it is the perfect companion to a conversation class or language exchange.

Spanish Demystified presents a straightforward approach to Spanish grammar, providing clear explanations of new material, a variety of examples to illustrate that material, and copious opportunities to practice what you learn. In addition to grammar points, you will learn key vocabulary through vocabulary lists and example sentences. The most common words also appear in the glossary in the back of the book. The audio recordings on the companion app will elucidate Spanish pronunciation.

Throughout the text, Spanish words are represented in **bold**. English translations appear in *italics*. For example:

> Spanish speakers in many regions of Latin America, when speaking colloquially, use the word **bien** (*well*) instead of **muy** to say *very*, *really*, or *quite*.

Oftentimes bold will also be used to highlight a particular grammar point. For example:

Use the definite article with days of the week to say *on*.

Celia va a la playa **el** viernes.   *Celia is going to the beach on Friday.*

Tengo clase **los** lunes.   *I have class on Mondays.*

In tables, Spanish words appear in Roman print and English words in italics. For example:

el niño	*little boy*
el chico	*boy*
el hermano	*brother*

Spanish Demystified features two kinds of practice: written and oral. While written practice predominates, it is no more important than oral practice, and I recommend that you read your written exercises, as well as example sentences and vocabulary lists, out loud. A basic pronunciation guide is provided in Chapters 1 and 2 with corresponding audio examples in the companion app. I encourage you to refer back to it when you have doubts about how to say new words. You will notice that English translations are provided for all exercises except the quizzes and tests. Use these when you have doubts about vocabulary, but try not to become dependent on translations, as it will hinder the development of Spanish fluency. The answers to both oral and written practice are provided in the answer key in the back of the book.

Oral practice will follow a number of different patterns. Most oral exercises have audio tracks that refer to tracks in the companion app. Some questions will ask you to change an example sentence according to new material. Others will require you to use the language you have learned to make original sentences about yourself or to complete existing sentences using the cues provided. In some exercises you will listen to the question; for others you will listen to the answer. For oral exercises that do not have audio tracks, you should still say your answers aloud. Here is an example of the type of oral practice you might see:

Talk about what you are going to do in the future by completing the following sentences about yourself using **ir a** + infinitive.

1. Hoy voy a... *Today I am going to . . .*

2. Esta noche... *Tonight . . .*

3. Mañana... *Tomorrow* . . .

4. El año que viene... *Next year* . . .

Written practice is presented in a variety of ways, including fill-in-the-blank, multiple-choice, and original writing exercises. Many written exercises have accompanying audio tracks that you can listen to and check your answers while practicing your listening skills. For fill-in-the-blank written practice that asks you to conjugate verbs, the subject is often provided in parentheses, even though a native speaker may not use the subject when writing or speaking. This is to help you know which verb conjugation to use. Take a look at this example:

Complete the sentences with the correct form of the verb in parentheses.

1. ¿(Tú) _____ esta noche? (salir) *Are you going out tonight?*

2. ¿Cuánto _____ este cuadro? (valer) *How much is this painting worth?*

3. (Yo) _____ la comida al trabajo. (traer) *I bring my lunch to work.*

4. (Yo) no le _____ sal a la sopa. (poner) *I don't put salt in the soup.*

Tables are used to present verb conjugations and new vocabulary. Tables are also used to highlight important information or to make comparisons. For example:

With this type of stem-changing verb, the **o** in the stem changes to **ue** for all forms except for **nosotros** and **vosotros**. Here is an example with the verb **poder** (*to be able to*).

Stem changes	Stem does not change
yo puedo	nosotros podemos
tú puedes	vosotros podéis
él/ella/usted puede	
ellos/ellas/ustedes pueden	

This book is made up of twenty chapters, divided into four parts of five chapters per part. Throughout the book you will be presented with quizzes and tests covering the material you have just learned.

Each chapter ends with a ten-question quiz that reviews the concepts you learned in that chapter. This quiz is *open-book*, but does not include English translations of the questions. You should try to achieve a score of 80 percent on the quiz before moving on to the next chapter.

Each part ends with a twenty-five-question part test. The part tests cover everything from the previous part, but will also build on knowledge you have learned up to that point. These are *closed-book* tests, and you should try to get 75 percent of the questions correct before moving on to the next part.

The book ends with a Final Exam. The Final Exam consists of fifty questions and will cover everything you learned in the book. It is a *closed-book* test. A good score is 75 percent or higher on the final exam.

These quizzes and tests are meant to help you evaluate your progress and manage your own learning. You will find the answers to the quizzes and tests in the answer key in the back of the book.

Language learning is an ongoing and incremental process. This book will serve you best if you do a little bit each day and review what you've learned regularly.

I hope you enjoy learning Spanish as much as I enjoyed *demystifying* it.

¡Buena suerte!   *Good luck!*

Spanish

DeMYSTiFieD®

Part One

Learning
the Basics

chapter 1

Introduction to Spanish

In this chapter you will review the Spanish you already know and learn how to recognize words that are similar in English and Spanish. You will learn the Spanish alphabet and how to pronounce consonants, vowels, and diphthongs.

CHAPTER OBJECTIVES

In this chapter, you will

- Uncover the Spanish you already know
- Learn about cognates
- Review the Spanish alphabet
- Practice pronouncing consonants, vowels, and diphthongs
- Learn about regional pronunciation

The Spanish You Already Know

Starting a new language can be intimidating, even downright scary. Luckily for you, you chose Spanish, a language that has crept into our everyday vocabulary in ways you may not even realize. This means that you not only have a few vocabulary words under your belt, but that you also have a basic idea of Spanish pronunciation. So take advantage of the spoken Spanish language environment around you, on TV or on the radio. Getting your ear accustomed to the sounds of Spanish will quickly improve your pronunciation and comprehension.

Borrowed Words and Place Names

English already uses a variety of Spanish words. You've probably ordered **tacos**, **tortillas**, or **guacamole** in a restaurant, danced **salsa,** or even petted a **Chihuahua** or an **iguana**. If you've traveled to **Los Angeles** or **San Francisco**, then you've surely spoken Spanish just by saying those city names. Finally, if you've swatted a **mosquito**, taken a **siesta**, or broken a **piñata**, then you're already putting your Spanish to use.

English also has a number of words that have their roots in Spanish, but which have been slightly changed as they have become anglicized. For instance, the English word *canyon* comes from the Spanish **cañón**; *hammock* comes from **hamaca**, and *ranch* comes from **rancho**.

Cognates

Spanish and English share a number of cognates, or words that have the same linguistic root and are therefore similar in spelling and meaning. Some cognates in English and Spanish are exactly the same, while others are so similar they are unmistakable. Although they will be pronounced differently in Spanish, you should be able to tell just by looking at cognates what their meanings are. Here are some examples. Can you guess their meaning?

Adjectives	Nouns	Verbs
arrogante	el actor	absorber
especial	el chocolate	adoptar
horrible	el debate	calcular
ideal	el doctor	decidir
liberal	el enigma	evaluar
natural	el error	facilitar

normal	el honor	imaginar
popular	la idea	limitar
radical	el mapa	organizar
sensual	la radio	utilizar

False Cognates.   Much to their embarrassment, some people have learned about false cognates the hard way. False cognates are words that are written similarly in English in Spanish but do not share a similar meaning. One of the most famous in Spanish is the word **embarazada**. It does not mean *embarrassed*, but rather *pregnant*. Here are some false cognates to be aware of:

Spanish Word	English Meaning
actual	*current*
asistir	*to attend*
la carpeta	*file folder*
comer	*to eat*
el compromiso	*commitment, duty*
constipado	*with a cold (as in having a cold)*
embarazada	*pregnant*
la librería	*bookstore*
la ropa	*clothing*
sensible	*sensitive*
el vaso	*drinking glass*

False Cognates in "Spanglish."   Among Spanish-speaking communities living in English-dominant environments, many of these false friends—and others—have been adopted into "Spanglish." This means they are used with the English meanings you would expect, not the ones originally intended in Spanish. For instance, **la carpeta** would be used to say carpet instead of *file folder*. In other cases, Spanish words are invented from their English counterparts. An example of this would be using **vacumear** to say *to vacuum*. (The actual Spanish term is **pasar la aspiradora**.) You may notice this code switching from time to time, especially in colloquial Spanish. So, when you hear someone saying they need to **vacumear la carpeta** instead of **pasar la aspiradora por la moqueta**, remember that while these types of linguistic adaptations and alterations can make it easier for English speakers to understand Spanish conversation, this is not "academic" Spanish and surely wouldn't fly in your Spanish 101 class or in Spanish-speaking countries with little Anglophone influence.

Written Practice 1

Now that you realize you knew more Spanish than you thought you did, try translating the following sentences into English. If there are any words you do not recognize, take a guess using the words you already know as clues.

1. Juan come tacos en un restaurante. _____.

2. El tequila es horrible. _____.

3. El actor es especial. _____.

4. El chocolate es delicioso. _____.

5. Carla y David adoptan a un niño. _____.

6. Emilia organiza la fiesta. _____.

7. Julia está embarazada. _____.

8. Jorge asiste a clase. _____.

The Spanish Alphabet and Pronunciation

Spanish pronunciation is very straightforward. Unlike English, almost everything is spelled as it sounds, and sounds as it is spelled, so once you learn the rules it's a snap!

This section will provide example sounds and words, which you can listen to on the audio CD. Additionally, you will see transliterations of each pronunciation in parentheses. Syllables are separated by hyphens and the syllable in bold is stressed. (For example, pronunciation of the word **famoso** is wrtten **fah-moh-soh**.) Accents and word stress will be covered in the next chapter; however, while you are practicing your pronunciation, keep in mind that when you see an accent mark (´) over a part of a word, it means that you should stress that part of the word.

While pronunciation sections in this book will provide transliterations to help you, transliteration should not act as a substitute for hearing the real thing. The best way to learn Spanish pronunciation is to master the basic sounds of Spanish and then interact with the language as much as possible: by listening to music and downloading lyrics, tuning into Spanish-language television, or conversing with Spanish speakers.

The Spanish Alphabet

Below you will find a complete table of the Spanish alphabet, including all the letters used in everyday Spanish. In older dictionaries, **ch** and **ll** are treated as separate letters, but for the sake of simplicity these have been integrated alphabetically into modern dictionaries. In the past, there have also been debates over whether **w** and **k** are considered true Spanish letters. They are used on a regular basis, however, in "borrowed" words such as **water** (*toilet*) or **kilo** (*kilogram*) and to refer to foreign words or names.

The list includes the letters, their names (just as we say "jay" for the letter *j* or "zee" or "zed" for the letter *z*, letters in Spanish also have names), the sound the letter makes, and an example word. Pronunciation is in parentheses. In the next section we will explore the variation of pronunciation of some of these letters more in depth, but this list can act as a simplified reference as you make your way through the book.

Listen to the letters of the alphabet and repeat the letter after each one. Keep listening and repeating until you can say the alphabet all the way through.

▶ Track 2

The Spanish Alphabet

Letter	Name	Sound	Example
a	a (*ah*)	*ah*	acto (**ahk**-*toh*)
b	be (*beh*)	*b*	bola (**boh**-*lah*)
c	ce (*seh*)	*s* (soft c) before e and i	centro (**sehn**-*troh*)
		k (hard c) everywhere else	campo (**kahm**-*poh*)
ch	che (*cheh*)	*ch*	chico (**chee**-*koh*)
d	de (*deh*)	*d*	dólar (**doh**-*lar*)
e	e (*eh*)	*eh*	evento (eh-**vehn**-*toh*)
f	efe (**eh**-*feh*)	*f*	famoso (fah-**moh**-*soh*)
g	ge (*hheh*)	throaty *h* (soft g) before e and i	gente (**hhehn**-*teh*)
		g (hard g) everywhere else	gol (*gohl*)
h	hache (**ah**-*cheh*)	silent	hola (**oh**-*lah*)
i	i (*ee*)	*ee*	isla (**ees**-*la*)
j	jota (**hho**-*ta*)	throaty *h*	junio (**hhoo**-*nee-oh*)

Letter	Name	Sound	Example
k	ka (*kah*)	*k*	kilo (**kee**-*loh*)
l	ele (**eh**-*leh*)	*l*	lima (**lee**-*mah*)
ll	elle (**eh**-*yeh*)	*y*	llave (**yah**-*veh*)
m	eme (**eh**-*meh*)	*m*	mano (**mah**-*noh*)
n	ene (**eh**-*neh*)	*n*	nota (**noh**-*tah*)
ñ	eñe (**eh**-*nyeh*)	*ny*	niña (**nee**-*nyah*)
o	o (*oh*)	*oh*	olé (*oh*-**leh**)
p	pe (*peh*)	*p*	padre (**pah**-*dreh*)
q	cu (*koo*)	*k*	quinta (**keen**-*tah*)
r	erre (**eh**-*rreh*)	slightly rolled in the middle of a word, rolled at the beginning of a word, after **l**, **n**, or **s**, or when **rr**	toro (**toh**-*roh*) Raquel (*rrah*-**kehl**) carro (**kah**-*rro*)
s	ese (**eh**-*seh*)	*s*	simple (**seem**-*pleh*)
t	te (*teh*)	*t*	taco (**tah**-*koh*)
u	u (*oo*)	*oo*	uva (**oo**-*bah*)
v	ve (*beh*) uve (*oo*-*beh*) (Spain)	soft *b*	vino (**bee**-*noh*)
w	doble v (**doh**-*bleh beh*) uve doble (Spain) (*oo*-*beh* **doh**-*bleh*)	*w*	Walter (**Wahl**-*tehr*)
x	equis (**eh**-*kees*)	*ks*	exacto (*ehk*-**sahk**-*toh*)
y	i griega (*ee gree*-**eh**-*ga*)	*y*	yo (*yoh*)
z	zeta (**seh**-*tah*)	*s*	azul (*ah*-**sool**)

Vowels

Spanish has five vowels: **a**, **e**, **i**, **o**, and **u**. The vowels in Spanish are always pronounced the same, and are never silent or shortened. Some advice: if you learn your vowels well you will sound like less of a "gringo." Listen to the vowels and example words, and repeat what you hear.

▶ **Track 3**

a The vowel **a** (*ah*) sounds similar to *a* in *father.* Practice saying these examples:

gato (**gah**-*toh*)	*cat*
sábado (**sah**-*bah-doh*)	*Saturday*
Panamá (*Pah-nah-***mah**)	*Panama*

e The vowel **e** (*eh*) sounds similar to the *e* in *met.* Remember that the **e** is pronounced even when it falls at the end of a word. Practice saying these examples:

este (**eh**-*steh*)	*this*
tres (*trehs*)	*three*
mente (**mehn**-*teh*)	*mind*

i The vowel **i** sounds like the *ee* in *seek.* Practice saying these examples:

mito (**mee**-*toh*)	*myth*
hilo (**ee**-*loh*)	*thread*
instinto (*een-***steen**-*toh*)	*instinct*

o The vowel **o** (*oh*) sounds like the *o* in *smoke.* Practice saying these examples:

sólo (**soh**-*loh*)	*only*
ropa (**rroh**-*pah*)	*clothing*
cosa (**koh**-*sah*)	*thing*

u The vowel **u** sounds similar to the *oo* in *food* or the *u* in *tune.* Note that **u** does not sound like the *u* in *union.* Hence, the country name **Cuba** (see below) is not pronounced as it is in English. Practice saying these examples:

Cuba (**koo**-*bah*)	*Cuba*
nudo (**noo**-*doh*)	*knot*
uno (**oo**-*noh*)	*one*

After the letter **q**, and in the groupings **gue** and **gui**, the **u** is silent in Spanish. Practice saying these examples:

queso (**keh**-*soh*)	*cheese*
guerra (**gueh**-*rra*)	*war*

The exception to the silent **u** in **gue** and **gui** occurs if the **u** has an umlaut (¨) over it. In this case, the **ü** and the following vowel are both pronounced, creating a diphthong. (See more on diphthongs below.) Practice saying these examples:

vergüenza (*behr-goo***ehn**-*sah*)	*shame*
pingüino (*peen-goo***een**-*oh*)	*penguin*

Oral Practice 1

 Track 4

Practice saying the words in the following list. Focus on the pronunciation of your vowels. Listen to the audio CD to check your pronunciation and word stress.

Spanish Word	Spanish Pronunciation	English Meaning
lata	**lah**-tah	tin can
moto	**moh**-toh	motorcycle
anda	**ahn**-dah	walk
onda	**ohn**-dah	wave
hindú	een-**doo**	Hindu
sangre	**sahn**-greh	blood
modelo	moh-**deh**-loh	model
octubre	ohk-**tuh**-breh	October
intestino	een-tehs-**tee**-noh	intestine

Diphthongs

You will notice that some words have pairs of vowels within the same syllable. These are called diphthongs. A diphthong is made by the combination of two vowels that retain their individual sounds but are treated as one syllable. Therefore, their pronunciation is relatively straightforward. It is important to know about diphthongs now so you can better understand word stress later.

Diphthongs are composed of one weak vowel (**i**, **u**, and sometimes **y**, which behaves like **i** at the end of a word) and one strong vowel (**a**, **e**, or **o**). Unless signaled by an accent (you will learn more about accents later on), the stress falls on the strong vowel. In the case of two weak vowels, the stress falls on the second vowel. Listen to these examples and repeat what you hear:

 Track 5

bueno (*boo**eh**-noh*)	good
aire (**ah**ee-reh*)	air
hoy (**oh**ee*)	today
oiga (**oh**ee-gah*)	listen
pausa (**pah**oo-sah*)	pause
Suiza (*soo**ee**-sah*)	Switzerland
fiel (*fee**ehl***)	faithful
agua (*ah-**goo**ah*)	water

NOTE *In the word* **agua**, *the stress of the word is on the first syllable, which is not the diphthong. The diphthong* **ua** *is represented as* **ooah** *and the* **ah** *sound of the* **a** *predominates because it is the strong vowel.*

Sometimes you will see two strong vowels together. These vowel combinations sound very similar to diphthongs, but are treated as separate syllables. Practice saying these examples:

marea (*mah-**reh**-ah*)	*tide*
feo (**feh**-*oh*)	*ugly*
aorta (*ah-**ohr**-ta*)	*aorta*

Oral Practice 2

 Track 6

Practice saying the words in the list and for each word write down how many syllables it has. It may help you to divide the syllables in each word with vertical lines. Remember, a diphthong counts as one syllable, but two strong vowels together count as two. Listen to each word on the audio CD, and check your answers in the back of the book.

Spanish Word	Number of Syllables	English Meaning
1. museo	_____	*museum*
2. suerte	_____	*luck*
3. nieto	_____	*grandchild*
4. cuidado	_____	*careful*
5. medio	_____	*half*
6. europeo	_____	*European*
7. real	_____	*real; royal*
8. Nicaragua	_____	*Nicaragua*

Consonants

Spanish consonants generally sound similar to their English counterparts, with a few variations and exceptions. For those that stray slightly from English pronunciation, the difference is slight enough that you will still be understood if you can produce something similar, so keep talking!

b and v The letters **b** and **v** are pronounced the same in Spanish, with two variations. At the beginning of a word or after **m** or **n**, both letters sound similar to the English *b* in *belt* or *boy*. Everywhere else, the **b** and **v** are softer, with the lips barely touching. Note that the **v** is never pronounced like the English *v*. Practice saying these examples:

▶ Track 7

Hard b and v
vida (**bee**-*dah*)	*life*
bola (**boh**-*lah*)	*ball*
ambos (**ahm**-*bohs*)	*both*

Soft b and v
saber (*sah*-**behr**)	*to know*
nave (**nah**-*beh*)	*ship*

c In Spanish, as in English, the **c** has a soft sound (*s*), like the *c* in *center* or the *s* in *song*, and a hard sound (*k*), like the *c* in *climate*. In Spanish, the soft **c** occurs in front of the vowels **e** and **i**. The hard **c** occurs everywhere else. Practice saying these examples:

Hard c
clima (**klee**-*mah*)	*climate*
carta (**kahr**-*tah*)	*letter*
vaca (**bah**-*kah*)	*cow*

Soft c
centro (**sehn**-*troh*)	*center*
cima (**see**-*mah*)	*top, summit*
ácido (**ah**-*see-doh*)	*acid, acidic*

Sometimes you will have a hard and soft **c** next to each other. Practice saying these examples:

acción (*ahk-see**ohn***)	*action*
acceder (*ahk-seh-**dehr***)	*to accede*
sección (*sehk-see**ohn***)	*section*

d The letter **d** also has soft and hard variations. At the beginning of a word or after an **n** or **l** it has a harder sound, similar to the English *d* in *dog*. When it falls between vowels or at the end of a word, the sound is much softer, similar to the *th* in the English word *then*, and said with the tongue between the teeth. Practice saying these examples:

Harder d
dolor (*doh-**lohr***)   *pain*
andar (*ahn-**dahr***)   *to walk*

Softer d
adulto (*ah-**dool**-toh*)   *adult*
Madrid (*mah-**dreed***)   *Madrid*

g The letter **g** has a soft sound (*hh*) and a hard sound (*g*). The soft **g** occurs in front of the vowels **e** and **i** and is represented here by *hh*. Note that the soft **g** sound is similar to the English *h*, but is actually a bit throatier, like the *ch* sound in Yiddish words, such as *chutzpah*. The hard **g** occurs everywhere else. The hard **g** sounds like the *g* in *egg* or *go*. Practice saying these examples:

Hard g
gato (***gah**-toh*)   *cat*
gol (***gohl***)   *goal*
guía (***gee**-ah*)   *guide*

Soft g
gente (***hhehn**-teh*)   *people*
ágil (***ah**-hheel*)   *agile*

h The letter **h** is always silent. Always! Practice saying these examples:
hola (***oh**-lah*)   *hello*
huevo (*oo**eh**-boh*)   *egg*

j The Spanish **j** sounds similar to the soft **g** sound, like a throaty *h* in English, and is represented here by the letters *hh*. The **j** is always pronounced the same, no matter where it is placed, even at the end of a word. Practice saying these examples:
caja (***kah**-hhah*)   *box*
jabón (*hhah-**bohn***)   *soap*
reloj (*rreh-**lohh***)   *watch*

ll   While the sound of the ll varies widely from region to region, it is safe to pronounce it similar to the *y* in *yellow.* Practice saying these examples:

amarillo (*ah-mah-**ree**-yoh*)   *yellow*
lluvia (**yoo**-*veeah*)   *rain*
millón (*mee-**yohn***)   *million*

ñ   The ñ sounds like the English *ny,* as in the word *canyon.* Practice saying these examples:

baño (**bah**-*nyoh*)   *bath; bathroom*
año (**ah**-*nyoh*)   *year*
señora (*she-**nyoh**-rah*)   *lady; madam*

q   The letter q is used to make the *k* sounds when followed by **ue** or **ui** (before **a**, **o**, and **u**, the *k* sound is made with the hard **c**.) Practice saying these examples:

pequeño (*peh-**keh**-nyoh*)   *small*
queso (**keh**-*soh*)   *cheese*
tequila (*teh-**kee**-lah*)   *tequila*

NOTE   *The* **qu** *sound we are used to in English is usually made with* **cu** *in Spanish to make words such as* **cuándo** *(when) and* **cuánto** *(how much).*

r   The **r** in Spanish does not sound very similar to any *r* sound in English. At the beginning of a word, after the letters **l**, **n**, or **s**, or when doubled, the **r** is rolled strongly toward the front of the tongue. This sound is represented here with *rr.* When it appears alone in the middle or at the end of a word, it is produced by making a single "turn" of the tongue against the roof of the mouth. To the English speaker, this may sound closer to the *d* in *ladder* than to the English *r* sound. Practice saying these examples:

Strong Roll
rana (**rrah**-*nah*)   *frog*
perro (**peh**-*rroh*)   *dog*
arriba (*ah-**rree**-bah*)   *above, up*

Soft "Turn"
mar (*mahr*)   *sea*
pero (**peh**-*roh*)   *but*
claro (**klah**-*roh*)   *of course*

s and z In Latin-American Spanish, the **s** and **z** are pronounced like the *s* sound in *see* (this varies in Spain). The *z* sound in the English word *zoo* does not exist in Spanish. This hard *s* sound is retained even when **s** or **z** falls at the end of a word. Practice saying these examples:

sol (*sohl*)	*sun*
casas (***kah**-sahs*)	*houses*
zapato (*sah-**pah**-toh*)	*shoe*
diez (*dee**ehs***)	*ten*

x The letter **x** generally sounds like the *ks* sound in *tracks*. However, depending on its origin, it can have an *h* sound, as in México (***meh**-hee-koh*), or an *sh* sound, as in Xela (***sheh**-lah*), a city in Guatemala. Practice saying these examples:

éxito (***eh**-ksee-toh*)	*success*
examen (*eh-**ksah**-mehn*)	*exam*
Ximena (*hee-**meh**-nah*)	*Ximena (woman's name)*

y The letter **y** can behave like a vowel in diphthongs (see diphthongs above) or like a consonant. When behaving like a consonant, the sound is very similar to the **ll** and can range from the *y* in *yes* to the *j* in *joy* depending on the region. In some regions, the sound falls somewhere in between (or nowhere near either)! Using the English *y* sound is generally a safe bet. Practice saying these examples:

yo (*yoh*)	*I*
ayer (*ah-**yehr***)	*yesterday*
playa (***plah**-yah*)	*beach*

Oral Practice 3

 Track 8

Practice saying the words in the list below. Focus on the pronunciation of your consonants and vowels. Listen to the audio CD to check your pronunciation and word stress.

Spanish Word	Spanish Pronunciation	English Meaning
rojo	***rroh**-hhoh*	*red*
hielo	*ee**eh**-loh*	*ice*

cuándo	*koo**ahn**-doh*	*when*
águila	*__ah__-gee-lah*	*eagle*
vocal	*boh-__cal__*	*vowel*
consonante	*con-soh-__nahn__-teh*	*consonant*
zanahoria	*sah-nah-__oh__-reeah*	*carrot*
palabra	*pah-__lah__-brah*	*word*
maquillaje	*mah-kee-__yah__-hheh*	*make-up*
gerente	*hheh-__rehn__-teh*	*manager*

Regional Variations in Pronunciation

The Spanish taught in this book will focus as much as possible on "standard" Latin-American Spanish. Of course, in a Spanish-speaking world that spans three continents and twenty-one countries, not to mention countries with large Spanish-speaking immigrant populations, the idea of "standard" is elusive. Some regional variants in pronunciation stand out, however. For instance, in most of Spain, the **z** and the "soft" **c** are pronounced like the *th* in *thin*. This makes spelling much easier, as the only letter that is pronounced as *s* is the actual letter **s**. Meanwhile, Argentineans and Uruguayans are famous for pronouncing the **ll** and the **y** like the sound made by the letter *s* in the word *pleasure*, or the letter *z* in *azure*. In some regions, such as the Caribbean and southern Spain, Spanish speakers literally **se comen las eses** (*eat their s's*) meaning that they drop the *s* sound in the middle or end of words. Although it may be difficult at first to adjust your ear to the accents of different regions, the differences shouldn't be great enough to impede communication.

QUIZ

Choose the closest approximate English sound for the letter or letters in bold.

1. **a**ves
   A. *th*
   B. *v*
   C. *b*

2. **ll**orar
   A. *y*
   B. *l*
   C. *ny*

3. ba**ñ**o
   A. *y*
   B. *n*
   C. *ny*

4. esto**y**
   A. *ee*
   B. *ye*
   C. *u*

5. lar**g**o
   A. *g*
   B. *j*
   C. *h*

6. **c**ualidad
   A. *qu*
   B. *k*
   C. *g*

7. ba**j**o
   A. *j*
   B. *g*
   C. *h*

8. **hola**

   A. *oh*
   B. *hoh*
   C. *hah*

9. **cuna**

   A. *oo*
   B. *yoo*
   C. *uh*

10. **diez**

   A. *z*
   B. *s*
   C. *b*

chapter 2

Talking About People and Things

In this chapter you will learn about nouns and gender, as well as how to use definite and indefinite articles. You will continue to practice your pronunciation by applying the basic rules of word stress. Finally, you will learn how to sound more "native" by using diminutives.

CHAPTER OBJECTIVES

In this chapter you will learn

- Nouns and gender
- Definite and indefinite articles and when to use them
- How to sound more fluent with the diminutive
- Rules for word stress

Nouns and Gender

In Spanish, all nouns (people, places, and things) are classified as either masculine or feminine. This does not necessarily mean that all masculine nouns are more "manly" or that all feminine nouns are more "womanly." Rather, the use of gender comes from the Latin word *genus*, which means *kind*. As such, the use of gender classifies words by kind: either masculine or feminine.

Nouns Referring to People

That said, nouns that refer to people generally do reflect their genders: *father* and *brother* are masculine; *mother* and *sister* are feminine. The same is true for animals. The gender of these types of words is easy to guess. Here are some examples:

Masculine		**Feminine**	
el niño	*little boy*	la niña	*little girl*
el chico	*boy*	la chica	*girl*
el hermano	*brother*	la hermana	*sister*
el padre	*father*	la madre	*mother*
el hijo	*son*	la hija	*daughter*
el nieto	*grandson*	la nieta	*granddaughter*
el primo	*cousin (male)*	la prima	*cousin (female)*
el abuelo	*grandfather*	la abuela	*grandmother*
el amigo	*friend (male)*	la amiga	*friend (female)*
el tío	*uncle*	la tía	*aunt*
el hombre	*man*	la mujer	*woman*
el sobrino	*nephew*	la sobrina	*niece*
el toro	*bull*	la vaca	*cow*
el perro	*dog*	la perra	*dog (female)*
el gato	*cat*	la gata	*cat (female)*
el chileno	*the Chilean man*	la chilena	*the Chilean woman*

As you have seen above, when talking about people, nouns ending in **-o** are masculine and nouns ending in **-a** are feminine. The **-o** is easily changed to an **-a** to make the masculine noun feminine.

In some cases, masculine nouns referring to people end in a consonant or **-e**. You can make these nouns feminine by adding an **-a** after the consonant, or by changing the **-e** to an **-a**.

Masculine	Feminine	
el autor	la autora	*author*
el profesor	la profesora	*teacher*
el jefe	la jefa	*boss*
el francés	la francesa	*Frenchman; Frenchwoman*
el español	la española	*Spanish man; Spanish woman*

Nouns ending in **-ista** refer to people as well, but can be either masculine or feminine depending on whether the person you are referring to is male or female. Many of these words are easy to use and remember because they are just English words + **-a**. To make these feminine, just change the article from masculine (**un; el**) to feminine (**una; la**). (You will learn more about articles later in this chapter.)

Masculine	Feminine	
el periodista	la periodista	*journalist*
el dentista	la dentista	*dentist*
el artista	la artista	*artist*
el capitalista	la capitalista	*capitalist*

Nouns ending in **-nte** also refer to people and can usually refer to either gender. Many of these words are also easy to remember because they are just English words + **-e**. Spanish speakers often change the **-e** to **-a** when referring to women, but not always.

Masculine	Feminine	
el presidente	la presidenta	*president*
el pariente	la parienta	*relative*
el sirviente	la sirvienta	*servant*

The following words usually keep the suffix **-nte**, even when referring to women.

Masculine	Feminine	
el estudiante	la estudiante	*student*
el cantante	la cantante	*singer*
el amante	la amante	*lover*

Finally, some nouns about people change endings irregularly depending on whether they are masculine or feminine.

Masculine		Feminine	
el actor	*actor*	la actriz	*actress*
el rey	*king*	la reina	*queen*

Nouns Ending in -*a* and -*o*

As you have seen above, when referring to people, as a general rule, nouns ending in **-o** are masculine, and almost all nouns ending in **-a** are feminine. This is often true when talking about things as well. Here are some examples:

Masculine		Feminine	
el libro	*book*	la casa	*house*
el museo	*museum*	la mesa	*table*
el trabajo	*work*	la playa	*beach*
el carro	*car*	la escuela	*school*
el dedo	*finger*	la cocina	*kitchen*
el cuarto	*room*	la fruta	*fruit*

Exceptions to the -a/-o Rule. Of course there are some exceptions to the **-a/-o** rule. For instance, some masculine nouns end in -a. Many of these, but not all, come from Greek roots and have the suffix **-ama**, **-ema**, **-ima**, or **-ista**. Some of the feminine nouns ending in -o are actually shortened versions of longer words, such as **moto/motocicleta** (*motorcycle*), or **disco/discoteca** (*discotheque*).

Masculine		Feminine	
el tema	*theme*	la mano	*hand*
el mapa	*map*	la disco	*disco*
el día	*day*	la foto	*photo*
el programa	*program*	la moto	*motorcycle*
el planeta	*planet*		
el sofá	*sofa*		
el idioma	*language*		
el problema	*problem*		

More Rules for Feminine Nouns

Words ending in **-tad**, **-dad**, **-tud**, **-ión**, and **-umbre** are always feminine.

la universidad	*university*	la canción	*song*
la ciudad	*city*	la costumbre	*custom*
la dificultad	*difficulty*	la profesión	*profession*
la virtud	*virtue*	la región	*region*

Nouns Without Rules

Some nouns don't follow any rules. In these cases you just have to use your memory.

Masculine		**Feminine**	
el coche	*car (Spain)*	la piel	*skin*
el parque	*park*	la leche	*milk*
el cine	*cinema/movies*	la clase	*class*
el arte	*art*	la noche	*night*
el viaje	*trip*	la calle	*street*
el pie	*foot*	la pared	*wall*
el café	*coffee*	la flor	*flower*
el postre	*dessert*	la miel	*honey*
el país	*country*	la sal	*salt*

Nouns with Two Genders

Some nouns change meaning according to gender. Here are some examples:

Masculine		**Feminine**	
el cura	*priest*	la cura	*cure*
el capital	*capital (money)*	la capital	*capital (city)*
el coma	*coma*	la coma	*comma*
el corte	*cut*	la corte	*court*
el final	*end*	la final	*sports final*
el policía	*police officer (male)*	la policía	*police department*

Written Practice 1

Write *m* for *masculine* or *f* for *feminine* for the following nouns. Use the word lists, the rules you've learned, and your own common sense to help you.

1. _____ pueblo   *town*
2. _____ muchacha   *girl*
3. _____ sala   *room*
4. _____ televisión   *television*
5. _____ caballo   *horse*
6. _____ muchedumbre   *crowd*
7. _____ clima   *climate*
8. _____ actitud   *attitude*
9. _____ cura   *priest*
10. _____ pan   *bread*
11. _____ novio   *boyfriend*
12. _____ gerente   *manager*
13. _____ alemana   *German*
14. _____ sal   *salt*
15. _____ drama   *drama*
16. _____ misión   *mission*
17. _____ maldad   *evil*
18. _____ monja   *nun*
19. _____ papa   *the pope*
20. _____ papa   *potato*

Definite and Indefinite Articles

In Spanish, definite and indefinite articles (*the, a, an,* and *some*) indicate both the gender of the noun (masculine or feminine) as well as the number (singular or plural).

Definite Articles

	Masculine	Feminine	
Singular	el	la	*the*
Plural	los	las	*the*

The articles **el** (singular) and **los** (plural) are used before masculine nouns to say *the*. The articles **la** (singular) and **las** (plural) are used before feminine nouns to say *the*.

El carro es azul.   *The car is blue.*
Las manzanas son deliciosas.   *The apples are delicious.*

Indefinite Articles

	Masculine	Feminine	
Singular	un	una	*a*
Plural	unos	unas	*some*

The article **un** is used before masculine nouns to say *a*. The article **una** is used before feminine nouns to say *a*. The article **unos** is used before plural masculine nouns to say *some*. The article **unas** is used before plural feminine nouns to say *some*.

Argentina es **un** país hermoso.	*Argentina is a beautiful country.*
Quiero **unas** cervezas frías.	*I want some cold beers.*

There are some feminine nouns that begin with the **a** sound that use the masculine article in the singular form, and the feminine in the plural. This is done to avoid the awkward sound of **a** and **a** together.

el águila	las águilas	un águila	unas águilas	*eagle(s)*
el arma	las armas	un arma	unas armas	*firearm(s)*
el agua	las aguas	un agua	unas aguas	*water(s)*
el hacha	las hachas	un hacha	las hachas	*hatchet(s)*

Written Practice 2

Rewrite the following sentences replacing the indefinite articles with definite articles and the definite articles with indefinite articles.

1. María tiene el perro. _____.

   María has the dog. María has a dog.

2. David quiere unos mapas. _____.

   David wants some maps. David wants the maps.

3. El libro está encima de la televisión. _____.

   The book is on top of the television. A book is on top of a television.

4. La vaca da leche. _____.

   The cow gives milk. A cow gives milk.

5. Unos hombres están en la cocina. _____.

Some men are in the kitchen. The men are in a kitchen.

6. Gonzalo vive en una ciudad. _____.

Gonzalo lives in a city. Gonzalo lives in the city.

7. Marta bebe una botella de agua. _____.

Marta drinks a bottle of water. Marta drinks the bottle of water.

8. Marco es el fundador de la empresa. _____.

Marco is the founder of the company. Marco is a founder of a company.

Use of Indefinite Articles

Spanish has various rules about when to use, and when not to use, indefinite articles. The indefinite articles (**un**, **unos**, **una**, **unas**) can generally be used when you want to say *a* or *some*. The exception to this rule is with professions. First, let's see a list of professions.

Professions

abogado/-a	*lawyer*	juez	*judge*
actor, actriz	*actor, actress*	mecánico/-a	*mechanic*
camarero/-a	*server*	músico/-a	*musician*
dentista	*dentist (m. or f.)*	policía	*police officer (m. or f.)*
doctor(a)	*doctor*	profesor(a)	*teacher*
médico/-a	*doctor*	maestro/-a	*teacher*
estudiante	*student (m. or f.)*	psicólogo/-a	*psychologist*
enfermero/-a	*nurse*	trabajador(a) social	*social worker*

When talking generally about people's professions, the article is omitted. Here are some examples:

Estela es **abogada**.	*Estela is a lawyer.*
Enrique es **músico**.	*Enrique is a musician.*

But, when discussion of professions gets more specific and the profession is modified by an adjective or phrase, the indefinite article is used.

Estela es **una buena abogada**.	*Estela is a good lawyer.*
Enrique es **un músico que trabaja mucho**.	*Enrique is a musician who works a lot.*

Written Practice 3

 Track 9

Complete the following sentences with **un, unos, una, unas,** or nothing, when appropriate. Refer to the rules you learned about gender to help you.

1. Charo es _____ mujer. *Charo is a woman.*
2. Miguelito es _____ niño. *Miguelito is a boy.*
3. Guatemala es _____ país diverso. *Guatemala is a diverse country.*
4. El chino es _____ idioma difícil. *Chinese is a difficult language.*
5. Hay _____ carros en la calle. *There are some cars in the street.*
6. Veo _____ personas enojadas. *I see some angry people.*
7. Ella vive en _____ ciudad grande. *She lives in a big city.*
8. Miguel es _____ buen profesor. *Miguel is a good teacher.*
9. Josué es _____ enfermero. *Josué is a nurse.*
10. Dame _____ mano. *Give me a (your) hand.*

Use of Definite Articles

The rules for when to use or not use the definite article (**el, los, la, las**) are more complicated. In general, the definite article can be used whenever we say *the* in English. However, sometimes the definite article is used in Spanish when we *don't* say *the* in English. Take a look at the following rules.

With Generic or Abstract Nouns

Use the definite article when speaking generally or abstractly about a noun. This rule trumps all others!

El amor es lindo.	*Love is beautiful.*
No me gusta **la carne**.	*I don't like meat.*
Los gatos son muy independientes.	*Cats are very independent.*
El verano es húmedo.	*Summer is humid.*

With Days of the Week

Use the definite article with days of the week to say *on*.

Celia va a la playa **el viernes**.	*Celia is going to the beach on Friday.*
Tengo clase **los lunes**.	*I have class on Mondays.*

With Languages

When talking about languages in a general way, as you have already learned, the definite article is used.

El chino es difícil.	*Chinese is difficult.*

The article is not used after verbs used in relation to languages, such as **hablar** (*to speak*), **saber** (*to know*), and **aprender** (*to learn*) or after the prepositions **en** (*in*), and **de** (*of*). This is similar to English.

Hablo **español**.	*I speak Spanish.*
Sara lee **en español**.	*Sara reads in Spanish.*
Es un libro **de español**.	*It's a Spanish book.*

However, when another verb or an adverb is in the mix, the definite article is used.

Katrina habla **bien el español**.	*Katrina speaks Spanish well.*
Pero **prefiere el portugués**.	*But she prefers Portuguese.*

With Some Countries, Cities, and States

Just as we say *the Ukraine* or *the Philippines* in English, some place names always take the definite article. Unfortunately there is no rule and these have to be memorized. Here are a couple of examples:

el Reino Unido	*the United Kingdom*
La Habana	*Havana*

Otherwise countries, cities, and states do not use the definite article in Spanish. Compare the following sentences.

Vivo **en Argentina**.	*I live in Argentina.*
Begoña viaja **a Nueva York**.	*Begoña travels to New York.*

but

El país de **Gales** está en **el Reino Unido**.	*The country of Wales is in the United Kingdom.*

With Titles

The definite article is used with titles when talking *about* people:

El señor Hernando tiene una llamada.	*Mr. Hernando has a phone call.*

But not when talking *to* them:

«**Señor Hernando**, usted tiene una llamada».	*"Mr. Hernando, you have a phone call."*

With Parts of the Body

The definite article is used with parts of the body and personal possessions when we would ordinarily use possessive pronouns, such as **mi** (*my*) or **su** (*his, her*) in English.

Me lavo **la cara**.	*I wash my face.*
Me como **las uñas**.	*I bite my nails.*

Written Practice 4

 Track 10

Complete the following sentences with **el, los, la, las**, or nothing, where appropriate. Refer to the rules you learned about gender to help you.

1. Manuel es de _____ Habana. *Manuel is from Havana.*

2. ¡_____ fiestas son divertidas! *Parties are fun!*

3. «Buenos días, _____ Doctor Cáceres». *"Good morning, Dr. Cáceres."*

4. _____ doctor Cáceres no está en la oficina. *Dr. Cáceres is not in the office.*

5. _____ clase es difícil. *The class is hard.*

6. Elisa vive en _____ Argentina. *Elisa lives in Argentina.*

7. _____ águila es un ave. *The eagle is a bird.*

8. _____ perros son buenas mascotas. *Dogs are good pets.*

9. Ellos no hablan _____ inglés. *They don't speak English.*

10. Patricia llega _____ lunes. *Patricia arrives on Monday.*

The Plural Form of Nouns

You have learned to recognize the plural form of nouns (people, places, and things) by the articles **los**, **las**, **unos**, and **unas**, and probably noticed that in Spanish, as often occurs in English, the plural forms of nouns end in -s. Here are some rules for making singular nouns plural.

For most nouns ending in a vowel, just add an -s to make it plural.

la casa	las casas	*house, houses*
el gato	los gatos	*cat, cats*
la llave	las llaves	*key, keys*
el espíritu	los espíritus	*spirit, spirits*

The exception to this rule is for nouns ending in a vowel whose last syllable is accented—a very rare case. In this case, add -es to make the plural form. This will add a syllable to the word and the written accent is maintained.

el colibrí	los colibríes	*hummingbird, hummingbirds*
el hindú	los hindúes	*Hindu, Hindus*

For most nouns ending in a consonant, add -es to make the plural form. Notice that for words ending in -ión, the written accent in dropped in the plural. Also note that by adding -es to the end of the word, you also add an extra syllable.

la piel	las pieles	*skin, skins; fur (as in a fur coat); furs*
la ciudad	las ciudades	*city, cities*
la nación	las naciones	*nation, nations*
el país	los países	*country, countries*

However, for nouns ending in **-z**, the plural is made by changing the **-z** to a **-c-** before adding **-es**.

| la voz | las voces | *voice, voices* |
| el lápiz | los lápices | *pencil, pencils* |

Notice that the word for *people*, **la gente**, is always singular, even though it refers to a plural concept.

La gente es simpática.   *The people are nice.*

Written Practice 5

Write the following singular nouns in their plural forms. Remember to make the article plural as well.

1. el árbol _____   7. el arma _____
2. el mes _____   8. una montaña _____
3. una rana _____   9. el pez _____
4. la televisión _____ 10. el huésped _____
5. el maní _____   11. la calle _____
6. el avión _____   12. un mapa _____

Diminutives

Spanish speakers often use words called diminutives, usually formed with the suffix **-ito**, to show fondness or affection, as well as to indicate smallness of size. Think of words like *kitty*, *doggie*, *booties*, or *cutie* in English.

To form the diminutive, drop the last **-a** or **-o** of a noun and add the endings **-ito**, **-ita**, **-itos**, or **-itas**, following the same rules for number and gender as with regular nouns. Note that for nouns ending in **-r**, **-n**, or **-e**, you don't need to drop the last letter, and the suffix **-cito** is generally used. For words that end in **-co** or **-ca**, the -c- changes to a **-qu-**.

un vaso de agua	*a glass of water*	un vasito de agua	*a small glass of water*
un café	*a coffee*	un cafecito	*a little coffee; a coffee*
Paco	*(nickname for Francisco)*	Paquito	*(little Francisco, Frankie)*

Diminutives can be used with nouns, adjectives, and adverbs. Depending on the region you are in, different suffixes may serve the same purpose: **cafecito** (*small coffee*), **cafelito** (*small coffee*), **cafecillo** (*small coffee*), **pequeñino** (*small, young*), **chiquillo** (*little boy*), **amiguete** (*friend*), **ratico** (*a little while*). You will even see diminutives of diminutives, such as **chiquitito** (*tiny*). Keep in mind that using the diminutive can make you sound more "native" in Spanish, but if you use it incorrectly, you could be misunderstood. For instance, in some instances **un amiguete** (from **amigo**) could mean *a male friend*, and in other instances it could refer to a guy with whom you have a romantic attachment.

The diminutive has many uses and connotations. You can use it simply to say something is small, for instance, **gatito** (*kitty*) or **casita** (*little house*). It can add shades of meaning or nuance; for instance, in Latin America you may hear people say **ahorita**, the diminutive of **ahora** (*right now*), to say *in a minute*. The **-ita** implies that *right now* might not be so immediate, but it will happen. **Un momentito** (from **momento**) is also a common way to say *just a moment*. The diminutive can also be added to names or titles to demonstrate familiarity or affection with friends or family, for instance, **papito** (*daddy*), **Miguelito** (*little Michael, Mikey*), or **abuelita** (*granny*). The famous **Evita Perón** got her name from the diminutive of **Eva**. Finally, the diminutive can also be used to diminish the importance of something. A little white lie could be **una mentirita** (from **mentira**); a problem that's not that bad could be **un problemilla**.

Pronunciation: Word Stress

Word stress is a key aspect of Spanish pronunciation, and refers to the syllable in a word that receives the emphasis when you are speaking. For instance, the stress in the English word *Spanish* is on the first syllable: ***Spa****nish*. The stress in the English word *apply* is on the second syllable: *ap****ply***.

The rules for word stress in Spanish are relatively straightforward, but remembering them and applying them effectively can take some time, so be patient. There are three basic guidelines for word stress.

▶ Track 11

1. If the word ends in a vowel, **n**, or **s**, the stress is on the second-to-last syllable. Listen to these examples: *so****bri****na, choco****la****te, ac****to****res, ****bo****tas, ****jo****ven, ****lla****man*. Most words fall into this category.

2. For words that end in a consonant other than **n** or **s,** the stress is on the last syllable. Listen to these examples: *an****dar****, lla****mar****, acti****tud****, fi****nal***.

3. An accent mark is placed over any stressed syllables that do not follow rules 1 and 2 above. Listen to these examples: *águila, avión, médico, francés*.

The only exceptions to rules 1, 2, and 3 are foreign words, which usually do not carry accent marks. For instance, **video** has the stress on the first syllable (remember, **e** and **o** are both strong vowels, so **video** has three syllables, **vi**-de-o).

And speaking of vowels, remember diphthongs from Chapter 1? Sometimes they can make applying the pronunciation rules a little more difficult. Remember that diphthongs count as one syllable, and should be counted as such when you are trying to figure out word stress. Listen to the stress for these words, which all have diphthongs and follow Rule 1.

Word	Stress	Meaning
remedio	re-**me**-dio	*remedy; solution*
agua	**a**-gua	*water*
farmacia	far-**ma**-cia	*pharmacy*

When you see an accent mark over a weak vowel, however, that vowel is stressed as a separate syllable. Listen:

| loteria | lo-te-**rí**-a | *lottery* |
| peluquería | pe-lu-que-**rí**-a | *hairdresser's* |

In these examples, **ía** is not a diphthong as it is in the word **farmacia** above. Here, the syllable -**ri** -is the stressed syllable in the word, dividing the **i** and **a** into two syllables.

Sometimes accents are used not to mark word stress, but rather to distinguish the meanings of words that are otherwise spelled identically, for instance:

el	*the*	él	*he*
si	*if*	sí	*yes*
tu	*your*	tú	*you*
que	*that*	qué	*what*

Oral Practice

 Track 12

Practice saying the following words, placing the stress on the correct syllable. Listen to the audio CD to check your answers. If you're still having trouble, use the Answer Key to see where the stress falls.

1.	joyería	*jewelry store*	11.	viernes	*Friday*
2.	héroe	*hero*	12.	preguntar	*to ask*
3.	llamada	*telephone call*	13.	pantalones	*pants*
4.	ciruela	*plum*	14.	difícil	*difficult*
5.	algodón	*cotton*	15.	ojo	*eye*
6.	almuerzo	*lunch*	16.	lápiz	*pencil*
7.	hígado	*liver*	17.	bolígrafo	*pen*
8.	miércoles	*Wednesday*	18.	pastel	*cake*
9.	alrededor	*around*	19.	cereales	*cereal*
10.	vehículo	*vehicle*	20.	restaurante	*restaurant*

QUIZ

Circle the letter of the word that best completes each sentence.

1. **Son las _____ de la casa.**
   A. llave
   B. llaves
   C. gato
   D. gatos

2. **_____ canciones son lindas.**
   A. El
   B. La
   C. Los
   D. Las

3. **Necesito _____ mapa.**
   A. un
   B. una
   C. unos
   D. unas

4. **No me gustan los _____.**
   A. águilas
   B. programas
   C. aguas
   D. armas

5. **Mercedes Hernando es _____ presidenta de la firma.**
   A. el
   B. los
   C. la
   D. las

6. **Su tío es _____ enfermero.**
   A. un
   B. una
   C. el
   D. —

7. **«Buenos días, _____ señora Brito».**
   A. —
   B. La
   C. El
   D. Una

8. **Hablo _____ español con mis padres.**
   A. —
   B. el
   C. un
   D. es

9. _____ capital de Paraguay es Asunción.

   A. El
   B. La
   C. Un
   D. Una

10. **Pedro es** _____.

    A. artista
    B. profesora
    C. suegra
    D. actriz

chapter 3

Talking About Actions and Possession

In this chapter you will learn about verbs, and how to talk about the present using regular verbs that end in **-ar** and the verb **ser.** You will learn how to ask questions and answer them affirmatively and negatively. You will learn the subject pronouns and how to talk about ownership and relationships using possessive adjectives. Finally, you will learn how to talk about nationalities.

CHAPTER OBJECTIVES

In this chapter you will learn

- Subject pronouns
- About verbs (regular and irregular) and their stems and endings
- How to talk about the present using *-ar* verbs and *ser*
- Countries and nationalities
- How to ask yes/no questions and how to answer them
- Possessive adjectives

Subject Pronouns

Subject pronouns (*I*, *you*, *we*, *they*, etc.) refer to the person or people who are doing the action in a sentence. These pronouns are important for conjugating verbs.

yo	*I*	nosotros/-as	*we*
tú	*you* (singular, informal)	vosotros/-as	*you* (plural, informal)
él	*he*	ellos	*they*
ella	*she*	ellas	*they*
usted	*you* (singular, formal)	ustedes	*you* (plural)

Nosotros and **vosotros** can also be feminine: **nosotras, vosotras**. What do you say when you're speaking to or about a gender-mixed group? As un-politically correct as it may seem, the men have it. Even if there is only one man in the mix, the masculine form (**nosotros, vosotros**) is used.

Tú, Usted, Vos, and Vosotros

Unlike English, Spanish has numerous ways to say *you*. Remember that in Spanish, the pronoun you choose can have wide social repercussions, so choose wisely!

Tú is used in informal situations to address one person. **Tú** is used throughout Spain and Latin America, although it is used more often in Spain with a wider variety of people. In general, it is safe to use **tú** with a relative (especially one younger than you), a friend, or a child. **Usted** is the formal way to say *you* and can be used to address a person you want to show a degree of respect to: someone older than you, a boss, a taxi driver, an official, a police officer, etc. Some social settings in Latin America are extremely formal and the **usted** form is more customary. A third form, **vos**, is used widely in certain regions, including Central America, Argentina, Uruguay, Paraguay, and the Andes. In some regions **vos** is used in addition to **tú,** and in other regions it is used instead of **tú**. Either way, **vos** is a very familiar form that should be reserved for intimate acquaintances. **Vos** will not be taught in this book, but you should be aware of its existence.

Another way that Spanish differs from English is that Spanish has various plural *you* forms. (Sometimes we try to make up for the lack of this possibility in English by saying *you guys*, or *y'all*.) **Ustedes**, the plural of **usted**, is most common in Latin America where it is used exclusively to address two or more people, of either gender, in both formal and informal situations. In writing, **usted** and **ustedes** are often shortened to Ud. and Uds. In Spain, **vosotros/-as**, the plural of **tú**, is used informally to address two or more people. **Vosotros/-as** will be taught, but not tested, in this book.

An Introduction to Verbs

You have probably already noticed some verbs appearing here and there in these lessons. We all know that verbs talk about actions, whether they be tangible actions (walking, sleeping) or more abstract (being). But there are a few things about Spanish verbs that are surprising and challenging for new language learners. First, in English, the infinitive of a verb is always signaled by the word *to*: *to walk, to sleep, to be*, etc. In Spanish, the infinitive of a verb is signaled by its ending: **-ar, -er**, or **-ir**: **andar** (*to walk*), **dormir** (*to sleep*), **ser** (*to be*).

Second, in English we always use the subject pronouns (*I, you, she, we, they,* etc.) to identify which conjugated form the verb takes: *I walk, you walk, she walks*, etc. Furthermore, English has very few conjugations and often uses auxiliary, "helping" verbs to form different tenses. In the future tense, for example, the helping word *will* is used, and the only thing that changes is the subject pronoun: *he will walk, they will walk, we will walk*.

In Spanish, however, conjugating verbs is a much more complex matter. Subject pronouns are almost unnecessary and are often left out. For instance, you can just as easily say **ando** (*I walk*) as **yo ando** (*I walk*). This is because the verb's ending largely tells you to whom the verb is referring: **ando** (*I walk*), **andas** (*you walk*), **andamos** (*we walk*). In addition, the tense or mood (future, past, conditional, etc.) is also indicated through the verb ending, for instance: **ando** (*I walk*), **andaré** (*I will walk*), **anduve** (*I walked*). This means that there are a lot of endings to deal with! Luckily verbs can be grouped according to type, which makes memorizing them easier. What's more, the third-person subject pronouns **él/ella** and **ellos/ellas** are conjugated the same as the second-person subject pronouns **usted/ustedes**, which simplifies things a bit more.

The Verb *Ser*

There are two verbs in Spanish that mean *to be:* **ser** and **estar**. **Ser** is used to express the essence of something or someone, the intrinsic qualities. Think, for example, of a person's gender, nationality, faith, or profession, or an object's characteristics such as classification, color, material, owner, or style. You will learn more about the differences between **ser** and **estar** in Chapter 10.

Ser is an irregular verb, and as such has its own special conjugation that must be memorized. Here is the present tense of **ser**:

Ser: Present Tense

yo soy	*I am*
tú eres	*you are* (singular informal)
él/ella/usted es	*he, she, it is, you are* (singular formal)
nosotros/nosotras somos	*we are*
vosotros/vosotras sois	*you are* (plural informal)
ellos/ellas/ustedes son	*they, you are* (plural)

You have already seen many examples of the present tense of the verb **ser** in this book. Here are a few more:

Verónica **es** venezolana.	*Veronica is Venezuelan.*
Carla y Carlos **son** católicos.	*Carla and Carlos are Catholic.*
Usted **es** bombero.	*You are a firefighter.* (formal)
La casa **es** pequeña.	*The house is small.*
¿Los libros **son** de Juan?	*Are the books Juan's?*

Oral Practice 1

Choose the phrases that best describe you and practice saying them aloud. If you don't see the appropriate identifier to describe you, just pretend, or even better, try to find the word that does.

Soy un hombre/una mujer.	*I'm a man/woman.*
Soy de Estados Unidos/Inglaterra /Gales/Australia/Irlanda.	*I'm from the United States/England/ Wales/Australia/Ireland.*
Soy estudiante/profesor(a)/ médico/-a/camarero/-a.	*I'm a student/teacher/doctor/server.*
Mi casa es pequeña/grande.	*My house is small/big.*
El español es fácil/difícil.	*Spanish is easy/difficult.*

Mis amigos son simpáticos/ extraños/divertidos.	*My friends are nice/strange/fun.*
Tú eres mi amigo/colega/pariente.	*You are my friend/colleague/relative.*
Ustedes son de España/América Latina.	*You are from Spain/Latin America.*

Countries and Nationalities

The verb **ser** is used when describing country of origin and nationality. When talking about place of origin, use **ser** + **de**. Here are some examples. Note that nationalities are not capitalized in Spanish.

Yo soy de Argentina.	*I am from Argentina.*
Soy argentino/argentina.	*I am Argentinean.*
Tú eres de España.	*You are from Spain.*
Eres español/española.	*You are Spanish.*
Ella es de Colombia.	*She is from Colombia.*
Es colombiana.	*She is Colombian.*
Ellos son de Alemania.	*They are from Germany.*
Son alemanes.	*They are German.*
Somos de Francia.	*We are from France.*
Somos franceses/francesas.	*We are French.*

We Are All Americans

When talking about people from the United States, or (**los**) **Estados Unidos**, describing nationality becomes more difficult. The word **americano** refers to all people living in **las Américas**, and therefore all Latin Americans, Mexicans, Canadians, and U.S. citizens. As a result, people may get offended if you say **soy americano** to mean, "I'm from the United States." To solve this problem, some people prefer to use the word **norteamericano** (*North American*), but this creates obvious problems since Canada and Mexico are also part of North America. In Spain, the word **estadounidense** is used, but this term is not familiar to many Latin Americans. So what is the answer? There's no easy one, but for now just stick to: **Soy de (los) Estados Unidos.**

Written Practice 1

 Track 13

Use the clues provided to make pairs of sentences similar to those previously shown. The first one has been done for you as an example.

Yo/Portugal/portuguesa <u>Yo soy de Portugal. Soy portuguesa.</u>

1. Tú/Brasil/brasileña _____.

2. Ella/Canadá/canadiense _____.

3. Ustedes/Japón/japoneses _____.

4. Nosotros/Rusia/rusos _____.

5. Usted/Austria/austriaca _____.

6. Él/Senegal/senegalés _____.

7. Yo/Grecia/griego _____.

Verb Stems and Endings

Spanish has regular and irregular verbs. Regular verbs fall into three categories: verbs ending in **-ar**, **-er**, and **-ir**, for instance, **hablar** (*to speak*), **comer** (*to eat*), and **vivir** (*to live*). For regular verbs, verbs in each category follow the same pattern of conjugation. **Ser** is an irregular verb because it isn't conjugated the same way as any other verb. It doesn't follow a pattern.

Spanish verbs, both regular and irregular, have two parts, the stem and the ending. Look at the stems and endings of these three regular verbs.

Verb	Stem	+	Ending	English Meaning
hablar	habl-	+	-ar	*to speak, talk*
comer	com-	+	-er	*to eat*
vivir	viv-	+	-ir	*to live*

When regular verbs are conjugated, or changed according to their subjects, only the ending changes. The stem stays the same. Here are some examples in the present tense:

yo hablo	*I speak, talk*
tú comes	*you eat*
ellos viven	*they live*

Verbs Ending in -*ar*: Present Tense

Verbs with the infinitive ending in **-ar** are the largest category of regular verbs. The meaning of some of these is quite easy to guess.

necesitar	*to need*	estudiar	*to study*

In order to conjugate **-ar** verbs in the present, simply drop the **-ar** and add the following endings to the stem: **-o, -as, -a, -amos, -áis, -an**. Here's an example with the verb **hablar** (*to speak, talk*):

Subject	Stem	Ending	Present Tense	
yo	habl-	-o	hablo	*I speak*
tú	habl-	-as	hablas	*you speak* (informal)
él/ella/usted	habl-	-a	habla	*he, she, it speaks, you speak* (formal)
nosotros	habl-	-amos	hablamos	*we speak*
vosotros	habl-	-áis	habláis	*you speak* (informal plural)
ellos/ellas /ustedes	habl-	-an	hablan	*they, you speak* (plural)

Remember that because the verb endings indicate who is carrying out the action, the subject pronoun is often omitted. For instance: **Hablo inglés** (*I speak English*).

Now, using the vocabulary you already know and a few **-ar** verbs, you can make an almost unlimited number of sentences—affirmative and negative, as well as questions. Here are some examples:

Yo **estudio** español.	*I study Spanish.*
¿**Estudias** español?	*Do you study Spanish?*
Enrique **trabaja** el lunes.	*Enrique works on Monday.*
Mariana **no canta**.	*Mariana doesn't sing.*

Some Regular Verbs Ending in -*ar*

ayudar	*to help*	estudiar	*to study*	necesitar	*to need*
bailar	*to dance*	ganar	*to win*	olvidar	*to forget*
buscar	*to look for*	gastar	*to spend*	organizar	*to organize*
cambiar	*to change*	hablar	*to speak, talk*	pasar	*to spend time, pass, happen*
caminar	*to walk*	importar	*to matter*	pagar	*to pay*

cantar	to sing	invitar	to invite	preguntar	to ask
cenar	to eat dinner	lavar	to wash	preparar	to prepare
cocinar	to cook	llamar	to call	quitar	to remove, leave
comprar	to buy	llegar	to arrive	regresar	to return
descansar	to rest	lavar	to wash	tomar	to take
enseñar	to teach, show	mandar	to send	trabajar	to work
escuchar	to listen	mirar	to look at	viajar	to travel
esperar	to wait for, hope	nadar	to swim	visitar	to visit

Uses of the Present Tense

In Spanish, as in English, the present tense can express a variety of meanings.

Ella **habla**. *She speaks. She is speaking. She does speak.*

Meaning often changes according to context, or with adverbs of time, such as **ahora** (*right now*), **mañana** (*tomorrow*), or **hoy** (*today*). For example:

Ella llega **ahora**. *She is arriving right now.*
Ella llega **mañana**. *She is arriving (She'll be arriving) tomorrow. She arrives (She'll arrive) tomorrow.*

In general, the present tense is used to describe the following situations:

1. Something happening at the moment.

   Lee el periódico. *He's reading the newspaper.*
   Clara **está** en Buenos Aires. *Clara is in Buenos Aires.*

2. Something that is generally true or happens regularly, as indicated by words such as **mucho** (*a lot*), **siempre** (*always*), or **nunca** (*never*).

   Estudio mucho los fines de semana. *I study a lot on weekends.*
   Trabajo en ventas. *I work in sales.*
   Ella siempre llega a **tiempo**. *She always arrives on time.*

3. Something happening in the near future.

Sari **regresa** el lunes.   *Sari returns/is returning on Monday.*
Nosotros **esperamos** aquí.   *We'll wait here.*

Written Practice 2

Complete these sentences using the present tense of the verb in parentheses.

1. (Nosotros) _____ (descansar) en la cama. *We rest in bed.*

2. Julia _____ (trabajar) mucho. *Julia works a lot.*

3. ¿Ustedes no _____ (cambiar) cheques de viajero? *You don't cash traveler's checks?*

4. (Nosotros) _____ (llevar) tu perro al veterinario. *We'll take your dog to the veterinarian.*

5. ¿Usted _____ (enseñar) español? *Do you teach Spanish?*

6. Javier nunca _____ (estudiar) los fines de semana. *Javier never studies on weekends.*

7. Ernesto y Juan _____ (necesitar) unos libros. *Ernesto and Juan need some books.*

8. (Yo) no _____ (llegar) a Quito hoy. (Yo) _____ (llegar) mañana. *I don't arrive in Quito today. I arrive tomorrow.*

Oral Practice 2

 Track 14

In order to speed up your ability to conjugate **-ar** verbs, try conjugating the following verbs with the subjects provided. Keep practicing until you can say the entire list fluently and quickly. Listen to the CD to check your pronunciation.

1. yo/llamar

2. tú/cocinar

3. ellos/cantar

4. usted/organizar

5. ella/buscar

6. nosotros/mirar

7. él/ganar

8. ustedes/ayudar

9. tú/hablar

10. yo/gastar

Making a Sentence Negative

Making sentences negative in Spanish is very straightforward. Just add the word **no** before the verb.

Regina **habla** inglés.	*Regina speaks English.*
Regina **no habla** inglés.	*Regina doesn't speak English.*
Tú **eres** mi novio.	*You are my boyfriend.*
Tú **no eres** mi novio.	*You are not my boyfriend.*

Asking Yes/No Questions

Asking questions that generate either a *yes* or *no* answer in Spanish is simple. The sentences stay the same, and only your voice intonation changes. To make a question, just raise your voice at the end of the sentence with a questioning tone. Remember that when writing questions in Spanish, you have to use an upside-down question mark at the beginning of the sentence or phrase.

¿Es tu padre?	*Is he your father?*
¿Eres el amigo de Camila?	*Are you Camila's friend?*

The Spanish language is very flexible, and in questions, words can be inverted in several ways to ask the same thing.

¿Carlos habla español?	*Does Carlos speak Spanish?*
¿Habla Carlos español?	
¿Habla español Carlos?	

Questions can also be used in the negative.

¿Carlos no habla español?	*Carlos doesn't speak Spanish?*
¿No habla español Carlos?	*Doesn't Carlos speak Spanish?*

Tag Questions

Spanish speakers often add tags such as **¿no?** and **¿verdad?** to the end of statements to make questions. These are similar to phrases such as *right?*, *isn't it?*, or *aren't you?* that English speakers add at the end of questions. Tag questions are often not "real" questions, but rather attempts to seek confirmation of something you think you already know. Note that in Spanish the written question marks fall only around the tag and your voice rises only with the tag.

Es tu padre ¿verdad?	*He's your father, right?*
Eres el amigo de Camila ¿no?	*Your Camila's friend, aren't you?*

Tags can also be used to confirm negative statements. Usually only **¿verdad?** is used in these cases.

Ellos no son de aquí ¿verdad?	*They're not from here, are they?*
Sara no habla español ¿verdad?	*Sara doesn't speak Spanish, does she?*

Answering Yes/No Questions

To answer yes/no questions, use a simple **sí** (*yes*) or **no** (*no*) followed by a restatement of the question.

¿Es tu padre?	*Is he your father?*
Sí, es mi padre.	*Yes, he's my father.*
No, no es mi padre.	*No, he's not my father.*

Tag questions are answered the same way.

Eres el amigo de Camila ¿no?	*You're Camila's friend, aren't you?*
Sí, soy el amigo de Camila.	*Yes, I'm Camila's friend.*
No, no soy el amigo de Camila.	*No, I'm not Camila's friend.*

Negative Expressions

When speaking in the negative, either when answering questions, asking questions, or making a statement, you can use a number of negative expressions. These expressions often add emphasis to what you are saying.

nada	*nothing, anything, at all*	nunca, jamás	*never*
nadie	*no one, anyone*	tampoco	*either/neither*

These expressions can be used before the verb in place of the word **no**.

¿Usted toma alcohol?	*Do you drink alcohol?*
No, nunca tomo alcohol.	*No, I never drink alcohol.*
No, jamás tomo alcohol.	*No, I never drink alcohol.*
Yo tampoco tomo alcohol.	*I don't drink alcohol, either.*

Or they can be used in addition to the word **no**, after the verb. Notice that unlike English, Spanish may use double negatives.

¿Usted toma alcohol?	*Do you drink alcohol?*
No, no tomo alcohol nunca.	*No, I never drink (alcohol).*
	(Literally: *No, I don't drink alcohol, ever.*)
Yo no tomo alcohol tampoco.	*I don't drink alcohol either.*

These words can be used similarly in questions, either in addition to the word *no* or instead of it. Again, they add emphasis, or disbelief, to the question.

¿Nunca comes carne?	*You never eat meat?*
¿No comes carne nunca?	*You never eat meat?*
	(Literally: *You don't eat meat, ever?*)
¿Tampoco comes carne?	*You don't eat meat either?*

Here are some more examples. Notice that when the word **nadie** substitutes for the subject pronoun the verb is conjugated as with **él** or **ella**.

Nadie habla español.	*No one speaks Spanish.*
No veo nada.	*I can't see anything.*
Yo tampoco.	*Me neither.*
Nunca como carne.	*I never eat meat.*
¿Nadie aquí es médico?	*No one here is a doctor?*
No me gusta nada.	*I don't like it at all.*

Oral Practice 3

 Track 15

Listen to the following questions that use the verb **ser**. Pause the CD after each question and say your answer. Then listen to the correct answer on the CD and repeat what you hear before moving on to the next question.

1. ¿Eres de Paraguay? *Are you from Paraguay?* (Sí)

2. Somos amigos ¿verdad? *We're friends, right?* (No)

3. ¿Es una bicicleta? *Is this a bike?* (Sí)

4. Ellas no son hermanas ¿verdad? *They aren't sisters, right?* (No)

5. Elena es psicóloga ¿no? *Elena is a psychologist, isn't she?* (Sí)

6. ¿Son de Buenos Aires Santos y Marisol? *Are Santos and Marisol from Buenos Aires?* (No)

7. ¿Tú no bailas salsa? *You don't dance salsa?* (No)

Possessive Adjectives

Possessive adjectives (*my, your, his, her, our, their*) are used to show ownership or possession of something, or a relationship to someone.

tu libro	*your book*
mi primo	*my cousin*
nuestra casa	*our house*

Unlike in English, possessive adjectives in Spanish can be singular or plural. Here are all of the possessive adjectives in their singular and plural forms:

Possessive Adjectives

Singular	Plural	
mi	mis	*my*
tu	tus	*your* (informal, singular)
su	sus	*his, her, your* (formal), *their*
nuestro/-a	nuestros/-as	*our*
vuestro/-a	vuestros/-as	*your* (informal)

Adjectives in Spanish agree with the words they modify. (You will be learning more about adjectives in Chapter 4.) Possessive adjectives are no exception and agree with the thing or person they are describing. Note that **tu(s)**, **mi(s)**, and **su(s)** agree only in number: singular or plural. This means that you add an s when the noun being described is plural.

mi prima	*my cousin*
mis primas	*my cousins*

tu libro	your book
tus libros	your books
su casa	his, her, your, their house
sus casas	his, her, your, their houses

Su(s) has four meanings: *his, her, your,* and *their.* In addition, it can mean *your* singular (**usted**) or *your* plural (**ustedes**).

Like most adjectives in Spanish, **nuestro** and **vuestro** agree in both gender and number with the nouns they modify. This means that **-o** changes to **-a** when the noun being described is feminine and an **-s** is added in the plural.

nuestro libro	our book	nuestros libros	our books
nuestra casa	our house	nuestras casas	our houses
vuestro libro	your book	vuestros libros	your books
vuestra casa	your house	vuestras casas	your houses

NOTE *Vuestro,* like *vosotros,* is used only in Spain and will not be tested in this book.

Written Practice 3

Use possessive adjectives and these words to translate the phrases below into Spanish: **madre** (*mother*), **padre** (*father*), **hijo** (*son*), **hija** (*daughter*), **hijos** (*children, sons*), and **padres** (*parents*).

1. my daughter _____

2. her son _____

3. your (informal) mother _____

4. our father _____

5. your (plural, formal) parents _____

6. their daughters _____

7. your (informal) father _____

8. our daughters _____

9. my children _____

10. their mothers _____

Now, can you write the well-known phrase *My house is your house* both informally and formally?

11. Informal: _____

12. Formal: _____

Write *Our house is your house* using the formal plural of *your*.

13. Plural: _____

Possession with *De*

De is often used to show possession, especially when the possessor needs to be introduced, clarified, or emphasized. The **de** clause is similar to the possessive *'s* in English. Note, however, that in Spanish, the phrase that identifies the owner comes after the thing that is possessed.

el hijo **de mi primo**	*my cousin's son*
	(Literally: *the son of my cousin*)
los zapatos **de mi madre**	*my mother's shoes*
las calles **de Cartagena**	*the streets of Cartagena (Cartagena's streets)*

The word **su(s)** has four meanings (*his, her, your, their*). Usually it is clear from the context of the sentence what the exact meaning is.

Alicia lee **su libro**.	*Alicia reads her book.*

However, when the meaning of **su** is unclear, you can use **de** to clarify possession.

Alicia lee **el libro de Manuel**.	*Alicia reads Manuel's book.*

NOTE *De + el becomes del.*

El libro del Señor Moreno   *Señor Moreno's book.*

This is only the case with the article el. The subject pronoun él (with an accent) does not contract: de él.

El libro de él.   *His book.*

Written Practice 4

Make phrases using the thing(s) plus **de** to show possession. Then write the translation below. The first one has been done for you.

Part A
El vaso/Pedro   *El vaso de Pedro.*   *Pedro's glass.*

1. Los exámenes/el profesor _____

2. Los monumentos/Europa _____

3. El perro/las niñas _____

4. El sueño/ella _____

5. Las canciones/Shakira _____

Now rewrite the phrases using a possessive adjective. The first one has been done for you.

Part B
Su vaso _____

1. _____

2. _____

3. _____

4. _____

5. _____

QUIZ

Circle the letter of the word that best completes each sentence.

1. _____ primos regresan mañana.
   A. Nuestra
   B. Nuestro
   C. Nuestras
   D. Nuestros

2. ¿_____ es francesa?
   A. Yo
   B. Tú
   C. Él
   D. Ella

3. Ustedes _____ simpáticos.
   A. es
   B. somos
   C. son
   D. sois

4. Hugo Chávez es _____.
   A. venezolano
   B. venezolana
   C. Venezolano
   D. Venezolana

5. _____ como carne. Soy vegetariano.
   A. Yo
   B. Nunca
   C. Siempre
   D. Sí

6. Yo _____ en el supermercado.
   A. nado
   B. compro
   C. bailo
   D. descanso

7. ¿_____ ustedes hoy?

   A. Llego

   B. Llega

   C. Llegamos

   D. Llegan

8. No, nosotros _____ mañana.

   A. llego

   B. llega

   C. llegamos

   D. llegan

9. Adán no habla ruso, _____

   A. verdad

   B. ¿verdad?

   C. ¿cómo?

   D. ¿así?

10. Sonia y yo tenemos una hermana. Ella es _____ hermana.

   A. mi

   B. mis

   C. nuestra

   D. nuestras

chapter **4**

Describing People and Things

In this chapter you will learn how to form adjectives and where to place them. You will learn how to exaggerate using superlatives. You will learn the infinitive and present tense for two more types of regular verbs as well as how to make questions using question words.

CHAPTER OBJECTIVES

In this chapter you will learn

- Adjectives and adjective placement
- The superlative of adjectives
- The question words *¿Qué?*, *¿Quién?*, *¿Cuál?*, and *¿Por qué?*
- Regular verbs ending in *-er*: Infinitive and present tense
- Regular verbs ending in *-ir*: Infinitive and present tense

Adjectives

Adjectives are used to modify, or describe, nouns. It is easy to recognize the meanings of some adjectives.

moderno   *modern*   inteligente   *intelligent*

An adjective in Spanish must agree in gender and number with the noun it modifies. You have seen examples of this with nationalities (**alemán**, **alemana**) and with possessive adjectives (**nuestro**, **nuestros**). Notice how the adjective changes in these examples.

el chico **alto**	*the tall boy*	(masculine singular)
la chica **alta**	*the tall girl*	(feminine singular)
los chicos **altos**	*the tall boys*	(masculine singular)
las chicas **altas**	*the tall girls*	(feminine singular)

Adjectives Ending in -o

Most descriptive adjectives in Spanish end in **-o** and have four forms: **-o**, **-a**, **-os**, **-as**. Notice how the endings of the adjectives often echo the endings of the nouns.

un libro barato	*a cheap (inexpensive) book*
una casa antigua	*an old house*
unos libros baratos	*some cheap (inexpensive) books*
unas casas antiguas	*some old houses*

Here are some common adjectives ending in **-o**:

alto	*tall*	gordo	*fat*
antiguo	*old, ancient*	hermoso	*beautiful*
amarillo	*yellow*	largo	*long*
atractivo	*attractive*	limpio	*clean*
bajo	*short*	lindo	*pretty*
barato	*cheap*	loco	*crazy*
blanco	*white*	malo	*bad*
bonito	*pretty*	moderno	*modern*
bueno	*good*	negro	*black*
caro	*expensive*	nuevo	*new*
cómodo	*comfortable*	pequeño	*small*

corto	*short*	rico	*rich; delicious*
delgado	*thin*	rojo	*red*
delicioso	*delicious*	rubio	*blond*
divertido	*fun*	simpático	*nice*
enfermo	*sick, ill*	sucio	*dirty*
feo	*ugly*	tímido	*shy*
frío	*cold*	viejo	*old*

Adjectives Ending in -e and -a

Some adjectives are an exception to the rule above in that they don't change when they modify a masculine or feminine noun. These adjectives ending in -e or -a have only two forms: singular and plural. To make the plural, simply add an -s.

la mujer elegante	*the elegant woman*	(singular)
las mujeres elegantes	*the elegant women*	(plural)
el niño idealista	*the idealistic child (m.)*	(singular)
los niños idealistas	*the idealistic children*	(plural)

Here are some common adjectives ending in -e:

alegre	*happy*	humilde	*humble*
amable	*friendly*	independiente	*independent*
eficiente	*efficient*	inteligente	*intelligent*
elegante	*elegant*	paciente	*patient*
enorme	*enormous, huge*	pobre	*poor*
fuerte	*strong*	triste	*sad*
grande	*big*	verde	*green*

Here are some common adjectives ending in -a. Notice that, with the exception of colors, these adjectives are abstract concepts applying to people.

egoísta	*selfish*	rosa	*pink*
idealista	*idealistic*	optimista	*optimistic*
hipócrita	*hypocritical*	pesimista	*pessimistic*
materialista	*materialistic*	realista	*realistic*
naranja	*orange* (color)	violeta	*violet* (color)

Adjectives Ending in a Consonant

Most adjectives ending in a consonant also have only two forms, singular and plural. They do not change for masculine and feminine. To make these adjectives plural, simply add -es, unless the adjective ends in a -z, in which case the -z becomes a -c-.

El examen es fácil.	*The test is easy.*
Los exámenes son fáciles.	*The tests are easy.*
La alumna es feliz.	*The student is happy.*
Las alumnas son felices.	*The students are happy.*

Here are some adjectives ending in a consonant:

azul	*blue*	gris	*gray*
difícil	*difficult*	joven	*young*
fácil	*easy*	normal	*normal*
feliz	*happy*	popular	*popular*

Note that adjectives of nationality, whether they end in a consonant or vowel, actually have four forms.

español	españoles	*Spanish (m.)*
española	españolas	*Spanish (f.)*

A few adjectives that end in a consonant actually take on masculine and feminine forms as well as singular and plural, such as those ending in -dor.

encantador	*charming*
hablador	*talkative*
trabajador	*hardworking*

La señora Guzmán es encantadora.	*Mrs. Guzmán is charming.*
Mi esposo es muy hablador.	*My husband is very talkative.*
Las camareras son muy trabajadoras.	*The waitresses are very hardworking.*

Written Practice 1

▶ Track 16

Complete each sentence with the proper form of the adjective in parentheses.

1. El chico _____ es mi hijo. (joven)

2. La bicicleta _____ es de mi mamá. (viejo)

3. Tegucigalpa es la capital _____. (hondureño)

4. Los zapatos _____ son _____. (azul, bonito)

5. Mis amigas son bastante _____. (materialista)

6. La clase de física es _____. (difícil)

7. Los padres de Camilo son _____. (amable)

8. La silla es _____, pero es _____. (caro, cómodo)

9. La comida _____ es _____. (francés, delicioso)

10. Éstos son unos niños _____. (feliz)

Written Practice 2

Now translate the previous sentences into English. Most of the vocabulary should be familiar to you. If you see a word you don't recognize, use the surrounding words to help you or look it up in the vocabulary index in the back of this book.

1. _____.

2. _____.

3. _____.

4. _____.

5. _____.

6. _____.

7. _____.

8. _____.

9. _____.

10. _____.

Adjective Placement

You may have noticed that in Spanish the adjective usually comes after the noun. This is the opposite of English syntax.

Es una niña **linda**.	*She's a pretty girl.*

Adjectives can also follow the verbs **ser** and **estar**, but they still must agree (in masculine, feminine, singular, and plural) with the nouns they are modifying.

Las manzanas **están deliciosas**.	*The apples are delicious.*
Tu amigo **está loco**.	*Your friend is crazy.*

Sometimes adjectives can precede the noun. In Spanish the rules are not hard and fast, so it's best to let your ear and eye get used to these constructions. Here are some common tendencies to be aware of.

Adjectives of quantity, such as **poco** (*little, few*) and **mucho** (*much, many, a lot*) generally come *before* the noun.

poco trabajo	*little work*
mucha amistad	*a lot of friendship*
pocos amigos	*few friends*
muchas mujeres	*many women*

Sometimes the placement of adjectives before or after the noun implies subtle differences in meaning.

un amigo **viejo**	*an old friend* (a friend who is old in years)
un **viejo** amigo	*an old friend* (a friend you have known for a long time)
el chico **pobre**	*the poor boy* (a boy with very little money)
el **pobre** chico	*the poor boy* (a boy to be pitied, one feels sorry for him)

The adjective **grande** (*big*) not only changes meaning according to its placement, but is shortened when used before a singular noun.

un hombre **grande**	*a big (tall) man*
un **gran** hombre	*a great man* (by deeds or reputation)
una mujer **grande**	*a big (tall) woman*
una **gran** mujer	*a great woman*

A few adjectives can either follow or precede the noun. When they precede a masculine singular noun, the adjective is shortened, but the meaning stays the same.

| un niño **bueno** | un **buen** niño | *a good boy* |
| un chico **malo** | un **mal** chico | *a bad kid* |

Ordinal numbers (*first, second, third*, etc.) usually precede the noun they modify. Notice how **primero** (*first*) and **tercero** (*third*) shorten to **primer** and **tercer** before a masculine singular noun. You will learn more about ordinal numbers in Chapter 5.

el **primer** piso	*the first floor*
la **primera** dama	*the first lady*
el **tercer** día	*the third day*
la **tercera** planta	*the third floor*

The adjectives **alguno** (*some, any*) and **ninguno** (*no, not any*) are also frequently placed before the noun. They take a written accent in the shortened form (before a masculine singular noun).

algunas personas	*some people*
algún motivo	*some reason*
ninguna duda	*no doubt*
ningún momento	*no time, never*

Oral Practice 1

 Track 17

Put the elements of the following sentences in the most logical order and say them aloud. Use the translations to help you. Listen to the recording to check your answers. Repeat what you hear.

1. un/trabaja/Miguel/edificio/en/enorme. _____.
   Miguel works in a huge office building.

2. amiga/una/Saskia/vieja/es. _____.
   Saskia is an old friend.

3. gran/un/Márquez/el/es/hombre/Señor. _____.
   Mr. Márquez is a great man.

4. gasto/dinero/no/mucho. _____.
   I don't spend a lot of money.

5. el/tercer/en/vive/piso/Adán. _____.

Adán lives on the third floor.

6. es/mi/esposa/mujer/la/rubia. _____.

The blond woman is my wife.

Superlatives and Diminutives of Adjectives

There are various ways to either intensify or tone down your use of adjectives. One way to intensify or even exaggerate your description is to add the suffix **-ísimo** to the end of an adjective to make the *superlative*. This grammatical structure doesn't exist in English, so the translation is a loose one, similar to *very*, *extremely*, or *most* in English. Note that your adjective with **-ísimo** still has to agree with the noun it modifies. Here are some examples:

«Carlota tiene mucha suerte. Su novio es **altísimo**, **guapísimo** y **riquísimo**. Ella está **contentísima**».

"Carlota is really lucky. Her boyfriend is very tall, really handsome, and extremely rich. She is really happy."

The suffix **-ito**, which indicates the *diminutive* for nouns, can also be applied to adjectives to add shades of meaning, or to express familiarity or affection. Use this construction with care, however, because it can also come off as belittling or derogatory when used inappropriately.

«Yo, en cambio, tengo un novio **bajito**, **feíto** y **gordito**. Pero tiene los ojos **azulitos** y la nariz **chiquita** y me quiere **muchísimo**».

"I, on the other hand, have a very short, kind of ugly, chubby little boyfriend. But he has those blue eyes and that cute little nose and he loves me a lot."

The adverbs **muy** (*very*), **demasiado** (*too*), and **bastante** (*quite, rather*) can also be used to modify adjectives. They come before the adjective and do not change according to gender or number; they always stay the same.

Ella es **muy** simpática.
Él es **demasiado** egoísta.
La comida es **bastante** buena.

She is very nice.
He is too selfish.
The food is quite good.

«Bien chevere»

When speaking colloquially, Spanish speakers in many regions of Latin America use the word **bien** (*well*) instead of **muy** to express *very*, *really*, or *quite*. They would say, for instance, **bien chévere** for *really cool*, **bien caro** for *very expensive*, or **bien grande** for *quite big*. Keep in mind that the use of **bien** in this context generally applies to spoken Spanish, rarely to written Spanish, and is considered colloquial. This usage is quite common (you could even say **bien común**), so incorporating it into your speaking vocabulary can help your Spanish sound less "textbook" and more "native."

Oral Practice 2

Practice saying the following sentences, modifying the adjectives in a number of different ways. Follow the example provided.

> La comida es buena: -ísima, muy, bastante (*The food is good.*)
>
> *La comida es buenísima. La comida es muy buena. La comida es bastante buena.*

1. El carro es viejo: -ísimo, muy, bastante, demasiado (*The car is old.*)
2. La caja es fuerte: -ísima, muy, bastante (*The box is strong.*)
3. El español es fácil: -ísimo, muy, bastante, demasiado, bien (*Spanish is easy.*)
4. Las joyas son caras: -ísimas, muy, bastante, demasiado (*The jewels are expensive.*)
5. Es una película violenta: -ísima, bastante, demasiado, bien (*The film is violent.*)

The Question Words ¿Quién?, ¿Qué?, ¿Cuál?, and ¿Por qué?

You've already learned how to ask yes/no questions in Spanish by using tone of voice or intonation. To ask information questions—questions that require longer or explanatory answers—you will use question words, equivalent to the

English *who*, *where*, *what*, *when*, *why*, and *how*. In this chapter we will begin with **¿Quién?** (*Who?*), **¿Qué?** (*Which? What?*), **¿Cuál?** (*Which? What?*), and **¿Por qué?** (*Why?*).

NOTE *All question words in Spanish have accents. The same words can also be used as connecting words when they appear without accents, as is the case with* **porque** *(= because—all one word), and* **que** *(= that). The accent denotes the interrogative use of the word and must be used every time you write a question.*

To make a question, begin with the question word, followed by the verb. If there is also a noun subject, it follows the verb. When writing, remember to begin your question with **¿** and end it with **?** When speaking, end your question with rising intonation. Practice saying these examples:

¿Quién es?	*Who is it?*
¿Quién trabaja los lunes?	*Who works on Mondays?*
¿Qué estudias?	*What do you study?*
¿Qué hace Pilar?	*What does Pilar do?*
¿Cuál es tu número de teléfono?	*What is your phone number?*
¿Cuál quieres?	*Which do you want?*
¿Por qué estudian español?	*Why do you study Spanish?*
¿Por qué no hablas?	*Why don't you talk?*

The question words **¿Quién?** and **¿Cuál?** in Spanish also have plural forms, **¿Quiénes?** and **¿Cuáles?**. The plural forms usually differentiate among a group and are used before a plural verb. Take a look at the following examples:

¿Quiénes son ustedes?	*Who are you?* (plural)
¿Quiénes van a la fiesta?	*Who is going to the party?*
¿Cuáles son tus películas preferidas?	*What are your favorite movies?*
¿Cuáles quieres?	*Which (ones) do you want?*

Variations of *¿Quién?*

The question word **¿Quién?** can be used with various prepositions to express a number of different ideas. To say *whom* or *to whom*, use the construction **¿A quién?** or **¿A quiénes?**. To say *of whom*, *about whom*, or *from whom*, use **¿De quién?** or **¿De quiénes?**, and to say *with whom*, use **¿Con quién?** or **¿Con quié-**

nes? Note that in many of these cases, saying *who* instead of *whom* has become common in colloquial English.

¿A quién buscas?	*Who(m) are you looking for?*
	(For whom are you looking?)
¿De quién hablas?	*Who(m) are you speaking about?*
	(Of whom are you speaking?)
¿Con quién vas a la fiesta?	*Who(m) are you going to the party with?*
	(With whom are you going to the party?)

Written Practice 3

 Track 18

Complete the questions using **¿Quién?**, **¿Quiénes?**, **¿Qué?**, or **¿Por qué?** to elicit the answers you see in the statements below. Use the translations to help you. When you have finished, listen to the answers on the audio CD.

1. ¿_____ habla francés? Enrique habla francés.
   _____ *speaks French? Enrique speaks French.*

2. ¿_____ toman el taxi? Mis amigos toman el taxi.
   _____ *are taking the taxi? My friends are taking the taxi.*

3. ¿_____ compra Sergio? Sergio compra un DVD.
   _____ *is Sergio buying? Sergio is buying a DVD.*

4. ¿_____ suban la montaña? Porque son muy aventureras.
   _____ *are they climbing the mountain? Because they are very*
   adventurous.

5. ¿_____ viaja a Cuba mañana? Marta viaja a Cuba mañana.
   _____ *is traveling to Cuba tomorrow? Marta is traveling to*
   Cuba tomorrow.

6. ¿_____ es de Guatemala. Myra es de Guatemala.
   _____ *is from Guatemala? Myra is from Guatemala.*

7. ¿A _____ escribe Matilde? Matilde escribe a su novio.
   To _____ *is Matilde writing? Matilde is writing to her*
   boyfriend.

8. ¿_____ escribe? Escribe un correo electronico.
   _____ *is she writing? She's writing an e-mail.*

¿Cuál? or ¿Qué?

It is often difficult for English speakers to know when to use **¿Cuál?** and when to use **¿Qué?**, since both words can have the meaning *What?* or *Which?* Here are a few rules to guide you:

- Use **¿Qué?** before a singular or plural noun to ask *Which?* or *What?*

¿Qué idiomas hablas?	*What languages do you speak?*
¿Qué libro estás leyendo?	*Which book are you reading?*

- Use **¿Qué?** to say *What?* when asking for a description or explanation.

¿Qué significa *azulejo*?	*What does "azulejo" mean?*
¿Qué haces?	*What do you do (for a living)?*

- Use **¿Qué?** with the verb **ser** to ask for a definition.

¿Qué es esto?	*What is this?*
¿Qué es un aguacate?	*What is an avocado?*

- Use **¿Cuál?** before forms of the verb **ser** to ask *What?* or *Which?* and before other verbs and the preposition **de** to ask *Which?*, *Which ones (out of a group)?*

¿Cuál es tu nombre?	*What is your name?*
¿Cuál de los bares prefieres?	*Which of the bars do you prefer?*
¿Cuáles son tus hijos?	*Which ones are your children?*
¿Cuáles quieres?	*Which ones do you want?*

Notice that **¿Cuál?** and **¿Qué?** can serve very similar purposes and express similar meanings, but must often change according to the grammatical context:

¿Qué libro quieres?	*Which book do you want?*

In this example, **¿Qué?** is used before a *singular noun* to ask *Which?* while in the next example, **¿Cuál?** is used before *the preposition* **de** to ask *Which?*

¿Cuál de los libros quieres?	*Which of the books do you want (out of a group)?*

In the next example, **¿Qué?** is used before a *plural noun* to ask *Which?*

¿Qué libros quieres?	*Which books do you want?*

And here you see **¿Cuáles?** used before a *verb* to ask *Which ones?*

¿Cuáles quieres?	*Which ones do you want?*

In the final example in this section, **¿Cuál?** is used with the verb **ser** to ask *Which?*

¿Cuál es el libro que quieres?   *Which is the book that you want?*

Written Practice 4

 Track 19

Complete the following sentences with **¿Qué?**, **¿Cuál?**, or **¿Cuáles?**.

1. ¿——— es la capital de Perú? *What is the capital of Peru?*

2. ¿——— música escuchas? *What music are you listening to?*

3. ¿——— es un higo? *What is a fig?*

4. ¿——— son tus canciones favoritas? *What are your favorite songs?*

5. ¿——— miras? *What are you looking at?*

6. ¿——— de los carros es el mejor? *Which car is the best?*

7. ¿——— tipo de helado quieres? *What kind of ice cream do you want?*

8. ¿——— tienes en la mano? *What do you have in your hand? (Which one do you have in your hand?)*

9. ¿——— es tu dirección de email? *What is your e-mail address?*

10. ¿——— es una esmeralda? *What is an emerald?*

Verbs Ending in *-er*: Present Tense

You've already learned how to conjugate the present tense of verbs ending in **-ar**, the first category of regular verbs. Verbs whose infinitive form ends in **-er** are the second category of regular verbs. There aren't many cognates in this group, so their meanings will have to be memorized.

In order to conjugate **-er** verbs, drop the **-er** and add the following endings to the stem: **-o, -es, -e, -emos, -éis, -en**. Here's an example with the verb **comer** (*to eat*):

Subject	Stem	Ending	Present Tense	
yo	com-	-o	com**o**	*I eat*
tú	com-	-es	com**es**	*you eat* (singular, informal)
él/ella /usted	com-	-e	com**e**	*he, she, it eats, you eat* (singular, formal)
nosotros	com-	-emos	com**emos**	*we eat*
vosotros	com-	-éis	com**éis**	*you eat* (plural, informal)
ellos/ellas /ustedes	com-	-en	com**en**	*they, you eat* (plural)

Remember that because the verb endings show the person being referred to, the subject pronoun is often omitted. For instance: **Como carne** (*I eat meat*). Here are some examples of sentences using **-er** verbs in the present:

Comen en un restaurante.	*They eat in a restaurant.*
No **bebo** alcohol.	*I don't drink alcohol.*
Leemos el periódico por la mañana.	*We read the newspaper in the morning.*
¿Pilar **cree** en extraterrestres?	*Does Pilar believe in aliens?*

Some Regular Verbs Ending in -er

aprender	*to learn*	deber	*to owe; to have to*
beber	*to drink*	leer	*to read*
comer	*to eat*	meter	*to put*
comprender	*to understand*	prometer	*to promise*
correr	*to run*	vender	*to sell*
creer	*to believe*	ver	*to see*

Written Practice 5

Complete these sentences using the present tense of the verb in parentheses.

1. ¿Tú _____ (creer) en Dios? *Do you believe in God?*

2. (Yo) no _____ (comprender) portugués. *I don't understand Portuguese.*

3. Ángela _____ (correr) por las mañanas. *Ángela runs in the mornings.*

4. ¿Qué _____ (ver) usted? *What do you see?*

5. La tienda _____ (vender) zapatos elegantes. *The store sells elegant shoes.*

6. Nosotras no _____ (prometer) nada. *We don't promise anything.*

7. Silvia y Rodrigo le _____ (deber) mil dólares al banco. *Silvia and Rodrigo owe a thousand dollars to the bank.*

8. (Yo) _____ (meter) la cartera en el equipaje de mano. *I put the wallet in the hand luggage.*

9. Ellos no _____ (aprender) muy rápido. *They don't learn very fast.*

10. ¿Qué tipo de libros _____ (leer) Juan José? *What type of books does Juan José read?*

Written Practice 6

Track 20

Choose the best verb to complete each sentence and conjugate it in the present. Use the vocabulary you have already learned and the following words to help you: **el cigarro** (*cigarette*), **la tienda** (*store*), **las verduras** (*vegetables*), **siempre** (*always*), **la revista** (*magazine*), **el parque** (*park*).

beber	ver	leer
comer	correr	vender

1. (Yo) no _____ agua. *I don't drink water.*

2. ¿Usted _____ el carro rojo? *Do you see the red car?*

3. Ellos no _____ cigarros en esta tienda. *They don't sell cigarettes in this store.*

4. Dario _____ mucha verdura. *Dario eats lots of vegetables.*

5. Mi madre siempre _____ la revista *Hola. My mother always reads the magazine* Hola.

6. Mónica y Luz _____ en el parque. *Mónica and Luz run in the park.*

Verbs Ending in *-ir*: Present Tense

Verbs with the infinitive ending in **-ir** are the third category of regular verbs. The meaning of some of these is quite easy to guess.

admitir   *to admit*   decidir   *to decide*

In order to conjugate **-ir** verbs, drop the **-ir** and add the following endings to the stem: **-o, -es, -e, -imos, -ís, -en**. Here's an example with the verb **vivir** (*to live*):

Subject	Stem	Ending	Present Tense	
yo	viv-	-o	vivo	*I live*
tú	viv-	-es	vives	*you live* (singular, informal)
él/ella/usted	viv-	-e	vive	*he, she, it lives, you live* (singular, formal)
nosotros	viv-	-imos	vivimos	*we live*
vosotros	viv-	-ís	vivís	*you live* (plural, informal)
ellos/ellas /ustedes	viv-	-en	viven	*they, you live* (plural)

Remember that because the verb endings show the person being referred to, the subject pronoun is often omitted. For instance: **Vivo en la ciudad.** (*I live in the city*.) Here are some examples of sentences using **-ir** verbs in the present:

Vivimos en Canadá.	*We live in Canada.*
Hugo **escribe** libros.	*Hugo writes books.*
¿**Sufres** de alguna enfermedad?	*Do you suffer from any illness?*
Mi hermano y yo **discutimos**.	*My brother and I argue.*

Some Regular Verbs Ending in *-ir*

abrir	*to open*	escribir	*to write*
admitir	*to admit*	recibir	*to receive*
asistir	*to attend*	subir	*to go up, climb, raise*
cubrir	*to cover*	sufrir	*to suffer*
discutir	*to discuss, argue*	vivir	*to live*

Written Practice 7

Complete these sentences using the present tense of the verb in parentheses.

1. María _____ (vivir) con sus padres. *María lives with her parents.*

2. (Yo) no _____ (abrir) la puerta a desconocidos. *I don't open the door to strangers.*

3. Nosotros _____ (escribir) emails. *We write emails.*

4. Carla _____ (subir) la montaña sola. *Carla climbs the mountain alone.*

5. ¿Ustedes _____ (asistir) a clase? *Do you attend class?*

6. Él no _____ (admitir) que tiene un problema. *He doesn't admit that he has a problem.*

7. ¿(Tú) no _____ (sufrir) del calor en Panamá? *You don't suffer from the heat in Panama?*

8. El niño no _____ (cubrir) la boca cuando estornuda. *The boy doesn't cover his mouth when he sneezes.*

9. Miguel y su esposa _____ (discutir) mucho. *Miguel and his wife argue a lot.*

10. ¿Usted _____ (recibir) dinero de sus padres? *Do you receive money from your parents?*

Oral Practice 3

Track 21

Choose the best verb to complete each sentence and put it in the present. Use the vocabulary you have already learned and the following words to help you: **jóvenes** (*young people*), **la ventana** (*window*), **las escaleras** (*stairs*).

abrir	escribir	vivir	admitir	subir

1. Nosotros _____ en Los Ángeles. *We live in Los Angeles.*

2. ¿Tú _____ libros? *Do you write books?*

3. Javier _____ las escaleras. *Javier climbs the stairs.*

4. Los bares no _____ a jóvenes. *Bars don't admit teenagers.*

5. Yo _____ la ventana por la mañana. *I open the window in the morning.*

QUIZ

Circle the letter of the word or phrase that best completes each sentence.

1. Jackie Kennedy era _____.
   A. un mujer elegante
   B. un elegante mujer
   C. una mujer elegante
   D. una elegantes mujer

2. Adán compra un _____.
   A. viejos carros
   B. carro viejo
   C. vieja moto
   D. moto vieja

3. Es un hombre popular. Tiene _____.
   A. mucho amigo
   B. amigo mucho
   C. muchos amigos
   D. amigos muchos

4. En general, los elefantes son _____.
   A. grandísimos
   B. chiquitos
   C. pequeñitos
   D. muchísimo

5. ¿_____ son tus libros?
   A. Cuál
   B. Cuáles
   C. Quién
   D. Quiénes

6. ¿_____ de las historias crees?

    A. Qué

    B. Cuál

    C. Quién

    D. Quiénes

7. **Elena y Marcos _____ mucho.**

    A. discute

    B. discutimos

    C. discutes

    D. discuten

8. **Rafael come _____.**

    A. carne

    B. leche

    C. Guatemala

    D. cigarros

9. ¿_____ **habla francés?**

    A. Quién

    B. Quiénes

    C. Qué

    D. Cuál

10. ¿_____ **tú no _____ a clase?**

    A. Qué; asiste

    B. Por qué; asiste

    C. Qué; asistes

    D. Por qué; asistes

chapter 5

Talking About Location and Time

In this chapter you will learn more question words and the verbs **estar** and **ir**. You will learn how to talk about time and place as well as the cardinal and ordinal numbers and how to say *hello* and *good-bye*.

CHAPTER OBJECTIVES

In this chapter you will learn

- The question words *¿Dónde?, ¿Cómo?, ¿Cuándo?,* and *¿Cuánto?*
- The present tense of the verbs *estar* and *ir*
- Expressions of time and place
- Cardinal and ordinal numbers
- Days, months, and seasons
- Hellos and good-byes

The Question Words *¿Dónde?*, *¿Cómo?*, *¿Cuándo?*, and *¿Cuánto?*

In Chapter 4, you learned how to ask questions with **¿Quién?** (*Who?*), **¿Qué?** (*What?, Which?*), **¿Cuál?** (*What?, Which?*), and **¿Por qué?** (*Why?*). Now we will move on to **¿Dónde?** (*Where?*), **¿Cómo?** (*How?*), **¿Cuándo?** (*When?*), and **¿Cuánto?** (*How much?*). When writing, remember to begin your question with **¿** and end it with **?** When speaking, finish your question with rising intonation. Practice saying these examples:

¿Dónde está Maribel?	*Where is Maribel?*
¿Dónde trabaja tu padre?	*Where does your father work?*
¿Cómo estás?	*How are you?*
¿Cómo va Carlos al médico?	*How is Carlos going to the doctor?*
¿Cuándo vienen tus primos?	*When are your cousins coming?*
¿Cuándo viajas a Costa Rica?	*When are you traveling to Costa Rica?*
¿Cuánto cuesta?	*How much does it cost?*
¿Cuántos años tienes?	*How old are you?*
	(Literally: *How many years do you have?*)

The question word **¿Cuánto?** (*How much?*) has singular, plural, masculine, and feminine forms: **¿Cuánto?, ¿Cuántos?, ¿Cuánta?,** and **¿Cuántas?**. That is, when used before a noun, **¿Cuánto?** agrees with the noun that follows. Take a look at the following examples:

¿Cuánto dinero tienes?	*How much money do you have?*
¿Cuánta sangría quiere usted?	*How much sangria do you want?*
¿Cuántos años tiene Alberto?	*How old is Alberto?*
¿Cuántas personas vienen?	*How many people are coming?*

When used before a verb, the generic form **¿Cuánto?** is used.

¿Cuánto quieres?	*How much do you want?*
¿Cuánto paga el trabajo?	*How much does the job pay?*

Written Practice 1

▶ Track 22

Choose the question words that will elicit the answers to the statements below. Follow the example and use the translations to help you.

Adán trabaja en el supermercado. ¿_Quién_____ trabaja en el supermercado?
Adán works at the supermarket.

1. Adán trabaja en el supermercado. ¿_____ trabaja Adán?
Adán works at the supermarket.

2. Adán gana cinco dólares por hora. ¿_____ gana Adán?
Adán earns five dollars an hour.

3. Adán va al trabajo a las siete. ¿_____ va Adán al trabajo?
Adán goes to work at seven.

4. Adán va al trabajo en bicicleta. ¿_____ va Adán al trabajo?
Adán goes to work by bicycle.

5. Adán tiene tres hermanas. ¿_____ hermanas tiene Adán?
Adán has three sisters.

6. Una de sus hermanas se llama Laura. ¿_____ se llama su hermana?
One of his sisters is named Laura.

7. Adán come en una cafetería después de trabajar. ¿_____ come Adán después de trabajar?
Adán eats at a café after work.

The Verb *Estar*

You will often see the question words **¿Dónde?** and **¿Cómo?** used with the verb **estar**. In Chapter 3 you learned that Spanish has two ways to say *to be*: **ser** and **estar**. While **ser** talks about the intrinsic qualities of something, **estar** is used to express a state or condition. Think about transient qualities, such as *how* or *where* something is.

Estar is irregular in the **yo** form. Otherwise, it follows the rules for **-ar** verbs in the present tense.

Estar: **Present Tense**

yo estoy	*I am*
tú estás	*you are* (singular, informal)
él/ella/usted está	*he, she, it is, you are* (singular, formal)
nosotros estamos	*we are*
vosotros estáis	*you are* (plural, informal)
ellos/ellas/ustedes están	*they, you are* (plural)

Estar has various uses. You will learn more about these in Chapter 10, but here are some examples to get you started:

1. To describe a feeling, temporary state, or condition.

¿Cómo **estás**?	*How are you?*
—**Estoy** bien, gracias.	*I'm fine, thank you.*

2. To talk about location.

¿Dónde **está** el supermercado?	*Where is the supermarket?*
—**Está** al lado de la farmacia.	*—It's next to the pharmacy.*

¿Cómo es? or ¿Cómo está?

Asking **¿Cómo está Raquel?** and **¿Cómo es Raquel?** are two very different questions. The former, as you already know, means *How is Raquel?* The answer could be, **Raquel está bien** (*Raquel is well*) or **Raquel está enferma** (*Raquel is sick*). **¿Cómo es Raquel?**, however, asks about Raquel's appearance or personality and could be translated as *What does Raquel look like?* or *What is Raquel like?* The answer could be, **Es alta, morena con ojos azules** (*She's tall, dark, with blue eyes*), **Es delgada con el pelo corto** (*She's thin with short hair*), or **Es inteligente y generosa** (*She is intelligent and generous*).

Written Practice 2

Complete the sentences with the correct form of **estar** in the present.

1. Sergio _____ en la cocina. *Sergio is in the kitchen.*

2. Cristina y Raúl _____ tristes. *Cristina and Raúl are sad.*

3. ¿(Tú) _____ aquí? *Are you here?*

4. Nosotros no _____ enojados. *We are not angry.*

5. La casa _____ sucia. *The house is dirty.*

6. ¿Ustedes _____ en mi clase de español? *Are you in my Spanish class?*

7. El museo _____ detrás de la estación. *The museum is behind the station.*

8. (Yo) _____ cansada. *I'm tired.*

Oral Practice 1

Answer the following questions about yourself. Use the same verb that appears in the question in your answer. If you don't see the appropriate identifier to describe you, just pretend, or even better, try to find the word that does.

1. ¿Cómo estás? _____ bien/mal/triste/contento(a).
   How are you? well/bad/sad/happy

2. ¿Dónde trabajas? _____ en una empresa/en una escuela/en una oficina.
   Where do you work? in a company/in a school/in an office

3. ¿Dónde vives? _____ en una casa/en un apartamento/en la ciudad/en el campo.
   Where do you live? in a house/in an apartment/in the city/in the country

4. ¿Cómo eres? _____ alto(a)/bajo(a)/moreno(a)/rubio(a)/flaco(a)/gordo(a).
   What do you look like? tall/short/brunette/blonde/thin/fat

Prepositions of Place and Location

When describing the location of something, asking for directions, or giving directions, it's important to know prepositions of place. Many of these are followed by the word **de** (*of*).

Prepositions of Place

alrededor (de)	*around*	detrás (de)	*behind*
al lado (de)	*next to*	en	*in, on*
antes (de)	*before*	encima (de)	*above, on*
atrás (de)	*behind*	enfrente (de)	*across (from), facing*
cerca (de)	*near*	entre	*between*
debajo (de)	*under*	frente a	*across from, facing*
delante (de)	*in front of*	lejos (de)	*far from*
después (de)	*after*	sobre	*on*

Here are some other important words to know when talking about place:

Here and There

a la derecha	*to/on the right*	a la izquierda	*to/on the left*
derecho	*straight ahead*	recto	*straight ahead*
aquí/acá	*here*	allí/allá	*over there*
ahí	*there* (closer than *allí/allá*)	al final (de)	*at the end (of)*

Here are some example answers to the question **¿Dónde está el teatro?** (*Where is the theater?*) (Note how **de** + **el** and **a** + **el** contract to **del** and **al**.)

Está **cerca del** museo.	*It is near the museum.*
Está **al lado de** la biblioteca.	*It is next to the library.*
Está **en** la calle Bolívar.	*It's on Bolívar street.*
Está **frente a** la playa.	*It's facing the beach.*
Está **allí**.	*It's over there.*

Asking ¿Dónde queda?

Another way to ask the location of something is to use the verb **quedar**. It is commonly used in place of **estar**.

¿Dónde **queda** el banco?	*Where is the bank?*
Mi casa **no queda** muy lejos de aquí.	*My house isn't very far from here.*

Locations and Landmarks

When asking for or giving directions, or talking about the location of something, you should know some key vocabulary.

la avenida	*avenue*	la estación de metro	*metro/subway station*
el barrio	*neighborhood*	la estación de tren	*train station*
la calle	*street*	la manzana	*block* (Spain)
el camino	*road/way/path*	la parada de autobús	*bus stop*
la carretera	*road/highway*	la periferia/los alrededores	*outskirts*
el centro	*center*	la plaza	*square*
la cuadra	*block*	la terminal de autobuses	*bus station*

As well as some important landmarks:

la biblioteca	*library*	el palacio	*palace*
la catedral	*cathedral*	el parque	*park*
el edificio	*building*	la playa	*beach*
la escuela	*school*	la plaza de toros	*bullring*
el estadio	*stadium*	el puerto	*port/harbor*
el gimnasio	*gym*	el río	*river*
el hotel	*hotel*	el supermercado	*supermarket*
la iglesia	*church*	el teatro	*theater*
el jardín	*garden*	la tienda	*store*
el museo	*museum*	el zoo	*zoo*

Oral Practice 2

 Track 23

Practice asking and answering questions about location by translating the following sentences into Spanish. Use the verb indicated in parentheses.

1. *Where is the beach? —It's over there.* (estar)

2. *Where is the bus stop? —It's in front of the hotel.* (quedar)

3. *Where are the palace and the cathedral? —They're at the end of the street.* (estar)

4. *Where is Juan Bravo Street? —It's in the center, near the train station.* (quedar)

5. *Where is the restaurant "La Limeña?" —It's here on the right, above the Hotel Excelsior.* (estar)

The Spanish-Speaking World

Whether you want to travel to Latin America, communicate with your neighbor down the street, or follow the World Cup broadcast on Univisión, there are plenty of good reasons to learn Spanish. As the third-most-spoken language in the world (after Mandarin Chinese and English), and the second-ranked native tongue, Spanish is spoken by hundreds of millions of people all over the world as a first or other language.

As you can see on the map, Spanish is an official language in twenty countries and the commonwealth of **Puerto Rico**. Countries with Spanish as an official language include: **España** (*Spain*) in Europe, **México**, **Guatemala**, **El Salvador**, **Honduras**, **Nicaragua**, **Costa Rica**, **Panamá**, **Cuba**, **la República Dominicana**, **Colombia**, **Venezuela**, **Ecuador**, **Peru**, **Bolivia**, **Chile**, **Argentina**, **Uruguay**, and **Paraguay** in Latin America, and **Guinea Ecuatorial** (*Equatorial Guinea*) in Africa.

The United States is home to almost 30 million Spanish speakers, a number that some believe will reach over 40 million by the year 2025. You will also find Spanish speakers in **Andorra** (*Europe*), and in **las Filipinas** (*the Philippines*), which was once a Spanish colony.

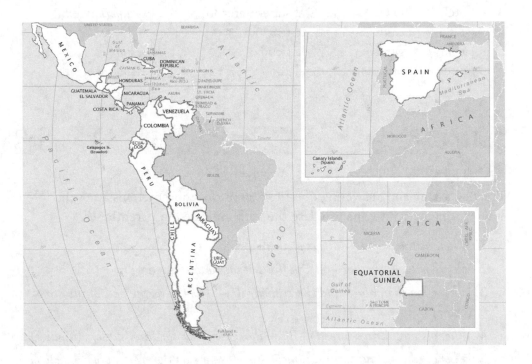

Spain, the birthplace of the Spanish language, is also host to a number of regional languages aside from Iberian Spanish, often referred to as **castellano** (*Castilian*). As debate and controversy arise over the use of Spanish in the United States, it is important to remember that the Spanish "motherland" itself has a diversity of languages. These include: **gallego** (*Galician*), **catalán** (*Catalan*), and **euskera** (*Basque*), as well as a number of smaller language groups.

The Verb *Ir*

You will often see the question words **¿Dónde?**, **¿Cómo?**, and **¿Cuándo?** used with the verb **ir** (*to go*). You'll notice that while **ir** is irregular and has its own conjugation, its verb endings are very similar to those of **ser** and **estar**, which should make it easier to memorize. Here is the present tense:

Ir: Present Tense

yo voy	*I go*
tú vas	*you go* (singular, informal)
él/ella/usted va	*he, she, it goes, you go* (singular, formal)
nosotros vamos	*we go*
vosotros vais	*you go* (plural, informal)
ellos/ellas/ustedes van	*they, you go* (plural)

Uses of *Ir*

Ir is an important verb to learn and memorize because it is used so often and in so many ways. Notice that **ir** is often used with the preposition **a** to talk about place. Remember that **a** + **el** contracts to **al**.

Voy a la playa en verano.	*I go to the beach in the summer.*
¿Cuándo **vamos** al aeropuerto?	*When are we going to the airport?*

Here are the uses of **ir** in the present.

- When talking about cities, states, and countries, use **ir** + **a** without the article (with the exception of countries that take the definite article, several of which you learned in Chapter 2).
  Ana María **va a** Filadelfia.   *Ana María is going to Philadelphia.*
  ¿Cómo **vas a** México?   *How are you going to Mexico?*

- When talking about modes of transportation, use **ir** + **en** without the article before the type of transportation.
  Voy a Nueva York **en tren**.   *I'm going to New York by train.*
  Van en avión a Canadá.   *They're going by plane to Canada.*

- When talking about walking, however, use **ir** + **a** to say *go by (or on) foot*.
  Voy a pie.   *I go by (on) foot/I walk.*

- As is the case with other verbs, the present tense of **ir** is often used to express the future. In this case, the present tense of **ir** would be translated as *is/are/am going*.
  Cristina **va** al zoo el domingo.   *Cristina is going to the zoo on*
                          Sunday.

  ¿**Vamos** al cine mañana?   *Are we going to the movies*
                          tomorrow?

Written Practice 3

▶ Track 24

Complete the following sentences with the correct conjugation of the verb **ir** in the present.

1. ¿Dónde (nosotros) _____ a comer? *Where are we going to eat?*

2. Alicia _____ a la iglesia los domingos. *Alicia goes to church on Sundays.*

3. ¿Ustedes _____ en tren, o _____ en autobús? *Are you going by train or are you going by bus?*

4. (Yo) _____ al teatro el viernes a las ocho. *I'm going to the theater on Friday at eight.*

5. Ellos _____ a las montañas. *They are going to the mountains.*

6. ¿Cómo (usted) _____ al parque? *How are you going to the park?*

7. (Nosotros) _____ a pie. *We're walking/We're going on foot.*

8. Tú nunca _____ al centro en carro. Siempre _____ en metro. *You never go downtown by car. You always go by subway.*

9. ¿Quiénes _____ a la fiesta? *Who is going to the party?*

10. ¿Cuándo (tú) _____ a Los Ángeles, hoy o mañana? *When are you going to Los Angeles, today or tomorrow?*

Cardinal Numbers

Now that you have learned the question *How many?* (¿**Cuanto?**) in Spanish, it's important to know how to count out your answer. Here are some useful cardinal numbers in Spanish. Listen to the CD to hear their pronunciation.

▶ **Track 25**

1	uno	19	diecinueve
2	dos	20	veinte
3	tres	21	veintiuno
4	cuatro	22	veintidós
5	cinco	23	veintitrés
6	seis	24	veinticuatro
7	siete	25	veinticinco
8	ocho	26	veintiséis
9	nueve	27	veintisiete
10	diez	28	veintiocho
11	once	29	veintinueve
12	doce	30	trcinta
13	trece	40	cuarenta
14	catorce	50	cincuenta
15	quince	60	sesenta
16	dieciséis	70	sctenta
17	diecisiete	80	ochenta
18	dieciocho	90	noventa

Notice how the numbers 16–29 are written as one word, but in essence they are made up of three words joined together:

dieciséis	=	diez + y + seis	=	*ten and six (16)*
veintinueve	=	veinte +y + nueve	=	*twenty and nine (29)*

Compound numbers after 30 are written as two words connected by the word **y** (*and*) . . .

32	treinta y dos	78	setenta y ocho
55	cincuenta y cinco	91	noventa y uno

Uno (*one*) is only used when counting, or when the number stands alone. Otherwise, **un** is used before masculine nouns and **una** before feminine nouns.

uno, dos, tres, cuatro,...	*one, two, three, four, . . .*
¿Cuántos días? **Uno./Un** día.	*How many days? One./One day.*
¿Cuántas hijas tienes? **Una./** **Una** hija.	*How many daughters do you have? One./One daughter.*
veinti**ún** años	*twenty-one years*
ciento **una** personas	*one hundred and one people*

For 100, **cien**, a shortened version of **ciento** is used. The numbers 200, 300, etc., are written as all one word and the plural **cientos** is used (**doscientos**). Note that unlike English, the word *hundred* in Spanish becomes plural after *one hundred*, giving the literal meaning of *two hundreds, three hundreds*, etc. Also note the slight variations of spelling.

100	cien (ciento)	600	seiscientos
200	doscientos	700	setecientos
300	trescientos	800	ochocientos
400	cuatrocientos	900	novecientos
500	quinientos		

For all other compound numbers **y** (*and*) is used only between the tens and the units (for numbers ending in the 30s and above). **Ciento** is used for compound numbers in the 100s.

101	ciento uno	143	ciento cuarenta y tres
102	ciento dos	375	trescientos setenta y cinco
140	ciento cuarenta	491	cuatrocientos noventa y uno
122	ciento veintidós	984	novecientos ochenta y cuatro

When compounds of **cien** are used to describe feminine nouns, the feminine form is used.

doscientos hombres	*two hundred men*
doscientas mujeres	*two hundred women*

Finally, the word **mil** (*thousand*) is never plural, but **millón** (*million*) and **billón** (*billion*) are.

1000	mil	1500	mil quinientos
2000	dos mil	1798	mil setecientos noventa y ocho
7000	siete mil	3460	tres mil cuatrocientos cincuenta

| 1,000,000 | un millón | 1,000,000,000,000 | un billón |
| 2,000,000 | dos millones | 5,000,000,000,000 | cinco billones |

Multiples of **millón** and **billón** use **de** before a noun.

un millón de dólares   *a million dollars*

Note that **billón** actually means *trillion* in English, following the British usage. To say *a billion* as it is meant in the United States, say **mil millones** (literally: *a thousand million*).

mil millones de euros   *a billion euros*
billones de personas   *trillions of people*

Oral Practice 3

▶ Track 26

Say the following numbers in Spanish.

1. 5	11. 505
2. 13	12. 657
3. 26	13. 829
4. 41	14. 1003
5. 58	15. 1492
6. 85	16. 1840
7. 99	17. 5000
8. 102	18. 7834
9. 137	19. 4,000,000
10. 450	20. 2,000,000,000

Now say the following phrases in Spanish. The singular form of the necessary vocabulary word is given to you in parentheses.

21. *two million dollars* (un dólar)

22. *one hundred and one women* (la mujer)

23. *five hundred things* (la cosa)

24. *thirty-one books* (el libro)

25. *two hundred and fifty-one girls* (la muchacha)

Ordinal Numbers

Ordinal numbers are used to talk about order. In Spanish, the ordinal numbers are:

primero	*first*	sexto	*sixth*
segundo	*second*	séptimo	*seventh*
tercero	*third*	octavo	*eighth*
cuarto	*fourth*	noveno	*ninth*
quinto	*fifth*	décimo	*tenth*

In Spanish, the ordinal numbers beyond **décimo** (*tenth*) are rarely used. For instance, to say *Carlos the Fifth*, use the ordinal number: **Carlos Quinto**. However, to say *Alfonso the Thirteenth* use the cardinal number **Alfonso Trece**.

Like adjectives, ordinal numbers agree in number and gender with the nouns they modify.

la **séptima** calle	*the seventh street*
las **primeras** damas	*the first ladies*

The words **primero** and **tercero** are shortened when used before masculine singular nouns.

el **tercer** piso	*the third floor*
el **primer** paso	*the first step*

Talking About Time

To ask the time, you can use:

¿Qué hora es?	*What time is it?*

To answer this question, use the verb **ser** plus the time. Use the singular form **es la** with times between 1:00 and 1:59 because 1:00 is considered singular.

Es la una.	*It is 1:00.*
Es la una y diez.	*It is 1:10.*

For all other times, use the plural form **son las** because the hours 2:00 to 12:59 are considered plural.

Son las cinco.	*It's 5:00.*
Son las ocho y media.	*It's 8:30.*

For the expressions **medianoche** (*midnight*) and **mediodía** (*noon*), use **es** and **es el**, respectively.

Es medianoche.	*It's midnight.*
Es el mediodía.	*It's noon.*

To ask at what time something will happen, use **¿A qué hora... ?** (*At what time . . . ?*).

¿A qué hora vas al gimnasio?	*At what time (When) are you going to the gym?*

To answer this question, use the preposition **a** (*at*) plus **la** (singular) or **las** (plural), depending on the time.

A la una.	*At 1:00.*
A las tres.	*At 3:00.*

For the expressions **medianoche** (*midnight*) and **mediodía** (*noon*), use **a** and **al**, respectively.

A medianoche.	*At midnight.*
Al mediodía.	*At noon.*

Expressing Time

There are several ways to express the time. You can always use the hour followed by **y** plus the minutes. You can also use **media** for *thirty* and **cuarto** for *quarter/fifteen*.

la una **y media**	*1:30*
las dos **y cuarto**	*2:15*
las siete **y veinticinco**	*7:25*

When naming specific minutes (25, 40, 33, etc.), Spanish speakers often drop the **y**.

las ocho **cuarenta**	*8:40*

To express times after half past the hour, you can use the word **menos** (*minus*) in place of **y**. Just remember to refer to the hour after the hour you want to speak about and then subtract the minutes. For example:

las ocho **menos veinte**	*7:40 (Literally: eight minus twenty)*
la una **menos cuarto**	*12:45 (Literally: one minus a quarter)*

As you may have noticed, the same time can be said in different ways. 3:50 can be **las cuatro menos diez** (literally: *four minus ten*) or **las tres (y) cincuenta** (literally: *three fifty*).

To describe the time of day, use **de la mañana** (*in the morning*), **de la tarde** (*in the afternoon*), and **de la noche** (*at night*). In most Spanish-speaking countries, morning ends at noon. The distinction between afternoon and evening may depend on where you are.

La tienda abre a las siete **de la mañana**.	*The store opens at seven in the morning.*
Empiezan a trabajar a las dos **de la tarde**.	*They start work at two in the afternoon.*
Vamos a las ocho **de la noche**.	*We're going at eight at night.*

Oral Practice 4

 Track 27

Practice saying the following times in as many ways as possible using **es la** or **son las** plus the hour and minutes. Listen to the CD to check your answers and pronunciation.

1. 12:45
2. 1:30
3. 3:50
4. 7:15
5. 8:45

Oral Practice 5

 Track 28

Listen to the following questions and answer them using the time in parentheses plus **de la mañana**, **de la tarde**, or **de la noche** depending on whether the answer is A.M. or P.M. Follow the example.

¿A qué hora van al teatro? (7:30)
Van al teatro a las siete y media.

What time are they going to the theater?

1. ¿A qué hora vas a clase? (mediodía)

    What time are you going to class?

2. ¿A qué hora abre el supermercado? (6:00 A.M.)

    What time does the supermarket open?

3. ¿A qué hora vamos a la playa? (2:00 P.M.)

    What time are we going to the beach?

4. ¿A qué hora llegas a casa? (8:45 P.M.)

    What time do you get home?

5. ¿A qué hora termina la obra? (10:00 P.M.)

    What time does the play end?

6. ¿Qué hora es? (1:15 P.M.)

    What time is it?

7. ¿A qué hora cenamos? (7:15 P.M.)

    What time are we having dinner?

Expressions of Time

To answer questions with **¿Cuándo?** (*When?*), there are several expressions you can use to express time.

anoche	*last night*	por la mañana	*in the morning*
ayer	*yesterday*	esta noche	*tonight*
hoy	*today*	por la noche	*at night*
esta mañana	*this morning*	esta tarde	*this afternoon*
mañana	*tomorrow*	por la tarde	*in the afternoon*

por semana	*per week*	por día	*per day*
por mes	*per month*		
la semana que viene/la próxima semana	*next week*		
el mes/año que viene/el próximo mes/año	*next month/year*		

¿Cuando vas al concierto?	*When are you going to the concert?*
Voy mañana por la noche.	*I'm going tomorrow night.*

Days of the Week

The days of the week are not capitalized in Spanish. The week, and therefore most calendars, usually start with **lunes** (*Monday*).

lunes	*Monday*	viernes	*Friday*
martes	*Tuesday*	sábado	*Saturday*
miércoles	*Wednesday*	domingo	*Sunday*
jueves	*Thursday*		

To say something happens *on* a certain day, use the article **el** with the day.

El jueves voy a Montreal.	*On Thursday I'm going to Montreal.*
Julio va a estar en Caracas **el martes**.	*Julio is going to be in Caracas on Tuesday.*

To say something happens regularly on a certain day, use the article **los**. In this case, **sábado** and **domingo** are made plural by adding an **-s**.

Voy a misa **los domingos**.	*I go to mass on Sundays.*
¿Qué haces **los viernes**?	*What do you do on Fridays?*

Months and Seasons

The months and seasons are also not capitalized in Spanish.

enero	*January*	la primavera	*spring*
febrero	*February*	el verano	*summer*
marzo	*March*	el otoño	*fall/autumn*
abril	*April*	el invierno	*winter*
mayo	*May*		
junio	*June*		
julio	*July*		
agosto	*August*		
septiembre *or* setiembre	*September*		
octubre	*October*		

noviembre	*November*
diciembre	*December*

To say something happens *in* a certain month or season, use **en** (*in*).

Tomo vacaciones **en agosto**.	*I take vacation in August.*
En invierno nieva.	*In winter it snows.*

Hellos and Good-Byes

You can learn all the verb conjugations in the world, but if you don't know how to say *hi*, you'll never get the conversation going. By the same token, if you can't say *bye*, it may be difficult for you to extricate yourself from an extended discussion. Here are some conversation starters and stoppers to help you out. You'll notice that almost all of these use words (nouns, adjective, and verbs) that you already know and follow the rules you have already learned. For instance, **Buenos días** (*Hello, Good morning*) follows the rule for noun/adjective agreement that you learned in Chapter 4. **¿Cómo estás?** uses a question word and the verb **estar** in the **tú** form, both of which you have learned. Here is a list of the most common and traditional hellos and good-byes. Listen to the CD to practice your pronunciation.

▶ Track 29

Hola	*Hello/Hi*
Buenos días	*Hello/Good morning*
Buenas tardes	*Good afternoon*
Buenas noches	*Good evening/Good night*
¿Cómo está(s)?	*How are you?*
Adiós	*Good-bye*
Hasta luego	*See you later* (Literally: *Until later*)
Hasta mañana	*See you tomorrow* (Literally: *Until tomorrow*)

Here are some colloquial variations for these phrases:

Buenas	*Good morning/afternoon/evening*
Muy buenas	*Good morning/afternoon/evening*
¿Qué tal?	*How are things?*
¿Cómo te va?	*How are you?*
¿Qué pasa?	*What's up?*

¿Cómo andas?	How are you?
¿Qué hubo?	What's up?
Chau/Chao	Bye

A typical exchange might go something like this:

Juan: ¡Hola! ¿Qué tal? *Hi! How are things?*

Ester: Muy bien, ¿y tú? *Great, and you?*

Juan: Muy bien, gracias. Bueno, me voy. ¡Chau! *Really great, thanks. OK,
I have to go. Bye!*

Ester: ¡Chau! ¡Adiós! *Bye! See you!*

QUIZ

Circle the letter of the word or phrase that best completes each sentence.

1. ¿_____ años tiene Paula?
   A. Cuánto
   B. Cuánta
   C. Cuántos
   D. Cuántas

2. ¿_____ queda el centro comercial?
   A. Qué
   B. Cuánto
   C. Cuándo
   D. Dónde

3. Mis padres _____ enojados.
   A. estoy
   B. estás
   C. está
   D. están

4. La calle Sol no está lejos. Está _____.
   A. cerca
   B. lejos
   C. entre
   D. frente

5. Van _____ la playa _____ pie.

   A. a; a

   B. a; en

   C. al; a

   D. al; en

6. doce + noventa y nueve = _____

   A. ciento doce

   B. ciento once

   C. cien y once

   D. ciento uno

7. Hay _____ días en una semana.

   A. cincuenta y dos

   B. trescientos sesenta y cinco

   C. doce

   D. siete

8. _____ tres de la mañana.

   A. Es la

   B. Son las

   C. Es

   D. Son

9. Yo no _____ a clase hoy.

   A. va

   B. van

   C. vamos

   D. voy

10. La tienda está cerrada _____ lunes.

   A. la

   B. los

   C. en

   D. a

PART ONE TEST

Circle the letter of the word or phrase that best completes each sentence.

1. **The closest English sound of the** c **in the word** centro **is** _____.

    A. *k*

    B. *s*

    C. *b*

    D. *v*

2. **The closest English sound of the** ho **in the word** hola **is** _____.

    A. *ho*

    B. *oh*

    C. *hoo*

    D. *oo*

3. **Yo soy** _____ **estudiante.**

    A. un

    B. una

    C. el

    D. —

4. _____ **casa es grande.**

    A. El

    B. La

    C. Los

    D. Las

5. **Tengo una** _____.

    A. foto

    B. mapa

    C. problema

    D. sofá

6. **In the word** farmacia, **the stress is placed on which sound?**

    A. far-

    B. -ma-

    C. -ci-

    D. -a

7. Tú no _____ nicaragüense, ¿verdad?

   A. es
   B. eres
   C. sois
   D. son

8. _____ aquí vive en la ciudad.

   A. Nadie
   B. Nunca
   C. Jamás
   D. Nada

9. Mis padres _____ inglés y español.

   A. habla
   B. hablas
   C. hablamos
   D. hablan

10. ¿Tú _____ los fines de semana?

    A. trabaja
    B. trabajan
    C. trabajo
    D. trabajas

11. ¿Son _____ amigos?

    A. tus
    B. nuestras
    C. nuestro
    D. mi

12. Mis piernas son muy _____.

    A. gordo
    B. gorda
    C. gordos
    D. gordas

13. Penélope Cruz y Javier Bardem son _____.

    A. español
    B. española
    C. españolas
    D. españoles

14. **Sofia Loren es una _____.**

    A. elegante mujeres

    B. mujer elegante

    C. elegantes mujer

    D. mujer elegantes

15. **El restaurante es muy, muy caro. Es _____.**

    A. carísimo

    B. carísima

    C. carito

    D. carita

16. **¿_____ no bailas?**

    A. Qué

    B. Por qué

    C. Quién

    D. Cuál

17. **¿_____ de los discos es de Los Fabulosos Cadillacs?**

    A. Qué

    B. Cuáles

    C. Quién

    D. Cuál

18. **¿Usted _____ la revista Hola?**

    A. lees

    B. lee

    C. leen

    D. leo

19. **Yo _____ maratones.**

    A. corre

    B. corres

    C. corro

    D. corren

20. **¿_____ cuesta la cartera?**

    A. Cuánto

    B. Cuándo

    C. Dónde

    D. Cómo

21. **Mauricio y Raúl _____ en la misma clase de inglés.**

    A. están
    B. está
    C. estoy
    D. estáis

22. **Tú y yo _____ al teatro en metro.**

    A. vas
    B. voy
    C. van
    D. vamos

23. **A las 10:00 p.m. decimos _____.**

    A. «Buenos días».
    B. «Buenas medianoches».
    C. «Buenas tardes».
    D. «Buenas noches».

24. **El número 125 se lee _____.**

    A. cien veinticinco
    B. ciento y veinticinco
    C. ciento veinticinco
    D. ciento veinte y clnco

25. **_____ doce y media.**

    A. Son las
    B. Es la
    C. Es
    D. Son

Part Two

Expressing Yourself in the Present

chapter 6

Using Common Irregular Verbs

In this chapter you will learn how to say *there is* and *there are* using the verb **hay**. You will learn the common irregular verbs **hacer**, **tener**, and **venir** and how to use them in expressions. You will also learn how to use conjunctions, talk about the weather, ask someone his or her age, and express obligation.

CHAPTER OBJECTIVES

In this chapter you will learn

- The verb form *hay*
- Conjunctions
- The verb *hacer* in the present
- Expressions with *hacer*
- How to talk about the weather
- The verbs *tener* and *venir* in the present
- Expressions with *tener*
- Expressing obligation with *hay que* and *tener que*

The Verb Form *Hay*

Saying *there is* or *there are* in Spanish is a simple matter of using the word **hay**. Unlike other Spanish verbs, which conjugate according to the subject, **hay** (a form of the verb **haber**), is always **hay** in the present tense, whether you are expressing the singular *there is* or the plural *there are*.

Hay leche en el frigorífico.	*There is milk in the fridge.*
Hay una cama en el cuarto.	*There is a bed in the room.*
Hay tres libros encima de la mesa.	*There are three books on the table.*

To ask the questions *Is there (any)* or *Are there (any)* use **¿Hay... ?**

¿Hay leche en el frigorífico?	*Is there any milk in the fridge?*
¿Hay dos camas en el cuarto?	*Are there two beds in the room?*

You may answer positively with **Sí, hay** or negatively with **No, no, hay**.

Sí, hay.	*Yes, there is./Yes, there are.*
Sí, hay leche en el frigorífico.	*Yes, there is milk in the fridge.*
No, no hay.	*No, there isn't./No, there aren't.*
No, no hay leche en el frigorífico.	*No, there isn't any milk in the fridge.*

For some Spanish language learners, the use of **hay** to say *there is* or *there are* can be confusing. It might help to remember that **hay** is actually the "impersonal" form of the verb **haber**. **Haber** is also used (as an auxiliary verb) to make compound forms of verbs, which you will learn later in this book.

Written Practice 1

 Track 30

Translate each sentence into Spanish using the vocabulary words in parentheses to help you.

1. *There is a chair* (una silla) *in the living room* (la sala de estar).

   _____.

2. *There are three parks* (parques) *in the city* (la ciudad).

   _____.

3. *Is there a restaurant* (un restaurante) *nearby* (cerca)?

¿————————————————————————————?

4. *—No, there isn't a restaurant nearby.*

————————————————————————————.

5. *Are there mountains* (montañas) *in Venezuela?*

¿————————————————————————————?

6. *—Yes, there are mountains in Venezuela.*

————————————————————————————.

7. *There is a telephone* (un teléfono) *in the room* (el cuarto).

————————————————————————————.

8. *There are fifteen bars* (bares) *in the neighborhood* (el barrio).

————————————————————————————.

Conjunctions

Conjunctions can help you create more complex sentences with very little effort. In addition, if you learn your conjunctions well, you can understand more shades of meaning when you listen to native speakers. Here are some common Spanish conjunctions that can always be used with the present tense you've already learned:

Conjunctions

y	*and*	sin embargo	*however*
o	*or, either*	así que	*so*
pero	*but*	es decir	*that is*
ni... ni	*neither . . . nor*	o sea	*in other words*
además	*furthermore*	por eso	*because of this*
encima	*furthermore, on top of that*	por lo tanto	*therefore*
sino	*but rather*	pues	*well, since, as, then*

You have already seen **y** (*and*) and **o** (*or*) used in this book. Here are some examples with other conjunctions from the list:

O vas tú, **o** voy yo.   *Either you go, or I go.*
Hay una lámpara, **pero** no funciona. *There is a lamp, but it doesn't work.*

Ni come carne **ni** bebe alcohol.	*He neither eats meat nor drinks alcohol.*
No es camarera, **sino** cliente.	*She isn't a waitress, but rather a customer.*
No hay piscina en el hotel; **sin embargo**, hay gimnasio.	*There isn't a pool at the hotel; however, there is a gym.*

NOTE *Before words beginning with **i**, the word **y** (and) becomes **e**. Before words beginning with **o**, the word **o** (or) becomes **u**.*

Uno **u** otro va a la fiesta.	*One or the other is going to the party.*
Estudio física **e** ingeniería.	*I study physics and engineering.*

Written Practice 2

Read the following passage describing a house. Then mark each statement true (T) or false (F). Use the vocabulary in the table to help you.

Household Vocabulary

el cuarto de baño	*bathroom*	estacionar	*to park*
el dormitorio	*bedroom*	la cocina	*kitchen*
el jardín	*yard*	el lugar	*room, space*
la terraza	*balcony*	la ventaja	*advantage*
el sótano	*basement*	la desventaja	*disadvantage*
el sitio para estacionar	*parking spot*	la gente	*the people*

La casa no es grande, sino pequeña. Sin embargo, hay dos cuartos de baño y tres dormitorios. Hay un jardín pero no hay ni patio ni terraza. Además, no hay sótano ni un sitio para estacionar. Por eso la gente estaciona en la calle. Sin embargo, la cocina es nueva y hay lugar para comer dentro. Por lo tanto hay ventajas y desventajas de la casa.

1. _____ The house is big.
2. _____ The house is small.
3. _____ The house has two bedrooms.
4. _____ The house has two bathrooms.
5. _____ The house has a patio but not a balcony.

6. _____ The house has a balcony but not a patio.

7. _____ The house doesn't have a patio or a balcony.

8. _____ The house has a basement.

9. _____ The house has a parking spot.

10. _____ People park on the street.

11. _____ The kitchen is new.

12. _____ The kitchen is tiny.

13. _____ The house has only disadvantages.

The Verb *Hacer*

Hacer is a verb that you will see over and over again used in a wide variety of ways. It is often translated as *to do* or *to make* but can take on many meanings according to context. While **hacer** is an irregular verb, its conjugations in the present tense are relatively straightforward—only the **yo** form strays from the **-er** verb pattern. In other tenses, however, **hacer** can become highly irregular, almost unrecognizable. Here is the present tense:

Hacer: Present Tense

yo hago	*I make/do*
tú haces	*you make/do* (singular, informal)
él/ella/usted hace	*he, she, it makes/does, you make/do* (singular, formal)
nosotros hacemos	*we make/do*
vosotros hacéis	*you make/do* (plural, informal)
ellos/ellas/ustedes hacen	*they, you make/do* (plural)

Uses of *Hacer*

As we mentioned above, **hace** has many uses. Here we will see some of the most common and most basic.

- **Hacer** is used with the meaning *to make*, often implying a sense of producing or creating.

  Rodolfo **hace** el almuerzo.   *Rodolfo makes lunch.*

  Hago la cama por la mañana.   *I make the bed in the morning.*

- It also means *to do*, used similarly in English.

  ¿Qué **haces**?   *What do you do?/What are you doing?*

  Camila no **hace** nada.   *Camila doesn't do anything/isn't doing anything.*

- In Spanish, **hacer** is used to talk about the weather.

  Hace frío.   *It's cold.*

  Hace buen tiempo.   *The weather is nice.*

- **Hacer** often means *to make* in the sense of making someone or something feel or do something. In this case it is used with direct object pronouns, which you will learn later in this book. You'll see the pronoun **me** (*me*) used before the verb in the following examples:

  Viajar **me hace** feliz.   *Traveling makes me happy.*

  Las películas tristes **me hacen** llorar.   *Sad movies make me cry.*

Idiomatic Expressions with *Hacer*

Hacer is used with a number of idiomatic expressions in which the meaning of the verb itself varies widely. Idiomatic expressions, by definition, cannot be understood by the individual words that make them up. Think of expressions in English, such as *to put your foot in your mouth* or *to throw a party*. If you tried to understand them literally, according to the meaning of each word, they wouldn't make sense. Therefore, these expressions with **hacer** and all the idiomatic expressions you learn in this book will be easier for you to understand if you don't try to translate them word for word, but rather focus on getting the gist. Here are a few common expressions with **hacer**:

hacer una broma	*to play a joke*
hacer caso	*to pay attention to*
hacer cola	*to form a line/to wait in line*
hacer daño	*to hurt, damage*
hacer dinero	*to make money*
hacer falta	*to be necessary*
hacer una fiesta	*to throw a party*
hacer la maleta	*to pack (one's suitcase)*

hacer una pregunta	*to ask a question*
hacer una visita	*to pay a visit*

Here are some examples of sentences using these expressions with **hacer**:

Enrique no **hace caso** al profesor.	*Enrique doesn't pay attention to the teacher.*
¿Quieres **hacer una pregunta**?	*Do you want to ask a question?*
El sol **hace daño** a la piel.	*The sun damages your skin.*

Keep in mind that the expression **hacer falta** is usually used in the third person singular (**él**) or plural (**ellos**) forms: **hace falta** or **hacen falta**. It can be followed by a noun or by the infinitive. While the expression means *to be necessary* it can also be translated as *to need*. Take a look at these examples:

No **hace falta** cerrar la puerta.	*It's not necessary to close the door. There's no need to close the door.*
Hace falta una silla.	*A chair is needed. (We need a chair.)*
Hacen falta profesores bilingües.	*Bilingual teachers are needed.*

Written Practice 3

Complete the following sentences with the present tense of **hacer**.

1. ¿_____ falta llevar identificación? *Is it necessary to bring ID?*

2. (Yo) _____ mil cosas a la vez. *I do a thousand things at once.*

3. Gerardo no _____ mucho dinero. *Gerardo doesn't make a lot of money.*

4. ¿Qué _____ (nosotros) hoy? *What shall we do today?*

5. Ellos _____ las maletas en el hotel. *They pack their suitcases in the hotel.*

6. Ustedes _____ demasiado. *You do too much.*

7. ¿Qué preguntas _____ los padres sobre la escuela? *What questions do parents ask about school?*

8. ¿Quién _____ las reglas? *Who makes the rules?*

9. Yo no _____ caso de las noticias. *I don't pay attention to the news.*

10. ¿Qué _____ (tú) los fines de semana? *What do you do on weekends?*

Talking About the Weather

Now that you know the verb **hacer**, you will be better prepared to talk about the weather. What better way to strike up a conversation? To ask about the weather, you can say:

¿Qué tiempo hace?   *How's the weather?/What's the weather like?*

Many of the expressions used to talk about the weather in Spanish use the verb **hacer** with a noun (**hacer calor**; literally: *it makes heat*). This is different from English, when we generally use the verb *to be* and an adjective (*It is cold*). Compare the Spanish and English constructions below.

Hace calor.   *It's hot.*
Hace frío.   *It's cold.*
Hace sol.   *It's sunny.*
Hace viento.   *It's windy.*
Hace fresco.
Hace fresquito. }   *It's cool.*
Hace buen tiempo.   *The weather is good./It's a nice day.*
Hace mal tiempo.   *The weather is bad.*

Using the verb **hay** you can make even more weather expressions.

Hay humedad.   *It's humid. (There's humidity.)*
Hay niebla.   *It's foggy. (There's fog.)*
Hay granizo.   *It's hailing. (There's hail.)*
Hay lloviznas.   *It's drizzling. (There are drizzles.)*
Hay neblina.   *It's misty. (There's mist.)*

You can use the verbs **llover** (*to rain*) and **nevar** (*to snow*).

Llueve.   *It's raining./It rains.*
Nieva.   *It's snowing./It snows.*

And finally, using the verb **estar** you can say even more about the weather.

Está nublado.	*It's cloudy.*
Está lloviendo.	*It's raining.*
Está nevando.	*It's snowing.*

The expressions **está lloviendo** and **está nevando** are used to talk about the weather at the moment of speaking. Compare these examples:

¿Qué tiempo hace ahora?	*What's the weather like right now?*
—Está nevando.	*—It's snowing.*
¿Qué tiempo hace en Alaska en invierno?	*What's the weather like in Alaska in the winter?*
—Nieva.	*—It snows.*

Written Practice 4

 Track 31

Make sentences to answer the following four questions using the phrases you just learned. Answers will vary depending on the climate where you live, but try to use as wide a variety of expressions as possible.

1. ¿Qué tiempo hace en invierno?

_____.

2. ¿Qué tiempo hace en verano?

_____.

3. ¿Qué tiempo hace en primavera?

_____.

4. ¿Qué tiempo hace en otoño?

_____.

The Verbs *Tener* and *Venir*

The irregular verbs **tener** (*to have*) and **venir** (*to come*) follow similar patterns of conjugation in the present tense. Learning them together should make them easier to memorize.

Tener: Present Tense

yo tengo	*I have*
tú tienes	*you have* (singular, informal)
él/ella/usted tiene	*he, she, it has, you have* (singular, formal)
nosotros tenemos	*we have*
vosotros tenéis	*you have* (plural, informal)
ellos/ellas/ustedes tienen	*they, you have* (plural)

Venir: Present Tense

yo vengo	*I come*
tú vienes	*you come* (singular, informal)
él/ella/usted viene	*he, she, it comes, you come* (singular, formal)
nosotros venimos	*we come*
vosotros venís	*you come* (plural, informal)
ellos/ellas/ustedes vienen	*they, you come* (plural)

Here are some examples of sentences using **tener** and **venir**. You'll notice that due to the nature of the verbs and their meanings in English, **venir** in the present is often, but not always, translated as *is/are/am coming*, while **tener** is often, but not always, translated as *has/have*.

¿**Vienes** con Roberto?	*Are you coming with Roberto?*
Vienen en coche.	*They are coming by car.*
Tengo tres hijos.	*I have three children.*
¿No **tienes** amigos?	*You don't have any friends?*

Written Practice 5

Complete the sentences with the preset tense of the verb in parentheses.

1. (Tú) _____ mi cartera. (tener) *You have my wallet.*

2. Trinidad _____ el sábado. (venir) *Trinidad is coming on Saturday.*

3. (Yo) no _____ ni idea. (tener) *I have no idea.*

4. ¿Ustedes _____ en avión? (venir) *Are you coming by plane?*

5. (Él) _____ muchos problemas. (tener) *He has a lot of problems.*

6. (Yo) _____ a las tres y media. (venir) *I'm coming at three-thirty.*

7. Laura y José no _____ hijos. (tener) *Laura and José don't have children.*

8. (Yo) nunca _____ a la oficina por la mañana. (venir) *I never come to the office in the morning.*

9. ¿(Nosotros) _____ planes esta noche? (tener) *Do we have any plans tonight?*

10. (Nosotros) _____ a ver los museos. (venir) *We are coming to see the museums.*

Uses of *Tener*

Tener is used a number of ways in Spanish, often in expressions that in English are used with the verb *to be*.

Tener to Talk About Age

When talking about age, the verb **tener** (*to have*) is used with **años** (*years*), or in the case of babies and young children, **meses** (*months*) or **semanas** (*weeks*). While in English we say *I'm seven* or *How old is he?*, in Spanish, you literally say *I have seven years*, or *How many years does he have?* To ask about someone's age, use the following questions:

¿Cuántos años tiene(s)?   *How old are you?*
                          (Literally: *How many years do you have?*)

¿Cuántos años tiene Ana?   *How old is Ana?*

To answer, simply use **tener** + **años** (or **meses** or **semanas**, etc.).

Tengo veinticinco años.   *I'm twenty-five.*
Ana tiene diecisiete años.   *Ana is seventeen.*
El bebé tiene dos meses.   *The baby is two months old.*

Tener to Talk About Feelings and Qualities

There are a great number of expressions with **tener** that are used to talk about feelings, states of being, and qualities. Again, you'll see **tengo** or **tienes/tiene/tienen** used with a noun in cases where we usually use *I am*, *he/she is*, or *you are* with an adjective in English. For instance, *I am hungry* is **Tengo hambre** (literally, *I have hunger*). Here are some more common useful expressions with **tener**:

Expressions with *Tener*

tener hambre	*to be hungry*	tener razón	*to be right*
tener sed	*to be thirsty*	tener sueño	*to be sleepy*
tener calor	*to be hot*	tener vergüenza	*to be ashamed*
tener frío	*to be cold*	tener prisa	*to be in a hurry*
tener éxito	*to be successful*	tener suerte	*to be lucky*
tener miedo	*to be scared*	tener lugar	*to take place*
tener ganas de (+ infinitive)	*to feel like*		

Here are some examples of these expressions used in sentences:

Tengo hambre.	*I'm hungry.*
¿Les tienes miedo a los perros?	*Are you afraid of dogs?*
La niña tiene sueño. Va a la cama.	*The girl is sleepy. She's going to bed.*

Using Idiomatic Expressions Correctly

Remember that these expressions are very common in Spanish, and that translating what you want to say directly from English into Spanish may get you into trouble. For example, **tengo calor** which literally translated means *I have heat* is used to say *I'm hot* or *warm*. You might say this on a sunny day or when the air conditioning is broken. If you translated *I'm hot* directly from English into Spanish, however, your result would be **estoy caliente**, which actually means *I'm turned on* (in a sexual sense). This is an expression you probably want to avoid when sweltering in a crowded elevator or when frolicking on a sunny beach with friends.

On a similar note, remember that the expression **tener ganas de** is followed by an infinitive. For example, **Tengo ganas de ir al cine.** *I feel like going to the movies.* It can also be used alone to answer questions. **¿Quieres ir al cine?** —

No, no tengo ganas. *Do you want to go to the movies? —No, I don't feel like it.* However, beware: If you say **tengo ganas** by itself, out of context, it can have sexual overtones.

Written Practice 6

▶ Track 32

Complete the following sentences in the present tense using an expression from the list. Use the context to help you figure out which expression to use.

tener trece años	tener suerte	tener calor	tener ganas de
tener frío	tener prisa	tener sueño	tener años
tener sed	tener razón		

1. Hace mucho sol en la playa hoy. (Yo) _____. *It's very sunny at the beach today. I . . .*

2. Hoy es el cumpleaños de Luis. Ya es adolescente. (Él) _____. *Today is Luis's birthday. He's finally a teenager. He . . .*

3. Tengo una cita con el médico a las tres y ya son las dos y cuarenta. ¡(Yo) _____! *I have an appointment with the doctor at three and it's already two-forty. I . . .*

4. ¡Ganaste la lotería! ¡(Tú) _____! *You won the lottery! You . . .*

5. Son las dos de la mañana. ¿Ustedes no _____? *It's two A.M. You . . .*

6. Está nevando. Nosotros _____. *It's snowing. We . . .*

7. Isabel está enferma. No _____ hacer nada. *Isabel is sick. She doesn't . . . doing anything.*

8. ¿(Usted) _____? ¿Quiere un vaso de agua? *You . . . ? Would you like a glass of water?*

9. ¿Cuántos _____ tu hija? Mi hija tiene cuatro. *How . . . your daughter? Mine is four.*

10. (Tú) _____. No es buena idea andar sola por la noche. *You . . . It's not a good idea to walk alone at night.*

Tener que and *Hay que* to Express Obligation

The verbs **tener** and **hay** can both be used with **que** + infinitive to express obligation. **Tener** is conjugated according to who is speaking. Look at these examples.

Tengo que...	*I have to . . .*
Tengo que irme.	*I have to go.*
Tengo que ir a clase.	*I have to go to class.*
¿Tengo que comer las espinacas?	*Do I have to eat the spinach?*
No tienes que cerrar la puerta.	*You don't have to close the door.*

Hay que can be used to express obligation, in the general sense of *have to*, similar to when we say *you have to* (meaning *one has to*) in English. Its exact meaning can also change according to context. In this example, it is not clear who is speaking, so a neutral translation is used.

Hay que hacer la maleta.	*One has to pack the bags./You have to pack your bags.*

However, in this example it is clear that the subject is *we*, so **hay que** can be translated as *we have to*.

Vamos a la playa mañana.	*We're going to the beach tomorrow.*
Hay que hacer la maleta.	*We have to pack our bags.*

Hay que can also be negative or interrogative, as shown in these examples:

¿**Hay que** hacer la maleta?	*Is it necessary to pack our bags?/Do we have to pack our bags?*
—No, **no hay que** hacer la maleta.	—*No, it's not necessary to pack our bags./No, we/you don't have to pack our/your bags.*

Written Practice 7

Translate the following sentences into Spanish using the verb in parentheses. Use the vocabulary you learned so far to help you.

1. *We have to sell the house.* (tener que/vender)

    _____.

2. *You have to wait in line.* (hay que/hacer cola)

    _____.

3. *I have to clean the bathroom.* (tener que/limpiar)

    _____.

4. *However, we don't have to do anything.* (tener/hacer nada)

    _____.

5. *It's sunny. We have to throw a party.* (hay que/hacer una fiesta)

    _____.

6. *Do you (singular) have to smoke?* (tener que/fumar)

    ¿_____?

7. *Do we have to make lunch?* (hay que/hacer)

    ¿_____?

8. *We have to arrive at 8:00.* (tener que/llegar)

    _____.

9. *You have to make the bed in the morning.* (hay que/hacer la cama)

    _____.

10. *You (plural) don't have to come to class tomorrow.* (tener que/venir)

    _____.

QUIZ

Circle the letter of the word or phrase that best completes each sentence.

1. _____ mucha gente en Nueva York.
   A. Hay
   B. No hay
   C. ¿Hay
   D. Hace

2. **No. En la casa _____ sótano.**
   A. hay
   B. no hay
   C. tiene
   D. no tiene

3. **La casa tiene siete dormitorios, cuatro cuartos de baño, jardín, terraza y tres sitios para estacionar. _____, es muy grande.**
   A. Pero
   B. O sea
   C. Sin embargo
   D. Sino

4. **¿Qué _____ Jorge? Es cineasta.**
   A. hago
   B. haces
   C. hace
   D. hacen

5. **Para mi cumpleaños siempre _____.**
   A. hago cola
   B. hago caso
   C. hago dinero
   D. hago una fiesta

6. **Hay mucho sol. _____.**
   A. Hace calor
   B. Hace viento
   C. Hace frío
   D. Hace fresco

7. **Paty y Eduardo _____ en metro.**

    A. viene

    B. vienen

    C. tiene

    D. tienen

8. **¿Qué _____ en Patagonia?**

    Está nevando.

    A. hora es

    B. tiempo hace

    C. hay

    D hay que

9. **Son las 2:59 y Rodrigo tiene clase a las 3:00. Rodrigo _____.**

    A. tiene prisa

    B. tiene miedo

    C. tiene éxito

    D. tiene vergüenza

10. **¿Cuántos años _____ Julio?**

    A. es

    B. hay

    C. tiene

    D. viene

chapter 7

Expressing Likes and Dislikes

In this chapter you will learn about stem-changing verbs, how to talk about *this one* and *that one* using demonstrative pronouns and adjectives, and how to talk about likes and dislikes.

CHAPTER OBJECTIVES

In this chapter you will learn

- Stem-changing verbs in the present
- Demonstrative pronouns and adjectives
- How to use *gustar* and similar verbs
- Indirect object pronouns
- How to talk about likes and dislikes

Stem-Changing Verbs in the Present Tense

As you probably remember from our introduction to verbs in Chapter 3, conjugated verbs in Spanish are made up of two parts, the stem and the ending. You learned three types of verbs with three types of endings: **-ar** (**hablar**, **llamar**), **-er** (**comer**, **aprender**), and **-ir** (**vivir**, **subir**).

With regular verbs, you learned that only the ending changes according to the person or subject pronoun. Look at this example with **hablar** (stem: **habl-**, ending: **-ar**).

> yo habl**o**
> tú habl**as**

For irregular verbs, both the stem and the ending may change. Look at this example with the irregular verb **venir**. Notice how the endings change *and* the stem changes from **ven-** to **vien-** in the **tú** form.

> yo **vengo**
> tu **vienes**
> nosotros **venimos**

In addition to regular and irregular verbs, there is a third category of Spanish verbs called stem-changing verbs. These verbs are semi-regular, in that they follow patterns, but within this pattern the stem changes as well as the endings. There are three types of stem-changing verbs: **o→ue**, **e→ie**, and **e→i**. Stem-changing verbs can end in **-ar**, **-er**, or **-ir**, and their endings change according to the rules for regular verbs.

O→UE Verbs

With this type of stem-changing verb, the **o** in the stem changes to **ue** for all forms, except for **nosotros** and **vosotros**. Here is an example with the verb **poder** (*to be able to*):

Stem changes	**Stem does not change**
yo **pue**do	nosotros **po**demos
tú **pue**des	vosotros **po**déis
él/ella/usted **pue**de	
ellos/ellas/ustedes **pue**den	

In this book, **o→ue** verbs will be indicated by (**ue**). Here is a list of common **o→ue** verbs:

O→UE Verbs

almorzar	*to have lunch*	mostrar	*to show*
contar	*to count*	mover	*to move*
costar	*to cost*	poder	*to be able to*
devolver	*to return, give back*	probar	*to prove, try, test*
dormir	*to sleep*	recordar	*to remember*
encontrar	*to find*	soñar	*to dream*
jugar	*to play*	volar	*to fly*
morir	*to die*	volver	*to return*

E→IE Verbs

With this type of stem-changing verb, the **e** in the stem changes to **ie** for all forms except for **nosotros** and **vosotros**. Here is an example with the verb **pensar** (*to think*):

Stem changes	Stem does not change
yo p**ie**nso	nosotros pensamos
tú p**ie**nsas	vosotros pensáis
él/ella/usted p**ie**nsa	
ellos/ellas/ustedes p**ie**nsan	

In this book, e→ie verbs will be indicated by **(ie)**. Here is a list of common e→ie verbs:

E→IE Verbs

advertir	*to warn*	hervir	*to boil*
cerrar	*to close*	mentir	*to lie*
comenzar	*to begin, start*	pensar	*to think*
confesar	*to confess*	perder	*to lose*
defender	*to defend*	preferir	*to prefer*
despertar	*to wake up*	querer	*to want, wish, love*
empezar	*to begin, start*	sentir	*to feel*
encender	*to light*	sugerir	*to suggest*
entender	*to understand*		

E→I Verbs

With this type of stem-changing verb, the **e** in the stem changes to **i** for all forms except for **nosotros** and **vosotros**. Here is an example with the verb **pedir** (*to ask for*):

Stem changes	Stem does not change
yo pido	nosotros pedimos
tú pides	vosotros pedís
él/ella/usted pide	
ellos/ellas/ustedes piden	

In this book, e→i verbs will be indicated by (i). Here is a list of common e→i verbs:

E→I Verbs

competir	to compete	perseguir	to pursue, chase
conseguir	to get, obtain, manage to	reír	to laugh
despedir	to say good-bye to; fire	repetir	to repeat
freír	to fry	seguir	to follow
gemir	to groan, moan	servir	to serve
medir	to measure	sonreír	to smile
pedir	to ask for		

NOTE *Verbs ending in -guir drop the u in the first person singular (yo) form.*
For example:

yo consigo   I obtain
yo sigo   I follow
yo persigo   I chase

Verbs ending in -eír maintain the accent on the i even when the stem changes.
For example:

yo sonrío
él ríe
ustedes fríen

Written Practice 1

 Track 33

Complete the sentences with the present tense of the verb in parentheses.

1. (Nosotros) _____ a la una de la tarde. (almorzar [ue])

   We eat lunch at one o'clock in the afternoon.

2. (Yo) _____ muy bien por la noche. (dormir [ue])

   I sleep very well at night.

3. (Ustedes) _____ las clases de español el viernes. (empezar [ie])

   You begin Spanish classes on Friday.

4. (Yo) no _____ las almejas. _____ los mejillones. (querer [ie], preferir [ie])

   I don't want the clams. I prefer the mussels.

5. ¿(Tú) _____ venir a cenar con nosotras? (poder [ue])

   Can you come eat dinner with us?

6. Cecilia nunca _____. (mentir [ie])

   Cecilia never lies.

7. El camarero _____ los platos. (servir [i])

   The waiter serves the dishes.

8. ¿Cuánto _____ el ceviche de mariscos? (costar [ue])

   How much does the seafood ceviche cost?

9. ¿Usted _____ que el restaurante es bueno? (pensar [ie])

   Do you think this restaurant is good?

10. El bebé _____ mucho. (sonreír [i])

    The baby smiles a lot.

11. Nosotros _____ de Sevilla esta noche, pero Luci no _____ hasta mañana. (volver [ue], volver [ue])

    We return from Seville tonight, but Luci doesn't come back until tomorrow.

12. (Yo) no _____ los huevos, los _____. (freír [i], hervir [ie])

    I don't fry the eggs, I boil them.

The Personal *A*

You may notice in this book, or in your study of Spanish, that the preposition **a** often appears before references to people. This is because Spanish uses the **a personal** *before the direct object* when the direct object is a *person* (or sometimes a pet). The **a personal** is not used with things. Compare these examples:

Vemos a Matilde.	*We see Matilde.*
Vemos una película.	*We see a movie.*

Here are some more examples of the **a personal**. Remember that **a** plus **el** contracts to **al**.

Llamo **a alguien**.   *I call someone.*

El policía persigue **al ladrón**.   *The police officer chases the burglar.*

The personal **a** is *not* used with the verb **tener**.

Tengo dos hijas.   *I have two daughters.*

Recognizing the Direct Object

You may learn to use the **a personal** just by hearing it and recognizing it in certain types of phrases and sentences. But those of you who are more grammatically inclined might be wondering, "How do I know when the person is a direct object?"

The direct object of a sentence is the noun or pronoun that receives the action of the verb. You can also think of this in terms of the subject acting on the object. A useful general rule is to ask *What?* or *Who(m)?* The answer is the direct object. Here are some examples in English:

I see **you**.

Who(m) do I see? I see you. "You" is the direct object.

Leonard reads **the book**.

What does Leonard read? He reads the book. "The book" is the direct object.

I'll call Mary tomorrow.

Who(m) will you call? You'll call **Mary**. "Mary" is the direct object.

So, when you are using a verb that acts upon a direct object that is a person or a pet, simply add **a** before it.

Quiero **a mi marido**.   *I love my husband.*
Marta despierta **a su amiga**.   *Marta wakes up her friend.*
Acariciamos **al perro**.   *We pet the dog.*

Written Practice 2

Complete the sentences with **a** or **al** where appropriate.

1. ¿Llamamos _____ Juan? *Shall we call Juan?*
2. Tenemos _____ tres gatos. *We have three cats.*
3. Ellos miran _____ la película. *They watch the movie.*
4. No conozco _____ señor Gutiérrez. *I don't know Mr. Gutiérrez.*
5. Llevo _____ mi amiga a la fiesta. *I'm taking my friend to the party.*
6. El jefe va a despedir _____ cinco personas. *The boss is going to fire five people.*

Demonstrative Adjectives and Pronouns

Demonstrative adjectives and pronouns are used to say *this, that, these,* and *those.* Before studying them, it's important to remember the difference between adjectives and pronouns. An adjective describes or modifies a noun. A pronoun is used in place of a noun and stands alone. Compare these examples:

Prefiero **este** vestido.   *I prefer this dress.*

In this example, **este** (*this*) is an *adjective* because it describes the noun **vestido**.

Prefiero **éste**.   *I prefer this one.*

In this sentence, **éste** (*this one*), with an accent over the e (é), is a *pronoun* because it replaces the words **este vestido** and stands alone.

Demonstrative Adjectives

In English, we have only one way to say *this* and one way to say *that,* in addition to the plural forms *these* and *those. This, that, these,* and *those* are the demonstrative adjectives. In Spanish, there are three demonstrative adjectives, each with four forms.

To say *this,* use the adjective **este** and its feminine and plural forms.

este camarero	*this waiter*	**estos** camareros	*these waiters*
esta galleta	*this cookie*	**estas** galletas	*these cookies*

Spanish has two ways to say *that*.

- The first is **ese**. **Ese** refers to something that is close to the person spoken to, but not to the speaker. It also has four forms.

ese cuchillo	*that knife*	**esos** cuchillos	*those knives*
esa cuchara	*that spoon*	**esas** cucharas	*those spoons*

- The second way to say *that*, **aquel**, refers to something that is far away from both the speaker and the person spoken to. The adjective **aquel** also has four forms. Remember that in the feminine and plural forms, the **ll** has a *y* sound.

aquel restaurante	*that restaurant*	**aquellos** restaurantes	*those restaurants*
aquella ciudad	*that city*	**aquellas** ciudades	*those cities*

Here are some example sentences using demonstrative adjectives:

¿Dónde compraste **esos** zapatos?	*Where did you buy those shoes?*
Estos caramelos son mis favoritos.	*These candies are my favorites.*
Aquella ciudad es demasiado peligrosa.	*That city is too dangerous.*

Written Practice 3

 Track 34

Complete the sentences with the correct demonstrative adjective according to the clues given in parentheses.

1. ¡_____ sopa está deliciosa! (*this*) *This soup is delicious.*

2. _____ cafetería es horrible. (*that [far]*) *That café is horrible.*

3. No me gustan _____ enchiladas. (*these*) *I don't like these enchiladas.*

4. ¿De dónde es _____ plato? (*that [near]*) *Where is that dish from?*

5. _____ camarones que preparas están muy ricos. (*those [near]*) *Those shrimp that you make are really tasty.*

6. ¿Usted conoce _____ bar de la esquina? (*that [far]*) *Do you know that bar on the corner?*

7. _____ pescado no es muy bueno. (*this*) *This fish is not very good.*

8. _____ huevos que comes son orgánicos. (*those [near]*) *Those eggs you're eating are organic.*

Demonstrative Pronouns

Demonstrative pronouns look very similar to demonstrative adjectives, and sound the same when spoken. The only thing that differentiates their spelling from that of adjectives is that they carry accent marks. Here is a list of all the demonstrative pronouns:

Singular masculine	Singular feminine	
éste	ésta	*this one* (here)
ése	ésa	*that one* (there)
aquél	aquélla	*that one* (over there)

Plural masculine	Plural feminine	
éstos	éstas	*these* (here)
ésos	ésas	*those* (there)
aquéllos	aquéllas	*those* (over there)

Remember that the demonstrative pronoun replaces a noun. Here are some examples:

¿Prefieres este vino o **ése**?	*Do you prefer this wine, or that one (near you)?*
—Prefiero **éste**.	*—I prefer this one.*
Aquél es bueno.	*That one is good.*

Notice how demonstrative pronouns are often used in conjunction with demonstrative adjectives.

Me gusta **este** reloj, pero prefiero **aquél**.	*I like this watch, but I prefer that one over there.*
Aquella playa es bonita, pero **ésta** es más tranquila.	*That beach is nice, but this one is calmer.*
Voy a **ese** restaurante, pero no voy a **aquél**.	*I go to that restaurant (near you) but I don't go to that one (over there).*

Sometimes you'll see the gender-neutral pronouns **esto**, **eso**, or **aquello** used to refer to something of which the gender is not known, such as a general concept or idea, or a thing. These words never carry a written accent and are not used to refer to people, except in a derogatory way.

Esto es un rollo.	*This is a drag.*
Esto es para ti.	*This is for you.*
¡**Eso** es!	*That's it!*
Por **eso**.	*That's why.*
No me gusta **aquello**.	*I don't like that one over there.*
Aquello es bueno.	*That one over there is good.*

Written Practice 4

 Track 35

Complete each sentence with the proper demonstrative pronoun. Use the clues in parentheses to help you.

1. ¿Qué camisa prefieres, _____ (*here*) o _____ (*there*)?

   Which shirt do you prefer, this one or that one?

2. Estos zapatos son más bonitos que _____ de la otra tienda (*over there*).

   These shoes are prettier than the ones from the other store.

3. No me gusta mucho esta paella. Prefiero _____ del Rincón Español (*over there*).

   I don't like this paella very much. I prefer that one from the Rincón Español.

4. Estos duraznos no están maduros, pero _____ que tienes están buenos (*there*).

   These peaches aren't ripe, but the ones you have are good.

5. Ese carro es caro. _____ es barato (*here*).

   That car is expensive. This one is cheap.

The Verb *Gustar*

You've already learned the stem-changing verbs **querer** (*to want, to love*) and **preferir** (*to prefer*), which can be used to talk about wants and preferences in the present. These verbs are relatively straightforward. Unfortunately for the student of Spanish, to say that one *likes* something is a little more complicated. Let's try to demystify it here.

To talk about liking something, use the verb **gustar**. Literally translated, the verb means *to be pleasing*. There is no verb that simply means *to like* in Spanish, but **gustar** is used to convey this idea. Compare the following translations of the Spanish sentence:

Me gusta la carne.   Literal translation: *Meat is pleasing to me.*
                            Meaning: *I like meat.*

In English, *I* agrees with *like*. In Spanish, **la carne** agrees with **gusta**. **La carne** is the subject of the sentence, and **gusta** is the verb. If the subject is plural, then the verb is plural: **gustan. Me gustan las manzanas.** *I like apples.* In this construction, **me** is actually an indirect object pronoun meaning *to me*. You will learn more about indirect objects below and in Chapter 12. Compare the following translations of the Spanish sentence:

Me gustan las empanadas. Literal translation: *Empanadas are pleasing to me.*
                              Meaning: *I like empanadas.*

Note that if the thing you like is singular, say **gusta**. If the thing you like is plural, say **gustan**.

Me gusta la paella.   *I like paella.*
Me gustan las verduras.   *I like vegetables.*

When talking about liking an action, the verb, or action, is usually treated as a singular subject.

Me gusta trabajar.   *I like to work. (Work is pleasing to me.)*
No **me gusta** volar en avión. *I don't like flying (by plane). (Flying [by plane] is not pleasing to me.)*

Indirect Object Pronouns

In order to talk about other people liking things, replace **me** with a different indirect object pronoun. Here are the indirect object pronouns:

Indirect Object Pronouns

Pronoun	Meaning	Can Be Used To Say
me	*to me*	*I like* / Me gusta(n)
te	*to you* (informal)	*You like* / Te gusta(n)

le	to him, to her	He, She, It likes / Le gusta(n)
le	to you (formal)	You like / Le gusta(n)
nos	to us	We like / Nos gusta(n)
os	to you (plural informal, Spain)	You like / Os gusta(n)
		They, You like / Les gusta(n)
les	to them, to you (plural)	

Here are some example sentences. Notice how the verb changes according to the thing that is liked, or pleasing, not the person doing the "liking."

Singular subject

¿**Te gusta** esta taberna?
Do you like this tavern?

Le gusta el vestido.
She likes the dress.

No **nos gusta** trabajar.
We don't like to work.

Plural subject

¿**Te gustan** los champiñones?
Do you like the mushrooms?

Le gustan los zapatos.
She likes the shoes.

No **nos gustan** nuestros trabajos.
We don't like our jobs.

Still Struggling

In order to figure out whether to use the singular or plural of **gustar**, match the singular verb with a singular noun and the plural verb with a plural noun.

Le gust**a el** teatr**o**. (singular verb; singular noun)   *He likes the theater.*
Le gust**an las** películ**as**. (plural verb; plural noun)   *He likes films.*

Written Practice 5

Complete the following sentences with **gusta** or **gustan**.

1. Me _____ el queso. *I like cheese.*

2. Le _____ las aceitunas. *He likes olives.*

3. ¿Les _____ esta música? *Do you like this music?*

4. No nos _____ ir a la playa. *We don't like going to the beach.*

5. Me _____ mucho los tacos. *I really like tacos.*

6. No les _____ los platos picantes. *They don't like spicy dishes.*

7. Le _____ la comida china pero no le _____ los rollos de primavera. *She likes Chinese food, but she doesn't like egg rolls.*

8. ¿Te _____ estudiar español? *Do you like studying Spanish?*

Clarifying *Gustar*

Because **le** can mean *to him, to her,* or *to you* (formal) and **les** can mean *to them* or *to you* (plural), sentences using **gustar** and these pronouns can be confusing. For example: **Le gusta la comida peruana**. In this sentence, who likes Peruvian food? (To whom is Peruvian food pleasing?) To him? To her? To you? In these cases a prepositional phrase with **a** is used to clarify who is doing the liking, or literally, who is being pleased. The indirect object pronoun remains before the verb.

A Juan le gusta la comida peruana. *Juan likes Peruvian food.*
A usted le gusta la comida peruana. *You like Peruvian food.*
A ella le gusta la comida peruana. *She likes Peruvian food.*

Often, this construction is used for emphasis, rather than clarification.

A Juan le gusta la comida peruana, *Juan likes Peruvian food, but me,*
pero **a mí** me gusta la comida   *I like Mexican food.*
mexicana.

In this case **a mí** is used to emphasize that *I* like Mexican food (as opposed to Juan, who likes Peruvian food).

Here are some examples of prepositional phrases used with **gusta**. Notice that you can use **a** + any person or name, or a personal pronoun.

Prepositional Phrases with Gusta

Singular		Plural	
a mí me gusta(an)	*I like*	**a nosotros/as** nos gusta(an)	*we like*
a tí te gusta(an)	*you like*	**a vosotros/as** os gusta(an)	*you like*
a él le gusta(an)	*he likes*	**a ellos** les gusta(an)	*they like*
a ella le gusta(an)	*she likes*	**a ellas** les gusta(an)	*they like*
a usted le gusta(an)	*you like*	**a ustedes** les gusta(an)	*you like*
a Juan le gusta(an)	*Juan likes*	**a Juan y José** les gusta(an)	*Juan and José like*
a Julieta le gusta(an)	*Julieta likes*	**a mis padres** les gusta(an)	*my parents like*

| a mi abuela le gusta(an) | *my grand-mother likes* | a Julieta y Juanita-les gusta(an) | *Julieta and Juanita like* |

Here are some more example sentences. Notice how the prepositional phrase matches the indirect object pronoun.

¿A ti te gusta el pollo?   *Do you like chicken?*
A Julieta le gustan las albóndigas. *Julieta likes meatballs.*
A mí no me gusta el teatro.   *I don't like the theater.*
A mis padres no les gusta mi novio. *My parents don't like my boyfriend.*

The prepositional phrase with a can also go at the end of the sentence.

Le gusta la comida Peruana a Daniel.
No le gusta beber soda a Miriam.

Written Practice 6

▶ Track 36

Complete each sentence with a plus person (pronoun, names, description, etc.). Use the translations to help you.

1. _____ no me gusta el ajo. *I don't like garlic.*

2. Pero _____ le gusta mucho el ajo. *But Eduardo likes garlic a lot.*

3. ¿Les gustan las sardinas _____? *Do you like sardines? (formal)*

4. _____ no le gustan nada los fideos. *Emilio doesn't like noodles at all.*

5. Nos gusta mucho este restaurante _____. *We like this restaurant a lot.*

6. _____ le gusta comer en casa. *My uncle likes to eat at home.*

7. ¿_____ te gusta cocinar? *Do you like to cook (informal)?*

8. ¿_____ le gusta cocinar? *Does your (informal) father like to cook?*

Using *Caer Bien* to Talk About Liking People

When talking about liking (or disliking) *people*, using **gustar** can be tricky. To say **No me gusta** or **Me gusta** about someone can imply romantic feeling, or mean that the person is or isn't your "type." Similarly, the verb **querer** can be tricky because to say **te quiero** means *I love you* or *I want you*, thereby expressing fairly strong feelings on the part of the speaker.

Luckily you have the expressions **caer bien** and **caer mal** at your disposal. The verb **caer** is a regular **-er** verb that literally means *to fall*, but changes meaning when used with **bien** (*well*) or **mal** (*badly*). Literally, **Me cae bien** means *He falls well to me*. But it is used to say *I am fond of him* or *I like him*. Remember that **caer bien** follows similar rules of agreement as **gustar** except that the subject usually goes at the beginning of the sentence. Take a look at these examples:

Juan **me cae bien**.	*I'm fond of Juan.*
A mí este tipo **me cae mal**.	*I don't like this guy.*

You can use **no caer bien** instead of **caer mal** to soften the blow.

El profesor **no me cae bien**.	*I'm not very fond of the professor.*

You can also talk about other people's likes and dislikes.

A Matilde **le cae bien** su cuñada.	*Matilde is fond of her sister-in-law.*
Le cae mal su suegra.	*He doesn't like his mother-in-law.*

The plural of **cae** is **caen**.

Me **caen** bien tus amigos.	*I like your friends.*

Other Verbs That Behave like *Gustar*

Spanish has several additional verbs that behave like **gustar**. These verbs also use the construction: indirect object pronoun + verb + subject. Once you learn the trick of using **gustar** you'll be able to greatly expand your vocabulary.

Encantar means *to love* something:

¡**Me encanta** el helado!	*I love ice cream.*
A Elena **le encantan** los dulces.	*Elena loves sweets.*

Molestar means *to annoy* or *to bother*.

¿**Te molesta** el humo?	*Does the smoke bother you?*

Parecer means *to appear* or *to seem* but can also be used to express prefer-
ence. It is a little different from the other example verbs in that an opinion with
parecer must be followed by **bien** (*fine*), **mal** (*bad*), or an adjective.

¿Qué te parece?	*What do you think?*
	(Literally: *How does it seem to you?*)
Me parece bien.	*It seems fine.*
La comida me parece buena.	*The food seems good.*
Los chicos me parecen normales.	*The guys appear normal.*

You learned the verb **quedar** to talk about location. When used with the
indirect object pronoun, **quedar** means *to have left (over)*.

No me queda nada del pastel.	*I don't have any cake left.*
¿Te quedan minutos en tu celular?	*Do you have any cell phone minutes left?*

Faltar means *to be lacking* something or *to be missing* or *to still need* something.

Nos falta una persona.	*We're missing one person.*

Ana:	¿Vas a comprar la casa?	*Are you going to buy the house?*
Bela:	No, me faltan cinco mil euros.	*No, I still need five thousand euros.*

 Still Struggling

Still struggling with all these personal pronouns? Notice how the prepositional
pronouns (**mí**, **ti**, **él**, **ella**, **nosotros**, **ellos**, **ustedes**) and the indirect object pronouns (**me**, **te**, **le**, **nos**, **les**) match.

A **mí me** gusta

A **ti te** encantan

A **él le** parecen

A **ella** no **le** quedan

A **nosotros nos** gusta

A **ellos les** falta

A **ustedes** no **les** molestan

Written Practice 7

 Track 37

Complete the sentences using an indirect object pronoun and the verb in each group.

caer

1. ¡A mí esa chica _____ muy mal! *I don't like that girl!*

2. ¿A usted _____ bien sus colegas? *Are you fond of your colleagues?*

molestar

3. A mí no _____ trabajar. *Working doesn't bother me.*

4. A Cecilia _____ los perros pequeños. *Small dogs annoy Cecilia.*

encantar

5. A mis abuelos _____ visitar a sus nietos. *My grandparents love visiting their grandchildren.*

6. A mí _____ los vinos chilenos. *I love Chilean wines.*

quedar

7. ¿A ti _____ más días de vacaciones? *Do you have any vacation days left?*

8. No _____ más dinero. *I have no more money left.*

parecer

9. A Julio no _____ buena idea. *To Julio it doesn't seem like good idea.*

10. ¿Qué _____ a ustedes la película? *What do you think of the movie?*

faltar

11. A Ernesto _____ amor. *Ernesto is lacking love.*

12. A nosotros _____ dos sillas. *We're missing two chairs.*

QUIZ

Circle the letter of the word or phrase that best completes each sentence.

1. **El pescado no _____ mucho.**
   A. costar
   B. costa
   C. cuesta
   D. cuestan

2. **Nosotros siempre _____ a las ocho de la mañana.**
   A. empezar
   B. empiezan
   C. empecemos
   D. empezamos

3. **El cliente _____ la cuenta.**
   A. pueda
   B. puede
   C. pide
   D. pida

4. **Yo _____ mi hija.**
   A. a tengo
   B. despierto
   C. despierto a
   D. hablo

5. **¿Les gusta _____ restaurante?**
   A. éste
   B. este
   C. esta
   D. esto

6. **Me gusta _____ sitio pero me encanta _____.**
   A. ése; aquel
   B. ése; aquél
   C. ese; aquel
   D. ese; aquél

7. **A mis padres no _____ mi corte de cabello.**

    A. le gusta

    B. les gusta

    C. le gustan

    D. les gustan

8. **¿_____ les gusta la comida mexicana?**

    A. A mí

    B. A usted

    C. A ustedes

    D. A Enrique

9. **Mercedes es muy amable. _____ bien.**

    A. Me gusta

    B. Me falta

    C. Me cae

    D. Me molesta

10. **¿Te _____ buena idea?**

    A. parece

    B. pareces

    C. parecen

    D. parecemos

chapter 8

Expressing Actions in Progress

In this chapter you will learn how to talk about actions in progress using present participles. You will learn how to use indefinite adjectives and pronouns to talk about things that are undefined and possessive pronouns to talk about possession. Finally, you will learn how to talk about things *you know* using **saber** and **conocer**.

CHAPTER OBJECTIVES

In this chapter you will learn

- The present progressive
- How to form present participles
- Indefinite adjectives and pronouns
- Possessive pronouns
- The verbs *saber* and *conocer*

The Present Progressive with *Estar*

The present progressive is used to describe actions taking place at the moment: *I am walking, She is reading, They are eating dinner.* The structure of the present progressive in Spanish is similar to English. Both use the verb *to be* plus the present participle, which in English is the *-ing* form of the verb. In Spanish, the verb **estar** is generally used to make the present progressive. Here is a quick review of the present tense of **estar**:

yo estoy	nosotros estamos
tú estás	vosotros estáis
él/ella/usted está	ellos/ellas/ustedes están

To form the present progressive, use the present tense of **estar** + present participle, which in Spanish ends in **-ando**, **-iendo**, or **-endo**. Here are some examples:

Estoy andando.	*I am walking.*	Está andando.	*He is walking.*
Está leyendo.	*She is reading.*	Estás leyendo.	*You are reading.*
Están cenando.	*They are eating dinner.*	Estamos cenando.	*We are eating dinner.*

The use of the present progressive differs between English and Spanish. In English we often use the present progressive to talk about the near future, for instance when saying *I'm arriving tomorrow*, or *I'm not going to the soccer game.* In Spanish, however, as you have already learned, the present tense is used for these types of situations: **Llego mañana** (*I'm arriving tomorrow*) or **No voy al partido de fútbol** (*I'm not going to the soccer game*). In Spanish, the present progressive is reserved for talking about actions taking place *at the moment of speaking* (not in the future, and not in the past). You've already seen an example of this with expressions such as **está nevando** (*it's snowing*) and **está lloviendo** (*it's raining*) to talk about the weather. Remember that these expressions say what the weather is at the moment, not in general. Here are some more examples:

Estoy hablando con mi madre.	*I am speaking to my mother (right now).*
Estamos esperando el autobús.	*We're waiting for the bus (right now).*

Some verbs, including **ir** (*to go*), **volver** (*to return*), **venir** (*to come*), **estar** (*to be*), and **poder** (*to be able*), are seldom used in the present progressive. Another verb that is rarely used in the progressive is **llevar** in the sense of *to wear*. *I'm wearing a red dress* would be translated as **Llevo un vestido rojo**.

The Present Progressive with *Ir* and *Seguir*

In addition to the verb **estar**, the verbs **ir** (*to go*) and **seguir** (*to continue, keep [on]*) can be used as an auxiliary with the present participle. These two verbs add a different shade of meaning. The verb **ir** sounds a bit more colloquial and gives the sense of *to go along* doing something or gives an immediate, simple feeling to a sentence. Look at this example.

El niño **va andando** a la escuela.   *The boy goes to school on foot.*
                                        The boy goes along walking to school.

Seguir, when used with the present participle, means *to keep (on) doing* something or *to continue* something. Here is an example:

Sigue hablando por favor.   *Keep speaking, please.*

The construction can also be used to express a future intention.

Seguimos trabajando mañana.   *We'll continue working tomorrow.*

Forming Present Participles

Present participles end in either **-ando**, **-endo**, or **-iendo**. There are a few simple rules about forming the present participle of a verb.

Present Participles of Regular Verbs

To make the present participle of regular **-ar** verbs, drop the **-ar** and add **-ando** to the stem.

Verb	Present Participle	Present Progressive
trabajar	trabajando	estoy trabajando
hablar	hablando	estás hablando
viajar	viajando	está viajando
comprar	comprando	estamos comprando

To make the present participle of regular -er and -ir verbs, drop the -er or -ir and add -iendo to the stem.

Verb	Present Participle	Present Progressive
comer	comiendo	están comiendo
aprender	aprendiendo	estás aprendiendo
sufrir	sufriendo	estamos sufriendo
vivir	viviendo	está viviendo

Present Participle of Stem-Changing Verbs

To make the present participle of -ir stem-changing verbs, drop the -ir, change e→i or o→u in the stem, and add -iendo at the end.

Verb	Present Participle	Present Progressive
pedir	pidiendo	está pidiendo
mentir	mintiendo	están mintiendo
dormir	durmiendo	estamos durmiendo
morir	muriendo	está muriendo

All other stem-changing verbs follow the rules for regular -ar and -er verbs.

Verb	Present Participle	Present Progressive
querer	queriendo	está queriendo
contar	contando	estamos contando

Some Irregular Present Participles

Some verbs take on orthographic, or spelling, changes in the present participle. Verbs that have a vowel before -er or -ir usually add -yendo to the stem.

Verb	Present Participle	Meaning
ir	yendo	*to go, going*
caer	cayendo	*to fall, falling*
creer	creyendo	*to believe, believing*
huir	huyendo	*to flee, fleeing*
construir	construyendo	*to build, building*
oír	oyendo	*to hear, hearing*
traer	trayendo	*to bring, bringing*
leer	leyendo	*to read, reading*

Some irregular verbs follow the same rules as stem-changing verbs and regular verbs.

Verb	Present Participle	Meaning
decir	diciendo	*to say, saying*
dar	dando	*to give, giving*
hacer	haciendo	*to make/do, making/doing*
saber	sabiendo	*to know, knowing*
tener	teniendo	*to have, having*

Other extremely short verbs merely maintain the first letter plus **-iendo**.

ser	siendo	*to be, being*
reír	riendo	*to laugh, laughing*
ver	viendo	*to see, seeing*

Written Practice 1

Track 38

Complete the sentences with the verb in parentheses in the present progressive. The pronoun has been indicated for you when necessary.

1. ¿Con quién _____? (tú/hablar) *With whom are you talking?*

2. _____ una casa en las montañas. (nosotros/construir) *We are building a house in the mountains.*

3. ¡Shhhh! Los niños _____. (dormir) *Shhhh! The kids are sleeping.*

4. ¿Julián _____. *El amor en los tiempos del cólera?* (leer) *Is Julian reading* Love in the Time of Cholera?

5. Mis padres _____ en la cocina. (comer) *My parents are eating in the kitchen.*

6. Laura y Marisa _____ tortillas. (hacer) *Laura and Marisa are making tortillas.*

7. Creo que mi amigo _____. (mentir) *I think my friend is lying.*

8. ¿_____ el Internet ahora? (tú/usar) *Are you using the Internet now?*

9. Mi madre _____ en la puerta. (esperar) *My mother is waiting at the door.*

10. Perdón, _____ la entrada del metro. (nosotros/buscar) *Excuse me, we're looking for the entrance to the subway.*

Written Practice 2

Choose the best verb form to complete each sentence. Use the rules you've learned and your common sense to help you.

1. Clara _____ un anillo de oro.
   (a) lleva
   (b) está llevando

2. Nosotros _____ al centro esta tarde.
   (a) vamos
   (b) estamos yendo

3. No puedo ir al centro ahora.
   (a) Trabajo
   (b) Estoy trabajando

4. ¿_____ con nosotros a la fiesta?
   (a) Vienes
   (b) Estás viniendo

5. No voy con ustedes a la fiesta. No _____.
   (a) puedo
   (b) estoy pudiendo

6. ¿Qué haces? _____ música.
   (a) Escucho
   (b) Estoy escuchando

Oral Practice

Say a few sentences about what you are doing at the moment using the present progressive. Use the following verbs or others you can think of.

estudiar   hablar   escribir   aprender   leer   hacer

Indefinite Adjectives

In Chapter 4 you briefly learned about the adjectives **alguno** (*one, some, any*) and **ninguno** (*no, not any*), which can come before or after the nouns they modify, and which carry an accent in their short forms (before the masculine singular noun). These, along with the adjective **cualquiera** (*any*) are called *indefinite* adjectives because they do not strictly define the nouns they describe. Indefinite adjectives can be used in many ways, including in common phrases.

ninguna parte	*nowhere*
ningún lado	*nowhere*
de ninguna manera	*no way*
alguna vez	*sometime, ever (once or at a future date)*
algunas veces	*a few times*
cualquier cosa	*anything*
cualquier lugar	*anywhere, any place*
en cualquier momento	*at any time*

The adjective **alguno** (and its forms) is generally used in affirmative statements and questions. **Alguno** shortens to **algún** before a singular masculine noun.

¿Tienes **algún dinero**?	*Do you have any money?*
—Tengo **algunas monedas**.	*—I have some change.*

The adjective **ninguno** (and its forms) is usually used in negative statements. **Ninguno** shortens to **ningún** before a singular masculine noun. **No** is used before a verb that is followed by **ninguno** to make a double negative.

No conozco **ningún restaurante** cerca.	*I don't know any restaurants nearby.*
Ninguna mujer está casada.	*None of the women is married.*

Notice how **alguno** can be used in negative expressions after the noun it modifies to mean *no* or *not any* and **ninguno** can precede the noun to express the same meaning.

sin duda **alguna**	*without a doubt*
sin **ninguna** duda	
no hay motivo **alguno**	*there isn't any reason*
no hay **ningún** motivo	

The singular adjective **cualquiera** is always shortened to **cualquier** before any noun, masculine or feminine, and is used to say *any (at all)*.

Cualquier libro es bueno.	*Any book is good.*
Cualquier persona puede aprender.	*Any person can learn.*

The singular form **cualquiera** is used after any noun (masculine or feminine) to say *whichever* or *any(one) (at all)*.

Toma **un autobús cualquiera**.	*Take any bus.*
No es **una niña cualquiera**.	*She's not just any girl.*

Indefinite Pronouns

The words **ninguno**, **alguno**, and **cualquiera** also lead a double life as pronouns. Remember that as with the demonstrative pronouns you learned in the last chapter, pronouns take the place of nouns and stand alone. You've already learned some of the indefinite pronouns that make negative statements: **nada** and **nadie**. Now you will learn some more affirmative and negative indefinite pronouns.

Indefinite Pronouns

alguien	*someone/somebody/anyone/anybody*
algo	*something*
alguno(s) (m.)	*some/somebody*
alguna(s) (f.)	*some/somebody*
cualquiera	*anybody*
nada	*nothing*
nadie	*no one/nobody/anyone/anybody*
ninguna (f.)	*none/nobody*
ninguno (m.)	*none/nobody*

Alguien and **nadie** refer to people. Use **alguien** to make affirmative statements and questions, and **nadie** to make negative statements.

Alguien está llamando.	*Someone is calling.*
¿Hay **alguien** en la cocina?	*Is there anyone/someone in the kitchen?*
¿**Alguien** quiere salir?	*Does anyone want to go out?*
Nadie está llamando.	*No one is calling.*
No, no hay **nadie** en la cocina.	*No, there's nobody/there isn't anybody in the kitchen.*

Algo and **nada** refer to things. Use **algo** with affirmative statements and questions, and **nada** with negative statements.

Tienes **algo** en el ojo.	*You have something in your eye.*
¿Estás haciendo **algo**?	*Are you doing something?*
No tengo **nada** en el ojo.	*I don't have anything in my eye.*
No, no estoy haciendo **nada**.	*No, I'm not doing anything.*

The pronouns **alguno**, **algunos**, **alguna**, and **algunas** are used to talk about people and sometimes things in affirmative statements and questions. **Ninguno** and **ninguna** are used in negative statements to talk about things and people. They are always singular. Both stand alone and are used in the place of nouns.

Ninguna está casada.	*None of them (f.) is married.*
Algunas son buenas.	*Some (f. pl.) are good.*

These pronouns can be used with **de** (*of*) to say *none of them* or *any of them*.

Ninguna de ellas está casada.	*None of them is married.*
No conozco a **ninguno de los dos**.	*I don't know either of them.*
¿Quieres **alguno de éstos**?	*Do you want any (one) of these?*
¿**Alguno de ustedes** quiere salir?	*Do any of you want to go out?*

Cualquiera is used before a singular verb to say *anybody*.

Cualquiera puede cocinar.	*Anyone can cook.*

Cualquiera can also be used before **de** (*of*) to say *either of them* or *any of them*. Notice that the verb following **cualquiera** is always singular.

Cualquiera de los dos es bueno.	*Either of them is good.*
Cualquiera de ustedes puede venir.	*Any of you can come.*

Double Negatives

Remember that in Spanish, double negatives are not only acceptable, but expected! Whereas in English we would say *There is nobody* or *There isn't anybody*, in Spanish you say **No hay nadie** (literally: *There isn't nobody*). When answering a question the double negative can become triple. For instance, to answer the question **¿Viene alguien?** (*Is someone coming?*) in the negative, you could answer **Nadie viene** (*no one is coming*) or **No, no viene nadie** (literally: *No, no one isn't coming*).

Notice that when **nada** or **nadie** comes at the beginning of an answer, it behaves as a subject and the double negative is not necessary.

¿Quién está llamando?	**Nadie** está llamando.
Who's calling?	*No one's calling.*
¿Alguien está llamando?	**No, nadie** está llamando.
Is someone calling?	*No, no one is calling.*

However, when it comes at the end of the sentence, the double negative is necessary.

¿Qué pasa?	No pasa **nada**.
What's going on?	*Nothing is going on.*
¿Pasa algo?	**No, no** pasa **nada.**
Is something going on?	*No, nothing is going on.*

Still Struggling

When using **nadie** and **nada**, it might help to match them with their respective question words.

  Nadie makes negative statements about people. Therefore it answers questions beginning with *who* or *someone*.

¿Quién…? ¿Alguien…?→Nadie

  Nada makes negative statements about things. Therefore it answers questions beginning with *what* or *something*.

¿Qué…? ¿Algo…?→Nada

Written Practice 3

Circle the letter of the word or phrase that best completes each sentence or mini-conversation.

1. ¿_____ está aquí?
   —No, no veo a _____.
   (a) Algo, nada
   (b) Alguien, nadie

2. ¿Estás diciendo _____?
   —No, no estoy diciendo _____.
   (a) algo, nada
   (b) alguien, nadie

3. No quiero ir a _____ lado.
   (a) ningún
   (b) ninguno

4. _____ de ellos son simpáticos.
   (a) Algunas
   (b) Algunos

5. No tiene _____ problema.
   (a) algún
   (b) ningún

6. ¿Tienes _____ en la mano?
   —No, no tengo _____.
   (a) algo, nada
   (b) alguien, nadie

7. ¿Quién quiere ir al teatro?
   —_____ quiere ir.
   (a) Nada
   (b) Nadie

8. Este trabajo tiene _____ ventajas, pero no muchas.
   (a) alguna
   (b) algunas

9. A los niños les gusta la escuela?
   —A _____ sí, y a otros no.
   (a) alguien
   (b) algunos

10. ¿Alberto sigue saliendo con Kara?
    —No, Alberto no está saliendo con _____ .
    (a) alguien
    (b) nadie

11. ¿Qué plato es el mejor?
    _____ plato de este restaurante es bueno.
    (a) Cualquier
    (b) Cualquiera

12. ¿Es difícil aprender a conducir?
    No, es fácil. _____ puede aprender.
    (a) Cualquier
    (b) Cualquiera

Possessive Pronouns

Spanish also has a number of pronouns to talk about *possession*. In English, these are pronouns such as *mine*, *yours*, and *theirs*. Compare the following pronouns to the possessive adjectives you learned in Chapter 3.

Adjective		Pronoun	
mi, mis	*my*	el mío, la mía	*mine*
		los míos, las mías	
tu, tus	*your*	el tuyo, la tuya	*yours*
		los tuyos, las tuyas	
su, sus	*your, their*	el suyo, la suya	*yours, theirs*
		los suyos, las suyas	
nuestro, nuestra	*our*	el nuestro, la nuestra	*ours*
nuestros, nuestras		los nuestros, las nuestras	

vuestro, vuestra	*your*	el vuestro, la vuestra	*yours (Spain)*
vuestros, vuestras		los vuestros, las vuestras	
su, sus	*your, their*	el suyo, la suya	*yours, theirs*
		los suyos, las suyas	

Remember that pronouns take the place of nouns. Possessive pronouns agree in number and gender with the nouns they replace. Look at these examples:

mi libro	*my book*	→ el mío	*mine*
tu imaginación	*your imagination*	→ la tuya	*yours*
su llave	*his, her, your key*	→ la suya	*his, hers, yours*
nuestras hijitas	*our little girls*	→ las nuestras	*ours*
sus calcetines	*your, their socks*	→ los suyos	*yours, theirs*

Here are the pronouns used in sentences:

¿Es mi libro o **el tuyo**?	*Is this my book or yours?*
Yo no tengo imaginación, pero **la tuya** es muy vívida.	*I don't have any imagination, but yours is very vivid.*
Yo tengo mi llave. **La suya** está allí.	*I have my key. Yours is over there.*
Sus ideas son más interesantes que **las nuestras**.	*Your ideas are more interesting than ours.*
Aquellos calcetines son **suyos**. Éstos son **míos**.	*Those socks are yours. These are mine.*

When used directly after the verb **ser**, the article (**el, la, los, las**) is usually dropped:

| Este libro **es mío**. | *This book is mine.* |
| Ese libro **es tuyo**. | *That book is yours.* |

Or it can be used for emphasis.

| La mejor idea **fue la mía**, **no la tuya**. | *The best idea was mine, not yours.* |

El suyo and its various forms can mean many things: *his, hers, theirs, yours.* You can replace this pronoun with a prepositional phrase (**de** + the article) to prevent ambiguity and clarify what you are saying. Remember that the initial article is usually dropped when used after the verb **ser**.

his	hers	theirs	yours
(el) de él	(el) de ella	(el) de ellos/ellas	(el) de usted/ustedes
(la) de él	(la) de ella	(la) de ellos/ellas	(la) de usted/ustedes
(los) de él	(los) de ella	(los) de ellos/ellas	(los) de usted/ustedes
(las) de él	(las) de ella	(las) de ellos/ellas	(las) de usted/ustedes

Here are some example sentences:

El Mercedes es **suyo.** ⎫
El Mercedes es **de él.** ⎭   *The Mercedes is his.*

Este vaso es **suyo.** ⎫
Este vaso es **de usted**. ⎭   *This glass is yours.*

Mi collar es barato. **El suyo** es caro. ⎫
Mi collar es barato. **El de ella** es caro. ⎭   *My necklace is cheap. Hers is expensive.*

Esta oficina no es de la señora
  Moreno. **La suya** está allí. ⎫
Esta oficina no es de la señora
  Moreno. **La de ella** está allí. ⎭   *This office is not Señora Moreno's. Hers is over there.*

Written Practice 4

Rewrite the sentences in Spanish, replacing the phrase in italics with the correct possessive pronoun.

1. Está comprando *nuestros boletos.* *He's buying our tickets.*

   _____ .

2. ¿Tienen *sus pasaportes?* *Do they have their passports?*

   ¿_____?

3. *Mi silla* no es cómoda. *My chair isn't comfortable.*

   _____ .

4. ¿Dónde está *su cartera?* *Where is her (his, your) wallet?*

   ¿_____?

5. *Mi tren* sale a las ocho. *Tu tren* sale a las nueve y cuarenta. *My train leaves at eight. Your train leaves at nine forty.*

   _____ .

6. Ésta es *nuestra parada*. La próxima es *la parada de ustedes*. *This is our stop. The next one is your stop (yours).*

_____.

For the following items, use prepositional phrases to clarify.

7. *Su pasaje (de ella)* es caro, pero *el pasaje de ustedes* es carísimo. *Her fare is expensive, but your fare (yours) is very expensive.*

_____.

8. Éstas son *las cosas de ella*. ¿Dónde están *sus cosas (de ustedes)*? *These are her things. Where are your things (yours)?*

The Verbs *Saber* and *Conocer*

Spanish has two ways to say *to know*: **saber** and **conocer**. In the present tense both are irregular in the **yo** form (**saber** is highly irregular in other tenses).

Saber: Present Tense

yo sé	*I know*
tú sabes	*you know* (singular, informal)
él/ella/usted sabe	*he, she, it knows, you know* (singular, formal)
nosotros sabemos	*we know*
vosotros sabéis	*you know* (plural, informal)
ellos/ellas/ustedes saben	*they, you know* (plural)

Conocer: Present Tense

yo conozco	*I know*
tú conoces	*you know* (singular, informal)
él/ella/usted conoce	*he, she, it knows, you know* (singular, formal)
nosotros conocemos	*we know*
vosotros conocéis	*you know* (plural, informal)
ellos/ellas/ustedes conocen	*they, you know* (plural)

The present participles are **sabiendo** and **conociendo**, but they are not used very often.

Distinguishing Between *Saber* and *Conocer*

Because they are translated the same, students of Spanish often confuse **saber** and **conocer**. However, they have distinct uses.

Conocer is used in the sense of *to be familiar with* or *to know personally*, often with people, places, or other specific nouns. Compare these sentences:

¿**Conoces** al rey de España?	*Do you know the king of Spain?*
¿**Sabes** quién es el rey de España?	*Do you know who the king of Spain is?*
No **conozco** a tu madre.	*I don't know your mother.*
No **sé** quién es tu madre.	*I don't know who your mother is.*

When used to talk about a place, **conocer** is usually used in the sense of having visited and had some experience of a place (versus having heard of it or simply knowing of its existence).

No **conozco** Bogotá, pero **sé** que es la capital de Colombia.	*I've never been to Bogotá, but I know it's the capital of Colombia.*
¿**Conoces** el bar de la esquina?	*Have you been to the bar on the corner?*
—No, pero **sé** que es bueno.	*—No, but I know it's good.*

Saber is used more often to talk about knowledge of facts, actions (verbs), and languages, and with clauses (that start with **que** or **quien**).

No **sé** inglés.	*I don't know English.*
¿**Sabes** nadar?	*Do you know how to swim?*
Tú no **sabes** nada.	*You don't know anything.*
Yo no **sé** que hacer.	*I don't know what to do.*
¿Quien **sabe** jugar fútbol?	*Who knows how to play soccer?*

NOTE *In Spanish you never say **saber cómo** to express knowing how to do something. Instead, **saber** is used followed by the infinitive. You will not see **conocer** followed by the infinitive.*

No sé llegar a la carretera.	**I don't know how to get to the highway.**
¿Sabes tocar el piano?	**Do you know how to play the piano?**

Conocer is also used to say *to meet*, but only the first time you meet someone, i.e., *to get acquainted with someone*.

Ayer **conocí** a un muchacho lindo.	*Yesterday I met a cute boy.*
Mis padres **se conocieron** en primaria.	*My parents met each other in elementary school.*

Of course both of these verbs are useful with the indefinite pronouns and adjectives you just learned.

¿Conoces a algún dentista?	*Do you know any dentists?*
—No, no conozco a ninguno.	*—No, I don't know any.*
¿Sabes algo de música?	*Do you know anything about music?*
—No, no sé nada.	*—No, I don't know anything.*

Finally, there are a few well-known expressions that use the verb **saber**:

¿Quién sabe?	*Who knows?*
No sé. / No lo sé.	*I don't know.*
Lo sé.	*I know.*
¿Yo qué sé?	*Don't ask me!/What do I know?*
Para que los sepas.	*For your information./Just so you know.*

Incidentally, **saber** also means *to taste*. It's usually used with **a** to say *tastes like*.

¿A qué **sabe**?	*What does it taste like?*
La sopa **sabe a** pescado.	*The soup tastes like fish.*

Written Practice 5

 Track 39

Complete the sentences with **saber** or **conocer** in the present or present participle.

1. (Yo) _____ a tres Argentinos. *I know three Argentineans.*

2. (Yo) no _____ dónde queda la parada de metro. *I don't know where the metro stop is.*

3. ¿_____ usted a mi esposo? *Do you know my husband?*

4. ¿(Tú) no _____ conducir? *You don't know how to drive?*

5. (Nosotros) _____ a mil personas en Miami. *We know a ton of people in Miami.*

6. Elvira no _____ París, pero _____ que en Francia hay buena comida. *Elvira has never been to Paris, but she knows that France has good food.*

7. Todavía estoy _____ a Marta, pero parece buena gente. *I'm still getting to know Marta, but she seems like a good person.*

8. ¿Ustedes _____ cuántas personas vienen a la fiesta? *Do you know how many people are coming to the party?*

9. (Yo) no _____ a nadie en esta clase. *I don't know anyone in this class.*

10. (Yo) no _____ su nombre, pero lo _____ de vista. *I don't know his name, but I recognize him by sight.*

QUIZ

Circle the letter of the word or phrase that best completes each sentence.

1. **Sergio _____.**
   A. es viajando
   B. esta viajando
   C. está viajando
   D. A, B, o C

2. **¿Tú _____ dinero?**
   A. estás ahorrando
   B. sigues ahorrando
   C. vas ahorrando
   D. A, B, o C

3. **Yo _____ una camisa verde.**
   A. está llevando
   B. lleva
   C. estoy llevando
   D. llevo

4. **Son las nueve da la noche. El bebé está _____.**
   A. durmiendo
   B. leyendo
   C. trabajando
   D. corriendo

5. ¿Qué sabes del idioma francés?

    —No sé _____.

    A. nada

    B. nadie

    C. alguien

    D. nunca

6. Compra _____ marca. Son todas iguales.

    A. cualquier

    B. cualquiera

    C. ningún

    D. algún

7. ¿_____ de ellas está hablando en español? No, _____ de ellas está hablando en español.

    A. alguna; alguna

    B. algunas; ningunas

    C. alguna; ninguna

    D. ningunas; ningunas

8. Mi libro es una novela, pero _____ de ella es un libro de poesía.

    A. él

    B. la

    C. ella

    D. el

9. ¡Tu casa es enorme! _____ es muy pequeña.

    A. El mío

    B. La mía

    C. La tuya

    D. El tuyo

10. Juan y Maya _____ cocinar.

    A. conocen

    B. conocen como

    C. saben

    D. saben como

chapter **9**

Using Reflexive Verbs

In this chapter you will learn a simple way to talk about the future using **ir**. You will learn some more irregular verbs in the present as well as reflexive and reciprocal verbs.

CHAPTER OBJECTIVES

In this chapter you will learn

- The future with *ir + a*
- Present tense of *poner*, *valer*, *traer*, and **salir**
- Reflexive verbs
- Reflexive verbs with multiple meanings
- Reciprocal verbs

The Future with *Ir* + *a*

In Chapter 5, you learned that the present tense can be used to express the future in cases such as **Mañana salgo a pescar** (*I'm going out fishing tomorrow*). Another simple and surefire way to express the future in Spanish is to use **ir a** + the infinitive of the verb that is taking place in the future. This is the same as saying *to be going to* in English.

Here is the structure of the future with **ir**:

yo voy
tú vas
él/ella/usted va + **a** + infinitive
vosotros vais
nosotros vamos
ellos/ellas/ustedes van

Look at these examples.

Voy a salir.	*I am going to go out.*
Vamos a bailar.	*We are going to dance/go dancing.*
Ellos **van a** beber algo.	*They are going to have a drink.*
¿**Vas a** cenar?	*Are you going to eat dinner?*

To talk about **hay** (*there is, there are*) or **no hay** (*there isn't, there aren't*) in the future, use **ir a** + the infinitive **haber**.

Va a haber una manifestación	*There is going to be a demonstration*
mañana.	*tomorrow.*

Usually the present tense of the verb **ir** can be used to say *going to* (a place) without using **ir a** beforehand.

Voy a la discoteca.	*I'm going to the dance club.*
El año que viene **vamos a** Irlanda.	*Next year we're going to Ireland.*

Written Practice 1

 Track 40

The following sentences are in the present tense. Rewrite them using the future with **ir a** + infinitive.

1. ¿Hacemos algo esta noche? *Are we doing something tonight?*

_____ *Are we going to do something tonight?*

2. Hablan con tus padres. *They're speaking with your parents.*

_____ *They're going to speak with your parents.*

3. ¿No puedes venir? *You can't come?*

_____ *You aren't going to be able to come?*

4. Vivo en las afueras de Madrid. *I live on the outskirts of Madrid.*

_____ *I'm going to live on the outskirts of Madrid.*

5. Tenemos tres hijos. *We have three children.*

_____ *We are going to have three children.*

6. ¿Hacen la cama? *Do they make the bed?*

_____ *Are they going to make the bed?*

7. Conozco a los padres de mi novio. *I know my boyfriend's parents.*

_____ *I'm going to meet my boyfriend's parents.*

8. Hay mucha gente en mi fiesta. *There are a lot of people at my party.*

_____ *There are going to be a lot of people at my party.*

Oral Practice

 Track 41

Talk about what you are going to do in the future by completing the following sentences about yourself using **ir a** + infinitive. Listen to possible answers on the CD.

1. Hoy voy a..._____ *(Today I am going to . . .)*

2. Esta noche..._____ *(Tonight . . .)*

3. Mañana..._____ *(Tomorrow . . .)*

4. El año que viene..._____ *(Next year . . .)*

5. Esta semana..._____ (*This week . . .*)

6. Después de aprender español..._____ (*After learning Spanish . . .*)

More Irregular Verbs in the Present Tense

In Chapter 6 you learned the verb **hacer**. Here's a review:

yo hago	*I make/do*
tú haces	*you make/do* (singular, informal)
él/ella/usted hace	*he, she, it makes/does, you make/do* (singular, formal)
nosotros hacemos	*we make/do*
vosotros hacéis	*you make/do* (plural, informal)
ellos/ellas/ustedes hacen	*they, you make/do* (plural)

Several other irregular verbs are conjugated similarly to **hacer** in the present tense. These are **poner** (*to put*), **valer** (*to be worth*), **traer** (*to bring*), and **salir** (*to leave, go out*). You'll notice that these verbs are only irregular in the first person **yo** form, and otherwise follow the rules for regular **-er** and **-ir** verbs.

	poner	**valer**	**traer**	**salir**
yo	pongo	valgo	traigo	salgo
tú	pones	vales	traes	sales
él/ella/usted	pone	vale	trae	sale
nosotros	ponemos	valemos	traemos	salimos
vosotros	ponéis	valéis	traéis	salís
ellos/ellas/ustedes	ponen	valen	traen	salen

Here are some example sentences using these verbs:

Ponen la mesa.	*They set the table.*
¿Dónde **pones** los abrigos?	*Where do you put the coats?*
Valgo mucho.	*I'm worth a lot.*
Vale diez dólares.	*It's worth ten dollars.*
¿**Traigo** a mi amigo?	*Should I bring my friend?*
Selena **trae** mi entrada.	*Selena is bringing my ticket.*
Salimos esta noche.	*We're going out tonight.*
Salen a las ocho.	*They leave at eight o'clock.*

Written Practice 2

Complete the sentences with the correct form of the verb in parentheses.

1. ¿(Tú) _____ esta noche? (salir) *Are you going out tonight?*

2. ¿Cuánto _____ este cuadro? (valer) *How much is this painting worth?*

3. (Yo) _____ la comida al trabajo. (traer) *I bring my lunch to work.*

4. (Yo) no le _____ sal a la sopa. (poner) *I don't put salt in the soup.*

5. Estos discos no _____ nada. (valer) *These records aren't worth anything.*

6. ¿Cuántos platos (tú) _____ en la mesa? (poner) *How many plates do you put on the table?*

7. (Yo) No _____ nada por las mañanas. (hacer) *I don't do anything in the mornings.*

8. Sonia nunca _____. Prefiere quedarse en casa. (salir) *Sonia never goes out. She prefers to stay at home.*

Asking *¿Cuánto vale?*

Although the verb **valer** technically means *to be worth*, it is often used to ask or talk about prices. There are several ways to do this in Spanish.

¿Cuánto cuesta?	*How much does it cost?*
¿Cuánto vale?	*How much does it cost?*
¿Cuánto es?	*How much is it?*

Traer or *Llevar*?

Knowing when to use **traer** (*to bring*) and when to use **llevar** (*to take*) can be tricky in Spanish. This is confused by the fact that in English we generally depend on the verb *to bring* to talk about moving something from one place to another. In Spanish, you should be able to distinguish the use of these two verbs by following one basic rule. **Llevar** is used to take something from where the speaker is to where the speaker isn't. **Traer** is used to bring something from where the speaker isn't to where the speaker is. Listen to these sample telephone conversations:

▶ Track 42

Ana:	Hola, Santiago. ¿Vienes a mi fiesta esta noche? *Hi Santiago. Are you coming to my party tonight?*
Santiago:	Sí, por supuesto. *Yes, of course.*

| Ana: | ¿Puedes **traer** una botella de vino? *Can you bring a bottle of wine?* |
| Santiago: | Claro que sí. **Llevo** un Malbec Argentino. *Of course. I'll take (bring) an Argentinian Malbec.* |

In the previous example we have to assume that Ana's party is going to be at her place, or at least in the place she is at the moment of speaking. (We can also make this assumption because she uses the verb **venir**, which, like **traer** is used when talking about going to a place the speaker is.) Now let's assume for a moment that Ana is having her party somewhere else, other than where she is at the moment of speaking, perhaps at a restaurant downtown. She's calling Santiago on her cell phone from the street. In this case, the dialogue would change to:

Ana:	Hola, Santiago. ¿Vas a mi fiesta esta noche? *Hi Santiago. Are you going to my party tonight?*
Santiago:	Sí, por supuesto. *Yes, of course.*
Ana:	¿Puedes **llevar** una botella de vino? *Can you take a bottle of wine?*
Santiago:	Claro que sí. **Llevo** un Malbec Argentino. *Of course. I'll take an Argentinian Malbec.*

Here, Ana says ¿**Puedes llevar una botella de vino?** because the party will not be taking place where she is at the moment she is speaking with Santiago. We can further infer this because she uses the verb **ir** (¿**Vas a mi fiesta esta noche?**) implying that the party will take place somewhere else.

Written Practice 3

 Track 43

Complete the following mini-dialogues with the correct form of **traer** or **llevar** in the present. Use the clues provided to help you.

1. Jonás y Clarisa están en el trabajo. *Jonas and Clarisa are at work (together).*

| Clarisa: | Jonás, ¿tú _____ tu almuerzo al trabajo o lo compras fuera? |
| Jonás: | Siempre _____ el almuerzo al trabajo. No lo compro nunca. |

2. Jonás y Clarisa están en casa. *Jonas and Clarisa are at home (together).*

> **Clarisa:**   Jonás, ¿tú _____ tu almuerzo al trabajo o lo compras fuera?
>
> **Jonás:**   Siempre _____ el almuerzo al trabajo. No lo compro nunca.

3. Ester está en casa y Eunice está en el trabajo. *Ester is at home and Eunice is at work.*

> **Ester:**   Quiero hacer una tortilla esta noche pero no tengo huevos.
>
> **Eunice:**   No te preocupes. Te _____ unos huevos después de trabajar.

4. Jorge y Hugo están en su trabajo. *Jorge and Hugo are at work (together).*

> **Jorge:**   Oye, Hugo, ¿vas a cenar en la casa de Julia esta noche?
>
> **Hugo:**   Claro que sí. Cocina muy bien.
>
> **Jorge:**   Bacán. (*Great*) ¿Vas a _____ a Catarina?
>
> **Hugo:**   ¡Por supuesto que la _____!

Reflexive Verbs

Reflexive verbs and reflexive pronouns throw many students of Spanish for a loop. These pesky pronouns show up everywhere, and using them correctly can often make the difference between sounding like a native or a novice.

A *reflexive verb* is one in which the action both is carried out by and happens to the subject of the verb, i.e., it reflects upon the subject. Such verbs are sometimes expressed in English by using words such as *herself, themselves,* and *myself,* i.e., *I scratch myself.* Oftentimes, however, Spanish reflexive verbs don't seem intuitively "reflexive" to an English speaker. For instance, the verb **vestirse** means *to get dressed.* Why not just say **vestir** and be done with it? Because the literal translation is *to dress oneself.* We say *to get dressed* when we need a rough equivalent in English. You'll see that many Spanish reflexive verbs are translated into English with the word *get.*

Probably the most familiar reflexive verb (whether you're aware of it or not) is **llamarse** (*to be named*). Literally translated, **llamarse** means *to call oneself.*

¿Cómo **te llamas**?	*What's your name?*
	(Literally: *What do you call yourself?*)
—**Me llamo** Norma.	—*My name is Norma.*
	(Literally: *I call myself Norma.*)

The infinitive form of the verb **llamarse** ends with **se**. **Se** is a reflexive pronoun that is tacked on to the end of the infinitive to show it is reflexive. All reflexive verb infinitives end with -**se**. As you can see in the previous example, a reflexive pronoun is also used when the verb is conjugated. Here are the reflexive pronouns shown with **llamarse**. Notice how each reflexive matches up with the subject pronoun that it "reflects."

Subject	**Reflexive pronoun and verb**
yo	**me** llamo
tú	**te** llamas
él/ella/usted	**se** llama
nosotros	**nos** llamamos
vosotros	**os** llamáis
ellos/ella/ustedes	**se** llaman

The reflexive pronouns can be translated as follows:

me	*myself*
te	*yourself*
se	*himself, herself, itself, yourself*
nos	*ourselves*
os	*yourselves, each other (Spain)*
se	*themselves, yourselves, each other*

Many reflexive verbs have to do with personal grooming.

afeitarse	*to shave (oneself)*
bañarse	*to bathe (oneself)*
cepillarse (el cabello, los dientes)	*to brush one's (hair, teeth)*
ducharse	*to shower (oneself)*
lavarse (la cara, las manos)	*to wash oneself (one's face, hands)*
maquillarse	*to put on (one's) makeup*
peinarse	*to comb one's hair*
ponerse	*to put on (one's clothes)*
quitarse	*to take off (an item of clothing)*
vestirse (i)	*to get dressed*

Other common reflexive verbs are:

acostarse (ue)	*to go to bed*
despedirse (i)	*to say good-bye*
despertarse (ie)	*to wake up*
divertirse (ie)	*to have fun*
dormirse (ue)	*to fall asleep*
enojarse	*to get angry*
equivocarse	*to be mistaken*
fijarse (en)	*to notice, to pay attention (to)*
levantarse	*to get up*
olvidarse (de)	*to forget*
quejarse	*to complain*
sentarse (ie)	*to sit down*
sentirse (ie)	*to feel*

You'll see that many verbs can have a slight, but important, change of meaning when they become reflexive.

Not reflexive		**Reflexive**	
dormir	*to sleep*	dormirse	*to fall asleep*
ir	*to go*	irse	*to go away, leave*
engañar	*to trick, fool*	engañarse	*to be mistaken, deceive oneself*
llevar	*to take*	llevarse	*to take away*
marchar	*to go, walk*	marcharse	*to leave*
poner	*to put*	ponerse	*to put on*
quedar	*to be, be left (over)*	quedarse	*to remain, stay*

Here are some example sentences with reflexive verbs. Notice the placement of the reflexive pronoun before the conjugated verb.

María **se acuesta** a las diez.	*María goes to bed at ten.*
No **me siento** bien.	*I don't feel well.*
¿Ustedes **se quedan** aquí?	*Are you staying here?*
¿**Te duchas** por la noche?	*Do you shower at night?*
Nos vamos.	*We're leaving.*
¿**Se marchan**?	*Are you leaving?*
Me olvidé de su cumpleaños.	*I forgot her birthday.*

Colloquially, Spanish speakers will sometimes use verbs reflexively with the same meaning as the non-reflexive form. Compare these examples:

¿Vienes?	¿**Te** vienes?	*Are you coming?*
Comí todo.	**Me** comí todo.	*I ate everything.*

NOTE *Possessive pronouns are not used when talking about parts of the body and items of clothing. Spanish prefers the definite article in this construction. Compare the following sentences in English and Spanish.*

*Juan se lava **la cara** y se cepilla* ***los dientes.***	Juan washes his face and brushes his teeth.
*Me quito **el abrigo**.*	I take off my coat.

Written Practice 4

Complete the following sentences with the correct reflexive pronoun: **me**, **te**, **se**, or **nos**.

1. Raquel _____ despierta a las siete de la mañana. *Raquel wakes up at seven in the morning.*

2. ¿Qué _____ vas a poner? *What are you going to wear?*

3. _____ lavamos las manos antes de comer. *We wash our hands before eating.*

4. Mis padres _____ fijan en todo. *My parents notice everything.*

5. _____ estoy vistiendo para salir a las diez. *I'm getting dressed to go out at ten.*

6. ¿Por qué no _____ sientas? *Why don't you sit down?*

7. ¿Cuántas veces por día _____ cepillas los dientes? *How many times a day do you brush your teeth?*

8. Orlando siempre _____ está quejando. *Orlando is always complaining.*

9. ¿A qué hora _____ marchan? *What time are you leaving?*

10. ¿_____ vamos o _____ quedamos? *Shall we leave or shall we stay?*

Placement of Reflexive Pronouns

When reflexive verbs are used in the present tense, or other simple tenses (tenses composed of a single word), the pronoun precedes the verb. With present participles and infinitives, however, the placement of the pronoun is more flexible in Spanish. It can go before the auxiliary "helping" verb, or be "tacked on" to the end of the infinitive or present participle.

Me voy a vestir.	Voy a vestir**me**.	*I'm going to get dressed.*
Me tengo que ir.	Tengo que ir**me**.	*I have to go.*
Se están divirtiendo.	Están divirtiéndo**se**.	*They are having fun.*

NOTE *Adding the reflexive pronoun to the end of the present participle changes the number of syllables and, therefore, may create the need for a written accent. In the example above, **divirtiendo** (no accent) becomes **divirtiéndose**. The accent is added to maintain the stress on the syllable **-tien-**, which is now the third-to-last syllable.*

*Conversely, you must remove the accent when removing the reflexive pronoun. **Diviertiéndose** becomes **Se están divirtiendo** (no accent). This is because **-tien-** reverts to being the penultimate syllable of a word ending in a vowel, and naturally takes the stress.*

Written Practice 5

Rewrite the following sentences, putting the pronoun in a different place than it appears.

1. Pienso quedarme hasta el final. *I'm thinking of staying until the end.*

_____.

2. Luis tiene que despertarse a las seis. *Luis has to wake up at six.*

_____.

3. Nos vamos a sentar aquí. *We are going to sit here.*

_____.

4. Silvia se está duchando. *Silvia is taking a shower.*

_____.

5. Manolo está engañándose con esta relación. *Manolo is deceiving himself with this relationship.*

_____ .

6. ¿Vas a ponerte un vestido o una falda? *Are you going to put on a dress or a skirt?*

¿_____?

Written Practice 6

Track 44

Now complete the conversation between two friends with the reflexive verbs in parentheses. You can listen to the full conversation on the CD recording.

Silvia: Manolo, ¿_____ (1. venirse) a mi fiesta esta noche? *Manolo, are you coming to my party tonight?*

Manolo: No creo. No _____ (2. divertirse) mucho en las fiestas. *I don't think so. I don't have a lot of fun at parties.*

Silvia: Siempre _____ (3. quejarse) y luego _____ (4. alegrarse) de estar allí. *You always complain, but later you're glad to be there.*

Manolo: Es que si voy, tengo que _____ (5. ducharse) y _____ (6. vestirse). No me apetece. *But if I go I have to shower and get dressed. I don't feel like it.*

Silvia: Si no _____ (7. venirse), Marta y Ana _____ van a _____ (8. enojarse). *If you don't come, Marta and Ana are going to get angry.*

Manolo: Ya hablé con Marta. Ella _____ (9. quedarse) en casa esta noche. Está enferma. *I already talked to Marta. She's staying at home tonight. She's sick.*

Silvia: ¿Y Ana? Sabes que _____ (10. fijarse) mucho en ti. *And Ana? You know she really has her eye on you.*

Manolo: Sí, lo sé. Pero no _____ (11. interesarse). Esa chica es rara. *Yes, I know. But I'm not interested. That girl is weird.*

Silvia: Bueno, como quieras. Vamos a _____ (12. divertirse) mucho sin ti. *Fine, as you wish. We're going to have fun without you.*

Reflexive Verbs with Multiple Meanings

Some reflexive verbs have a variety of meanings and uses, and it's a good idea to try to get them under your belt. The Spanish language is very rich in idiomatic expressions, and the combinations are endless. Here are just a few useful common reflexive verbs with multiple meanings.

Encontrarse

Encontrar means *to find*. The reflexive **encontrarse** is most often used in the sense *to meet* or *to run into*. In this case it's used with the preposition **con** (*with*).

¿Dónde **nos encontramos**?	*Where are we going to meet?*
Me encontré con Susana en la fiesta.	*I ran into Susana at the party.*

Encontrarse is also used to talk about feelings. In this case it means *to feel*, but could literally be thought of as *I find myself feeling*.

¿**Te encuentras** bien, Carlos?	*Are you feeling O.K., Carlos?*
—No, **me encuentro** muy solo.	*—No, I'm feeling very lonely.*

Imagine you've gone out with friends and you suddenly feel sick or tired. See how this and other reflexive verbs can help you express yourself.

No **me encuentro** bien. **Me tengo que** ir a casa.	*I'm not feeling well. I have to go home.*

Finally, **encontrarse** can also mean *to be located*. Again, this has the sense of *to find itself*.

¿Dónde **se encuentran** los baños?	*Where are the bathrooms?*
—**Se encuentran** en el pasillo, a la derecha.	*—They are in the hallway, on the right.*

Quedarse

Incidentally, the verb **quedar**, non-reflexively, aside from meaning *to be left* also means *to arrange to meet* or *to make plans* as well as *to meet*. (You'll see that **quedar, quedarse, encontrar,** and **encontrarse** have a lot in common with each other.)

¿A qué hora **quedamos**?	*What time are we meeting?*
—**Quedamos** a las ocho en el centro comercial.	*—Let's meet at 8:00 at the mall.*

In its reflexive form, the verb **quedarse** can mean *to stay*.

Me quedo en casa.	*I'm staying home.*
¿Nos quedamos o nos vamos?	*Shall we stay or shall we go?*

Quedarse also means *to keep*. In this case it's used with the preposition con (*with*).

Me quedo con éste.	*I'll stick with this one.*
Te puedes quedar con el cambio.	*You can keep the change.*

Quedarse is also used in way that is difficult to translate, but has the general meaning of *to be left*, suggesting how something or someone *ends up*. These are often used in the past tense (preterit), which you will learn later.

Me quedé sin trabajo.	*I lost my job.* (Literally: *I was left without work.*)
Rodrigo se quedó dormido en el sofá.	*Rodrigo fell asleep on the couch.* (Literally: *Rodrigo ended up asleep on the couch.*)

In this sense, quedarse can be used in numerous ways. Here are just a few more common expressions:

quedarse en blanco	*to space out, blank out*
quedarse dormido	*to fall asleep*
quedarse helado	*to be scared stiff*
quedarse atrás	*to stay/get left behind*

Ponerse

Finally, you learned above that poner means *to put* and ponerse means *to put on* or *wear*.

¿Te vas a poner una corbata?	*Are you going to put on a tie?*
Marisa nunca se pone falda.	*Marisa never wears a skirt.*

In addition, ponerse can mean *to get* in the sense of *to become*.

Si como almejas me pongo enferma.	*If I eat clams I get sick.*

Here are a few common expressions that use ponerse in the sense of *to become* or *to get*.

ponerse mal/enfermo	*to get sick*
ponerse bien	*to get better*
ponerse de acuerdo	*to come to an agreement*
ponerse en contacto	*to get in touch*

Ponerse is also used in the sense of *to put oneself (in a certain position)*.

ponerse de pie	*to stand up*
ponerse de rodillas	*to kneel*

Finally, **ponerse a** can be used to mean *to start*.

Me pongo a hablar y no puedo parar.	*I start talking and I can't stop.*
Se puso a llover.	*It started to rain.*

Written Practice 7

Circle the letter of the word or phrase that best completes each sentence.

1. No me _____ bien. Me voy a sentar un rato. *I don't feel well. I'm going to sit down for a minute.*
   (a) quedo
   (b) encuentro
   (c) pongo

2. Nada más llego a casa y se _____ a llover. *No sooner do I arrive home than it starts to rain.*
   (a) queda
   (b) encuentra
   (c) pone

3. Cuándo veo una serpiente me _____ helado. *When I see a snake I get scared stiff.*
   (a) quedo
   (b) encuentro
   (c) pongo

4. Ustedes se _____ aquí y yo voy a buscar a Orlando. *You stay here, and I'll go look for Orlando.*

   (a) quedan

   (b) encuentran

   (c) ponen

5. ¿En dónde y a qué hora nos _____? *Where and what time are we meeting?*

   (a) quedamos

   (b) encontramos

   (c) ponemos

6. ¿Se _____ con la falda azul, señora? *Are you going to take the blue skirt, ma'am?*

   (a) queda

   (b) encuentra

   (c) pone

7. ¿Cómo te _____, Paty? Tienes mal aspecto. *How are you feeling, Paty? You don't look well.*

   (a) quedas

   (b) encuentras

   (c) pones

8. Julia siempre se _____ gafas oscuras. *Julia always wears dark glasses.*

   (a) queda

   (b) encuentra

   (c) pone

9. Cuando empieza la música me _____ a bailar. *When the music begins I start to dance.*

   (a) quedo

   (b) encuentro

   (c) pongo

10. Las toallas se _____ en el armario. *The towels are kept in the closet.*

   (a) quedan

   (b) encuentran

   (c) ponen

Reciprocal Verbs

As you have seen in some of the examples above, the personal pronouns **se**, **nos**, and **os** can also be used reciprocally (with **ustedes**, **nosotros**, and **vosotros**), meaning that instead of the action reflecting on the speaker, the action passes between or among two or more people. In this form, the personal pronouns have the sense of *each other* or *one another*. Look at the following examples:

¿Ustedes **se conocen**?   *Do you know each other?*
—¡Claro que **nos conocemos**!   *—Of course we know each other!*
Los dos perros **se están mirando**. *The two dogs are looking at each other.*
Nosotros **nos entendemos** bien. *We understand each other well.*

QUIZ

Circle the letter of the word or phrase that best completes each sentence.

1. Esta noche (yo) _____ salir con mis amigos.
   A. va
   B. voy
   C. va a
   D. voy a

2. _____ un examen mañana.
   A. Va haber
   B. Va a ver
   C. Va a haber
   D. Voy a haber

3. ¿Cuánto _____ el reloj?
   A. valgo
   B. vales
   C. vale
   D. valen

4. ¿Tú _____ tomate en la ensalada?

    A. pones

    B. sales

    C. traes

    D. vales

5. ¿Vas a la fiesta esta noche en casa de Elena?

    —Sí, y voy a _____ a Catarina.

    A. traer

    B. llevar

    C. traigo

    D. llevo

6. Los niños _____ lavan las manos antes de comer.

    A. me

    B. te

    C. se

    D. nos

7. No _____ bien. Voy a casa.

    A. me encuentra

    B. me siento

    C. siento

    D. encuentro

8. Tania _____ a las once de la noche y _____ a las siete de la mañana para ir a trabajar.

    A. se acuesta; se despierta

    B. se levanta; se despierta

    C. se despierta; se acuesta

    D. se levanta; se acuesta

9. _____. Me voy a casa.

    A. Me quedo

    B. No me quedo

    C. No me voy

    D. No me marcho

10. **¿Conoces a Marco?**

    —No. _____.

    A. Nos conocemos

    B. No nos conocemos

    C. Me conoce bien

    D. Nos conocemos bien

chapter **10**

Making Comparisons

In this chapter you will learn how to compare things that are similar and how to compare things that are different. You will learn to use the superlative to talk about the *biggest* or *best* in a category and how to make exclamations with ¡Qué! And finally you will learn when to use **ser** and when to use **estar** to say *to be*.

CHAPTER OBJECTIVES

In this chapter you will learn

- How to make comparisons
- Superlative adjectives
- Exclamations with *¡Qué!*
- When to use *ser* and *estar*

Making Comparisons

In English, when we want to compare two things, we often use comparative adjectives, for example: *She's prettier than her sister, This house is smaller than the other one,* or *The book is more interesting than the movie.* We can also compare actions by using comparative adverbs. For instance, *You walk more quickly than I do* or *Emilia sings better than Ana.* Finally, you can also compare nouns: *There are more single women than single men* or *More people speak Spanish than French.* As you can see, in English these comparatives are usually expressed by saying *more . . . than* or by adding *-er* to the comparative word.

Comparisons of Inequality

To compare two things that are unequal in Spanish, use the construction **más... que** (*more . . . than*). The comparative is most often used with adjectives: **más** + adjective + **que**. Compare these sentences with and without the comparative.

Larisa es alta.	*Larisa is tall.*
Yo no soy alta.	*I am not tall.*
Larisa es **más alta que** yo.	*Larisa is taller than me.*
Adán está contento.	*Adán is happy.*
Enrique no está contento.	*Enrique is not happy.*
Adán está **más contento que** Enrique.	*Adán is happier than Enrique.*

This construction can also be used with adverbs or nouns: **más** + adverb + **que** or **más** + noun + **que**.

El metro va **más rápido que** el bus.	*The metro goes faster than the bus.*
No tengo **más dinero que** tú.	*I don't have more money than you.*

When **más** is followed by a *number*, the construction **más... de** is used.

El televisor plasma cuesta **más de quinientos dólares**.	*The plasma TV costs more than five hundred dollars.*

However, if the sentence is *negative*, **que** is used before a number.

No tengo **más que veinte minutos**.	*I only have twenty minutes.*

You can also use the construction **menos... que** (*less . . . than*) to talk about inequality.

Enrique está **menos contento**
   que Adán.

Enrique is less happy than Adán.

Tengo **menos dinero que** *tú*.

I have less money than you.

While **más... que** (or **menos... que**) compares two things explicitly, you can use them alone, without **que**, to make implied comparisons:

El año pasado estaba gorda, pero
   ahora estoy **más delgada**.

*Last year I was fat, but now I'm
   thinner (than I was last year).*

Parecen **más contentos** hoy.

*They seem happier today (than they
   did yesterday, or last week).*

Irregular Comparatives of Inequality

Spanish also has a few irregular comparatives. Note that we have the same phenomenon in English. Just as we say *better* (instead of *more good* or *gooder*), or *worse* (instead of *more bad* or *badder*), in Spanish, the words **bueno**, **malo**, **grande**, and **pequeño** have irregular comparatives.

Adjective		Comparative	
bueno	*good*	mejor/mejores	*better*
malo	*bad*	peor/peores	*worse*
grande	*big*	mayor/mayores	*bigger/older*
pequeño	*little*	menor/menores	*"littler"/younger*

Here are some example sentences. Notice that the irregular comparative words do not change according to gender (but do change in the plural). They are followed by **que** when a comparison follows, but can also stand alone to make implied comparisons.

La sopa es mala. Es **peor que**
   la mía.

The soup is bad. It's worse than mine.

Este libro es bueno pero los otros
   son **mejores**.

*This book is good, but the others are
   better.*

The words **mayor** and **menor** are used only to talk about age. Otherwise, **grande** and **pequeño** are used to talk about size.

Mi hermana es **menor que** yo.

My sister is younger than I.

¿Tus hermanos son **mayores** o
   menores?

Are your siblings older or younger?

Esta casa es **más grande**   *This house is bigger than yours, . . .*
que la tuya...
... pero es **más pequeña**   *. . . but it is smaller than mine.*
que la mía.

Mejor and **peor** are also the comparatives of the adverbs **bien** and **mal**.

Juan canta **mejor que** Pablo.   *Juan sings better than Pablo.*
Yo creo que Juan canta **peor**.   *I think Juan sings worse.*

Written Practice 1

Complete the sentences with a comparative of the word (adjective, noun, or adverb) in parentheses using **más** with **que** or **de** when applicable.

1. Ahora mi vida es (complicada) _____ antes.

   Now my life is more complicated than before.

2. Los mariscos en Lima son (buenos) _____ los mariscos en Cuzco.

   The seafood in Lima is better than the seafood in Cuzco.

3. Yo tengo (miedo) _____ mi hermana.

   I am more scared than my sister.

4. Este cuarto está (limpio) _____ el otro.

   This room is cleaner than the other one.

5. Ángela tiene (dos mil dólares) _____ en el banco.

   Ángela has more than two thousand dollars in the bank.

6. John habla español (mal) _____ Raquel.

   John speaks Spanish worse than Raquel.

7. ¿Trabajas (horas) _____ tu jefe?

   Do you work more hours than your boss?

8. No quiero pagar (ciento cincuenta dólares) _____ la noche.

   I don't want to pay more than a hundred and fifty dollars a night.

9. Begoña parece (estudiosa) _____ Nieves.

   Begoña seems more studious than Nieves.

10. Mi madre tiene (paciencia) _____ mi padre.

   My mother has more patience than my father.

11. Carmen tiene sólo **23** años. Es (pequeña) _____ yo, pero parece (grande) _____ .

   *Carmen is only **23** years old. She's younger than me, but she looks older.*

12. Creo que Mel Gibson tiene (seis) _____ hijos.

   I think Mel Gibson has more than six children.

Comparatives of Equality

To compare two things that are equal, the construction changes depending on whether you are comparing nouns, adjectives, adverbs, or verbs. To compare adjectives, use **tan** + adjective + **como** (*as . . . as*). Compare these sentences with and without the comparative.

Marco es alto. Su hermano también es alto.	*Marco is tall. His brother is also tall.*
Marco es **tan alto como** su hermano.	*Marco is as tall as his brother.*
Su primer disco es bueno. Su segundo disco también es bueno.	*Their first album is good. Their second album is also good.*
Su segundo disco es **tan bueno como** el primero.	*Their second album is as good as their first.*

The same construction is used for adverbs.

Marta habla **tan rápido como** yo.	*Marta speaks as fast as I do.*
Este perfume huele **tan bien como** el otro.	*This perfume smells as good as the other one.*

For nouns, the comparison is different. The construction **tanto... que** (*as much . . . as, as many . . . as*) is used. Notice how **tanto** changes in gender and number according to the noun it modifies.

tanto	*as much (m.)*
tanta	*as much (f.)*
tantos	*as many (m. pl.)*
tantas	*as many (f. pl.)*

Here are some example sentences:

Tengo **tanto trabajo como** mis colegas.	*I have as much work as my colleagues.*
Catalina no tiene **tanta música** en su iPod **como** Adán.	*Catalina doesn't have as much music on her iPod as Adán.*
No conozco **tantos lugares como** Luisa.	*I haven't been to as many places as Luisa (has).*
Yo conozco a **tantas personas como** tú.	*I know as many people as you do.*

Using *Igual* to Make Equal Comparisons

Spanish speakers will often use the phrase **igual de** to make equal comparisons. You'll notice that **tan** and **tanto** usually describe an amount, or degree of similarity: *as tall, as much, as many, as fast.* The word **igual** literally means *equal,* but in this sense is commonly translated as *just as* or *equally* and can refer also to similarities in quality or existence: *they dress the same, they look the same.* The construction **igual de** can be followed by an adjective or **bien** or **mal** and will definitely give a native flavor to your speech. Take a look at these examples:

Ana: ¿Cómo va el trabajo? *How is the work going?*
Patricia: **Igual de** mal. *Just as bad (as before).*

In the previous example, **igual de** is followed by **mal**.

Juan: ¿Quién es más listo, René o André? *Who is smarter, René or André?*
Eva: Son **igual de** listos. *They're equally smart.*

Here, **igual de** is followed by an adjective, **listos** (*smart*).

NOTE *The adjective **igual** is invariable in this construction. It does not agree in number with the noun.*

When followed by a noun, use the construction **igual que** to say *just like.*

Ana: ¿Cómo es Maya? *What does Maya look like?*
Patricia: Es **igual que** su madre. *She looks just like her mother.*

Juan: ¿Felipe se viste bien? *Does Felipe dress well?*
Eva: Sí, se viste **igual que** yo. *Yes, he dresses just like me.*

In both of these cases, **igual que** is followed by a noun, noun phrase, or pronoun: **su madre** and **yo**.

Notice how similar ideas can be expressed in different ways.

Felipe se viste **tan bien como** yo.   *Felipe dresses as well as I do.*

Felipe se viste **igual que** yo.   *Felipe dresses just like me.*

Felipe y yo nos vestimos **igual de** bien.   *Felipe and I dress equally well.*

Oral Practice 1

 Track 45

Imagine that you are trying to decide where to live, **Nueva York** (*New York*) or **Boston**. Make sentences comparing the two cities, following the example, and say them aloud.

Boston es pequeña. Nueva York no es pequeña.

Boston es más pequeña que Nueva York.

1. El metro en Nueva York es grande. El metro en Boston no es grande.

2. El metro en Nueva York es muy sucio. El metro en Boston es un poco sucio.

3. Nueva York es cara. Boston también es cara.

4. Nueva York tiene mucho tráfico. Boston no tiene tanto tráfico.

5. En Nueva York hay muchas diversiones. En Boston hay menos diversiones.

6. Hace frío en Nueva York. También hace frío en Boston.

7. Los restaurantes en Nueva York son muy buenos. Los restaurantes en Boston son buenos.

Superlative Adjectives

Once you know comparatives, superlatives are easier to learn. Superlatives are used to talk about a noun or nouns in comparison with a larger group of nouns. In English, the superlative is expressed with phrases such as *the most intelligent* or *the best* or *the brightest*. To make the superlative in Spanish use **el/la/los/las**

+ noun + **más** + adjective + **de**. This may look confusing at first, but these examples will clarify this construction.

adjective	Ana es una chica **guapa**.	*Ana is a pretty girl.*
comparative	Ana es **más guapa que** Cuqui.	*Ana is prettier than Cuqui.*
superlative	Ana es **la chica más guapa de** la clase.	*Ana is the prettiest girl in the class.*

The superlative can either use or omit the noun. When it omits the noun, it retains the definite article. In this case it is important to know the gender of the noun you are describing.

Ana es **la más guapa de** la clase.	*Ana is the prettiest in the class.*
Juan es **el más alto de** su familia.	*Juan is the tallest in his family.*
Esta ciudad **es la más populosa del** país.	*This city is the most populated in the country.*
Estos zapatos son **los más caros de** la tienda.	*These shoes are the most expensive in the store.*

Notice that while the superlative uses **de** to show a noun or nouns that stands out among a group explicitly, you can use the superlative without **de** or the noun to make an implied comparison with a group. For example:

Cuqui es guapa, pero **la más guapa** es Ana.	*Cuqui is pretty, but the prettiest (of the group, class, etc.) is Ana.*
Estos zapatos son caros, pero **los más caros** son ésos.	*These shoes are expensive, but the most expensive (of the store, that I own, etc.) are those.*

Irregular Superlative Adjectives

As with comparatives, the adjectives **bueno**, **malo**, **pequeño**, and **grande** have irregular superlative forms. Remember that **mayor** and **menor** refer to age.

Adjective		Superlative		
bueno	*good*	el/la mejor	los/las mejores	*the best*
malo	*bad*	el/la peor	los/las peores	*the worst*
grande	*big*	el/la mayor	los/las mayores	*the biggest/oldest*
pequeño	*little*	el/la menor	los/las menores	*the "littlest"/youngest*

Here are some example sentences:

Antonio saca buenas notas.   Antonio gets good grades.

Antonio saca las **mejores**   Antonio gets the best grades in the class.

.

yo.   Elisa is younger than me.

menor   Elisa is the youngest sister in the family.

ative expressions in the following sentences with the

_____ ciudad _____ grande _____ los Estados Unidos.

iggest city in the United States.

_____ actriz _____ famosa _____ España.

Penélope Cruz is the most famous actress in Spain.

3. Hugo Chávez es _____ presidente _____ polémico _____ Latinoamérica.

Hugo Chávez is the most controversial president in Latin America.

4. Las ruinas de Machu Picchu son _____ _____ conocidas _____ Perú.

The ruins at Machu Picchu are the most well known in Peru.

5. Chimborazo es _____ pico _____ alto _____ Ecuador.

Chimborazo is the highest peak in Ecuador.

6. El aceite de oliva de España _____ _____ mejor _____ mundo.

Spanish olive oil is the best in the world.

7. La cultura maya es _____ _____ antigua _____ Mesoamérica.

The Mayan culture is the oldest in Mesomerica.

8. Las fiestas de Cali son _____ fiestas _____ divertidas _____ Colombia.

The parties in Cali are the most fun parties in Colombia.

Comparatives and Superlatives with Verbs

The same structures you learned for comparing nouns, adjectives, and adverbs can also generally be used with verbs. The phrase **más que** (*more than*) can also be used to make unequal comparisons of actions. This usage is very similar to English, and is simply the verb followed by **más que**.

Byron habla **más que** yo.	*Byron talks more than me.*
Carlota estudia **más que** sus compañeras de clase.	*Carlota studies more than her classmates.*

To make equal comparisons of actions, you can use **tanto como** or **igual**. Note that **tanto como** refers to *how much* the action takes place (*as much as . . .*) and **igual** refers to *the manner in which* it takes place (*the same . . .*).

María habla **tanto como** yo.	*María talks as much as I do.*
María y yo hablamos **igual**.	*María and I talk the same (way).*

This second example can also be phrased using **que**, as you learned earlier.

María habla **igual que** yo.	*María talks the same as me.*

The superlative is a little more complicated, and is not as easily translatable from English. The general construction is **ser** + article + noun + **que más** followed by the verb. As you saw with the superlatives of adjectives, the noun can be included or omitted.

Byron es **el chico que más** habla.	*Byron is the kid who talks the most.*
Byron es **el que más** habla.	*Byron is the one who talks the most.*
Carlota es **la alumna que más** estudia.	*Carlota is the pupil who studies the most.*
Carlota es **la que más** estudia.	*Carlota is the one who studies the most.*

Comparisons and superlatives can also be made using the adverbs **mejor** and **peor**.

El queso azul huele **peor que** otros tipos de queso.	*Blue cheese smells worse than other kinds of cheese.*
El queso azul es **el queso que peor** huele.	*Blue cheese is the cheese that smells the worst.*

| El pianista Chucho Valdés **toca mejor que** otros músicos. | *The pianist Chucho Valdés plays better than other musicians.* |
| El pianista Chucho Valdés es **el que mejor toca**. | *The pianist Chucho Valdés plays the best.* |

When the subject is plural, the verb is conjugated according to the subject. The adverbs, however, do not have plural forms.

| Nosotros somos **los que más** gastamos. | *We're the ones who spend the most.* |
| Los chocolates franceses son **los que mejor** saben. | *French chocolates are the ones that taste the best.* |

Written Practice 3

After each comparative sentence, write a superlative sentence that follows, omitting the noun. Follow the example.

Juliana canta mejor que yo. *Juliana sings better than I (do).*
Juliana es la que mejor canta.

1. David lee menos que sus hermanos. *David reads less than his brothers (do).*

   _____.

2. Este carro corre más que aquéllos. *This car runs faster than those (do).*

   _____.

3. Nosotros pagamos más que ellos. *We pay more than they (do).*

   _____.

4. Este perro ladra más que aquéllos. *This dog barks more than those (do).*

   _____.

5. Mi hija habla más que las tuyas. *My daughter talks more than yours (do).*

   _____.

6. Mi diamante brilla más que los de Tiffany's. *My diamond sparkles more than Tiffany's (do).*

   _____.

The Exclamation ¡Qué!

In English we often use the exclamation *What a . . .*! to show surprise, outrage, or other extreme emotion. In Spanish this is expressed with the word ¡**Qué**... ! followed by a noun. Note that, when used to express negative emotions, many of these expressions can sound rather harsh, so think before you speak!

¡Qué sorpresa!	*What a surprise!*
¡Qué idiota!	*What an idiot!*

When the noun is modified by an adjective, use **más** between the noun and the adjective. Note that in this context **más** can be used with **bueno** and **malo**.

¡Qué ciudad **más** bonita!	*What a beautiful city!*
¡Qué libro **más** bueno!	*What a great book!*
¡Qué idea **más** estupida!	*What a stupid idea!*
¡Qué chico **más** malo!	*What a bad kid!*

¡**Qué**... ! can also be used with an adjective to say *How . . .*!

¡Qué lindo!	*How beautiful!*
¡Qué ridículo!	*How ridiculous!*
¡Qué triste!	*How sad!*

There are number of common expressions that use ¡**Qué**... ! Here are a few examples:

¡Qué bueno!	*How great!*
¡Qué rico!	*How delicious!*
¡Qué barbaridad!	*How awful! My goodness!*
¡Qué vergüenza!	*What a disgrace!*
¡Qué pena! ¡Que lástima!	*What a shame!*
¡Qué rollo! *(Spain, Cuba)*	*What a pain!*

Oral Practice 2

 Track 46

Respond to each of the situations below. Use the exclamations you just learned or try to come up with some new ones of your own. Answers will vary. Follow the example shown here:

> You find out your friend just got a new job.
> *¡Qué bueno! ¡Qué noticias más buenas! ¡Qué alegría!*

1. You hear your friend's father is in the hospital.
2. You are eating a delicious meal.
3. You hear your friend's husband has been cheating on her for years.
4. You just finished watching a fantastic movie with a friend.
5. Your friend recommends visiting Mexico.

Ser or Estar?

When to use **ser** and **estar** is one of the great conundrums facing students of Spanish. Adjusting to two ways to say *to be* does not come very naturally to English speakers. The good news is that by learning a few rules, memorizing a number of examples, and flexing your analytical muscles just a bit, you should be able to understand the majority of the uses of **ser** and **estar**. The bad news is that some uses of **ser** and **estar** may elude you well into intermediate and advanced Spanish. The important thing is not to be put off by the potential confusion caused by these two verbs. You will make mistakes, but sometimes making a mistake is the best way to learn, so onward ho!

You learned in Chapter 3 that **ser** is used to express the essence of something or someone, its intrinsic qualities. You were given examples, such as a person's gender, nationality, faith, or profession, or an object's characteristics such as classification, color, material, owner, or style. In Chapter 5, you learned that **estar** is used to express a state or condition. You were asked to think about transient qualities, such as how or where something is located. Use **estar** to talk about something at the moment, today, or right now. Use **ser** if something is generally always the same. These are the basic differences between **ser** and **estar**. **Ser** is steadfast and abiding; **estar** is fickle and inconstant.

Rules for Using *Ser*

Use **ser** in the following cases.

1. To talk about general, permanent, physical characteristics (tall, short, blond, brunette).
   Ella **es** alta, morena y guapa.   *She is tall, dark, and pretty.*

2. For permanent temperaments (versus temporary emotional states).
   Carlos **es** triste.   *Carlos is a sad person (in general).*

3. To describe nationality or place of origin.
   Es colombiana.   *She is Colombian.*
   Es de La Paz.   *It (He, She) is from La Paz.*

4. To express time and dates.
   Son las ocho de la noche.   *It is eight o'clock at night.*

5. To express quantities.
   Somos tres personas.   *There are three of us.*
   Es mucho.   *It is a lot.*

6. Before nouns.
   Es médico.   *He's a doctor.*
   Eres una persona simpatica.   *You are a friendly person.*
   Es el presidente de Perú.   *He's the president of Peru.*

Rules for Using *Estar*

Use **estar** in the following cases.

1. To describe temporary or changeable physical characteristics (pale, flushed, open, closed, dirty, clean).
   El pez **está** vivo.   *The fish is alive.*
   Estás muy pálido.   *You are so pale.*
   La tienda **está** abierta.   *The store is open.*
   Mi casa **está** sucia.   *My house is dirty.*

2. For temporary emotional states (happy, sad, stressed out, angry).
   Estoy estresada.   *I'm stressed.*
   ¿**Están** enojados?   *Are they angry?*

3. To talk about location.
   ¿Dónde **está** el banco?   *Where is the bank?*
   Camila **está** en el baño.   *Camila is in the bathroom.*

4. With adverbs and adverb phrases (*She's doing well*), and present participles (*It's raining, I'm laughing*).

Está bien.	*It's OK.*
Está lloviendo.	*It's raining.*

Let's take a closer look at the temporary versus permanent emotional and physical states. These are some of the most challenging distinctions for students of Spanish to grasp. On the bright side, having both **ser** and **estar** at your disposal means that you can express yourself with more subtlety, employing a wider range of meaning. Remember, using **ser** + a descriptive adjective in these cases generally implies that someone or something is *always* that way. Using **estar** + a descriptive adjective means that the person or thing is like this *at the moment of speaking*, but may be different in an hour, next week, or next year.

Eva **es** bonita.	*Eva is pretty. (She is a pretty woman.)*
Eva **está** bonita hoy.	*Eva is pretty today. (She has just had a haircut and is wearing a flattering blouse.)*
Carlos **es** triste.	*Carlos is sad. (He's a sad, depressed soul.)*
Carlos **está** triste.	*Carlos is sad. (He is sad right now, because his cat died.)*
Luis **es** feo.	*Luis is ugly. (He is generally an unattractive person.)*
La situación **está** fea.	*The situation is ugly. (Right now the situation is bad.)*

Don't be too worried about mixing up **ser** and **estar** in these situations. It is considered quite complimentary to tell someone ¡**Qué guapo estás!** (*You look great!*) even if the implication is that the state is only temporary. Next, we will look at some descriptive adjectives that truly change meaning according to context.

Words That Change Meaning with *Ser* and *Estar*

There are some words that change meaning significantly depending on whether they are paired with **ser** or **estar**. Here are some examples:

ser borracho/-a	*to be a drunkard*	estar borracho/-a	*to be drunk (temporarily)*
ser callado/-a	*to be a quiet person*	estar callado/-a	*to be silent (even if you generally talk)*
ser listo/-a	*to be smart, intelligent*	estar listo/-a	*to be ready*
ser aburrido/-a	*to be boring*	estar aburrido/-a	*to be bored*

A friend living in Madrid once told her male (and quite attractive) roommate, ¡**Estás bueno!** (*You're hot!*). For sure he was quite flattered, but what she meant was **Eres bueno** (*You're a good guy*). Watch out for these distinctions, or you might find yourself saying **Soy lista** (*I'm smart*) instead of **Estoy lista** (*I'm ready to go*). While both may be true, using **ser** may make you sound a bit conceited.

Written Practice 4

Complete the sentences with the present tense of **ser** or **estar**.

1. Los bancos _____ cerrados los domingos. *The banks are closed on Sundays.*

2. No quiero bañarme. El agua _____ fría. *I don't want to bathe. The water is cold.*

3. Yo _____ lista para salir. *I'm ready to go out.*

4. ¿Ustedes _____ argentinos o uruguayos? *Are you Argentineans or Uruguayans?*

5. Cuidado con el plato, _____ caliente. *Careful with the plate, it's hot.*

6. Esta película _____ aburrida. No quiero ver más. *This movie is boring. I don't want to see any more (of it).*

7. ¡Qué guapo (tú) _____ con este corte de pelo! *You're so handsome with this haircut!*

8. Ester _____ muy callada. Nunca habla. *Ester is very quiet. She never speaks.*

9. Mil dólares _____ mucho dinero. *A thousand dollars is a lot of money.*

10. Vamos a casa. Los niños _____ cansados. *Let's go home. The kids are tired.*

11. Nosotros no _____ preparados para el exámen. *We are not prepared for the exam.*

12. Marcela y José _____ generosos. Siempre me invitan a comer. *Marcela and José are generous. They always treat me to dinner.*

QUIZ

Circle the letter of the word or phrase that best completes each sentence.

1. **Mi hermano estudia _____ yo.**
   A. más
   B. más que
   C. más de
   D. menos de

2. **Unas buenas botas de cuero cuestan _____ cien dólares.**
   A. menos
   B. más de
   C. menos que
   D. más

3. **Este hotel es _____ otro.**
   A. peor que el
   B. peor el
   C. más malo del
   D. más malo que

4. **¡Eres _____ tu madre!**
   A. tanto
   B. tanto como
   C. igual
   D. igual que

5. **Cecilia es _____ más inteligente de la clase.**
   A. la
   B. el
   C. las
   D. los

6. **Su último disco es bueno, pero _____ de todos es el primero.**
   A. el mejor
   B. la mejor
   C. el más mejor
   D. la más buena

7. **Me encanta Buenos Aires. ¡Qué ciudad _____ bonita!**

   A. qué

   B. más

   C. es más

   D. es

8. **Hoy es mi cumpleaños. _____ contenta.**

   A. es

   B. está

   C. soy

   D. estoy

9. **¿Nos vamos? Esta fiesta ya _____ aburrida.**

   A. es

   B. está

   C. soy

   D. estoy

10. **Los BMW _____ carros caros.**

    A. es

    B. está

    C. son

    D. están

PART TWO TEST

Circle the letter of the word or phrase that best completes each sentence.

1. **En la casa hay dos baños; sin embargo, _____ sótano.**
   A. hay
   B. no hay
   C. hace
   D. no hace

2. **¿Qué _____ Camila?**
   —Es bióloga.
   A. tiene
   B. hace
   C. haces
   D. tienes

3. **Está nevando. _____.**
   A. Está lloviendo
   B. Hace calor
   C. Hace frío
   D. Hay lloviznas

4. **¿Cuántos años _____ Inés?**
   A. es
   B. tiene
   C. está
   D. hace

5. **Nosotros _____ hacer los deberes.**
   A. tenemos
   B. hay
   C. tenemos que
   D. hay que

6. **¿Cuánto _____ las papas?**
   A. cuesta
   B. cuestan
   C. costar
   D. cuesto

7. **Elena mira a _____.**

   A. sus hijos
   B. su carro
   C. la vista bonita
   D. la televisión

8. **¿Prefieres _____ blusa o aquélla?**

   A. este
   B. éste
   C. esta
   D. está

9. **¿_____ a ti los zapatos de la tienda del centro?**

   A. Te gusta
   B. Te gustan
   C. Les gusta
   D. Les gustan

10. **_____ no me cae bien Kara.**

    A. A mí
    B. A ti
    C. A él
    D. A nosotros

11. **Haroldo está _____ muy rápido.**

    A. conducir
    B. conduce
    C. conduciendo
    D. va a conducir

12. **No puedo hablar ahora porque _____ trabajando.**

    A. estoy
    B. está
    C. están
    D. estás

13. **¿Conoces a _____ de Costa Rica?**

    —No, no conozco a _____.
    A. algo; nada
    B. alguien; nada
    C. algo; nadie
    D. alguien; nadie

14. **Este carro es de mis padres. Es _____.**
    A. mío
    B. tuyo
    C. suyo
    D. nuestro

15. **¿Usted _____ tocar un instrumento?**
    A. conoce
    B. sabe
    C. conoce a
    D. sabe a

16. **Nosotros no _____ comprar la casa.**
    A. vamos
    B. vamos a
    C. ir a
    D. van a

17. **Estoy cansada. _____ temprano.**
    A. Me voy a acostar
    B. Voy me a acostar
    C. Voy a me acostar
    D. Voy acostarme

18. **Yo siempre _____ los viernes.**
    A. valgo
    B. salgo
    C. traigo
    D. pongo

19. ¿_____ mucha ropa a Brasil?

    A. Vas a llevar

    B. Vas a traer

    C. Vas a salir

    D. Vas a ir

20. No voy a Brasil. _____ aquí.

    A. Quedo

    B. Me quedo

    C. Quedo me

    D. Quedarme

21. El Toyota cuesta $17,000 y el Lexus cuesta $38,000.

    A. El Toyota es más caro que el Lexus.

    B. El Toyota es menos caro que el Lexus.

    C. El Toyota es igual de caro que el Lexus.

    D. El Toyota es tan caro como el Lexus.

22. El Lexus cuesta _____ $35,000.

    A. más

    B. más que

    C. más de

    D. menos que

23. ¿Crees que la comida peruana es _____ la comida mexicana?

    A. más bueno que

    B. más bueno de

    C. mejor que

    D. mejor de

24. ¿Tu novia es estrella de cine? _____

    A. ¡Qué idiota!

    B. ¡Qué interesante!

    C. ¡Qué vergüenza!

    D. ¡Qué horror!

25. Linda _____ una mujer graciosa. Siempre _____ riendo.

    A. es; es

    B. está; está

    C. es; está

    D. está; es

Part Three

Moving Beyond the Present

chapter **11**

Making Commands

In this chapter you will learn how to make formal and informal commands using the imperative mood and reflexive verbs as well as how to make your commands more polite. You will also learn the present tense of two more irregular verbs and how to recognize and use direct object pronouns.

CHAPTER OBJECTIVES

In this chapter you will learn

- Formal commands
- Familiar commands
- First-person plural commands
- Commands with reflexive verbs
- How to make commands more polite
- The irregular verbs *dar* and *decir*
- Direct object pronouns

Making Commands with the Imperative Mood

The imperative is the verb form used when making commands or when telling people what to do. The title of Pedro Almodóvar's Oscar-winning film, **Hable con ella** (*Talk to her*), uses the imperative. Here are some more examples:

Mire usted el carro.	*Look at the car.*
Venga conmigo.	*Come with me.*
Crucemos la calle.	*Let's cross the street.*

Generally, commands are issued in the second-person singular and plural (**tú**, **vosotros**, **usted**, **ustedes**) or in the first-person plural (**nosotros**). Learning commands can be challenging, because some of the conjugations are new and different. However, because many of them are conjugated the same as the subjunctive, learning them now will give you a preview of the subjunctive mood, which is discussed in Chapter 16.

You might have noticed in the examples above that the personal pronoun is usually dropped in the command (or imperative) forms. However, the pronouns **usted** or **ustedes** may be used after the verb; this makes the order sound more formal.

Formal Commands

Formal commands are given with **usted** (*you*) and **ustedes** (*you* plural). Creating the verb forms for formal commands is basically a game of "switcharoo." Verbs ending in **-ar** that usually end in **-a** or **-an** in the present will end in **-e** and **-en** in the imperative. Verbs ending in **-er** or **-ir** that usually end in **-e** or **-en** in the present will end in **-a** and **-an** in the imperative. Just remember: **ar→e** and **er/ir→a**.

Infinitive	Present		Imperative (formal)	
hablar	habla	hablan	hable	hablen
comer	come	comen	coma	coman
vivir	vive	viven	viva	vivan

For stem-changing and irregular verbs, the same ending pattern (that is, the switcharoo) holds; but in these cases, constructing the imperative takes a few more steps. For most verbs, except for a few irregular exceptions, the first thing you need to do is recall the **yo** form. This serves as the root for making the imperative. For regular verbs, the **yo** form and the stem are one and the same (for **hablar**, it is **habl-**), but for stem-changing and irregular verbs, they may be different. Drop the **-o** from the **yo** form and add **-e** or **-en** to **-ar** verbs, and **-a** or **-an** to **-ir** or **-er** verbs. Look at these examples. The root is bolded for you.

	Infinitive	Present yo form	Imperative (formal)	
Regular	hablar	**habl**o	hable	hablen
	comer	**com**o	coma	coman
	vivir	**viv**o	viva	vivan
Stem-changing	pensar	**piens**o	piense	piensen
	dormir	**duerm**o	duerma	duerman
Irregular	poner	**pong**o	ponga	pongan
	venir	**veng**o	venga	vengan
Other	conducir	**conduzc**o	conduzca	conduzcan

Verbs ending in **-gar** and **-car** change to **-gue** and **-que** in the subjunctive.

Infinitive	Usted	Ustedes
buscar	busque	busquen
llegar	llegue	lleguen

Of course, as is always the case in Spanish, there are a few irregular exceptions:

Infinitive	Usted	Ustedes
dar	dé	den
estar	esté	estén
ir	vaya	vayan
ser	sea	sean
saber	sepa	sepan

Here are some more examples using formal commands:

Vaya al médico.	*Go to the doctor.*
Hable más despacio por favor.	*Speak more slowly, please.*
Doble a la izquierda.	*Turn left.*

Negative formal commands are exactly the same. Simply put **no** before the verb.

No hable.	*Don't talk.*
No vaya.	*Don't go.*
No anden solos.	*Don't walk alone.*

Written Practice 1

Make formal commands with the following verbs. Write both the singular (**usted**) and plural (**ustedes**) forms.

	usted	ustedes
1. abrir	_____	_____
2. doblar	_____	_____
3. correr	_____	_____
4. subir	_____	_____
5. prometer	_____	_____
6. buscar	_____	_____
7. hacer	_____	_____
8. salir	_____	_____
9. decir	_____	_____
10. tomar	_____	_____
11. volver	_____	_____
12. poner	_____	_____
13. oír	_____	_____
14. andar	_____	_____
15. contar	_____	_____
16. huir	_____	_____

Written Practice 2

For each question, answer using formal commands. For questions using **yo** (singular), answer using the **usted** form. For questions using **nosotros** (plural) answer using the **ustedes** form. Make the sentence negative if you see (**no**) and positive if you see (**sí**).

1. ¿Salimos ahora? *Shall we go out?* Sí, _____
2. ¿Tomo la medicina? *Should I take the medicine?* No, _____
3. ¿Vuelvo en seguida? *Should I come back right away?* Sí, _____

4. ¿Vamos a comer? *Shall we go eat?* Sí, _____

5. ¿Pido la cuenta? *Should I ask for the check?* Sí, _____

6. ¿Traemos a los hijos? *Should we bring the kids?* No, _____

7. ¿Vengo con ustedes? *Should I come with you?* Sí, _____

8. ¿Hablo con mi jefe? *Should I talk to my boss?* No, _____

Familiar Commands

Unlike formal commands, familiar (informal) commands are simple to construct in the affirmative and more complicated in the negative. In addition, familiar commands have more irregular verb forms. In this book we will focus only on the singular (**tú**) familiar commands.

Informal Affirmative Commands

The affirmative familiar command, also called the imperative, is the same as the present **usted** form of the verb.

Infinitive	Familiar Imperative
hablar	habla
comer	come
vivir	vive
pensar	piensa
dormir	duerme
pedir	pide
conducir	conduce
llegar	llega

Here are the irregular forms of familiar singular commands:

decir	**di**
hacer	**haz**
ir	**ve**
poner	**pon**
salir	**sal**
ser	**sé**
tener	**ten**
venir	**ven**

Here are some examples of familiar commands in sentences:

Sé bueno.	*Be good.*
¡**Ten** cuidado!	*Be careful!*
Ven con nosotras.	*Come with us.*
Pide la cuenta, por favor.	*Ask for the check, please.*

Informal Negative Commands

To make the negative of familiar (informal) commands, use **no** before the **tú** form of the subjunctive of the verb. This basically means adding an **-s** to the end of the *singular formal* commands that you already learned.

Infinitive	Formal Affirmative Command	Informal Negative Command
hablar	hable	**no** hables
comer	coma	**no** comas
vivir	viva	**no** vivas
pensar	piense	**no** pienses
dormir	duerma	**no** duermas
pedir	pida	**no** pidas
conducir	conduzca	**no** conduzcas
llegar	llegue	**no** llegues

The same rule holds true for the irregular verbs. Notice how the accents change for the verb **dar**.

Infinitive	Formal Affirmative	Informal Negative
dar	**dé**	**no des**
estar	esté	**no** estés
ir	vaya	**no** vayas
ser	sea	**no** seas
saber	sepa	**no** sepas
decir	diga	**no** digas
hacer	haga	**no** hagas
poner	ponga	**no** pongas
venir	venga	**no** vengas

Here are some examples of the familiar (informal) negative imperative in sentences:

No **seas** malo.   *Don't be bad.*
No **tengas** miedo.   *Don't be afraid.*
No le **des** más vueltas.   *Don't think about it any more.*
No **conduzcas** tan rápido, por favor.   *Don't drive so fast, please.*

NOTE *In Spain, the plural familiar command is used (**vosotros**). In the rest of Latin America, however, if you want to tell a group of people what to do, use the plural formal command (**ustedes**).*

Written Practice 3

Make familiar commands with the following verbs. Give both the affirmative and the negative forms.

	Affirmative +	Negative −
1. abrir	_____	_____
2. doblar	_____	_____
3. correr	_____	_____
4. subir	_____	_____
5. tener	_____	_____
6. buscar	_____	_____
7. salir	_____	_____
8. decir	_____	_____
9. tomar	_____	_____
10. volver	_____	_____
11. traer	_____	_____
12. oír	_____	_____
13. andar	_____	_____
14. contar	_____	_____
15. huir	_____	_____

Written Practice 4

 Track 47

For each question, answer using the imperative. Answer in the affirmative or negative depending on the clue provided (**Sí** or **No**).

1. ¿Salgo ahora? *Should I go out now?* Sí, _____

2. ¿Como una manzana? *Should I eat an apple?* No, _____

3. ¿Vuelvo mañana? *Should I come back tomorrow?* Sí, _____

4. ¿Voy a cenar? *Should I go eat?* No, _____

5. ¿Hago eso? *Should I do that?* No, _____

6. ¿Traigo dinero? *Should I bring money?* Sí, _____

7. ¿Vengo con Emilio? *Should I come with Emilio?* Sí, _____

8. ¿Hablo con mi jefe? *Should I talk to my boss?* No, _____

First-Person Plural Commands

To express *let's* in Spanish, we use commands in the first-person plural, formed with the subjunctive of **nosotros**. For those of you unfamiliar with the subjunctive, never fear. For regular verbs and e→ie stem-changing verbs, just do the "switcharoo" using the **nosotros** form. Look at these examples:

Infinitive	Present	First-Person Plural Imperative
hablar	hablamos	hablemos
comer	comemos	comamos
vivir	vivimos	vivamos
pensar	pensamos	pensemos
querer	queremos	queramos

For stem-changing verbs ending in **-ir,** use the changes you have already seen in the present participle of these verbs: e→i and e→ie verbs use **i** in the stem, and o→ue verbs use **u**. The ending does the switcharoo as with regular **nosotros** commands.

Infinitive	Present	First-Person Plural Imperative
dormir	dormimos	durmamos
mentir	mentimos	mintamos
pedir	pedimos	pidamos

The **nosotros** imperative for irregular verbs is made by adding **-mos** to the formal singular commands. Note that the accent is dropped for **dar** and **estar**.

Infinitive	Formal Singular Imperative	First-Person Plural Imperative
dar	dé	**demos**
estar	esté	**estemos**
ser	sea	**seamos**
saber	sepa	**sepamos**

Here are some examples of the commands in the first-person plural:

| **Andemos** juntos. | *Let's walk together.* |
| **Durmamos** en un hotel. | *Let's sleep in a hotel.* |

The only exception is the verb **ir**, which uses the present in the affirmative to say *let's* . . .

| **Vamos** a la tienda ahora. | *Let's go to the store now.* |

. . . and the imperative in the negative.

| No vayamos a la tienda. | *Let's not go to the store.* |

If you are wary of using the first-person command, you can replace it with a question using **nosotros** in the present tense. This gives the meaning of *Shall we?* and softens the command into a request.

| **¿Escribimos** el email ahora? | *Shall we write the email now?* |
| **¿Pedimos** un vinito? | *Shall we order some wine?* |

Or you can use **ir a** + infinitive to express *let's*.

| **Vamos a** bailar. | *Let's go dancing.* |
| **Vamos a** celebrar tu cumpleaños. | *Let's celebrate your birthday.* |

Written Practice 5

Make commands in the first-person plural (**nosotros**) using the following phrases.

1. Volver a casa. _____ *Let's go home.*

2. Hacer algo. _____ *Let's do something.*

3. Comer fuera. _____ *Let's eat out.*

4. Seguir adelante. _____ *Let's go ahead.*

5. Ir a la playa. _____ *Let's go to the beach.*

6. Traer algo de comer. _____ *Let's bring something to eat.*

Commands with Reflexive Verbs

Reflexive verbs are treated differently in affirmative and negative commands (as are direct object pronouns, which you will learn later in this chapter). Here's a reminder of the personal (reflexive) pronouns used with reflexive verbs:

me	os
te	nos
se	se

In *affirmative commands*, both formal and informal, the pronoun is "tacked on" to the end of the verb. Note that the verb needs to maintain the stress in the same place that it has in the present; this means placing a (´) on the *third-to-last syllable* in the imperative (this kind of accent, on the antepenultimate syllable, is called **esdrújula**).

Olvídese de eso.	*Forget about that.*
Váyanse a casa.	*Go home.*
Levántate.	*Get up.*
Lávate las manos.	*Wash your hands.*

In the *negative imperative*, formal, and informal, the personal pronoun is placed *before* the verb.

No se olvide de eso.	*Don't forget about that.*
No se vayan a casa.	*Don't go home.*
No te levantes.	*Don't get up.*
No te laves las manos.	*Don't wash your hands.*

For first-person (**nosotros**) commands, the **-s** of **-emos** is dropped in the affirmative.

Sentemos + nos = **Sentémonos.**   *Let's sit down.*

Levantemos + nos =   *Let's get up.*
    Levantémonos.

With first-person (**nosotros**) commands, the reflexive verb **irse** uses **vamos** in the affirmative and **vayamos** in the negative.

Vamos + nos = **Vámonos.**   *Let's go.*

No nos vayamos.   *Let's not go.*

If you are wary of using the first-person (**nosotros**) command in the reflexive form, you can replace it with a first-person plural question in the present tense. This gives the meaning of *Shall we?* and softens the command into a request.

¿Nos vamos?   *Shall we go?*

¿Nos sentamos?   *Shall we sit down?*

Oral Practice 1

▶ Track 48

Answer the following questions making commands following the pronoun given in parentheses. Give both affirmative and negative answers for each.

1. ¿Me fijo? (tú) *Should I pay attention?*

2. ¿Nos callamos? (ustedes) *Should we be quiet?*

3. ¿Me acuesto? (usted) *Should I go to bed?*

4. ¿Nos olvidamos del asunto? (nosotros) *Should we forget about it?*

5. ¿Me siento aquí? (tú) *Should I sit here?*

6. ¿Me visto? (usted) *Should I get dressed?*

7. ¿Nos paramos allí? (nosotros) *Shall we stop here?*

8. ¿Nos quedamos? (ustedes) *Shall we stay?*

9. ¿Me pongo al teléfono? (tú) *Should I get on the phone?*

10. ¿Voy a hablar con ustedes? (usted) *Should I go talk to you?*

Making Commands More Polite

The imperative is a verb form that is used to issue commands, literally to tell—not ask—someone to do something. As a result it can often sound quite brusque, even rude.

There are a few ways to sound a little more polite. One way is to use the formal commands with the words **usted** or **ustedes**: **Siga usted adelante**. Another way is to follow the command with polite phrases, such as **por favor** (*please*), **cuando pueda** (*when you have a moment*), or **si fuera tan amable** (*if you would be so kind*). A final way to sound more polite is to use phrases that ask or request, rather than tell, someone to do something. These fall into three main categories:

Expressions with **querer** (*to want, like*) can be used in a variety of ways to say you want something.

- **Quisiera** is the most polite, and means *I would like*: **Quisiera una empanada, por favor** (*I'd like an empanada, please*).

- **Quería** and **querría** are other ways to use **querer** and can also mean *I would like*: **Querría ir al Hotel Quinta Real, por favor** (*I'd like to go to the Quinta Real Hotel, please*).

- You can simply say **Quiero** (*I want*); however, this will sound rude unless softened with one of the above phrases.

Compare the following sentences. Which is more polite?

Tráeme el periódico, **por favor**.	*Bring me the newspaper, please.*
Quisiera el periódico, **por favor**.	*I'd like the newspaper, please.*

Expressions with **gustar** (*to be pleasing*) can be used similarly to **querer**. **Me gustaría** means *I would like* and can be used for any requests. Compare the following sentences. Which is more polite?

Venga a hablar conmigo, **por favor**.	*Come talk to me, please.*
Me gustaría hablar con usted, cuando pueda.	*I'd like to talk with you, when you have a chance.*

Poder (*to be able*) can be used in a number of ways as well.

- **Podría** or **Podrías** can be used in a question to say *Could you?*:
  ¿**Podría** traer el periódico, por favor?   *Could you bring the newspaper, please?*

- **Puede** and **Puedes** can be used similarly, although a bit less formally, to say *Can you?* Compare the following sentences:

Cierra la puerta. *Close the door.*
¿**Puedes cerrar** la puerta? *Can you close the door?*

As you travel through the Spanish-speaking world, or speak with people from different Spanish-speaking countries, you'll notice that usage varies regionally. In Spain, the use of the imperative is quite common, without being rude, even when speaking to service workers or older people. It's not surprising to hear someone walk into a bar and say, **"Dame una cerveza"** (*Give me a beer*) or **"Ponme un vinito"** (*Give me*, or literally *"Put before me"* a glass of wine). In fact, rarely will you hear someone speaking to a server or bartender with the word **quisiera**, a usage that is much more common in Latin America. This use of the imperative often sounds abrupt to people from more linguistically formal countries like Mexico or Colombia, where many of the niceties presented above are more common.

The Irregular Verbs *Dar* and *Decir*

Dar (*to give*) and **decir** (*to say, tell*) will complete our list of common irregular verbs in the present tense.

You will notice that **dar** is conjugated similarly to **ir**. The present participle is **dando**. Compare **dar** with **ir**:

	dar	**ir**
yo	doy	voy
tú	das	vas
él/ella/usted	da	va
nosotros	damos	vamos
vosotros	dais	vais
ellos/ellas/ustedes	dan	van

The verb **decir** is similar to **i→e** stem-changing verbs, such as **pedir**, but the first person is different. The present participle is **diciendo**. Compare **decir** with **pedir**:

	decir	**pedir**
yo	digo	pido
tú	dices	pides

él/ella/usted	dice	pide
nosotros	decimos	pedimos
vosotros	decís	pedís
ellos/ellas/ustedes	dicen	piden

Expressions with *Dar*

Dar is used in a number of expressions.

da igual, da lo mismo	*it doesn't matter*

(This expression is very common in Spain, but it borders on rude in much of Latin America, where **no me importa** is more acceptable.)

dar chance, oportunidad	*to give a chance; opportunity*
dar las gracias	*to thank*
darse cuenta	*to realize*
darse por vencido	*to give up*
dar un paseo	*go for a walk*
dar la mano	*to shake hands*

Expressions with *Decir*

There are a number of common uses of **decir** that will be very helpful to you.

¿Qué quiere decir...?	*What does . . . mean?*
Dime.	*Tell me./ Go on./ Yes?*
¡No me digas!	*You don't say!*
Es decir...	*that is (to say)*
Digi yo	*in my opinion*

NOTE *The Spanish answer the telephone with **¿Dígame?** or **¿Diga?**. This literally means Tell me (it's a formal command, sometimes used with an object pronoun). While each Latin American country has its own way of answering the phone, it is common to use **¿Aló?** or simply **¿Sí?**.*

Direct Object Pronouns

The *direct object* is a noun that receives the action of a verb. Determining whether a noun is a direct object can be difficult. There are a few ways to go about this:

1. A direct object always comes after a *transitive* verb. A transitive verb cannot exist without a direct object. Compare these sentences:

El niño lee el libro.   *The child reads the book.*

In this sentence, **lee** (*reads*) is a transitive verb and **el libro** (*the book*) is the direct object. In the next example, **lee** (*reads*) is an *intransitive* verb. It stands alone and is not followed by a direct object.

El niño lee.   *The child reads.*

2. Often, if you see a preposition (**a**, **con**, **en**, etc.) before the noun, that noun is usually considered an *indirect object*. The exception is the use of the **a personal**, which can make things a bit trickier. When the personal **a** is used, the person following the verb + **a** is generally a direct object.

Yo veo **a Juan**.   *I see Juan.*
Susana compra **chicle**.   *Susana buys gum.*

In these examples, **Juan** and **chicle** are both *direct objects*.
   In the next examples, **Ángela** and **Leticia** are both *indirect objects*. They are preceded by the prepositions **a** (*not* personal a) and **con**. Remember: If the word **a** can be translated into English as *to*, the noun following it is likely an *indirect object*.

Yo le doy el libro **a Ángela**.   *I give the book to Ángela.*
Ella habla **con Leticia**.   *She talks to Leticia.*

NOTE *Hablar (a, con) almost always takes the indirect object.*

3. Make the sentence into a question by asking *What?* or *Who(m)?* about the action of the verb. (Or, if you're feeling adventurous, ask ¿**Qué?** or ¿**Quién?**) The "thing" or "person" answer is the direct object that follows the verb.

Susana compra **chicle**.   *Susana buys **what**? Susana buys*
                                          ***chewing gum**.*
Yo veo a **Juan**.   *I see **whom**? I see **Juan**.*

Written Practice 6

Look at the following sentences. If the sentence has a *direct object*, write **sí** and circle it. If it does not have a direct object, write **no**.

1. _____ Camino al supermercado. *I walk to the supermarket.*
2. _____ Compro tomates. *I buy tomatoes.*
3. _____ No comemos galletas. *We don't eat cookies.*
4. _____ Celia está hablando con mi hermano. *Celia is talking to my brother.*
5. _____ ¿Toma azúcar con su café? *Do you take sugar in your coffee?*
6. _____ No pienses en eso. *Don't think about that.*

Using Direct Object Pronouns

You know that the direct object is a noun. In previous chapters you learned that a pronoun may replace a noun. So logically, the *direct object pronoun* is a pronoun *that replaces the direct object noun*. The direct object pronouns in Spanish are:

me	*me*	nos	*us*
te	*you* (familiar)	os	*you* (plural familiar)
lo	*him, it* (masculine)	los	*them* (masculine)
	you (formal)		*you* (plural)
la	*her, it* (feminine)	las	*them* (feminine)
	you (formal, feminine)		*you* (plural, feminine)

Direct object pronouns are used instead of nouns in order to avoid repetition and redundancy. Look at this mini-dialogue:

—Oye, ¿quién tiene mi cartera?　—*Hey, who has my wallet?*
—Yo tengo tu cartera. ¿Quieres　—*I have your wallet. Do you want*
　tu cartera?　　　　　　　　　*your wallet?*
—Sí, quiero mi cartera, por favor.　—*Yes, I want my wallet, please.*

Did you notice the repetition of the word **cartera**? (How could you not, right?) To sound more natural and reduce such repetition, replace **cartera** with the direct object pronoun **la**. Why **la**? Because **la cartera** is a feminine noun and the direct object pronoun **la** is feminine. Here, **la** means *it*. Look at a new version of the dialogue using direct object pronouns:

—Oye, ¿quién tiene mi cartera?	—*Hey, who has my wallet?*
—Yo **la** tengo. ¿**La** quieres?	—*I have it. Do you want it?*
—Sí, **la** quiero, por favor.	—*Yes, I want it, please.*

In affirmative statements, negative statements, and questions, the direct object pronoun goes before the verb. Here are some pairs of examples when the direct object is a thing. Notice how **lo** replaces a masculine singular noun, and **las** replaces a plural feminine noun.

No recomiendo **este libro**.	*I don't recommend this book.*
No **lo** recomiendo.	*I don't recommend it.*
Pongo **las maletas** en el salón.	*I'm putting the suitcases in the living room.*
Las puse en el salón.	*I put them in the living room.*

Now here are some pairs of examples when the direct object is a person. Notice how the direct object pronoun replaces the noun in bold.

Invité a **Gabriela**.	*I invited Gabriela.*
La invité.	*I invited her.*
La maestra felicita a **las niñas**.	*The teacher congratulates the girls.*
La maestra **las** felicita.	*The teacher congratulates them.*
¿El hombre ve a **los muchachos**?	*Does the man see the boys?*
¿El hombre **los** ve?	*Does the man see them?*

And finally, here are some examples using the direct object pronouns **me**, **te**, and **nos**:

Él **me** llamó ayer.	*He called me yesterday.*
Te veo todos los días.	*I see you every day.*
¿**Nos** van a escuchar bien?	*Are they going to listen carefully to us?*

With commands (the imperative), the direct object pronoun, like the reflexive pronouns, gets tacked on *to the end of the verb* in affirmative commands, and is placed *before* the verb in negative commands.

Lláma**lo** mañana.	*Call him tomorrow.*
No **las** toque.	*Don't touch them.*

With present participles and infinitives the pronoun can precede the auxiliary (conjugated) verb, or be tacked on to the end of the present participle or the infinitive.

Lo vamos a llamar mañana.   *We're going to call him tomorrow.*
Vamos a llamar**lo** mañana.   *We're going to call him tomorrow.*

Oral Practice 2

 Track 49

Repeat the following sentences, replacing the direct object with a direct object pronoun. In the first three the direct object is in bold text for you. In the last five you have to figure it out for yourself. Listen to the answers on the CD. There may be more than one possible answer.

1. Pongo **los vasos** encima de la mesa. *I'll put the glasses on the table.*
2. Quiero usar **tu computadora**. *I want to use your computer.*
3. ¿Podrías pagar **el alquiler** mañana? *Could you pay the rent tomorrow?*
4. Voy a ver a David esta tarde. *I'm going to see David this afternoon.*
5. No compres DVDs pirateados. *Don't buy pirated DVDs.*
6. Lleve una botella de vino. *Take a bottle of wine.*
7. Bebemos café todos los días. *We drink coffee every day.*
8. ¿Vamos a ver la película *Amores Perros* esta noche? *Shall we see the movie Amores Perros tonight?*

Written Practice 7

Look at the phrases below and match each phrase with its translation. Some may have more than one answer, so use the process of elimination to help you.

1. _____ Lo ve   a. *He calls us*
2. _____ La tengo   b. *I have it*
3. _____ La veo   c. *I call you*
4. _____ Te llamo   d. *You have me*

5. _____ Me ve		e.	*He sees it*
6. _____ Nos llama		f.	*She sees me*
7. _____ Me tienes		g.	*She loves me*
8. _____ Los tiene		h.	*I see her*
9. _____ La amo		i.	*I love her*
10. _____ Me ama		j.	*He has them*

Leísmo

In Spain, one very often hears the pronoun **le** used instead of **lo** to say *him*. This practice is so common and has become so much a part of daily speech that not only does the **Real Academia Española** condone it, but also many Spaniards will tell you that using **lo** is actually incorrect.

Some examples of **leísmo** are, for instance, saying **le veo** for *I see him* or **le llamé** for *I called him*. Sometimes **leísmo** bleeds into the use of **les** as well. **Les quiero** for *I love them* or **Les vi ayer** for *I saw them yesterday* (instead of **los** or **las**).

If you are planning on living in or traveling to Spain, it will be important to be able to recognize **leísmo** when you hear it. Who knows, you may even come away doing it yourself!

QUIZ

Circle the letter of the word or phrase that best completes each sentence.

1. **Usted está enfermo. _____ al hospital.**
   - A. Va
   - B. Vaya
   - C. Ve
   - D. Vayan

2. **No _____ conmigo ustedes. Yo no puedo ir.**
   - A. cuenta
   - B. cuentan
   - C. cuente
   - D. cuenten

3. ¡Shh! No _____ tan alto. Todo el mundo te oye.

   A. habla

   B. hablas

   C. hable

   D. hables

4 _____ a tu padre. Quiere hablar contigo.

   A. Llame

   B. Llama

   C. Llamen

   D. Llaman

5. ¿Vas a México? _____ un regalo, por favor.

   A. cómprame

   B. cómpreme

   C. me compra

   D. me compre

6. No _____ de su abrigo. Hace frío.

   A. olvídese

   B. se olvida

   C. se olvide

   D. olvida

7. _____ aquí. No debemos viajar por la noche.

   A. Dormimos

   B. Durmamos

   C. Duerme

   D. Duerma

8. ¿Qué quiere _____ "alrededor"?

   A. dar

   B. decir

   C. diga

   D. dé

9. **¿Conoces a Eugenia?**

   —Sí, _____ conocí ayer.

   A. le

   B. lo

   C. la

   D. se

10. **¿Tienes las llaves?**

    —No, _____ dejé en casa.

    A. el

    B. los

    C. la

    D. las

chapter **12**

Using the Future and the Conditional

In this chapter you will learn the simple future and conditional tenses. You will learn how to use indirect object pronouns as well as the pronoun **lo**. Finally, you will learn the augmentative forms of nouns.

CHAPTER OBJECTIVES

In this chapter you will learn

- The future tense
- Indirect object pronouns
- The pronoun *lo*
- The conditional
- Expressions to say *no* and *yes*
- Augmentative forms of nouns

The Future Tense

You've already learned how to use the future with **ir a**, roughly equivalent to the English future with *to be going to*: **Van a comer** (*They're going to eat*). You have also learned that the Spanish present tense can express the English future with *will*, especially when used with a preposition of time: **Te llamo mañana** (*I'll call you tomorrow*).

Spanish has another way to express the future: the future tense. The future tense is rather easy to learn, although it is not always necessary to use it, since there are so many options for expressing the future (how ironic, right?).

To form the *future* tense, add the endings **-é, -ás, -á, -emos, -éis, -án** to the infinitive of the verb.

	hablar	**comer**	**vivir**	**estar**
yo	hablaré	comeré	viviré	estaré
tú	hablarás	comerás	vivirás	estarás
él/ella/usted	hablará	comerá	vivirá	estará
nosotros	hablaremos	comeremos	viviremos	estaremos
vosotros	hablaréis	comeréis	viviréis	estaréis
ellos/ellas/ustedes	hablarán	comerán	vivirán	estarán

There are a number of irregular verbs that use a unique stem to construct the future, instead of the infinitive. Only the **yo** form is given here, but the endings for the other conjugations are the regular future endings.

decir	**dir**é	saber	**sabr**é
hacer	**har**é	poner	**pondr**é
querer	**querr**é	salir	**saldr**é
caber	**cabr**é	tener	**tendr**é
haber	**habr**é	valer	**valdr**é
poder	**podr**é	venir	**vendr**é

Remember that the verb **haber** is used in the form **hay** to say *there is/there are*. Similarly, the future is usually used in the third person, **habrá**, to say *there will be*:

Mañana **habrá** una reunión importante.   *Tomorrow there will be an important meeting.*

Uses of the Future Tense

In general, the future tense is used to express a more distant future than **ir a**. This is comparable to English.

Iré a Cuba el año que viene.   *I'm going to Cuba next year.*

The future tense can also sound a bit more formal than the future expressed with **ir a**.

El señor Olivera **volverá** en   *Mr. Olivera will return in a moment.*
seguida.

The Future Progressive

The future with **estar** can be used in the future as an auxiliary verb to form the future progressive, which can be translated as . . . *will be -ing.* Remember that progressive tenses use **estar** + the present participle, or **-ndo** form. Look at this example:

¿Vienes a la fiesta el viernes?   *Are you coming to the party on Friday?*
—No puedo. **Estaré viajando**.   *—I can't. I'll be traveling.*

Future of Uncertainty

The future tense in Spanish also has a use that has no equivalent in English. It is called the *future of uncertainty*, and is used to express—you guessed it—uncertainty or wondering. For instance, if you hear an unexpected knock on the door, you can say, **¿Quién será?** (*Who could it be?*). Note that the future progressive can also be used in this sense. Here are some more examples:

Situation: It is a Friday afternoon at work and there's almost no one at the office.
¿**Habrá** alguien en la reunión?   *(I wonder) will there be anyone at the meeting?*

Situation: Your friend goes into the other room to talk on her cell phone.
¿Con quién **estará hablando**?   *Who(m) could she be talking to?*

Similarly, the future of uncertainty can be used to express *probability*, or a *supposition*.

Situation: Your mother just called twice in a row, and the phone rings again.
Será mi madre.   *That would be my mother.*

Situation: Your friend doesn't show up to class on Tuesday.
Estará enfermo.   *He's probably sick.*

Written Practice 1

Rewrite the following sentences in the future tense.

1. Nosotros no cabemos todos en el carro. *We don't all fit in the car.*
   _____ *We won't all fit in the car.*

2. ¿Qué dicen sobre el examen? *What do they say about the exam?*
   _____ *What will they say about the exam?*

3. Un día voy a México. *One day I'll go to Mexico.*
   _____ *One day I'll go to Mexico.*

4. ¿Vuelves en avión? *Are you returning by plane?*
   _____ *Will you return by plane?*

5. Malena ve los murales de Diego Rivera. *Malena sees Diego Rivera's murals.*
   _____ *Malena will see Diego Rivera's murals.*

6. ¿Cuánto vale un diamante? *How much is a diamond worth?*
   _____ *How much could a diamond be worth?*

7. Nunca hago ningún viaje. *I never take any trips.*
   _____ *I'll never take any trips.*

8. ¿Quién está llamándome? *Who's calling me?*
   _____ *Who could be calling me?*

Oral Practice 1

 Track 50

Read the dialogue aloud, putting the verbs in parentheses in the future as you go along. Then listen to the entire dialogue on the CD and follow along to check your answers and pronunciation.

Claudia: Oye Jorge, ¿les _____ (1. decir) algo a tus padres sobre el accidente del carro? *Hey, Jorge. Are you going to say anything to your parents about the car accident?*

Jorge: No creo. Sólo _____ (2. crear) problemas. *I don't think so. It will only make trouble.*

Claudia: Pero tus padres _____ (3. querer) saber que pasó ¿verdad? *But your parents will want to know what happened, right?*

Jorge: Claro que sí, pero si se lo digo, _____ (4. dejar) de mandarme dinero para mis gastos. *Of course, but if I tell them, they'll stop sending me money for my expenses.*

Claudia: _____ (5. ser) por algo, ¿no? O sea, estás siendo un poco irresponsable, ¿no crees? *Well, it's for a reason, right? I mean, you are being a little irresponsible, don't you think?*

Jorge: Tú no conoces a mis padres. Si yo les cuento lo del carro, _____ (6. haber) un lío. Se _____ (7. poner) furiosos.¡Y el accidente ni fue por mi culpa! *You don't know my parents. If I tell them about the car it will be a disaster. They'll flip out. And the accident wasn't even my fault!*

Claudia: Ya veo. ¿Así que lo _____ (8. esconder) para siempre? *I see. So you're going to hide it forever?*

Jorge: Efectivamente, y _____ (9. usar) el dinero que me mandan para arreglar el carro. *Exactly, and I'll use the money they send me to fix the car.*

Claudia: Y tus padres nunca se _____ (10. dar) cuenta de nada. *And they'll never realize a thing.*

Jorge: No, nunca se _____ (11. dar) cuenta de nada. *Nope, they'll never realize a thing.*

Indirect Object Pronouns

You learned in Chapter 11 that a direct object pronoun takes the place of a noun—the direct object. The indirect object pronoun can also take the place of a noun, or it can appear in addition to the noun it represents—an indirect object noun. Here are the indirect object pronouns in Spanish.

me	*(to) me*
te	*(to) you* (familiar)
le	*(to) him, her, it, you* (formal)

nos	*(to) us*
os	*(to) you* (plural familiar, Spain)
les	*(to) them, you* (plural)

You probably noticed that the indirect and direct object pronouns are nearly identical. The only differences are:

Direct Object	Indirect Object
lo, la	le
los, las	les

Using Indirect Object Pronouns

In order to use indirect object pronouns successfully, you first need to be able to recognize the indirect object noun. Because the indirect object is a little trickier than the direct object, let's begin by recognizing it in English. Then you'll study the Spanish equivalents.

The indirect object tells where (the direction in which) the direct object is going. This will almost always be translated in English as *to* or *for*.

Yo **le** mando dinero **a Juani**.

I send money to Juani. (I send Juani money.)
Juani = indirect object
money = direct object

In the previous example, the money is going *to Juani*. Therefore, ***Juani*** is the indirect object.

You can also identify the indirect object by asking the questions *To whom?* or *For whom?*

Yo **le** di un carro **a ella**.

*I gave **her** a car. (I gave a car to her.)*
her = indirect object
car = direct object

In this example, *to whom* did I give a car? *To her.* Therefore, *her* is the indirect object.

Furthermore, in Spanish, the indirect object is often used with verbs of *giving, informing,* or *communicating,* such as **dar** (*to give*), **traer** (*to bring*), **decir** (*to tell*), **mostrar** (*to show*), **llevar** (*to take*), **hablar** (*to speak*), **mandar** (*to send*), or **ofrecer** (*to offer*).

Oral Practice 2

Practice saying these combinations to get used to using and understanding indirect object pronouns. Only one translation is given, but others are possible.

1. Le mando	*I send to him*		Le manda	*He sends to him*	
Le mandamos	*We send to him*				
2. Les mando	*I send to them*		Les manda	*She sends to them*	
Les mandamos	*We send to them*				
3. Le explico	*I explain to her*		Le explica	*He explains to her*	
Le explicamos	*We explain to her*				
4. Les explico	*I explain to them*		Les explican	*They explain to them*	
Les explicamos	*We explain to them*				
5. Le hablo	*I speak to him*		Le hablas	*You speak to him*	
Le hablan	*You (plural) speak to him*				
6. Les hablo	*I speak to them*		Les hablas	*You speak to them*	
Les hablan	*They speak to them*				

Indirect Object Pronouns with Prepositions

Using indirect object pronouns is tricky for several reasons. First, as you may have noticed above, indirect object pronouns are often used with a prepositional phrase that contains **a** + *noun* or *subject pronoun*. Even when this prepositional phrase (**a** + *noun* or *subject pronoun*) appears in the sentence, the indirect object pronoun is always present. This is very different from English, which uses *either* the pronoun *or* the noun.

> *I talk **to him**.*   or   *I talk **to Pedro**.*

With Spanish verbs, you use the indirect object pronoun alone or the indirect object pronoun with the prepositional phrase (with a noun or subject pronoun). Note that it is quite common to see the pronoun and the prepositional phrase with the same verb in a sentence. Compare these:

> Yo **le** hablo.   *I talk **to him**.*
> Yo **le** hablo **a Pedro**.   *I talk **to Pedro**.*

You may notice the similarity between the use of these pronouns and prepositional phrases and those used with **gustar** in Chapter 7. In fact, this is the same construction.

With **le** and **les**, the noun referred to can be unclear (both masculine and feminine); therefore the prepositional phrase with **a** (with the noun or subject pronoun) is used for clarity.

Luisa **le** prestará dinero.	*Luisa will lend **him/her/you** money.*
Luisa **le** prestará dinero **a Sergio**.	*Luisa will lend **Sergio** money.*
Les mandamos ropa.	*We send **them/you** clothes.*
Les mandamos ropa **a las víctimas del huracán**.	*We send clothes to **the hurricane victims**.*

In the case of **me**, **te**, **os**, and **nos**, the noun referred to is usually clear; when the prepositional phrase (with noun or subject pronoun) is used, it is used for emphasis.

No **me** hables.	*Don't talk **to me**.*
No **me** hables **a mí**.	
Papá **nos** dará las llaves.	*Daddy will give **us** the keys.*
Papá **nos** dará las llaves **a nosotras**.	

When used with ***con*** (*with*), **mí** and **ti** become **conmigo** (*with me*) and **contigo** (*with you*). When you wish to say *with himself* or *with herself*, use **consigo mismo** or **consigo misma**.

Sergio nunca habla **contigo**.	*Sergio never talks to you.*
Ven **conmigo**.	*Come with me.*
Él chico juega fútbol **consigo mismo**.	*The boy plays soccer alone (with himself).*

Still Struggling

Sometimes the direct object is implied, not stated. This can make it confusing for Spanish learners to know which pronoun to use. Compare these sentences:

Le dije.   *I told (it to) him.*
Lo dije.   *I said it.*

The indirect object, **le** (*him, to him*), is used in the first example to refer to the person to whom you are telling information. The direct object (*it*) is implied. The direct object, **lo** (*it*), is used in the second example to refer to the information being conveyed.

When you don't see the prepositions *to* or *for*, it's helpful to try to ask yourself a number of questions to identify if you should use the direct object pronoun:

Am I referring to a person or a pet? The indirect object almost always refers to a person or domesticated animal.

Is there an implied direct object that I'm missing? Finding the implied direct object will usually reassure you that you need an indirect object pronoun.

Which verb am I using? Remember that verbs of communicating (**hablar**, **decir**) almost always communicate to an indirect object.

Placement of the Indirect Object Pronoun

The indirect object pronoun, like the direct object pronoun, precedes the verb if the verb is conjugated, and can either precede the auxiliary verb or be tacked on to the end of the infinitive or the present participle.

Miguel no **me** dijo la verdad.	*Miguel didn't tell **me** the truth.*
¿**Le** vas a mandar un email **a tu madre**?	*Are you going to send **your mother** an email?*
¿Vas a mandar**le** un email **a tu madre**?	*Are you going to send **your mother** an email?*
El agente **nos** mostró tres casas.	*The agent showed **us** three houses.*

In the imperative, the pronoun is tacked on to the end of the verb form in the affirmative, and precedes the verb in the negative.

Escríbe**le a tu madre**.   *Write (to) your mother.*
No **le** escribas **a tu madre**.   *Don't write (to) your mother.*

Written Practice 2

Rewrite the following sentences making the singular indirect object nouns and their pronouns plural, and the plural indirect object nouns and their pronouns singular. Follow the example.

Tienes que entregarle los informes al jefe. *You have to deliver the reports to the boss.*

Tienes que entregarles los informes a los jefes. *You have to deliver the reports to the bosses.*

1. No les mandes el paquete a ellas. *Don't send them the package.*
   _____ *Don't send her the package.*

2. Dile a tu hermano que venga. *Tell your brother to come.*
   _____ *Tell your brothers to come.*

3. ¿El cantante nos está hablando a nosotras? *Is the singer talking to us?*
   _____ *Is the singer talking to me?*

4. La profesora les habla a sus alumnos. *The teacher talks to her students.*
   _____ *The teacher talks to her student.*

5. Penélope te dio un beso a ti. *Penélope gave you a kiss.*
   _____ *Penélope gave you (plural) a kiss.*

6. No le des la espalda a tu amiga. *Don't turn your back on your friend.*
   _____ *Don't turn your back on your friends.*

7. Le mando una tarjeta de Navidad a mi pariente. *I send a Christmas card to my relative.*
   _____ *I send a Christmas card to my relatives.*

Written Practice 3

Complete the sentences with the appropriate *direct* or *indirect object pronoun*.

1. Invité a Jorge a la fiesta. *I invited Jorge to the party.*

   _____ invité a la fiesta. *I invited him to the party.*

2. Elena visitará a su abuela en junio. *Elena will visit her grandmother in June.*

   Elena _____ visitará en junio. *Elena will visit her in June.*

3. Mándale un abrazo a tu esposa. *Give your wife a hug (for me).*

   _____ manda un abrazo. *Give her a hug (for me).*

4. Le dejaré una buena propina al camarero. *I'll leave the waiter a good tip.*

   _____ dejaré una buena propina. *I'll leave him a good tip.*

5. Los turistas miran los cuadros. *The tourists look at the paintings.*

   Los turistas _____ miran. *The tourists look at them.*

6. Nuestros vecinos nos saludan a nosotros. *Our neighbors greet us.*

   Nuestros vecinos _____ saludan. *Our neighbors greet us.*

7. El sábado voy a recoger a mi madre. *Saturday I'm going to pick up my mother.*

   El sábado _____ voy a recoger. *Saturday I'm going to pick her up.*

8. Silvia nunca ve a sus primos. *Silvia never sees her cousins.*

   Silvia nunca _____ ve. *Silvia never sees them.*

The Pronoun *Lo*

So far you've learned **lo bueno, lo malo y lo feo del español** (*the good, the bad, and the ugly of Spanish*). One of the most useful things in the Spanish language is the pronoun **lo**. You've learned how to use this word as a direct object. It can also be used in a number of situations to refer to the thing that is not quite defined—similar to the way we say *the good thing* or *the bad thing* in English. In Spanish you don't say **la cosa buena** but rather **lo bueno**. Here are some more examples of **lo** + adjective:

lo bueno	*the good thing*	lo malo	*the bad thing*
lo difícil	*the hard thing*	lo mejor	*the best thing*
lo divertido	*the fun thing*	lo peor	*the worst thing*
lo extraño	*the weird/strange thing*	lo raro	*the weird/strange thing*
lo increíble	*the incredible thing*	lo único	*the only thing*

These expressions are often followed by **es que**.

Lo bueno es que tengo trabajo.   *The good thing is that I have work.*
Lo malo es que lo odio.   *The bad thing is that I hate it.*

The Conditional

The conditional is rather straightforward as far as verb moods and tenses go. It's almost always roughly equivalent to the auxiliary *would* in English.

¿Tú **harías** paracaidismo?   *Would you ever go skydiving?*
—No, no lo **haría** nunca.   *—No, I would never do it.*
Quisiera un kilo de manzanas,   *I would like a kilo of apples, please.*
    por favor.

Forming the Conditional

Forming the conditional is relatively easy. To form the present conditional, add the endings **-ía**, **-ías**, **-ía**, **-íamos**, **-íais**, **-ían** to the infinitive of the verb.

Conditional

	hablar	comer	vivir	estar
yo	hablaría	comería	viviría	estaría
tú	hablarías	comerías	vivirías	estarías
él/ella/usted	hablaría	comería	viviría	estaría
nosotros	hablaríamos	comeríamos	viviríamos	estaríamos
vosotros	hablaríais	comeríais	viviríais	estaríais
ellos/ellas/ustedes	hablarían	comerían	vivirían	estarían

The same verbs that are irregular in the future are irregular in the conditional and the same stems are used. Note that only the **yo** form is given in the following table, but that the endings for the other conjugations are the regular endings of the conditional.

Irregular Verbs in the Conditional

decir	**diría**	poner	**pondría**
hacer	**haría**	salir	**saldría**
querer	**querría**	tener	**tendría**

caber	**cabría**	valer	**valdría**
haber	**habría**	venir	**vendría**
poder	**podría**		
saber	**sabría**		

Use of the Conditional

As mentioned previously, you can use the conditional almost any time you would use *would* in English.

Yo no la **llamaría** tan temprano.	*I wouldn't call her so early.*
¿Dónde **irías** de vacaciones, a España o a Argentina?	*Where would you go on vacation, Spain or Argentina?*

One main difference is that in English the auxiliary *would* is also used to talk about things you *used to* do in the past. In English, one might say, *When I was younger I* **would** *go to the park with my mother.* In Spanish, the *imperfect* past tense, covered in Chapter 14—not the conditional—is used to express these repeated actions in the past.

There are times when the conditional isn't translated as simply *would*. For instance, in Spanish, the conditional is often used to speculate about the past. In English this use of the conditional could be translated as *must have been* or *would have been*. (This usage is similar to the use of the future of uncertainty, which speculates about the present or future.)

Después de trabajar tanto **estarían** cansados.	*After working so much they must have been tired.*
Ayer **caminaríamos** quince millas.	*Yesterday we must have walked fifteen miles.*

When used in the conditional, the verb **poder** is translated as *could* and is usually followed by the infinitive to make polite requests.

¿Me **podrías comprar** unos huevos?	*Could you buy me some eggs?*

When used in the conditional, the verb **deber** is translated as *should* and is usually followed by the infinitive to give advice.

Deberías ir al médico.	*You should go to the doctor.*

Written Practice 4

 Track 51

Complete the following sentences with the conditional, using the verbs in parentheses.

1. A mí me _____ (gustar) aprender árabe. *I'd like to learn Arabic.*

2. ¿Tú _____ (viajar) solo por el mundo? *Would you travel around the world alone?*

3. Nosotros no _____ (saber) llegar al aeropuerto. *We wouldn't know how to get to the airport.*

4. ¿Usted _____ (poder) abrir la puerta, por favor? *Could you open the door, please?*

5. José nunca _____ (venir) con nosotras. *José would never come with us.*

6. Yo _____ (vivir) sola, pero es demasiado caro. *I would live alone but it's too expensive.*

7. Yo _____ (decir) que está durmiendo. *I would say that he's sleeping.*

8. Yo _____ (ir) al baile, pero primero _____ (tener) que comprar un vestido. *I would go to the dance, but I'd have to buy a dress first.*

Oral Practice 3

 Track 52

Practice saying these expressions for *no*, *yes*, and *maybe*. Listen to the CD to help you with your pronunciation and intonation.

Saying No		**Saying Yes**	
creo que no	*I don't think so*	creo que sí	*I think so*
la verdad es que no	*actually, no*	me temo que sí	*I'm afraid so*
en absoluto	*absolutely not*	la verdad es que sí	*actually, yes*

para nada	*no way*	sí, como no	*yeah, sure*
¿estás loco?	*are you crazy?*	claro	*sure*
nunca/jamás	*never*	por supuesto	*of course*

Saying *Maybe*

| quizás | *maybe* | | *maybe* |
| tal vez | | | |

Now read the questions out loud and answer them using the expressions you learned.

1. ¿Harías puenting? *Would you go bungee jumping?*

2. ¿Te raparías el cabello? *Would you shave your head?*

3. ¿Comerías insectos? *Would you eat insects?*

4. ¿Viajarías solo a un país hispanohablante? *Would you travel alone to a Spanish-speaking country?*

5. ¿Te harías cirugía plástica? *Would you get plastic surgery?*

6. ¿Adoptarías a un niño de otra cultura? *Would you adopt a child from another culture?*

7. ¿Escribirías un libro? *Would you write a book?*

8. ¿Te casarías con alguien veinte años mayor? *Would you marry someone twenty years older?*

Oral Practice 4

 Track 53

Now answer the following questions using the conditional. Use the models to help you. Then make up some sentences of your own.

1. ¿Cómo te prepararías para un viaje a Sudamérica? *How would you prepare for a trip to South America?*

   hacer la maleta / renovar el pasaporte / comprar un boleto de avión / leer una guía turística *pack my suitcase / renew my passport / buy a plane ticket / read a travel guide*

2. ¿Qué harías en el caso de un incendio en tu edificio? *What would you do if there were a fire in your building?*

llamar a 911 / agarrar la cartera / salir despacio por la escalera *call 911 / grab my wallet / exit slowly via the stairs*

3. ¿Qué harías como turista en Latinoamérica? *What would you do as a tourist in Latin America?*

hacer un cursillo de español en Antigua, Guatemala / escalar los Andes / visitar las playas de Panamá *take a short Spanish course in Antigua, Guatemala / climb the Andes / visit the beaches of Panama*

Augmentative Forms of Nouns

In Chapter 2 you learned how to make the diminutive using suffixes such as **-ito** and **-illo**. Spanish often uses augmentative forms as well. These add suffixes such as **-ón, -ona, -ote, -ota**, and **-azo, -aza** to nouns and adjectives.

bueno   buen**azo**   buen**ote**
grande   grand**ón**   grand**ote**

Augmentative suffixes can be used to accentuate a word or thought, or to indicate large size or intensity. Please note that these suffixes are often used to make insults or pejorative comments. You might be most familiar with the word **cabrón**, which literally means *he-goat* or *big goat* and is used to refer to someone who is especially aggressive or mean (although it has other uses which are not appropriate to go into here!) Most of these uses are slangy or colloquial, and should be approached *very* cautiously by a non-native speaker.

Written Practice 5

Practice making augmentatives using the words and suffixes provided.

1. -ote, -azo beso   *kiss*   _____ *big kiss*
2. -ona   mujer   *woman*   _____ *big, shapely woman*
3. -ote   padre   *father*   _____ *pimp*
4. -ona   mandar *to order* _____ *bossy woman*

Augmentative suffixes are often used in "standard" (or non-slangy) Spanish to make new words from other words. Practice making augmentatives using the words and suffixes provided.

5. -ón/ona	llorar	*to cry*	_____	*someone who cries a lot*
6. -ón	caja	*box*	_____	*drawer*
7. -ón	rata	*rat*	_____	*mouse* (seems backward, doesn't it?)
8. -ón	cintura	*waist*	_____	*belt*
9. -azo	flecha	*arrow*	_____	*love at first sight*

QUIZ

Circle the letter of the word or phrase that best completes each sentence.

1. (Yo) _____ los deberes mañana.
   A. hará
   B. hace
   C. haré
   D. hice

2. ¿_____ comida en la fiesta?
   A. estará
   B. será
   C. estará habiendo
   D. habrá

3. José _____ devolverá el dinero a mí.
   A. me
   B. te
   C. se
   D. le

4. _____ daré flores a mi novia para San Valentín.
   A. La
   B. Le
   C. Se
   D. Las

5. No voy a _____ de la sorpresa.

   A. le hablar

   B. la hablar

   C. hablarle

   D. hablarla

6. Lo fácil será reparar el carro. _____ será explicarles el accidente a mis padres.

   A. Lo fácil

   B. Lo difícil

   C. Lo divertido

   D. Lo bueno

7. ¿Ustedes _____ con nosotros al cine?

   A. iría

   B. irías

   C. irían

   D. iríais

8. ¿Escalarías el monte Kilimanjaro?

   —_____. **Me encantan las montañas**.

   A. Creo que no

   B. Tal vez

   C. Jamás

   D. Claro que sí

9. Voy a llegar tarde. _____ llamar a mis padres.

   A. Debería

   B. Querría

   C. Podría

   D. Habría

10. Fue amor a primera vista. Fue _____.

   A. un besazo

   B. una llorona

   C. un flechazo

   D. un cinturón

chapter **13**

Talking About the Past with the Preterit

In this chapter you will learn how to express actions in the past using the preterit (simple past) tense for regular and irregular verbs. You will also learn how to use direct and indirect pronouns together to make double object pronouns and how to sound more native by using adjectives as nouns.

CHAPTER OBJECTIVES

In this chapter you will learn

- The preterit tense of regular verbs
- Double object pronouns
- How to use adjectives as nouns
- The preterit of irregular verbs

The Preterit Tense

In Spanish there are many ways to talk about the past, and as you become more proficient, you'll learn a variety of compound tenses. However, the two verb tenses that you will use most often to talk about the past are the *preterit* and the *imperfect*. The tense you use depends on the context of the sentence. We will begin with the preterit.

The meaning of the preterit is similar to the simple past in English.

anduve	*I walked*
vimos	*we saw*
comieron	*they ate*

The preterit is generally used to describe completed actions in the past.

Salí anoche.	*I went out last night.*
¿**Terminaste** tu ensayo?	*Did you finish your essay?*
No me **llamaron** *ayer.*	*They didn't call me yesterday.*

In contrast, the Spanish imperfect is used to talk about past actions that are descriptive, were not completed, or that did not have a distinct beginning or end. You will learn more about the imperfect in Chapter 14.

Preterit of *-ar* Verbs

In the preterit, **-ar** verbs take one set of endings, and **-er** and **-ir** verbs take another.

Preterit of -ar Verbs

	hablar	
yo	habl**é**	*I talked/spoke*
tú	habl**aste**	*you talked/spoke (singular, informal)*
él/ella/usted	habl**ó**	*he, she, it talked/spoke, you talked/ spoke (singular, formal)*
nosotros	habl**amos**	*we talked/spoke*
vosotros	habl**asteis**	*you talked/spoke (plural, informal)*
ellos/ellas/ustedes	habl**aron**	*they, you talked/spoke (plural)*

NOTE *The **nosotros** form (**-amos**) is the same for the present tense and the preterit. Context will help you decide whether the verb is in the present or past.*

Here are some example sentences using **-ar** verbs in the preterit:

Anoche **estudiamos** hasta las tres de la madrugada.	*Last night we studied until three in the morning.*
La fiesta **se acabó** a la una.	*The party ended at one o'clock.*
¿**Jugaste** fútbol ayer?	*Did you play soccer yesterday?*

Preterit of *-er* and *-ir* Verbs

The endings are the same for **-er** and **-ir** verbs.

Preterit of *-er* and *-ir* Verbs

	comer		vivir	
yo	com**í**	*I ate*	viv**í**	*I lived*
tú	com**iste**	*you ate*	viv**iste**	*you lived*
él/ella/usted	com**ió**	*he, she, it, you ate*	viv**ió**	*he, she, it, you lived*
nosotros	com**imos**	*we ate*	viv**imos**	*we lived*
vosotros	com**isteis**	*you ate*	viv**isteis**	*you lived*
ellos/ellas/ustedes	com**ieron**	*they, you ate*	viv**ieron**	*they, you lived*

NOTE *The **nosotros** form (**-imos**) is also the same for the present tense and the preterit for **-er** and **-ir** verbs.*

Here are some example sentences using **-er** and **-ir** verbs in the preterit:

Anoche **comimos** en un buen restaurante.	*Last night we ate at a good restaurant.*
¿**Condujiste** solo a Chicago?	*Did you drive alone to Chicago?*

Stem-Changing Verbs in the Preterit

Stem-changing verbs ending in **-ar** and **-er** do not show a stem change in the preterit. They follow the same patterns as **-ar** and **-er** regular verbs. **Salir** is also "regular" in the preterit.

	pensar	**entender**	**salir**
yo	pensé	entendí	salí
tú	pensaste	entendiste	saliste
él/ella/usted	pensó	entendió	salió
nosotros	pensamos	entendimos	salimos
vosotros	pensasteis	entendisteis	salisteis
ellos/ellas/ustedes	pensaron	entendieron	salieron

Stem-changing verbs ending in **-ir** *do* change in the preterit. In the third-person singular (**él**, **ella**, **usted**) and third-person plural (**ellos**, **ellas**, **ustedes**), the **e→i** and the **o→u** in the ste*m*.

pedir	**dormir**
pedí	dormí
pediste	dormiste
pidió	durmió
pedimos	dormimos
pedisteis	dormisteis
pidieron	durmieron

Spelling Changes in the Preterit

Verbs that end in **-gar**, **-car**, and **-zar** have spelling changes in the first person singular preterit (**yo**). Other forms are regular.

	llegar	buscar	empezar
yo	lle**gué**	bus**qué**	empe**cé**

Verbs ending in **-uir**, **-aer**, **-eer,** and **-oír** show a spelling change in the third-person singular (**él**, **ella**, **usted**) and third-person plural (**ellos**, **ellas**, **ustedes**).

	construir	**leer**	**oír**	**caer**
yo	construí	leí	oí	caí
tú	construiste	leíste	oíste	caíste
él/ella/usted	**construyó**	**leyó**	**oyó**	**cayó**
nosotros	construimos	leímos	oímos	caímos
vosotros	construisteis	leísteis	oísteis	caísteis
ellos/ellas/ustedes	**construyeron**	**leyeron**	**oyeron**	**cayeron**

Exceptions to this rule are verbs ending in **-traer**, such as **traer** (*to bring*) and **atraer** (*to attract*). They are irregular.

Written Practice 1

Practice forming the preterit with the following verbs and the subjects indicated.

	nadar	tocar	creer	jugar	vender
yo	_____	_____	_____	_____	_____
tú	_____	_____	_____	_____	_____
él/ella/usted	_____	_____	_____	_____	_____
nosotros	_____	_____	_____	_____	_____
ellos/ellas/ustedes	_____	_____	_____	_____	_____

	escribir	huir	repetir	almorzar	sentir
yo	_____	_____	_____	_____	_____
tú	_____	_____	_____	_____	_____
él/ella/usted	_____	_____	_____	_____	_____
nosotros	_____	_____	_____	_____	_____
ellos/ellas/ustedes	_____	_____	_____	_____	_____

Uses of the Preterit

The most important rule for the preterit is that it is used to describe actions in the past that are completed.

Mis padres **llegaron** ayer.	*My parents arrived yesterday.*
Ayer **corrí** tres millas.	*Yesterday I jogged three miles.*
¿A qué hora **empezó** a llover?	*What time did it start raining?*
Yasmín **viajó** a Perú.	*Yasmín traveled to Peru.*
Construyeron un edificio nuevo.	*They built a new building.*

The following adverbial words or phrases that refer to the past will often tip you off that the preterit should be used.

ayer	*yesterday*
anteayer	*the day before yesterday*
anoche	*last night*
el otro día	*the other day*
la semana pasada	*last week*
el mes pasado	*last month*
el año pasado	*last year*

The completed actions in the past expressed with the preterit can be single events, repeated events, or part of a chain of events, but these events have to begin, occur, or end at a precise moment.

Fui a la comisaría tres veces.	*I went to the police station three times.*
Trabajé de nueve a cinco.	*I worked from nine to five.*
Encendí el celular y **llamé** a mi madre.	*I turned on the cell phone and called my mom.*

The preterit can also state the beginning or the end of an action.

El niño **empezó** a llorar.	*The child started to cry.*

Written Practice 2

Rewrite the following sentences in the preterit.

1. Yo pago cien dólares por esta camisa. *I pay a hundred dollars for this shirt.*
   _____ *I paid a hundred dollars for this shirt.*

2. Nosotros comenzamos a estudiar. *We begin to study.*
   _____ *We began to study.*

3. Selena y su hermana duermen hasta el mediodía. *Selena and her sister sleep until noon.*
   _____ *Selena and her sister slept until noon.*

4. María estudia mucho. *María studies a lot.*
   _____ *María studied a lot.*

5. ¿Tú compras los remedios? *Do you buy the medicine?*
   _____ *Did you buy the medicine?*

6. El bebé casi no llora. *The baby barely cries.*
   _____ *The baby barely cried.*

7. Mis padres no me creen. *My parents don't believe me.*
   _____ *My parents didn't believe me.*

8. ¿Ustedes piden arroz con leche? *Do you order rice pudding?*
   _____ *Did you order rice pudding?*

Oral Practice 1

Complete the sentences using the adverbial phrases to say what you did in the past. Follow the example, creating sentences with a variety of verbs.

> *Esta mañana me levanté, me cepillé los dientes, tomé un café y agarré el autobus.* **This morning I got up, brushed my teeth, drank a cup of coffee, and grabbed the bus.**

Ayer…
Anteayer…
Anoche…
El otro día…
La semana pasada…
El verano pasado…
El año pasado…
En invierno…

Double Object Pronouns

Now that you've learned how to use direct and indirect object pronouns, we will learn what to do when they occur together in a single sentence. Look at this example in English:

I lent José the car.	No object pronouns.
I lent **him** the car.	Indirect object pronoun *(to) him.*
I lent **it to him**.	Direct object pronoun *it* and indirect object pronoun *(to) him.*

Spanish has similar constructions.

> José compró el carro para nosotros. *José bought us the car.*

The previous example has no object pronouns.

> José **nos** compró el carro **(para nosotros)**.   *José bought **us** the car.*

The previous example has an indirect object pronoun **nos** (*[for] us*).

> José **nos lo** compró.   *José bought **it for us**.*

The previous example has an indirect object pronoun **nos** (*[for] us*) and a direct object pronoun **lo** (*it*).

Placement of Double Object Pronouns

When indirect and direct object pronouns appear together in the same sentence in Spanish, the order is always:

Indirect object pronoun   +   Direct object pronoun

The indirect object pronouns **le** or **les** become **se** when they precede **lo, la,** or **los.**

Indirect object pronoun +	Direct object pronoun
me	me
te	te
le→se	lo, la, los, las
nos	nos
os	os
les→se	lo, la, los, las

For example:

Yo **le** presté **el carro a José**.	*I lent José the car.*
Yo ~~le~~ **se lo** presté.	*I lent it to him.*
Silvia **les** mandó **una carta a sus padres**.	*Silvia sent her parents a letter.*
Silvia ~~les~~ **se la** mandó.	*Silvia sent it to them.*

As with single object pronouns, double object pronouns precede the conjugated verb form.

No **me lo** mandes.	*Don't send it to me.*
—Pero ya **te lo** mandé ayer.	*—But I already sent it to you yesterday.*

As with single object pronouns, double object pronouns are tacked on to the end of an affirmative command. Note the written accent mark indicating that the normally stressed syllable is retained.

Mánda**melo** mañana.	*Send it to me tomorrow.*

Object pronouns can either precede the conjugated verb or be tacked on to the end of the present participle or the infinitive.

No puedo mand**ártelo** mañana.   *I can't send it to you tomorrow.*
No **te lo** puedo mandar mañana.

Still Struggling

Remember, when using double object pronouns you cannot have two "**l**" pronouns in a row. The "**l**" changes to "**s**" in order to make the string of pronouns easier to pronounce.

le + lo → se lo   le + los → se los
le + la → se la   le + las → se las

Written Practice 3

Match each short phrase with its English translation.

1. _____ mándamelo   a. he bought them for me
2. _____ mándaselo   b. send it to her
3. _____ nos lo mandaron   c. he bought them for you
4. _____ se lo mandó   d. buy it for me
5. _____ me las compró   e. send it to me
6. _____ te las compró   f. she sent it to them
7. _____ cómpramelo   g. buy it for them
8. _____ cómpreselo   h. they sent it to us

Written Practice 4

Rewrite the following sentences substituting the direct and indirect objects with pronouns.

1. Laurita me presta el libro a mí. *Laurita lends me the book.*

   _____ *Laurita lends it to me.*

2. Estamos comprando flores para los vecinos. *We're buying flowers for the neighbors.*

   _____ *We're buying them for them.*

3. El profesor les explica las reglas a los niños. *The teacher explains the rules to the kids.*

   _____ *The teacher explains them to them.*

4. Explícame el problema, por favor. *Explain the problem to me, please.*

   _____ *Explain it to me, please.*

5. ¿Quieren prestarle su paraguas a mi amigo? *Can you lend my friend your umbrella?*

   _____ *Can you lend it to him?*

6. Mercedes les da indicaciones a los turistas. *Mercedes gives the tourists directions.*

   _____ *Mercedes gives them to them.*

7. No te confiaré mis problemas. *I'm not going to (I won't) talk to you about my problems.*

   _____ *I'm not going to (I won't) talk to you about them.*

8. Mi jefe me invitó a un café. *My boss treated me to a cup of coffee.*

   _____ *My boss treated me to it.*

Using Adjectives as Nouns

You already learned that you can use **lo** + an adjective to express *the good thing* (**lo bueno**) or *the only thing* (**lo único**). You can also use the definite article (**el**, **la**, **los**, or **las**) with the adjective to express ideas such as *the old one* (**el viejo**) or *the new one* (**la nueva**). You may have heard of the classic comedy duo Laurel and Hardy. Well, in Spanish they are called **el gordo y el flaco** (*the fat one and the thin one*). Here are some examples using this construction. Remember that **a** + **el** makes **al**.

▶ Track 54

Ester:	¿Qué te parece la nueva jefa?	*What do you think of the new boss?*
Araceli:	¿**La nueva**? Es simpática ¿no crees?	*The new one? She's nice, don't you think?*
Ester:	Bueno, creo que al asistente le cae mal.	*Well, I don't think the assistant likes her.*
Araceli:	¿A qué asistente? ¿**Al gordo** o **al flaco**?	*Which assistant? The fat one or the thin one?*
Ester:	**Al flaco**.	*The thin one.*
Araceli:	Sí, tienes razón.	*Yeah, you're right.*

* * *

Carlos:	¿Qué gorro te gusta más, **el azul** o **el blanco**?	*Which cap do you like better, the blue one or the white one?*
Miguel:	A mí me gusta **el azul**.	*I like the blue one.*
Carlos:	¿O tal vez **el rojo**?	*Or maybe the red one?*
Miguel:	No, **el rojo** no. Te queda mejor **el azul**.	*No, not the red one. The blue one looks better on you.*

Written Practice 5

Practice making nouns from the following noun/adjective combinations. Follow the example.

1. Los chicos jóvenes. <u>Los jóvenes</u>

2. Las mujeres bellas _____

3. La niña rubia _____

4. El alumno pequeño _____

5. La camisa verde _____

6. Los carros grandes _____

7. Las mujeres altas _____

8. Las películas serias _____

The Preterit of Irregular Verbs

Many students shudder at the thought of learning the Spanish preterit because of the number and variety of irregular verb forms. Never fear! These can be organized into groups to help make memorization easier.

Ser and Ir

Ser (*to be*) and ir (*to go*) are conjugated exactly the same in the preterit. Learn one and you'll know them both.

	ser	ir
yo	fui	fui
tú	fuiste	fuiste
él/ella/usted	fue	fue
nosotros	fuimos	fuimos
vosotros	fuisteis	fuisteis
ellos/ellas/ustedes	fueron	fueron

You can usually tell the meaning from the context.

Rodrigo **fue** a Chile.	*Rodrigo went to Chile.*
Me fui a las ocho.	*I left at eight.*
Violeta Chamorro **fue** presidenta de Nicaragua.	*Violeta Chamorro was the president of Nicaragua.*

Decir and Traer

Other verbs similar to **traer** (*to bring*) in the preterit include **atraer** (*to attract*) and **contraer** (*to contract*). Other verbs similar to **decir** (*to say*) include **traducir** (*to translate*) and **producir** (*to produce*).

	decir	traer
yo	dije	traje
tú	dijiste	trajiste
él/ella/usted	dijo	trajo
nosotros	dijimos	trajimos
vosotros	dijisteis	trajisteis
ellos/ellas/ustedes	dijeron	trajeron

Chapter 13 TALKING ABOUT THE PAST WITH THE PRETERIT 257

Dar and Ver

The verbs **dar** and **ver** are conjugated similar to -er and -ir verbs in the preterit, except they don't take the written accent.

	dar	ver
yo	di	vi
tú	diste	viste
él/ella/usted	dio	vio
nosotros	dimos	vimos
vosotros	disteis	visteis
ellos/ellas/ustedes	dieron	vieron

Querer, Hacer, and Venir

Other verbs similar to **hacer** (*to make; to do*) in the preterit include **rehacer** (*to do again*), **deshacer** (*to undo*), and **satisfacer** (*to satisfy*). Other verbs similar to **venir** (*to come*) include **prevenir** (*to prevent*) and **intervenir** (*to intervene; to take part*).

	querer	hacer	venir
yo	quise	hice	vine
tú	quisiste	hiciste	viniste
él/ella/usted	quiso	hizo	vino
nosotros	quisimos	hicimos	vinimos
vosotros	quisisteis	hicisteis	vinisteis
ellos/ellas/ustedes	quisieron	hicieron	vinieron

Poner, Poder, Saber, and Caber

Other verbs similar to **poner** (*to put*) in the preterit include **imponer** (*to impose*), **suponer** (*to suppose*), **exponer** (*to expose*), and **componer** (*to compose*).

	poner	poder	saber	caber
yo	puse	pude	supe	cupe
tú	pusiste	pudiste	supiste	cupiste
él/ella/usted	puso	pudo	supo	cupo
nosotros	pusimos	pudimos	supimos	cupimos
vosotros	pusisteis	pudisteis	supisteis	cupisteis
ellos/ellas/ustedes	pusieron	pudieron	supieron	cupieron

Tener, Andar, Estar

Other verbs similar to **tener** (*to have*) in the preterit include **mantener** (*to maintain*), **retener** (*to retain*), **contener** (*to contain*), **entretener** (*to entertain*), **sostener** (*to sustain*), and **obtener** (*to obtain*).

	estar	**tener**	**andar**
yo	estuve	tuve	anduve
tú	estuviste	tuviste	anduviste
él/ella/usted	estuvo	tuvo	anduvo
nosotros	estuvimos	tuvimos	anduvimos
vosotros	estuvisteis	tuvisteis	anduvisteis
ellos/ellas/ustedes	estuvieron	tuvieron	anduvieron

Written Practice 6

Complete the sentences with the preterit form of the verbs in parentheses.

1. ¿Tú _____ (ir) a clase ayer? *Did you go to class yesterday?*

2. Ellos no nos _____ (decir) nada sobre la reunión. *They didn't tell us anything about the meeting.*

3. Salí una vez con él, pero no me _____ (atraer) mucho. *I went out once with him, but I wasn't very attracted to him.*

4. Carla no quería pedir disculpas, pero lo _____ (hacer) de todos modos. *Carla didn't want to apologize, but she did anyway.*

5. ¿Tienes los apuntes de la clase del lunes? Yo no_____ (poder) ir. *Do you have the class notes from Monday? I couldn't go.*

6. Nosotros _____ (ir) en dos taxis, porque no _____ (caber) todos en uno. *We went in two taxis because we didn't all fit in one.*

7. ¿Dónde _____ (estar) anoche? *Where were you last night?*

8. Mis amigos llegaron tarde del aeropuerto porque _____ (tener) problemas en la aduana. *My friends arrived late from the airport because they had trouble in customs.*

Written Practice 7

▶ Track 55

Read the following dialogue. Then answer the questions using complete sentences. Try using direct and indirect object pronouns in your answers where possible.

Patricia: ¿Dónde conociste a Anabel? *Where did you meet Anabel?*

Oscar: Mmm... ¿Por qué? *Mmm . . . Why do you ask?*

Patricia: Porque nunca conozco a nadie, y tú siempre tienes suerte con las chicas. *Because I never meet anyone, and you always have luck with girls.*

Oscar: Pues la conocí en línea. *Well, I met her online.*

Patricia: ¡Nooooo! ¡Imposible! Pero tú eres un tipo normal, atractivo. ¿Tuviste que ir al Internet? ¿No pudiste conocer a nadie de una manera más normal? *No! That's impossible! But you're a regular guy, and good-looking. Did you have to go to the Internet? Couldn't you meet anyone in a more traditional way?*

Oscar: Hay mucha gente normal en línea. Ahora todo el mundo lo hace. ¿Tú nunca te metiste en línea? *There are lots of normal people online. These days everybody does it. Haven't you ever gone online?*

Patricia: ¡Para nada! Bueno, entonces, dime. ¿Cómo lo hiciste? *No way! So anyway, tell me. How did you do it?*

Oscar: Pues me metí en el sitio Web y puse mi perfil. Escribí a varias chicas... uy uy uy, y salí con unas muy raras. *Well, I went to the website and I set up my profile. I wrote to a few girls . . . ay, yay, yay, and I went out with a few very unusual ones.*

Patricia: ¿Ves? Te dije. El Internet está lleno de gente rara. *You see? I told you. The Internet is full of strange people . . .*

Oscar: Bueno... cuando vi el perfil de Anabel me pareció interesante y le escribí. *Well, . . . when I saw Anabel's profile she seemed interesting, and I wrote to her.*

Patricia: ¿Y cuándo la viste, qué pasó? *And when you saw her, what happened?*

Oscar: Uuuy... Fue amor a primera vista. Fuimos a tomar un café y... *Ooh . . . It was love at first sight. We went out for coffee, and . . .*

Patricia: ¿Café? ¿Solamente? *Coffee? Only coffee?*

Oscar: Es que tengo una regla de sólo tomar café durante la primera cita. Así es más fácil escaparse si la cosa no sale bien. *I have a rule that we only have coffee on the first date. That way it's easier to get away if things aren't going well.*

Patricia: Ah, claro, escaparte de todas las chicas 'normales' del Internet. *Oh, I see, to get away from all the "normal" girls you meet on the Internet.*

Oscar: Calla... Como te dije, fue un flechazo. La vi y casi no pude hablar... Se me erizó la piel. Se me puso la piel de gallina. Es que es una mujer impresionante. Le di mi teléfono y me llamó al día siguiente. Así empezó todo. *Shush . . . Like I said, it was a bolt from the blue (love at first sight). I saw her and I could barely speak. . . . The hair stood up on my neck. I got goose bumps. She's an impressive woman. I gave her my phone number and she called me the next day. That's how it all started.*

Patricia: Así que me lo recomiendas, lo del Internet. *So, you're recommending it, the Internet thing.*

Oscar: ¡Por supuesto que te lo recomiendo! *Of course I'm recommending it!*

1. ¿Dónde conoció Oscar a Anabel? *Where did Oscar meet Anabel?*

_____

2. ¿Por qué quiso Patricia saber dónde la conoció? *Why did Patricia want to know where he met her?*

_____

3. ¿Qué piensa Patricia de concertar citas en línea? *What does Patricia think of online dating?*

_____

4. ¿Anabel fue la primera chica que Oscar conoció por Internet? *Was Anabel the first girl that Oscar met online?*

_____

5. ¿Dónde fueron Anabel y Oscar en la primera cita? *Where did Oscar and Anabel go on their first date?*

_____

6. ¿Cómo se sintió Oscar cuando vio a Anabel? *How did Oscar feel when he saw Anabel?*

_____

7. ¿Cuándo llamó Anabel a Oscar? *When did Anabel call Oscar?*

_____

8. ¿Crees que Patricia se meterá en un sitio Web para concertar citas en línea? *Do you think Patricia will try online dating?*

_____

Oral Practice 2

Answer the following questions about yourself using the preterit.

1. ¿Qué hiciste anoche? *What did you do last night?*
2. ¿Dónde fuiste durante tus últimas vacaciones? *Where did you go on your last vacation?*
3. ¿Dónde estuviste ayer a las tres de la tarde? *Where were you yesterday at* 3:00 *P.M.?*
4. ¿Quién fue tu primer amor? ¿Cómo lo/la conociste? *Who was your first love? How did you meet him/her?*
5. ¿Cuándo viniste a vivir en tu casa actual? *When did you come to live in your current home?*
6. ¿Cuándo fue la última vez que viste a tus padres? ¿Dónde fue? *When was the last time you saw you parents? Where was it?*
7. ¿Saliste alguna vez en una cita a ciegas? ¿Cuándo? ¿Qué hicieron? ¿Qué tal estuvo? *Have you ever gone out on a blind date? When? What did you do? How was it?*

QUIZ

Circle the letter of the word or phrase that best completes each sentence.

1. **Cynthia y Josué _____ el año pasado.**
   A. se casarán
   B. se casan
   C. se casarían
   D. se casaron

2. **Ayer Leticia y yo _____ al teatro.**
   A. fui
   B. fue
   C. fuimos
   D. fueron

3. **Adán _____ a su esposa por Internet.**
   A. conoció
   B. construyó
   C. huyó
   D. empezó

4. **Encontré un suéter perfecto para ti y _____ compré.**
   A. me lo
   B. se la
   C. te lo
   D. te la

5. **¿Katrina le devolvió a Sergio su libro?**
   —Sí, _____ dio anteayer.
   A. le lo
   B. le la
   C. se lo
   D. se la

6. **No recibí su informe. _____ mañana, por favor.**
   A. Mándemela
   B. Mándemelo
   C. Mándeselo
   D. Mándenosla

7. **¿Te gusta la galleta salada o la galleta dulce?**

    —Me gusta _____.

    A. lo salado

    B. la salada

    C. el salada

    D. las saladas

8. **¿Tú _____ en mi clase de biología?**

    A. estuviste

    B. tuviste

    C. anduviste

    D. viste

9. **Yo no _____ mentir, pero _____ que hacerlo.**

    A. tuve; quise

    B. quise; tuve

    C. hice; quise

    D. quise; hice

10. **Mis amigos llegaron _____.**

    A. anoche

    B. mañana

    C. pasado mañana

    D. la semana que viene

chapter 14

Describing Actions in the Past with the Imperfect

In this chapter you will learn how to express actions in the past using the imperfect and imperfect progressive tenses for regular and irregular verbs. You will also learn how to make expressions with **ir a**, **volver a**, and **acabar de**. Finally, you will learn how to make and use adverbs and how to talk about time using the verb **hacer**.

CHAPTER OBJECTIVES

In this chapter you will learn

- The imperfect tense
- The imperfect progressive tense
- How to use *ir a*, *volver a*, and *acabar de*
- How to form and use adverbs
- How to talk about time using the verb *hacer*

The Imperfect Tense

In Spanish, the imperfect, along with the preterit, is used to talk about past actions. Whereas you learned that the preterit is used to talk about completed actions, the imperfect is used to talk about actions *that do not have a clear beginning or end*. These actions often take place over a period of time, but the beginning and end of this period are not specified. The imperfect can be translated a number of ways in English:

Cuando **era** joven, **iba** a la playa.   *When I **was** young, I **would go** to the beach.*

Caminábamos por el malecón.   *We **used to walk** along the boardwalk.*

Leía cuando llamó mi novio.   *I **was reading** when my boyfriend called.*

Tenía dos perros.   *I **had** two dogs.*

The Imperfect of -*ar* Verbs

Luckily, the imperfect has hardly any irregular forms. All **-ar** verbs follow the same pattern. Drop the **-ar** and add the endings **-aba**, **-abas**, **-aba**, **-ábamos**, **-abais**, **-aban**.

Note that there is no stem change in the imperfect for stem-changing **-ar** verbs.

	hablar	**pensar**	**dar**
yo	hablaba	pensaba	daba
tú	hablabas	pensabas	dabas
él/ella/usted	hablaba	pensaba	daba
nosotros	hablábamos	pensábamos	dábamos
vosotros	hablabais	pensabais	dabais
ellos/ellas/ustedes	hablaban	pensaban	daban

Imperfect of -*er* and -*ir* Verbs

To make the imperfect of **-er** and **-ir** verbs, drop the ending **-er** or **-ir** and add **-ía**, **-ías**, **-ía**, **-íamos**, **-íais**, **-ían**. Note that there is no stem change in the imperfect for stem-changing **-er** and **-ir** verbs.

	comer	**pedir**	**decir**
yo	comía	pedía	decía
tú	comías	pedías	decías

él/ella/usted	comía	pedía	decía
nosotros	comíamos	pedíamos	decíamos
vosotros	comíais	pedíais	decíais
ellos/ellas/ustedes	comían	pedían	decían

Imperfect of Irregular Verbs

There are only three irregular verbs in the imperfect. Hurray!

	ser	**ir**	**ver**
yo	era	iba	veía
tú	eras	ibas	veías
él/ella/usted	era	iba	veía
nosotros	éramos	íbamos	veíamos
vosotros	crais	ibais	veíais
ellos/ellas/ustedes	eran	iban	veían

Written Practice 1

Practice forming the imperfect of the following verbs in the forms shown.

1. tú / encontrar   _____
2. ellas / ver   _____
3. usted / salir   _____
4. yo / cerrar   _____
5. nosotros / mantener   _____
6. tú / decir   _____
7. ustedes / irse   _____
8. nosotros / platicar   _____
9. yo / hacer   _____
10. nosotras / ser   _____

Uses of the Imperfect

There are quite a few uses of the imperfect, although they all fall into the category of past actions that have no clear beginning or end.

The imperfect is used to describe continuing, customary, or habitual actions in the past. This is often translated as *would* or *used to* in English.

Dábamos una vuelta todas las mañanas.	*We would go for a stroll every morning.*
Mi tía **jugaba** a las cartas todos los jueves.	*My aunt used to play cards every Thursday.*

Often you will see the imperfect describe a continuing action that gets interrupted (usually by the preterit).

Miraba la televisión cuando **sonó** el teléfono.	*I was watching television when the phone rang.*

There are a number of adverbs of time and adverbial phrases that imply a continuing action and signal the use of the imperfect when used in the past.

cada día	*each/every day*
todos los días	*every day*
un día sí, un día no	*every other day*
con frecuencia	*frequently*
frecuentemente	*frequently*
generalmente	*generally*
todas los lunes, martes, etc.	*every Monday, Tuesday, etc.*
a menudo	*often*
cada semana	*each/every week*
todas las semanas	*every week*
siempre	*always*
a veces	*sometimes*
varias veces	*several times*
de vez en cuando	*from time to time*

For example:

Veía mi telenovela **cada día**.	*I watched my soap opera every day.*
Cuando era joven, **salía** muy **a menudo**.	*When I was younger I used to go out often.*

The imperfect is also used for descriptions in the past.

Un día en verano **hacía** sol.	*One day in the summer it was sunny.*
Eran las seis de la mañana	*It was six in the morning and I was*
y **corría** en el parque.	*jogging in the park.*

The imperfect is used to describe certain mental activities, such as thoughts and feelings, in the past. The imperfect is used because mental activity rarely happens at a precise moment and is usually part of an ongoing process. Verbs that fall in this category and are usually used in the imperfect include **querer** (*to want; to love*), **sentir** (*to feel*), **preferir** (*to prefer*), **desear** (*to desire*), **poder** (*to be able to*), **pensar** (*to think*), **creer** (*to believe*), and **saber** (*to know*).

Sabía que te **conocía** de algún lugar.	*I knew I recognized you from somewhere.*
Mariluz no **pensaba** que la **iban** a despedir.	*Mariluz didn't think they were going to fire her.*

The imperfect is also used to talk about time and age in the past.

Che Guevara **tenía** veinticinco años cuando viajó por Suramérica.	*Che Guevara was twenty-five when he traveled around South America.*
Eran las tres de la madrugada.	*It was three in the morning.*

Here is a recap of the uses of the imperfect. Remember that all uses fall under the category of past actions that have no clear beginning or end.

- To describe continuing, customary, or habitual actions in the past, often translated as *was . . . ing*, *would*, or *used to* in English. Sometimes these actions will be "interrupted" by the preterit.
- When past actions are modified by certain adverbs of time and adverbial phrases, such as **siempre** or **con frecuencia**.
- To make a description in the past.
- To describe certain mental activities, such as thoughts and feelings, using verbs such as **sentir** and **pensar**.
- To talk about time and age in the past.

Written Practice 2

▶ Track 56

Complete the following story using the verbs in parenthesis in the imperfect.

Cuando Rodrigo _____ (1. ser) pequeño _____
(2. vivir) en un barrio de Lima. En verano le _____ (3. gustar)
pasar todo el día en la calle. _____ (4. jugar) fútbol en el
parque con los otros niños. Ellos _____ (5. tirar) piedras a
los faroles y _____ (6. comprar) helados cuando
_____ (7. tener) un poco de dinero de sobra. Por las noches,
Rodrigo _____ (8. volver) a casa a cenar con su abuela y
sus hermanos. Sus padres _____ (9. trabajar) hasta muy
tarde y llegaban sólo para decirle buenas noches. A veces Rodrigo
_____ (10. ir) a la playa con sus primos. No _____
(11. saber) nadar pero _____ (12. meterse) en el agua,
_____ (13. tomar) el sol, _____ (14. comer)
ceviche y _____ (15. beber) chicha morada. A Rodrigo le
_____ (16. encantar) el verano en Lima.

NOTE *Chicha morada is a traditional Peruvian soft drink made of purple corn.*

Oral Practice 1

Using the imperfect, complete each of the following sentences about yourself
when you were younger. If the sentence doesn't apply to you, invent something!

1. *When I was young* . . .   Cuando era joven _____.
2. *My friends and I always* . . .   Mis amigos y yo siempre _____.
3. *I only . . . from time to time*   Sólo _____ de vez en cuando.
4. *Every weekend my family* . . .   Todos los fines de semana mi familia ____.
5. *Every year on my birthday* . . .   Cada año en mi cumpleaños _____.
6. *During the summers* . . .   Durante los veranos _____.

The Imperfect Progressive Tense

The imperfect progressive, like the present progressive you learned in Chapter 8, is used for graphic descriptions of continuous actions. It is generally translated as *was . . . -ing* in English and is very similar to some uses of the simple imperfect. The difference is that the imperfect progressive emphasizes that an action *was in progress* at a given time.

To form the imperfect progressive, use **estar** in the imperfect with the present participle (**-ndo** form). Note that the verbs **ir** and **venir** are rarely used in the imperfect progressive.

Estaba bailando.	*He was dancing.*
Estaban viendo el partido.	*They were watching the match.*

but

Iban al concierto.	*They were going to the concert.*

Often, the imperfect progressive is interrupted by the preterit.

Estaba hablando con mi jefe cuando me **interrumpiste**.	*I was talking to my boss when you interrupted me.*
Estaban viendo el partido cuando **empezó** a llover.	*They were watching the match when it began to rain.*

One nice thing about the imperfect progressive is that it is relatively easy to conjugate and is always translated the same way in English, so you can use it in a pinch to express past progressive actions.

Written Practice 3

Change the following sentences from the imperfect to the imperfect progressive.

1. La chica platicaba con sus amigas. *The girl was chatting with her friends.*

_____

2. ¿Qué decías? *What were you saying?*

_____

3. Los niños jugaban baloncesto. *The kids were playing basketball.*

_____

4. Mercedes no comía nada. *Mercedes wasn't eating anything.*

_____

5. Los vecinos chismeaban. *The neighbors were gossiping.*

_____

6. ¿Usted veía el reportaje? *Were you watching the news report?*

_____

Using *Ir a*, *Volver a*, and *Acabar de*

There are certain verbs that have special uses. **Ir** (*to go*), **volver** (*to return*), and **acabar** (*to finish*) can be used to say: *I was going to do it* (**ir a**), *I just did it* (**acabar de**), and *I'll do it again* (**volver**).

In the imperfect, the construction **ir a** (**iba a...**) + the infinitive is used to say *was going to*.

Iba a llamarte pero se me olvidó.	*I was going to call you, but I forgot.*
¿No **ibas a comprar** comida hoy?	*Weren't you going to buy groceries today?*

In the present, future, and preterit, the construction **volver a** + the infinitive is used to talk about *doing something again*. Note that in certain expressions both the present and future of **volver** can denote a future action.

Lo vuelvo a repitir.	*I'm saying it again.*
Te vuelvo/volveré a llamar.	*I'll call you back.*
Volvió a intentar.	*He tried again.*

The verb **acabar** usually means *to end* or *to finish*. **Se acabó** means *it ended*; **se acabaron las entradas** means *the tickets are all sold out*. But **acabar** has another use. In the present it is used to mean *just* as in *I just talked to her*. This usage can be a little confusing to English speakers, because in Spanish the present tense of the verb denotes something that just ended in the recent past.

Acabo de hablar con ella.	*I just talked to her.*
Acaban de llegar.	*They just arrived.*

The imperfect of **acabar de** is used to say *had just* as in *I had just talked to her*. It is often coupled with the preterit.

Adán **acababa de llegar** cuando **se cayó** y **se rompió** el brazo.	*Adán had just arrived when he fell and broke his arm.*

Written Practice 4

Complete the following sentences in Spanish.

1. *They had just gone to the store.* _____ a la tienda.

2. *I've just seen a movie.* _____ una película.

3. *I'll see you again tomorrow.* _____ mañana.

4. *Were you going to say something?* ¿_____ algo?

5. *They were going to visit me.* _____

6. *They lied again.* _____

Adverb Formation

Adverbs describe or modify verbs, adjectives, or other adverbs. Earlier in this chapter you learned some adverbial phrases that describe how often or when an action takes place. You may have noticed that two of them, **generalmente** (*generally*) and **frecuentemente** (*frequently*) ended in **-mente**. The suffix **-mente** is the equivalent of the English *-ly* and is added to the end of adjectives to make adverbs.

To form an adverb, take the *feminine* form of the adjective and add **-mente**.

adjective	feminine form	adverb	
estupendo	estupenda	estupendamente	*stupendously*
feliz	feliz	felizmente	*happily, luckily*
evidente	evidente	evidentemente	*evidently*

Here are some examples of adverbs in use.

Raúl: Te toca trabajar por la mañana? *Is it your turn to work in the morning?*

Andrea: Felizmente, no. *Luckily not.*

Evidentemente acaban de llegar a este país.   *They obviously just arrived to this country.*

In colloquial speech the adjectives **rápido** (*fast*) and **lento** (*slow*) are often used as adverbs, without the suffix.

Maneja muy **rápido**.   *She drives very fast.*

Adverbs are often used with the imperfect to describe actions in the past.

Dormían **profundamente**.	*They slept (were sleeping) soundly.*
Normalmente trabajaba de nueve a cinco.	*Normally he worked from nine to five.*

Adverbs can also be formed by using **con** followed by a noun.

con cuidado	*with care*	cuidadosamente	*carefully*
con cariño	*with affection*	cariñosamente	*affectionately*
con dificultad	*with difficulty*	difícilmente	*with difficulty*

Trate a su suegra **con cuidado**.	*Treat your mother-in-law with care.*
Háblame **con cariño**, por favor.	*Talk to me with affection, please.*

or they can be formed by using **sin** followed by a verb.

sin cesar	*incessantly, without stopping*
sin querer	*without wanting to*
Lo hice **sin querer**.	*I didn't mean to. (I did it inadvertently.)*
Hablaba **sin cesar**.	*He talked incessantly.*

Written Practice 5

Complete the sentences by forming adverbs from the adjectives in parentheses.

1. (franco) _____, no me gusta la política. *Frankly, I don't like politics.*

2. (afortunado) _____, las tiendas están abiertas este domingo. *Luckily, the stores are open this Sunday.*

3. Mi marido cocina (divino) _____. *My husband cooks divinely.*

4. Terminé el examen (difícil) _____. *I finished the exam with difficulty.*

5. Lo hacía (perfecto) _____. *He did it perfectly.*

6. Ella está (completo) _____ loca. *She is completely crazy.*

Irregular Adverbs

Some adverbs do not follow any pattern and simply have to be memorized. You have already learned some of these up to now in this book.

bastante	*quite*	mucho	*a lot*
bien	*well*	muy	*very*
demasiado	*too*	nunca	*never*
despacio	*slowly*	poco	*little*
mal	*badly*	siempre	*always*

¡Los españoles hablan **demasiado** rápido!	*The Spanish speak too fast!*
Siempre miro antes de abrir la puerta.	*I always look before opening the door.*
Shakira baila **muy bien**.	*Shakira dances very well.*

Expressions of Time with *Hacer*

The verb **hacer** is used in a number of expressions of time in Spanish.

Time Expressions with *Hace* in the Present

When used with the present tense, **hace** expresses actions that in English are expressed with the present perfect tense (*has/have been*). It describes *for how long* something has been happening, up to the present. Either of the following constructions can be used:

hace + length of time + **que** + present tense of verb
present tense of verb + **desde hace** + length of time

Here are some examples:

Hace un año **que estoy** en Buenos Aires.	*I've been in Buenos Aires for a year.*
Estoy en Buenos Aires **desde hace** un año.	*I've been in Buenos Aires for a year.*
Hace tres meses **que** Sarah **estudia** español.	*Sarah has been studying Spanish for three months.*
Sarah **estudia** español **desde hace** tres meses.	*Sarah has been studying Spanish for three months.*

To make the negative, simply put **no** before the present tense of the verb.

Hace un año que **no voy** a la playa.   *I haven't gone to the beach for a year.*
Enrique **no ve** a su familia **desde**   *Enrique hasn't seen his family for ten*
    hace diez años.   *years.*

There are a variety of ways to ask the question *How long has . . . ?* using this time expression with **hacer**.

¿Hace cuánto tiempo que... ?   *How long has/have . . . ?*
¿Cuánto tiempo hace que... ?   *How long has/have . . . ?*
¿Hace cuántas horas que... ?   *How many hours has/have . . . ?*
¿Hace cuántos días/meses/años   *How many days/months/years has/*
    que... ?   *have . . . ?*
¿Hace mucho que... ?   *Has it been a long time that . . . ?*

Here are some example questions and answers.

¿Hace cuánto tiempo que   *How long has Veronica been sick?*
    Verónica está enferma?
—**Desde hace** dos semanas.   —*For two weeks.*
¿Cuántos años hace que Enrique   *How long has it been since Enrique*
    no come carne?   *stopped eating meat?*
—Creo que no come carne **desde**   —*I think he hasn't eaten meat for*
    hace unos cuatro años.   *about four years.*

Finally, you can use the question **¿Desde hace cuándo... ?** (*Since when . . .?*) to ask about the point in time (**cuando**) that a certain action began. The answer will be in the form of a day, date, or time.

¿Desde hace cuándo estás   —*Since when have you been waiting?*
    esperando?
—**Desde** las cuatro.   —*Since four o'clock.*

Oral Practice 2

 Track 57

Answer the first five questions about yourself. Then make questions that will elicit the answers in the following five statements.

1. ¿Hace cuánto tiempo que no ves a tus padres? *How long has it been since you last saw your parents?*

2. ¿Cuánto tiempo hace que vives en tu casa actual? *How long have you lived in your current house?*

3. ¿Hace cuánto tiempo que estudias español? *How long have you studied Spanish?*

4. ¿Desde hace cuándo usas este libro? *Since when have you been using this book?*

5. ¿Cuánto tiempo hace que te interesa la cultura latina o española? *How long have you been interested in Latino or Spanish culture?*

6. Hace tres días que no abro el libro de español. *I haven't opened a Spanish book for three days.*

7. Hace un semestre que estoy en la universidad. *I've been in college for one semester.*

8. No hablo español desde el lunes pasado. *I haven't spoken Spanish since last Monday.*

9. Hace un mes que viajo por Centroamérica. *I've been traveling in Central America for a month.*

10. Mi tía nada todas las mañanas desde hace treinta años. *My aunt has been swimming every morning for thirty years.*

Time Expressions with *Hacía* in the Imperfect

As you have learned, **hacía** is the imperfect of **hacer**. When used with the imperfect tense, **hacía** expresses actions that in English would be expressed with the past perfect tense (*had been*). It describes *for how long* something *had been happening*. The form is very similar to expressions with **hace** except that the imperfect replaces the present.

   hacía + length of time + **que** + imperfect tense of verb

Here are some examples:

Hacía un mes que Valeria **conocía** a Tito.   *Valeria had known Tito for a month.*

Hacía cinco años que no **iba** al dentista.   *I hadn't gone to the dentist for five years.*

NOTE *The verb tenses for each use of **hacer** match:*
- ***Hace** is used with the **present** to say **have been**.*
- ***Hacía** is used with the **imperfect** to say **had been**.*

Time Expressions with *Hace* in the Preterit

When used with the preterit, **hace** means *ago*. Again this usage differs from the English. Either of the following constructions can be used:

hace + length of time + **que** + preterit tense of verb
preterit tense of verb + **hace** + length of time

Here are some example sentences:

Hace media hora **que terminé** los deberes.	*I finished my homework half an hour ago.*
Silvio **fue** a Cuba **hace** una semana.	*Silvio went to Cuba a week ago.*

Questions to elicit this construction are the same as those that elicit **hace** with the present, but instead are followed by the preterit.

¿Hace cuánto que...?	*How long ago did . . . ?*
¿Hace cuánto tiempo que...?	*How long ago did . . . ?*
¿Cuánto tiempo hace que...?	*How long ago did . . . ?*
¿Hace mucho tiempo que...?	*Was it a long time ago that . . . ?*
¿Hace cuántos días/meses/ minutos que...?	*How many days/months/minutes ago did . . . ?*
¿Hace mucho que...?	*Was it a long time ago that . . . ?*

For example,

¿Hace mucho estrudiaste español?	*Was it a long time ago that you studied Spanish?*
—Sí, hace siglos.	*—Yes, it was ages ago.*

Hace and the preterit can also be used to answer questions with **¿Cuándo?**

¿Cuándo llegaste?	*When did you arrive?*
—**Hace una hora**.	*—An hour ago.*

Compare the difference between declarations containing **hace** with the present and **hace** with the preterit.

Hace quince años que **toco** el violonchelo.	*I've been playing the cello for fifteen years. (She still plays [continues to play] the cello.)*
Hace quince años que **toqué** el violonchelo.	*I played the cello fifteen years ago. (She probably hasn't touched the cello in fifteen years.)*

Ways to Talk About Lengths of Time

There are a number of ways to talk about how long ago something happened beyond mere **años, meses, días, horas,** and **minutos** (*years, months, days, hours, and minutes*). Many of these are common and/or colloquial and will help your Spanish sound more fluent and a little less "textbook."

un rato (un ratito, un ratico)	*a while (a little while)*
mucho rato	*a long while, a long time*
un tiempo (un tiempito)	*a while*
mucho tiempo	*a long time*
un par de horas/días/años	*a couple hours, days, years*
hace poco	*a little while ago*
hace mucho	*a long time ago*
hace siglos	*ages (Literally: centuries) ago*

Here are some example sentences using these time expressions.

¿Hace **mucho rato** que María se fue?	*Did María leave a long time ago?*
—No, se fue hace **un ratito.**	*—No, she left a little while ago.*
—Se fue hace **poco.**	*—She left a little while ago.*
Terminé hace **un par de horas.**	*I finished a couple of hours ago.*

Written Practice 6

Complete the following questions and responses with the appropriate words according to the timeline.

Imagina que es diciembre del año 2008. *Imagine that it is December 2008.*

1963: Carlos estudia en la Universidad de los Andes. *Carlos studies at the University of the Andes.*

1971: Carlos llega a los Estados Unidos. *Carlos arrives in the United States.*

1972: Carlos conoce a su futura esposa. *Carlos meets his future wife.*

1974: Carlos tiene a su primer hijo. *Carlos has his first child.*

1975: Carlos compra una casa. *Carlos buys a house.*

1982: Carlos viaja a Colombia con su familia. *Carlos travels to Colombia with his family.*

Mayo de este año: Carlos tiene a su primer nieto. *Carlos has his first grandchild.*

Septiembre de este año: Carlos se jubila de su trabajo. *Carlos retires from his job.*

1. ¿Hace cuánto tiempo que _____ Carlos en la Universidad de los Andes? *How long ago did Carlos study at the Universidad de los Andes?*

2. Carlos llegó a los Estados Unidos _____ treinta y siete años. *Carlos arrived in the U.S. thirty-seven years ago.*

3. Carlos _____ a su esposa _____ treinta y seis años. *Carlos met his wife thirty-six years ago.*

4. Carlos _____ a su primer hijo _____ treinta y cuatro años. *Carlos had his first child thirty-four years ago.*

5. ¿_____ cuántos años que compró Carlos una casa? *How many years ago did Carlos buy a house?*

6. ¿_____ viajó Carlos a Colombia con su familia? *How long ago did Carlos travel to Colombia with his family?*

7. Carlos _____ a su primer nieto hace
_____ meses. *Carlos had his first grandchild
seven months ago.*

8. ¿_____ cuántos meses que Carlos
_____ de su trabajo? *How many months ago did
Carlos retire from his job?*

Oral Practice 3

Answer the following questions about yourself using the preterit and **hace**.

1. ¿Hace cuántas horas te levantaste? *How many hours ago did you get up?*

2. ¿Hace cuánto tiempo que empezaste a estudiar español? *How long ago
did you start studying Spanish?*

3. ¿Hace cuánto tiempo que hablaste con un amigo o una amiga? *How long
ago did you speak to a friend of yours?*

4. ¿Cuánto tiempo hace que compraste los zapatos que llevas puesto? *How
long ago did you buy the shoes you're wearing?*

QUIZ

Circle the letter of the word or phrase that best completes each sentence.

1. Cuando vivías en Washington, ¿ _____ mucho a los museos?

   A. vas

   B. ibas

   C. irás

   D. irías

2. Eran las ocho de la mañana y _____ sol.

   A. hacía

   B. hace

   C. hará

   D. haría

3. Patricio y Ester _____ cuando vieron a Luis.

   A. estaba caminando

   B. estaban caminar

   C. estaban caminando

   D. estando caminan

4. ¿Tienes hambre, Eugenia?

   —No, gracias. _____ de comer.

   A. acabo

   B. vuelvo

   C. volveré

   D. iba

5. _____ hace sol en Santo Domingo, pero hoy está nublado.

   A. Normalmente

   B. Felizmente

   C. Afortunadamente

   D. Difícilmente

6. Tócalo _____. Es frágil.

   A. con cariño

   B. con cuidado

   C. sin querer

   D. sin parar

7. **¿Cuánto tiempo hace que Elvira no _____ carne?**

   —Desde hace cinco años.

   A. come

   B. comió

   C. ha comido

   D. comería

8. **¿Desde hace cuándo que tienes esas botas?**

   —Desde _____.

   A. dos años

   B. tres semanas

   C. el año pasado

   D. un mes

9. **_____ cinco años que salía con Luque.**

   A. Hace

   B. Hizo

   C. Hacía

   D. Hago

10. **¿Hace cuántos años que estudiaste en Antigua?**

    —_____ en Antigua hace tres años.

    A. Estudio

    B. Estudiaba

    C. Estudié

    D. Estoy estudiando

chapter **15**

Using the Preterit and the Imperfect

In this chapter you will learn when to use the preterit and when to use the imperfect. You will learn about a handful of verbs that change meaning when conjugated in the preterit and imperfect. Finally, you will learn the relative pronouns and adjectives.

CHAPTER OBJECTIVES

In this chapter you will learn

- When to use the preterit versus imperfect
- Verbs that change meaning in the preterit and imperfect
- Relative pronouns and adjectives

Preterit Versus Imperfect

You have learned the two most common ways of talking about the past in Spanish—the preterit and the imperfect. You know how to conjugate each tense. Now you will need to learn when to use each one. Most of the rules have already been set out. Here, we will simply make some comparisons between the two and give you more practice in using them appropriately.

Specific Versus General

In Chapter 13, you learned that the *preterit* is used to describe actions that were completed at a definite time in the past. The *preterit* tells specifically when something took place—it can be seen as an "x" on a timeline.

Salí anoche.	*I went out last night.*
¿**Terminaste** tu ensayo?	*Did you finish your essay?*
No me **llamaron** ayer.	*They didn't call me yesterday.*

The *preterit* is also used to refer to an action that was repeated multiple times in the past, or for a number of actions that happened successively and that are completed.

Te **llamé** tres veces anoche.	*I called you three times last night.*
Me desperté, **me levanté** y **me duché**.	*I woke up, got out of bed, and took a shower.*

In Chapter 14, you learned that the *imperfect* is used to talk about actions or to make descriptions that do not have a clear beginning or end. These actions often take place over a period of time, but the end point of the action or actions is not known or not designated.

Tenía dos perros.	*I had (used to have) two dogs.*
Marta **estaba** enferma.	*Marta was sick.*

This use of the *imperfect* includes actions that were repeated regularly or habitually in the past, often expressed as *would* or *used to* in English.

Cuando **era** joven, **iba** a la playa con mucha frecuencia.	*When I was young, I would go to the beach frequently.*
Caminábamos por el malecón todos los días.	*We used to walk along the boardwalk every day.*

You also learned that both tenses, preterit and imperfect, may be associated with certain expressions of time.

NOTE *These expressions are not exclusively used with the preterit or the imperfect, but are often associated with one or the other.*

The expressions in the first of the two following lists are used with the preterit to describe an exact point in time. The expressions in the second list are used with the imperfect to denote frequency or continuity—something that was customary or habitual in the past.

Time Expressions: Preterit Versus Imperfect

Time expressions commonly used with the *preterit*

anoche	*last night*
el año pasado	*last year*
anteayer	*the day before yesterday*
ayer	*yesterday*
hace un día/año/mes	*a day/year/month ago*
el otro día	*the other day*
el lunes/martes/miércoles, etc.	*on Monday/Tuesday/Wednesday, etc.*
el mes pasado	*last month*
la semana pasada	*last week*
a las dos/tres/cuatro etc.	*at two/three/four o'clock etc.*
hace tiempo/un rato	*a while ago*

Time expressions commonly used with the *imperfect*

cada día	*each/every day*
un día sí, un día no	*every other day*
todos los días	*every day*
frecuentemente	*frequently*
con frecuencia	*frequently*
generalmente	*generally*
todos los lunes/martes, etc.	*every Monday/Tuesday, etc.*
a menudo	*often*
cada semana	*each/every week*
todas las semanas	*every week*
siempre	*always*
a veces	*sometimes*
de vez en cuando	*from time to time*
varias veces	*several times*

Written Practice 1

Rewrite the following sentences changing the verb tense from preterit to imperfect, and the word **ayer** to **a menudo**.

1. El dueño del apartamento estuvo aquí ayer. *The apartment owner was here yesterday.*

   _____

2. Caminé al trabajo ayer. *I walked to work yesterday.*

   _____

3. Ellos me lo dijeron ayer. *They told me yesterday.*

   _____

4. Ví a Elmer ayer. *I saw Elmer yesterday.*

   _____

5. Gorky recibió los emails que mandé ayer. *Gorky received the emails I sent yesterday.*

   _____

6. Pedimos el pollo con arroz ayer. *Yesterday we ordered chicken with rice.*

   _____

Written Practice 2

Rewrite the following sentences changing the verb tense from imperfect to preterit, and the words **con mucha frecuencia** to **hace dos días**.

1. Iba a clase de yoga con mucha frecuencia. *I used to go to yoga class very frequently.*

   _____

2. ¿Tú hacías la comida con mucha frecuencia? *Did you often prepare the meals?*

   _____

3. Ellos veían a los vecinos con mucha frecuencia. *They often saw the neighbors.*

   _____

4. Nosotros la visitábamos con mucha frecuencia. *We would visit her often.*

_____

5. Comía carne con mucha frecuencia. *I often ate meat.*

_____

6. Sarita venía a mi casa con mucha frecuencia. *Sarita often came to my house.*

_____

Setting the Scene (Description) versus Interrupted Actions

You learned in Chapter 14 that the imperfect is used to make descriptions in the past. Often, if the two tenses appear in the same sentence, the preterit can be seen as "interrupting" the imperfect.

¿Qué **hacían** los alumnos cuando **entró** el profesor?
What were the students doing when the professor came in?

Hacía buen día cuando de repente **empezó** a llover.
The weather was nice when it suddenly started to rain.

The imperfect also "sets the stage" for actions in the preterit. In other words, it describes the environment or conditions prevailing when something happened or took place.

No **quería** ir al colegio, pero mis padres me **obligaron**.
I didn't want to go to school, but my parents made me.

Anoche **llovía** cuando **salimos**.
Last night it was raining when we went out.

Written Practice 3

Complete each sentence with one verb in the imperfect and one in the preterit.

1. Yo _____ (acostarse) cuando _____ (sonar) el teléfono. *I was getting into bed when the phone rang.*

2. Después de cenar, Marco _____ (encontrarse) mal y _____ (jurar) no comer más en el restaurante *La Gran Muralla*. *After dinner, Marco wasn't feeling well and swore he'd never eat again at La Gran Muralla restaurant.*

3. _____ (ser) las ocho cuando nosotros _____ (levantarse).
   It was eight A.M. when we got up.

4. María _____ (querer) hablar con Pedro, pero él _____ (irse).
   María wanted to chat with Pedro, but he left.

5. Tú no _____ (saber) el secreto, pero Marta te lo _____ (contar).
   You didn't know the secret, but Marta told it to you.

6. Luis _____ (dormir) cuando _____ (sonar) la alarma. *Luis was sleeping when the alarm rang.*

Uses of the Preterit and the Imperfect

You have seen three areas where the preterit and the imperfect differ from one another specifically. Let's review all of the uses of the preterit and the imperfect.

Uses of the Imperfect

Use the imperfect:

1. To describe past actions that have no clear beginning or end.
2. To describe continuing, customary, or habitual actions in the past.
3. For descriptions in the past, or to set the stage for another action.
4. To describe certain mental activities, such as thoughts and feelings.
5. To talk about time and age in the past.

Uses of the Preterit

Use the preterit:

1. To describe actions in the past that are completed.
2. To describe repeated events or a chain of events that took place during specific periods of time.
3. To signal the beginning or the end of an action.
4. To interrupt ongoing actions.

Written Practice 4

Complete the following passage by putting the verbs in parentheses in the imperfect or the preterit, according to the context. Use the following vocabulary to help you.

a su alrededor	*around her*	destacar	*to stand out*
cabello rizado	*curly hair*	una furgoneta	*van*
un cartel	*sign*	un huipil	*traditional Guatemalan blouse*
darse cuenta	*to realize*	un suspiro de alivio	*sigh of relief*

En 2005, cuando Sara _____ (1. terminar) la universidad, _____ (2. decidir) ir a Latinoamérica a estudiar español. _____ (3. escoger) Guatemala porque le _____ (4. interesar) la cultura Maya. _____ (5. querer) estudiar tres meses y después viajar por el país.Un día _____ (6. meterse) en Internet, _____ (7. elegir) una escuela de idiomas en Panajachel y _____ (8. matricularse) por email. _____ (9. decidir) vivir con una familia para tener una experiencia más auténtica. Ese mismo día _____ (10. comprar) el boleto de avión. _____ (11. ir) a viajar en junio y _____ (12. sentirse) un poco nerviosa porque sería su primer viaje a Centroamérica y no _____ (13. hablar) ni una palabra de español. Cuando _____ (14. llegar) el cinco de junio en el aeropuerto La Aurora de Guatemala _____ (15. darse) cuenta de que _____ (16. estar) en un país totalmente distinto al suyo. Mucha gente _____ (17. hablar) español, pero muchas personas _____ (18. hablar) en idiomas que ella no _____ (19. entender). Las mujeres _____ (20. llevar) trajes típicos con huipiles de muchos colores. _____ (21. haber) muchos turistas, pero Sara _____ (22. destacar) mucho con su cabello rizado y su estatura de 1,80. Por eso _____ (23. pensar) que sería fácil para la dueña de la escuela de idiomas encontrarla. Pero cuando _____ (24. mirar) a su alrededor, no _____ (25. ver) a nadie. Sara _____ (26. empezar) a sentirse un poco perdida. De repente _____ (27. aparecer) una mujer guatemalteca con un cartel que _____ (28. decir) «Escuela de Idiomas Tz'utujil» y Sara _____ (29. dar) un suspiro de alivio._____ (30. irse) con la mujer que_____ (31. llamarse) Andrea en una furgoneta verde. Así _____ (32. empezar) una aventura que Sara nunca olvidaría.

Verbs That Change Meaning in the Preterit and the Imperfect

Several verbs change meaning depending on whether they are used in the preterit or imperfect.

Conocer

In the preterit, **conocer** means *to meet*. In the imperfect it means *to know* or *to be familiar with*.

Conocí a Amparo hace siete años.	*I met Amparo seven years ago.*
No **conocía** bien a Juan en aquel entonces.	*I didn't know Juan very well back then.*

Saber

In the preterit, **saber** means *to find out* or *to learn*. In the imperfect it means *to know*.

¿**Sabías** que José Manuel está casado?	*Did you know that José Manuel is married?*
—Sí, lo **supe** ayer.	*—Yes, I found out yesterday.*

Querer

In the preterit affirmative, **querer** means *to want to do something and actually accomplishing it*. In the imperfect affirmative **querer** means *to want to do something* but does not necessary imply that the action was carried out.

Marco **quiso** salir.	*Marco wanted to go out (and he did).*
Marco **quería** salir, pero no tenía dinero para el autobús.	*Marco wanted to go out, but he didn't have money for the bus.*

In the negative preterit, **no querer** means *to refuse*. In the imperfect, **no querer** means *to not want to*.

No quise ir a clase.	*I refused to go to class (so I didn't).*
No quería ir a clase.	*I didn't want to go to class (but I did anyway).*

Poder

In the preterit, **poder** means *to be able to do something and succeeding in doing it*. In the imperfect, **poder** means *to be able to do something*, but the action was not necessarily carried out.

Por lo menos **pude** ir a clase ayer.   *At least I was able to go to class yesterday.*

Podía ir a clase ayer, pero no fui.   *I could go (could have gone) to class yesterday, but I didn't.*

In the negative preterit, **no poder** means *to be unable to do something despite trying*. The implication is that the person tried, but was unable.

El prisionero no **pudo** escapar   *The prisoner couldn't escape from de la cárcel.   prison (but he tried).*

Tener que

In the preterit, **tener que** means *to have to do something and doing it*. In the imperfect, **tener que** means *to have to (to be obliged to) do something*, but the action was not necessarily carried out.

Tuve que ir al médico.   *I had to go to the doctor's (and I went).*
Tenía que ir al médico, pero   *I had to (needed to) go to the doctor's, no había citas.   but there weren't any appointments.*

Written Practice 5

 Track 58

Listen to each situation and then circle the letter of the word or phrase that best answers the question.

1. **Silvia:**   Oye, Roberto, María Elena me dice que te conoció ayer.
   Roberto: Sí, nos conocimos en el elevador. Es muy simpática.
   Q: Roberto and María Elena met for the first time yesterday.

   (a) True

   (b) False

   (c) Not enough information

2. **Silvia:**   Oye, Roberto, María Elena me dice que ustedes se conocían bien en la universidad. ¿Es verdad?

Roberto: Fue hace tiempo, pero sí nos conocíamos muy bien.

Q: Roberto and María Elena met in college.

(a) True

(b) False

(c) Not enough information

3. **Rosa:** Mirta, ¿sabías que el director renunció a su puesto?

Mirta: Sí, lo supe hace unos minutos.

Q: Mirta has known for quite some time that the director resigned.

(a) True

(b) False

(c) Not enough information

4. **Elsa:**   ¿Qué tal estuvo el teatro anoche?

Ernesto: Carmen no quería ir...

Q: Ernesto and Carmen didn't go to the theater.

(a) True

(b) False

(c) Not enough information

5. **David:** Dicen que es imposible huir de la prisión Supermax.

Cristal: Es verdad. No pudo huir nadie.

Q: Prisoners have tried to escape from the Supermax.

(a) True

(b) False

(c) Note enough information.

Relative Pronouns and Adjectives

You have already learned that pronouns replace antecedent nouns. A relative pronoun is related to a noun that has already been introduced (hence its name). In English, the relative pronouns are *that*, *which*, *who*, *whose*, and *whom*.

In order of simplicity and frequency of use, the Spanish *relative pronouns* are:

que	*that*, *which*, *who*, or *whom*
quien, quienes	*who* or *whom*
el que, la que, los que, las que	*the one who* or *the ones who* or *which*

You have probably already used and seen relative pronouns a hundred times by now. **Que** is the most common one. Look at the story in Written Practice 5. Can you find any examples of the word **que**? Let's look at one of them.

Apareció una mujer con un cartel **que** decía «Escuela de Idiomas Tz'utujil».	*A woman appeared with a sign **that** said "Tz'utujil Language School."*

Relative pronouns introduce a clause that modifies a preceding noun. Look at the example sentence below. The clause **que (yo) toco** (relative pronoun + subject + verb) modifies the noun subject of the sentence, **el instrumento.** The rest of the sentence (**es el bajo**), contains the verb and the object of the main clause.

El instrumento **que toco** es el bajo.	*The instrument (**that**) I play is the bass.*

It may be easier to think of the relative pronoun as joining two phrases that talk about a shared noun. In the following example, the shared noun is **aventura** (*adventure*). The clause **que nunca olvidaría** (*that she would never forget*) describes the **aventura**: She would never forget it.

Sara tuvo una aventura.	*Sara had an adventure.*
Nunca olvidaría la aventura.	*She would never forget the adventure.*
Sara tuvo una aventura **que** nunca olvidaría.	*Sara had an adventure (that) she would never forget.*

NOTE *In English, the relative pronoun can often be omitted. In Spanish, it must be included in the sentence.*

Sara tuvo una aventura **que** nunca olvidaría.	*Sara had an adventure (that) she would never forget.*
El instrumento **que** toco es el bajo.	*The instrument (that) I play is the bass.*

The Relative Pronoun *Que*

As you have seen, the most common relative pronoun is **que**. **Que** can refer to either people or things, and can be translated into English as *that, which, who,* or *whom*.

La mujer **que** grita está enojada.	*The woman **who** is yelling is angry.*
La actriz **que** conocí es famosa.	*The actress **whom** I met is famous.*

La leche **que** compraste está mala. *The milk **that** you bought is spoiled.*

La casa, **que** se vende, es muy *The house, **which** is for sale, is very*
cara. *expensive.*

Que is invariable, whether the noun it refers to is singular or plural, masculine or feminine. It usually follows the noun it refers to. It can also come after a preposition, but only when referring to a thing, as in the examples below. Remember that **de** + **el** = **del** and **a** + **el** = **al**.

El apartamento **que** vi era *The apartment that I saw was too*
demasiado pequeño. *small.*

El apartamento **del que** hablas *The apartment that you're speaking*
es de mi hijo. *about is my son's.*

Éste es el bar **al que** vamos todos *This is the bar that we go to every*
los viernes. *Friday.*

Written Practice 6

Combine the following sentences with **que** to make a single sentence. Follow the example.

Leo la novela. La novela es de Vargas Llosa. → *La novela que leo es de Vargas Llosa.*

1. Veo el huipil. Es de Guatemala. *I see the huipil. It is from Guatemala.*

_____

2. Hablo de la película. La película es de Luis Buñuel. *I talk about the film. The film is by Luis Buñuel.*

_____

3. Me gusta el chavo. Es mexicano. *I like the guy. He is Mexican.*

_____

4. El bebé llora. El bebé está cansado. *The baby is crying. The baby is tired.*

_____

5. Tú tienes el anillo. Es de plata peruana. *You have the ring. It's made of Peruvian silver.*

_____

6. El hombre edita el libro. El hombre es super inteligente. *The man is editing the book. The man is extremely intelligent.*

_____

7. Pienso en el restaurante. El restaurante es muy caro. *I'm thinking about the restaurant. The restaurant is very expensive.*

_____

8. Los volcanes están alrededor del lago Atitlán. Los volcanes no son activos. *The volcanos are around Lake Atitlán. The volcanos are not active.*

_____

The Relative Pronoun *Quien*

Whereas **que** can refer to people or things, **quien** (*who* or *whom*) refers only to people. The plural form of **quien** is **quienes**.

El chico **que** habla es mi hermano.	The boy **who** is talking is my brother.
Las personas con **quienes** trabajo son muy inteligentes.	The people with **whom** I work are very smart.

Que usually follows the noun it refers to; **quien** often appears after a preposition. After a preposition, **quien** *must* be used when talking about a person. (**Que** is only used after a preposition to describe a thing.)

El tipo **con quien** fui al cine es mi primo.	The guy with whom I went to the movies with is my cousin.
Mi amiga es la persona **en quien** estoy pensando.	My friend is the person who(m) I'm thinking about.

but . . .

El grupo **del que** hablo toca cumbia.	The group I'm talking about plays cumbia.

When the pronoun refers to a person who functions as the *direct object* of the verb in the relative clause, either **que** or **quien** can be used. In this case, the personal **a** is used with **quien**, but not with **que**.

La mujer **a quien** vi anoche es mi ex novia.	The woman with whom I saw last night is my ex-girlfriend.
La mujer **que** vi anoche es mi ex novia.	The woman that I saw last night is my ex-girlfriend.

How do you know when the relative pronoun is in the direct object position or in the subject position? Compare the following phrases:

Subject Position
El chico **que** habla... = *The boy who speaks* . . .

In this case, the entire phrase is the subject of the sentence. **El chico** agrees with **habla** and **quien** ties them together. The **a personal** is not used.

Direct Object Position
El chico **a quien** (yo) veo... = *The boy who(m) I see* . . .

Here, if you reorganize the phrase, you'll see that **chico** is the *direct object* of the verb (**veo**) in the relative clause: **yo veo al chico**. **Quien** refers to the boy, and therefore to the direct object. Notice that it takes the **a personal**.

In addition, the relative pronoun is usually a direct object when you can omit it in the English translation. Here are some more examples:

Direct object	Subject
El amigo a quien llamo...	El médico, quien trabaja en el hospital, ...
The friend (who[m]) I'm calling . . .	*The doctor, who works in the hospital,* . . .
El amigo al que llamo...	El señor que está sentado allí...
The friend that I'm calling . . .	*The gentleman who is sitting over there* . . .
Los amigos a los que espero...	
The friends (that) I'm waiting for . . .	
Los amigos a quienes espero...	
The friends (whom) I'm waiting for . . .	

Written Practice 7

Complete the following sentences with **que**, **quien**, or **quienes**.

1. No conozco a la persona de _____ hablas.

2. El béisbol es algo en _____ no tengo interés.

3. Los niños para _____ compramos los regalos están enfermos.

4. El hombre a _____ conociste ayer es médico.

5. Esa señora _____ ves allí es senadora.

6. El restaurante del _____ hablas es de cuatro estrellas.

7. El profesor con _____ hablamos es muy estricto.

8. Las señoras _____ ves en el mercado empiezan a trabajar a las cuatro de la mañana.

The Relative Pronoun *El Que*

El que has four forms: **el que**, **la que**, **los que**, **las que**. These can be used in the subject or object position and can refer to people or things. They agree in number and gender with the nouns they refer to. In English they are translated as *the one who*, or *the ones who*. Take a look at these examples. Notice how **el que** can replace the noun it refers to.

El profesor que nos enseña es muy estricto.	*The professor who teaches us is very strict.*
El que nos enseña es muy estricto.	*The one who teaches us is very strict.*

They can also be used to emphasize the noun.

Mi hermana llega.	*My sister is arriving.*
La que llega es mi hermana.	*The one who is arriving is my sister.*

El que, **la que**, **los que**, and **las que** can be used to replace **que** and **quien** when you want to be very precise.

Las amigas **que** conocí en la universidad están de visita.	*My friends who(m) I met at the university are visiting.*
Mis amigas, **las que** conocí en la universidad, están de visita.	*My friends, the ones I met in college, are visiting.*

The pronouns **el cual**, **la cual**, **los cuales**, and **las cuales** can replace **el que**, **la que**, **los que**, and **las que** but are not common in colloquial usage and sound very formal.

When used after prepositions, **el que**, **la que**, **los que**, and **las que** mean *which*. You already learned that **que** and **quien** can come after short prepositions, such as **de**, **con**, or **en**. The longer forms of **el que**, **la que**, **los que**, and **las que** are usually used after longer prepositions, such as **alrededor de** (*around*), **atrás de** (*behind*), **encima de** (*above*), **durante** (*during*), etc. They are also often used after **por**, **sin**, and **para**, which otherwise might cause confusion when used with **que**.

Look at these examples. Both the noun and its relative pronoun have been bolded for you.

La clase durante **la que** dormí fue muy aburrida.	*The class during which I slept was very boring.*
El parque alrededor **del que** corremos es bastante grande.	*The park around which we jog is quite large.*

In these situations, **el cual**, **la cual**, **los cuales**, and **las cuales** may be used instead, since the style is rather complex and formal. Look at these examples. Both the noun and its relative pronoun have been bolded for you.

Los días durante **los cuales** esperamos los resultados de las pruebas parecían eternos.	*The days during which we waited for the test results seemed endless.*
Ésas son **las razones** por **las cuales** no puedo acudir a clase.	*These are the reasons why (for which) I can't go to class.*

The Relative Pronouns *Lo que* and *Lo cual*

Lo que and **lo cual** are neuter pronouns, which means they are used to refer to nouns whose genders we don't know. The phrase **lo que** in particular is very useful in Spanish.

No entiendo **lo que** me estás diciendo.	*I don't understand **what** you're telling me.*
Lo que necesitas es un buen masaje.	***What** you need is a good massage.*

Lo que and **lo cual** can also refer to general actions, which do not have genders.

Fuimos a la playa sin él, **lo cual** lo enojó mucho.	*We went to the beach without him, which made him really angry.*
Ayer hice dos horas de ejercicio, **lo que** me dejó cansadísima.	*Yesterday I did two hours of exercise, which left me very tired.*

The difference between **lo que** and **lo cual** is that **lo cual** can only refer to something specific (to refer to something that is known or has been mentioned). **Lo que** can be used like **lo cual** or, additionally, to refer to something that hasn't been mentioned yet or which remains unspecified.

Lo que me dijiste ayer fue increíble.	*What you told me yesterday was unbelievable. (***Lo cual*** could not be used here, since the specific item, event, or circumstance has not yet been mentioned.)*
Ayer me dijiste que ganaste un millón de dólares, **lo que/ lo cual** es increíble.	*Yesterday you told me you won a million dollars, which is incredible. (Here* **lo cual** *can also be used, since the topic has already been introduced.)*

Written Practice 8

Circle the letter of the pronoun that best completes each sentence. (Choose all that apply.)

1. _____ hablaba contigo es el presidente del banco.

  (a) El que

  (b) La que

  (c) Lo que

2. _____ te estoy diciendo es que te quiero mucho.

  (a) El que

  (b) Lo que

  (c) Lo cual

3. Hay una mesa encima de _____ están las llaves.

  (a) la cual

  (b) la que

  (c) lo cual

4. _____ salieron en el periódico son futbolistas.

  (a) El que

  (b) Los que

  (c) El cual

5. El autobús en _____ llegamos fue incómodo.

   (a) el cual

   (b) el que

   (c) que

6. Ayer me subieron el sueldo, _____ me dejó super feliz.

   (a) lo que

   (b) lo cual

   (c) el cual

The Relative Adjective *Cuyo*

The relative adjective **cuyo** means *whose* in English, and has four forms that agree with the noun it modifies: **cuyo, cuya, cuyos, cuyas**.

La chica, **cuyo equipaje** perdió la aerolínea, se quedó sin ropa.	*The girl, whose luggage the airline lost, ended up without any clothes.* (Here, **cuyo** agrees with **equipaje**.)
El diputado, **cuya hija** robó dinero, está metido en un escándalo.	*The senator, whose daughter stole money, is in the middle of a scandal.* (Here, **cuya** agrees with **hija**.)

Written Practice 9

Complete the sentences with the proper form of **cuyo**.

1. La pintora _____ cuadro ganó el premio es amiga mía. *The painter whose painting won the prize is a friend of mine.*

2. El compositor _____ música se toca en el Teatro Nacional tiene ochenta años. *The composer whose music is played in the National Theater is eighty years old.*

3. Sandra, _____ padres vienen de El Salvador, vive en Chicago. *Sandra, whose parents come from El Salvador, lives in Chicago.*

4. Mi cuñado, _____ familia es muy rica, tiene casas en Europa y el Caribe. *My brother-in-law, whose family is very rich, has houses in Europe and the Caribbean.*

5. Mi amiga, _____ postales llegaron ayer, está en Mozambique. *My friend, whose postcards arrived yesterday, is in Mozambique.*

6. Ernesto es un economista _____ trabajo es mundialmente conocido. *Ernesto is an economist whose work is world-renowned.*

QUIZ

Circle the letter of the word or phrase that best completes each sentence.

1. Yo _____ tres veces el año pasado.
   A. viajé
   B. viajaba
   C. viajará
   D. viajaría

2. Las niñas _____ francés todos los lunes.
   A. estudiaba
   B. estudiaban
   C. estudió
   D. estudiaron

3. Cuando Maya _____ joven, pasaba mucho tiempo con su abuela.
   A. fue
   B. estuvo
   C. estaba
   D. era

4. Anoche Mercedes no _____ a la fiesta porque no _____ bien.
   A. fue; se sintió
   B. iba; se sintió
   C. fue; se sentía
   D. iba; se sentía

5. Nosotros _____ cuando _____ el teléfono.
   A. dormíamos; sonaba
   B. dormíamos; sonó
   C. dormimos; sonaba
   D. dormimos; sonó

6. Yo _____ ir a la universidad porque mis padres me ayudaron a pagarla.

   A. podía

   B. no podía

   C. pude

   D. no pude

7. Frank no conoció a Julia hoy. Ya _____ del trabajo.

   A. se conoció

   B. se conocieron

   C. se conocía

   D. se conocían

8. La película _____ vimos era fenomenal.

   A. que

   B. quien

   C. la cual

   D. A, B, o C

9. La compañía en _____ trabajo tiene muy buenos beneficios.

   A. que

   B. la que

   C. la cual

   D. A, B, o C

10. Santiago Calatrava es un arquitecto _____ obras están por todo el mundo.

    A. cuyo

    B. cuyos

    C. cuya

    D. cuyas

PART THREE TEST

Circle the letter of the word or phrase that best completes each sentence.

1. **¿Quieres ir a la playa? _____ con nosotros.**
   A. Ven
   B. Viene
   C. Venga
   D. Vengas

2. **¿Usted quiere ir al parque? _____ a la derecha.**
   A. Dobla
   B. Doble
   C. Doblas
   D. Dobles

3. **Es temprano. No _____ todavía.**
   A. levántate
   B. levantes te
   C. te levantas
   D. te levantes

4. **¿Viste a Rafael?**
   —Sí, _____ vi ayer.
   A. le
   B. lo
   C. la
   D. los

5. **Su equipaje es muy pesado. _____ aquí.**
   A. Lo mete
   B. Métfrom
   C. Le meta
   D. Métalo

6. **Irene y Ester _____ en dos semanas.**
   A. salen
   B. saldrán
   C. salgan
   D. salieron

7. Mañana nosotros _____ clase a las doce en vez de la una.

    A. tengamos

    B. tendremos

    C. tuviéramos

    D. teníamos

8. Yo _____ daré los aretes a Juanita.

    A. lo

    B. la

    C. le

    D. los

9. ¿Prefieres _____ directamente a ellas?

    A. decirlas

    B. decirles

    C. les decir

    D. las decir

10. Odio los animales. _____ un gato.

    A. Jamás adoptaría

    B. Creo que adoptaría

    C. Quizás adoptaría

    D. La verdad es que sí adoptaría

11. Selena _____ en Santa Cruz de 1999 a 2000.

    A. vive

    B. vivirá

    C. vivió

    D. viva

12. Claudia ya sabe que vas a la fiesta. Yo _____ dije ayer.

    A. se lo

    B. le lo

    C. la lo

    D. se la

13. Mi familia _____ de vacaciones a Patagonia el año pasado.

    A. fui

    B. fue

    C. era

    D. va

14. **Entre los carros rojos y los carros negros, me gustan más _____.**

    A. el negro

    B. la negra

    C. los negros

    D. las negras

15. **Anoche _____ a estudiar a las 7:00 y no _____ hasta las 11:00.**

    A. empezamos; terminemos

    B. empecemos; terminemos

    C. empezamos; terminamos

    D. empecemos; terminamos

16. **Cuando vivíamos en Honduras, _____ mucho a la playa.**

    A. éramos

    B. íbamos

    C. vamos

    D. somos

17. **Jorge _____ veinte años cuando salió del país por primera vez.**

    A. tenía

    B. tenías

    C. tenían

    D. teníamos

18. **¿Acabas de llegar?**

    —Sí, llegué hace _____.

    A. mucho tiempo

    B. un siglo

    C. un ratito

    D. un par de horas

19. **_____ una semana que Valerie se casó con Javi.**

    A. Hacía

    B. Hace

    C. Hay

    D. Desde

20. **Hable _____ por favor, que no le entiendo.**
    A. rápido
    B. despacio
    C. bastante
    D. demasiado

21. **Cuando vivía con mi abuela, siempre _____ a cartas.**
    A. jugamos
    B. jugábamos
    C. juguemos
    D. jugaron

22. **Elvira _____ cuando _____ el ladrón.**
    A. durmió; entró
    B. durmió; entraba
    C. dormía; entró
    D. dormía; entraba

23. **¿A ti _____ tanto cocinar cuando estabas soltero?**
    A. te gustó
    B. te gustaba
    C. te gustabas
    D. te gustaste

24. **Mateo _____ salir, pero tenía demasiados deberes.**
    A. quiso
    B. quería
    C. no quiso
    D. no quería

25. **El chico _____ vimos anoche es mi primo.**
    A. a que
    B. quien
    C. a quien
    D. A, B, o C

Part Four

Mastering the Subjunctive

chapter 16

Introduction to the Subjunctive

In this chapter you will learn the theory behind the subjunctive mood. You will learn how to conjugate the present subjunctive of regular, stem-changing, and irregular verbs as well as when to use the subjunctive to express doubt or uncertainty.

CHAPTER OBJECTIVES

In this chapter you will learn

- About the subjunctive mood
- Present subjunctive of regular verbs
- Present subjunctive of stem-changing verbs
- Present subjunctive of irregular verbs
- How to use the subjunctive to express doubt and uncertainty

The Subjunctive

The verb tenses you have learned so far are all in the indicative mood. The indicative mood is used to present objective facts: things that happened, are happening, or will happen. In this chapter we introduce the subjunctive mood.

Students of Spanish often roll their eyes at the mention of the subjunctive. Not only does it mean learning yet another set of endings and irregular verb conjugations; the subjunctive also has no ready equivalent in English. Students can't depend on translation to understand the subjunctive (although ideally you should be depending less and less on translation in general!).

The subjunctive needn't be scary, however. First of all, we actually *do* have the subjunctive in English. We just don't use it very often, and we rarely refer to it as such. Look at these examples:

We ask that **you be** quiet during   (instead of *you are*)
   the show.
If **I were** richer, I'd buy a house.   (instead of *I was*)

Second, once you learn it, you might find yourself pleased to have the subjunctive at hand. Musicians will find it pleasant to say and beautiful to hear. Poets will understand that it can be used to express a range of subtlety that we don't have in English. For grammarians, it represents a whole new frontier of language to be mastered.

As we have said, the indicative (present, future, preterit, imperfect) is used to present *objective* facts: things that are happening, will happen, or already happened. The subjunctive is used to present the *subjective*: doubt, desire, uncertainty, hope, emotion, opinions, and future possibility (versus future reality). Here are some examples:

Subjunctive/Subjective	Indicative/Objective
No creo que lo **sepa**.	¡Claro que **sabe**!
I don't think he knows it.	*Of course he knows!*
Espero que **vaya** Ana al evento.	Ana **fue** al evento.
I hope Ana goes to the event.	*Ana went to the event.*
Es importante que **seas** honesto.	Siempre **soy** honesto.
It's important that you be honest.	*I'm always honest.*

First, you will learn the subjunctive conjugations of regular, stem-changing, and irregular verbs. This should feel familiar, as the conjugations are almost identical to some of the commands (imperatives) you learned in Chapter 11. We will then introduce two general categories of situations where the subjunctive is used: (1) situations expressing *doubt* and *uncertainty*, and (2) situations expressing *wishes* and *desires*. Finally, you will learn the *impersonal expressions* that are commonly followed by the subjunctive and a special use of the subjunctive to refer to things that may or may not exist.

Present Subjunctive of Regular Verbs

You will recall that the formal commands you learned in Chapter 11 are conjugated like the subjunctive. Remember that it is a game of "switcharoo." Verbs ending in **-ar** that usually end in **-a** or **-an** in the indicative will end in **-e** and **-en** in the subjunctive. Verbs ending in **-er** or **-ir** that usually end in **-e** or **-en** in the indicative will end in **-a** and **-an** in the subjunctive. Just remember:

ar→e and **er/ir→a**

For almost all verbs, with the exception of a few irregulars, first you take the **yo** form of the verb and drop the **-o**, leaving the root of the subjunctive. For regular verbs, this root is the verb stem (i.e., **hablar → habl-**). After you drop the **-o**, add the regular present subjunctive endings. Don't forget that in the subjunctive the vowel **e** is used in the ending for **-ar** verbs and **a** for **-er** and **-ir** verbs. For **-ar** verbs add the endings **-e, -es, -e, -emos, -éis, -en**. For **-er** and **-ir** verbs add **-a, -as, -a, -amos, -áis, -an**.

Regular Verbs

	hablar	comer	vivir
Yo form:	hablo	como	vivo
Root:	habl-	com-	viv-
yo	hable	coma	viva
tú	hables	comas	vivas
él/ella/usted	hable	coma	viva
nosotros	hablemos	comamos	vivamos
vosotros	habléis	comáis	viváis
ellos/ellas/ustedes	hablen	coman	vivan

Written Practice 1

Conjugate the verb in parentheses in the present subjunctive.

1. yo _____ (beber)

2. tú _____ (viajar)

3. nosotros _____ (abrir)

4. ella _____ (mandar)

5. ellos _____ (correr)

6. usted _____ (escribir)

7. yo _____ (hablar)

8. tú _____ (sonreír)

Present Subjunctive of Stem-Changing Verbs

For stem-changing verbs the same ending pattern holds. There are some variations in the stem, however.

For stem-changing verbs ending in **-ar** and **-er**, use the root from the present indicative **yo** form *except* for the **nosotros** and **vosotros** forms, which retain the stem of the infinitive.

Stem-Changing: -ar

	pensar	**contar**
Yo form:	pienso	cuento
Root:	piens-/pens-	cuent-/cont-
yo	piense	cuente
tú	pienses	cuentes
el/ella/usted	piense	cuente
nosotros	pensemos	contemos
vosotros	penséis	contéis
ellos/ellas/ustedes	piensen	cuenten

Stem-Changing: -er

	perder	**volver**
Yo form:	pierdo	vuelvo
Root:	pierd-/perd-	vuelv-/volv-
yo	pierda	vuelva
tú	pierdas	vuelvas
él/ella/usted	pierda	vuelva
nosotros	perdamos	volvamos
vosotros	perdáis	volváis
ellos/ellas/ustedes	pierdan	vuelvan

For e→ie and o→ue stem-changing verbs ending in **-ir**, use the root from the **yo** form of the present indicative *except* for the **nosotros** and **vosotros** forms, which use **i** in the root for e→ie verbs and **u** for o→ue verbs. You saw this pattern in the first-person plural commands presented in Chapter 11 and in the present participle.

Stem-Changing: -ir (e→ie and o→ue)

	mentir	dormir
Yo form:	miento	duermo
Root:	mient-/mint-	duerm-/durm-
yo	mienta	duerma
tú	mientas	duermas
él/ella/usted	mienta	duerma
nosotros	mintamos	durmamos
vosotros	mintáis	durmáis
ellos/ellas/ustedes	mientan	duerman

For **e→i** stem-changing verbs ending in **-ir** use the root from the **yo** form of the present indicative and keep the same root throughout all conjugated forms. You might remember this pattern from the first-person plural commands presented in Chapter 11 and from the present participle.

Stem-Changing: -ir (e→i)

	pedir	seguir
Yo form:	pido	sigo
Root:	pid-	sig-
yo	pida	siga
tú	pidas	sigas
él/ella/usted	pida	siga
nosotros	pidamos	sigamos
vosotros	pidáis	sigáis
ellos/ellas/ustedes	pidan	sigan

Written Practice 2

Conjugate the verb in parentheses in the present subjunctive.

1. nosotros _____ (medir [i])

2. tú _____ (contar [ue])

3. él _____ (pedir [i])

4. nosotras _____ (perder [ie])

5. ustedes _____ (mostrar [ue])

6. yo _____ (volver [ue])

7. ellas _____ (rendir [i])

8. nosotros _____ (morir [ue])

Present Subjunctive of Irregular Verbs

Most irregular verbs and verbs with spelling changes in the **yo** form follow the rules for regular verbs in the present subjunctive. Take the **yo** form of the present indicative, drop the **-o,** and add the present subjunctive endings.

	conocer	**salir**	**venir**
yo	conozca	salga	venga
tú	conozcas	salgas	vengas
él/ella/usted	conozca	salga	venga
nosotros	conozcamos	salgamos	vengamos
vosotros	conozcáis	salgáis	vengáis
ellos/ellas/ustedes	conozcan	salgan	vengan

Here are more examples in the **yo** form. Remember: The present subjunctive endings are **-e, -es, -e, -emos, -éis, -en** for **-ar** verbs and **-a, -as, -a, -amos, -áis, -an** for **-er** and **-ir** verbs.

Infinitive	**Present Indicative**	**Present Subjunctive**
decir	digo	diga
hacer	hago	haga
oír	oigo	oiga
poner	pongo	ponga
tener	tengo	tenga
traer	traigo	traiga
valer	valgo	valga
conducir	conduzco	conduzca
traducir	traduzco	traduzca
construir	construyo	construya
caber	quepo	quepa

Some irregular verbs are entirely irregular in the subjunctive. Some of these may be familiar to you from your study of the command (imperative) forms of irregular verbs.

	ser	**estar**	**ir**	**dar**	**saber**
yo	sea	esté	vaya	dé	sepa
tú	seas	estés	vayas	des	sepas
él/ella/usted	sea	esté	vaya	dé	sepa
nosotros	seamos	estemos	vayamos	demos	sepamos
vosotros	seáis	estéis	vayáis	deis	sepáis
ellos/ellas/ustedes	sean	estén	vayan	den	sepan

Spelling Changes in the Present Subjunctive

Remember the pronunciation and spelling rules that you learned in Chapter 1? You may recall that the **g** and **j** in **ga** (*ga*) and **ja** (*hha*) sound different, but the **g** and **j** in **ge** (*hhe*) and **ja** (*hha*) sound the same. This is because **g** becomes a soft **g** (*hh*) when followed by the vowels **i** and **e**. The same is true for **c** preceding a vowel. The sound of **c** is hard, **ca** (*k*), when followed by **a** and **o**, but soft or sibilant, **ci**, **ce** (*s*), when followed by **i** or **e**.

When conjugating verbs, it's important to maintain the sounds you hear in the infinitive. Because the subjunctive uses the "switcharoo," changing a's to e's, the sounds of some consonants might inadvertently change unless you follow some important spelling rules.

For verbs ending in **-zar**, the **-z-** (*s*) changes to **-c-** in the subjunctive, because it precedes **e** in these forms. This may seem counterintuitive to you, but keep in mind that in Spain, where Spanish originated, **za**, **zo**, **zu**, and **ce** all have the same initial sound (*th*). In New World Spanish, the Latin American soft (*s*) sound must also be maintained.

Infinitive	Subjunctive
empezar (ie)	empiece
rechazar	rechace
utilizar	utilice

For verbs ending in **-ger** and **-gir** the **-g-** changes to **-j-** in the subjunctive, because it precedes **-a**, and we want to maintain the soft sound (*hh*).

Infinitive	Subjunctive
elegir	elija
corregir	corrija
escoger	escoja
recoger	recoja

For verbs ending in **-car**, the **c** changes to **-qu-** (*k*) in the subjunctive, to maintain the hard (*k*) sound.

Infinitive	Subjunctive
buscar	busque
marcar	marque
tocar	toque

For verbs ending in **-gar**, the **-g-** changes to **-gu-** in the subjunctive, again to maintain the hard (*g*) sound.

Infinitive	Subjunctive
pagar	pa**gue**
llegar	lle**gue**
ligar	li**gue**

Written Practice 3

Conjugate the verb in parentheses in the present subjunctive.

1. tú _____ (querer [ie])
2. usted _____ (empezar [ie])
3. nosotros _____ (ser)
4. ella _____ (venir)
5. él _____ (valer)

6. tú _____ (poner)
7. yo _____ (salir)
8. nosotros _____ (tragar)
9. ustedes _____ (ir)
10. ellos _____ (estar)

Using the Subjunctive to Express Doubt and Uncertainty

The first thing you'll probably notice about the subjunctive is that it is often preceded by the word **que**. Although the subjunctive does not always follow the word **que** (for instance, when **que** is a relative pronoun), when **que** is used as a conjunction, that's a sign that the subjunctive may follow.

The subjunctive expresses *doubt* or *uncertainty*. Compare the following use of the subjunctive and the indicative:

Indicative: when you're sure	Subjunctive: when you're not sure
Sandra no **viene** a casa.	**No creo que** Sandra **venga** a casa.
Sandra is not coming over.	*I don't think Sandra is coming over.*
No **voy a aprobar** el examen.	**Dudo que apruebe** el examen.
I'm not going to pass the exam.	*I doubt I'll pass the exam.*
Adán no **sabe** español.	**Es dudoso que** Adán **sepa** español.
Adán doesn't know Spanish.	*It's doubtful Adán knows Spanish.*

Verbs Signaling Doubt or Uncertainty

There are certain verbs that signal the use of the subjunctive to express doubt or uncertainty.

dudar que	*to doubt that*	no parecer que	*to not seem that*
negar que	*to deny that*	no pensar que	*to not think that*
temer que	*to fear that; to suspect that*	no estar seguro de que	*to not be sure that*
no creer que	*to not believe that*	no suponer que	*to not suppose that*

Here are some example sentences that express doubt or uncertainty. The verb in the main clause is in the indicative; the verb in the subordinate clause (after **que**) is in the subjunctive.

No estoy segura de que venga.	*I'm not sure she's coming.*
Temo que Miguel **no sepa** la dirección.	*I fear that Miguel might not know the address.*

Impersonal Expressions Signaling Doubt or Uncertainty

There are many impersonal expressions that signal the use of the subjunctive (following **que**) to express doubt or uncertainty.

no es cierto que	*it's not true that*	es posible que	*it's possible that*
es dudoso que	*it's doubtful that*	es probable que	*it's probable that*
es imposible que	*it's impossible that*	no es probable que	*it's not probable that*
es improbable que	*it's improbable that*	puede ser que	*it could be that*

Here are some example sentences that use impersonal expressions ending in **que** followed by the subjunctive to express doubt or uncertainty.

Puede ser que todo **salga** bien.	*It could be that everything turns out ok.*
Es posible que me **den** el trabajo.	*It's possible that they'll give me the job.*

You may ask why the expressions *it's impossible* and *it's probable* are said to convey doubt and uncertainty. At first glance, they seem fairly unambiguous. There are a few possible explanations. First, languages don't always make sense or follow logical rules. (Sorry!) Second, they belong to a longer list of impersonal expressions formed with **es... que**, all of which introduce the subjunctive (see Chapter 17). Furthermore, have you ever thought *It's impossible that she'll be there* and then she shows up after all!? Isn't that a different idea from imagining *She won't be there (at all)*? So in a sense, *impossibility* when used in this context also expresses *possibility*, therefore, uncertainty.

Written Practice 4

 Track 59

Complete the following sentences with the present subjunctive of the verbs in parentheses.

1. Es posible que nosotros _____ (llegar) hoy. *It's possible that we'll arrive today.*

2. El chico niega que la culpa _____ (ser) suya. *The boy denies that it is his fault.*

3. No creo que Luís me _____ (amar). *I don't think Luis loves me.*

4. Temo que el partido _____ (perder) las elecciones. *I fear the party will lose the elections.*

5. No es cierto que todos los estudiantes _____ (trabajar) en la cafetería. *It's not true that all the students work in the cafeteria.*

6. No estoy convencida de que ellos _____ (estar) casados. *I'm not convinced they're married.*

7. No parece que Catalina _____ (querer) quedarse aquí. *It doesn't seem that Catalina wants to stay here.*

8. No estoy seguro de que tú _____ (estar) preparado. *I'm not sure that you're ready.*

Verbs and Expressions Signaling the Indicative

Now compare the expressions that introduce the subjunctive (listed above) with the following expressions that trigger the indicative. These expressions generally imply *certainty* or *objectivity*. Recognizing them will help you make the distinction with those that trigger the subjunctive.

creer que	to believe that	es verdad que	it's true that
pensar que	to think that	es cierto que	it's certain that
saber que	to know that	está claro que	it's clear that
no dudar que	to not doubt that	es evidente que	it's evident that
no negar que	to not deny that	es obvio que	it's obvious that
estar seguro de que	to be sure that	no hay duda de que	there's no doubt that

Written Practice 5

 Track 60

Complete the following sentences in the present subjunctive or the present indicative, depending on the context.

1. Es verdad que no me _____ (gustar) los chicharrones. *It's true that I don't like pork rinds.*

2. La madre duda que sus hijos _____ (hacer) los deberes. *The mother doubts that her children will do their homework.*

3. ¿No crees que nosotros _____ (ir) al campo? *You don't think that we're going to the country?*

4. Es obvio que Luis te _____ (amar). *It's obvious that Luis loves you.*

5. Puede ser que él ya _____ (saber) tu secreto. *It could be that he already knows your secret.*

6. Es evidente que Catalina no _____ (querer) quedarse aquí. *It's evident that Catalina doesn't want to stay here.*

7. Es imposible que ustedes dos se _____ (conocer). *It's impossible that you two know each other.*

8. Claro que (nosotros) _____ (caber) todos. *Of course we'll all fit.*

Using the Subjunctive to Express Ambivalence

There are other cases of the subjunctive's expressing uncertainty that do not use the conjunction **que**. These usually follow the words **cuando**, **donde**, **como**, and sometimes **quien**, as well as expressions such as **el que**, **la que**, and **lo que**. These expressions are used to express ambivalence, in the same way we use *-ever* in English to say *whatever, whenever, however,* or *whomever.* They are grouped under doubt and uncertainty because the outcome is unclear: If you don't really care what happens next, the future remains uncertain. Here are some examples that also give additional approximations in English.

¿Dónde comemos?	*Where shall we eat?*
—Donde **sea**.	*—Wherever. (It doesn't matter.)*
¿Cuándo quieres ir?	*When do you want to go?*
—Cuando tú **digas**.	*—Whenever you say so. (Just give the word.)*
¿Cómo vamos, en tren o en taxi?	*How are we going, by train or taxi?*
—Como **quieras**.	*—However you want. (It's up to you.)*
¿A quién invitamos a la boda?	*Whom shall we invite to the wedding?*
—A quien **sea**.	*—Whomever. (I don't care.)*
¿Pido cualquier cosa?	*Can I order anything (at all)?*
—¡Si! Pide lo que te **guste**.	*—Yes! Order whatever you want.*

Oral Practice

Because **ser** and **querer** are most commonly used in expressions of ambivalence, memorizing the following combinations will help you with fluency. Practice saying them aloud.

como quieras	*however you want*	como sea	*however (it doesn't matter)*
cuando quieras	*whenever you want*	cuando sea	*whenever (it's up to you)*
donde quieras	*wherever you want*	donde sea	*wherever (I don't care)*
lo que quieras	*whatever you want*	lo que sea	*whatever (either way)*

Using the Subjunctive to Express Future Uncertainty

In addition to phrases expressing *whenever, whatever,* etc., **cuando** (*when*) is also used to talk about future uncertainty. This is one of the most difficult concepts for students of Spanish to master. Basically, the subjunctive is used after **cuando** to talk about something that hasn't happened yet. For instance, *I'll let her know when I see her.* This is included under the category of future uncertainty since it's not certain when (or if) the two people will see each other. The indicative (not subjunctive) is used after **cuando** when talking about habitual or repeated actions, such as *I always fall asleep when I read before bed.* This is something that objectively happens: There is no uncertainty. Take a look at these examples:

Indicative: Always or usually happens

Cuando me **llama**, me da piel de gallina.	*I get goose bumps when (every time) he calls me.*
Siempre me quemo **cuando voy** a la playa.	*I always burn myself when I go to the beach.*
Ester suda mucho **cuando hace** ejercicio.	*Ester sweats a lot when she exercises.*

Subjunctive: Will likely or may happen in the future

Te llamaré **cuando llegue**.	*I'll call you when I get in.*
Silvia viene **cuando termine** su trabajo.	*Silvia will come when she finishes her work.*
José será famoso **cuando publiquen** su libro.	*José will be famous when they publish his book.*

Future Uncertainty with Other Conjunctions

In addition to **cuando**, the subjunctive is used after a number of conjunctions to signal incomplete events or uncertainty in the future. Now that you've mastered the use of **cuando**, these should be a cinch, since they are also followed by the subjunctive when they refer to an action that has not yet been completed.

antes de que	*before*	a pesar de que	*despite*
en cuanto	*as soon as*	tan pronto como	*as soon as*
a menos que	*unless*	sin que	*without*
para que	*so that; in order that*		

Here are some example sentences.

Termino el trabajo **antes de que te vayas**.	*I'll finish the work before you leave.*
Abrimos los regalos **en cuanto lleguen** los primos.	*We'll open the presents as soon as the cousins arrive.*
Pongo el plato en el microondas **para que se caliente**.	*I'll put the dish in the microwave so that it warms up.*

Written Practice 6

Complete the following sentences with the present subjunctive or the indicative, depending on the context.

1. Ponga sus cosas donde _____ (querer). No me importa. *Put your (singular) things wherever you want. It doesn't matter to me.*

2. Cuando _____ (viajar) en avión, siempre voy en primera clase. *When I fly, I always go first class.*

3. ¿Me traes una servilleta cuando _____ (poder)? *Can you bring me a napkin whenever you have a chance?*

4. Hacemos lo que tú _____ (decir). *We'll do whatever you say.*

5. Para que (ustedes) lo _____ (saber), no hay clase hoy. *Just so you know, there's no class today.*

6. Vamos en taxi, en metro, caminando, como _____ (ser), pero vamos ya. *We can go by taxi, metro, walking, however (you want), but let's go already.*

7. Gasto demasiado dinero cuando _____ (comer) fuera. *I spend too much money when I eat out.*

8. A menos que _____ (haber) un metro de nieve, tenemos que ir al colegio. *Unless there is a meter of snow, we have to go to school.*

QUIZ

Circle the letter of the word or phrase that best completes each sentence.

1. **No estoy segura de que Ignacio me _____.**
   A. ama
   B. ame
   C. amo
   D. amar

2. **Es cierto que Jorge _____ una casa en Marbella.**
   A. tenga
   B. tengo
   C. tiene
   D. ten

3. **Es imposible que me _____ para ese empleo.**
   A. escogen
   B. escojan
   C. escogían
   D. escogieron

4. **Creo que el bebé no _____ hablar.**
   A. sabe
   B. sepa
   C. sé
   D. saben

5. **Mamá, te llamaremos cuando _____.**
   A. llegamos
   B. lleguemos
   C. vamos a llegar
   D. llegaremos

6. **¿Adónde iremos de vacaciones?**
   —Adonde tú _____.
   A. quieres
   B. quieras
   C. quiera
   D. quiere

7. Tenemos que organizar la fiesta de cumpleaños de Rogelia sin que ella lo _____.

   A. sepa
   B. quepa
   C. ponga
   D. haga

8. Es obvio que el criminal _____ mintiendo.

   A. esté
   B. está
   C. sea
   D. es

9. No te preocupes. Puede ser que todo _____ bien.

   A. salga
   B. sale
   C. salgas
   D. sales

10. Cuando _____, siempre llevo mi almohada.

   A. viajo
   B. viaje
   C. viaja
   D. viajaba

chapter 17

More About the Subjunctive

In this chapter you will learn even more about the subjunctive. You will learn how to use it to express wishes, wants, and desires and how to ask about something that you're not sure exists. You'll also learn some impersonal expressions that take the subjunctive and finally you'll have a chance to review everything you've learned about the subjunctive mood.

CHAPTER OBJECTIVES

In this chapter you will learn

- How to use the subjunctive to express wishes, wants, and desires
- Impersonal expressions that take the subjunctive
- How to talk about the intangible using the subjunctive

Using the Subjunctive to Express Wishes, Wants, and Desire

You learned in Chapter 16 that the subjunctive is used to express subjectivity: doubt, desire, uncertainty, hope, and future possibility (versus future reality). The indicative, on the other hand, expresses objective facts: things that happened, are happening, or will happen.

You've studied the ways the subjunctive can talk about doubt and uncertainty. Now you will learn how to use the subjunctive to express *desire*. For the purpose of this book, desire covers *wanting, wishing, hoping, requesting,* and *suggesting*. Because making commands is actually an expression of desire—you want someone to do something—it also covers *commanding, ordering,* and *insisting*.

Verbs Signaling Wishes, Wants, and Desire

There are certain verbs expressing desire that trigger the subjunctive when the subject in the subordinate clause is *different* from the subject of the main clause.

desear que	*to desire, wish that*	prohibir que	*to prohibit that*
esperar que	*to hope that*	querer que	*to want that*
insistir que	*to insist that*	recomendar que	*to recommend that*
pedir que	*to ask that*	rogar que	*to beg that*
preferir que	*to prefer that*	sugerir que	*to suggest that*

Here are some examples using verbs followed by **que** + the subjunctive to express desire. The verb in the main clause is in the indicative. The verb in the subordinate clause (after **que**) is in the subjunctive.

Prefiero que no lo **hagas**.	*I prefer that you not do it.*
Mi madre **insiste que vaya** al médico.	*My mother insists that I go to the doctor.*

Impersonal Expressions Signaling Wishes, Wants, and Desire

There are several impersonal expressions that signal the use of the subjunctive to express desire.

es aconsejable que	*it's advisable that*	es mejor que	*it's better that*
hace falta que	*it's necessary that*	es necesario que	*it's necessary that*

Here are examples of these impersonal expressions followed by a clause in the subjunctive.

Es necesario que vayas a clase.   *It's necessary that you go to class.*
Es mejor que llamemos a   *It's better if/that we call the police.*
    la policía.

NOTE *The negative of these impersonal expressions and verbs also takes the subjunctive, not the indicative.*

No es necesario que me **llames**.   *It's not necessary that you call me.*
No hace falta que lo **digas**.   *It's not necessary that you say it.*
No quiero que te **vayas**.   *I don't want you to go.*

Indirect Commands with the Subjunctive

Indirect commands can be formed with **que** + the subjunctive. Note that this construction contains only the subordinate clause of a normal sentence with the subjunctive. This is similar to saying **Quiero que...** but dropping the **Quiero.**

Quiero que se vayan.   *I want them to leave.*
¡Que se vayan!   *Have them leave!*
¡Que me **llames!**   *Call me!*
Que ganen el partido.   *May they win the game.*

Subjunctive with *Ojalá*

Ojalá is a Spanish exclamation of Arabic origin that literally means *God willing* or *May Allah grant*. The subjunctive is always used after **Ojalá que** to say *If only . . .* , *Let's hope . . .* , or *May. . . .* There are several popular songs that use this poetic word, which can also help you learn the subjunctive. ***Ojalá que llueva café en el campo*** (*If only it would rain coffee in the countryside*), by the Dominican **merengue** artist Juan Luis Guerra is a popular song that has also been performed by the Mexican rock group **Café Tacuba**. One of the most powerful songs by the Cuban **cantautor** (*singer-songwriter*) and protest singer Silvio Rodríguez is called ***Ojalá***. In it, he appears to be singing about a lost love that he can't erase from his memory. He makes many wishes in the subjunctive, such as **ojalá que la luna pueda salir sin ti** (*may the moon be able to come out without you*); **ojalá pase algo que te borra de pronto** (*may something happen to erase [the memory of] you soon*). Singing along with these songs and others can help you get the sound of the subjunctive into your head.

Written Practice 1

Complete each sentence with the present subjunctive of the verb in parentheses.

1. Les pedimos que _____ (hacer) una donación. *We ask that you make a donation.*

2. Le rogamos que _____ (lavarse) las manos después de usar el servicio. *We beg you to wash your hands after using the restroom.*

3. Que (ellos) _____ (decir) lo que quieran. *May they say what they want.*

4. Ojalá que (tú) _____ (tener) algo de dinero. *Let's hope that you have some money.*

5. No hace falta que (ella) _____ (hablar) tan alto. *It's not necessary that she talk so loudly.*

6. Prefiero que usted _____ (utilizar) la puerta de atrás. *I prefer that you use the back door.*

7. Es mejor que los niños no _____ (correr) en la calle. *It's better if the children don't run in the street.*

8. La ley prohíbe que los médicos _____ (hablar) de sus pacientes. *It is prohibited for doctors to talk about their patients.*

Impersonal Expressions and the Subjunctive

You've already learned a number of impersonal expressions that use **es... que** that precede the subjunctive. Here is a complete list. Note that there is an additional category: expressions of *emotion* and *opinion*. In fact, as long as the context implies subjectivity, you can put almost any adjective between **es** and **que** to produce the subjunctive.

Doubt and Uncertainty

no es cierto que	*it's not true that*	es posible que	*it's possible that*
es dudoso que	*it's doubtful that*	es probable que	*it's probable that*
es imposible que	*it's impossible that*	no es probable que	*it's not probable that*
es improbable que	*it's improbable that*		

Still Struggling

We can't teach you every Spanish expression that goes with the subjunctive, so you should try to learn to evaluate when the subjunctive might be used according to what you already know. Here is a good way to do this analysis: Whenever you see **que**, ask yourself a series of questions. Is the idea expressed before **que** objective or subjective? Does it express doubt or desire? Is it a command? Does it express emotion? An opinion? Future uncertainty? Ambivalence? Has the action come to pass, or is it still up in the air?

Command and Desire

es aconsejable que	*it is advisable that*	es mejor que	*it's better that*
hace falta que	*it's necessary that*	es necesario que	*it's necessary that*

Emotion and Opinion

es bueno que	*it's good that*	es una lástima que	*it's a shame that*
es difícil que	*it's unlikely that*	es malo que	*it's bad that*
es importante que	*it's important that*	es triste que	*it's sad that*
es increíble que	*it's incredible that*		

Here are some example sentences using impersonal expressions and the subjunctive.

Es mejor que vayas al médico.	*You'd better go to the doctor. (It's a good idea for you to go to the doctor.)*
Es possible que gane las elecciones.	*It's possible that he wins the election. (He may win the election.)*

Expressions That Don't Take the Subjunctive

Even more important than memorizing a list of expressions that take the subjunctive is to remind yourself of the impersonal expressions that *don't* take it, since the list is shorter and easier to remember. Again, the majority of the following expressions imply objective facts. Here is a review of the *impersonal expressions that take the indicative* (see also Chapter 16):

es cierto que	*it's true that*	es evidente que	*it's evident that*
está claro que	*it's clear that*	es obvio que	*it's obvious that*
no hay duda de que	*there's no doubt that*	es verdad que	*it's true that*

Written Practice 2

In each sentence you will see an expression with **que** that hasn't been introduced yet. Try to evaluate whether it will take the present subjunctive or the present indicative. Conjugate the verb accordingly.

1. Siento que ella no _____ (tener) tiempo para verte. *I'm sorry she doesn't have time to see you.*

2. No empezamos a comer hasta que _____ (llegar) nuestros invitados. *We won't be eating until our guests arrive.*

3. Alejandro conoce la ley porque _____ (ser) abogado. *Alejandro knows the law because he's a lawyer.*

4. Quizás nosotros _____ (ir) a la playa mañana. *Perhaps we'll go to the beach tomorrow.*

5. Me alegro mucho de que (tú) _____ (estar) feliz en tu nueva casa. *I'm really glad you're happy in your new house.*

6. Me gusta que ella _____ (cantar). *I like that she sings.*

7. Por supuesto que los niños _____ (estudiar) mucho. *Of course the children study a lot.*

8. Es extraño que no _____ (haber) nadie en la calle. *It's strange that there's no one in the street.*

Questioning Existence with the Subjunctive

There is a final use of the subjunctive that asks if something exists or is used when you are seeking something that may or may not exist. This type of question or discussion stays in the subjunctive until it is *answered in the affirmative*, where it takes the indicative. Look at the following pattern:

¿Hay una tienda por aquí que **esté** abierta a esta hora? (subjunctive)

Is there a store near here that is open at this hour?

—**No, no** hay ninguna tienda por aquí que **esté** abierta. (subjunctive)

—*No, there's no store near here that's open.*

—**Sí,** hay una tienda a la vuelta que **está** abierta hasta medianoche. (indicative)

—*Yes, there is a store around the corner that is open until midnight.*

As you can see, in the first example, the speaker is asking about a store that may or may not exist. In the second example, when the second speaker answers *no*, the store still does not exist. In the last example, the speaker declares that the store definitely exists, so he or she uses the indicative.

In these indefinite situations with the subjunctive, when a person or persons are the direct object, the personal **a** is not used.

Busco un médico **que hable** español. (subjunctive)

I'm looking for a doctor who speaks Spanish.

¿Hay un médico **que hable** español por aquí? (subjunctive)

Is there a doctor who speaks Spanish near here?

—Sí, conozco **a** un médico que **habla** español (indicative)

Yes, I know a doctor who speaks Spanish.

In the third situation, the answer is in the affirmative. This declaration is a certainty. Thus, the indicative is used with the personal **a**.

Subjunctive for the Traveler

The subjunctive used to express things that may or may not exist is very useful when traveling. Keep it in mind when asking for directions or help, or when negotiating a hotel room. For example, if you need to find an ATM that accepts international credit cards, just say **Busco un cajero automático que acepte tarjetas internacionales.** If you get sick and need an English-speaking doctor, you might say, **Necesito un médico que hable inglés.** Perhaps you are shown an unacceptable hotel room. You can suggest something nicer with **¿Hay otro cuarto que**

tenga vista? (*Is there another room that has [might have] a view?*) Or if you need to leave your baggage while you step out for a minute, just say, **¿Hay un lugar donde pueda dejar el equipaje?** (*Is there somewhere I can leave my luggage?*)

Oral Practice

 Track 61

Complete the following sentences with the present indicative or present subjunctive, depending on whether the person or thing being referred to is definite or indefinite. Say the complete sentence aloud. Then listen to the audio CD to check your answers and pronunciation.

1. ¿Venden zapatos que _____ (tener) tacones altos? *Do you sell shoes that have high heels?*

2. Necesito un dentista que _____ (trabajar) cerca. *I need a dentist who works nearby.*

3. Busco alguien que _____ (saber) de computadores. *I'm looking for someone who knows about computers.*

4. Me ofrecieron un trabajo que _____ (pagar) bien. *They offered me a job that pays well.*

5. ¿Conocen algún hombre soltero que _____ (vivir) en mi ciudad? *Do you know any single men who live in my city?*

6. Viven en una casa que _____ (tener) una vista linda. *They live in a house with a beautiful view.*

7. Nadie aquí _____ (tener) cambio. *No one here has change.*

A Review of the Subjunctive

Here is a quick review of the subjunctive:

1. Used to present subjective ideas.

   Es importante que aprendas   *It's important that you learn the*
      el subjuntivo.   *subjunctive.*

2. Is usually, but not always, signaled by **que**.

   Insisto que hables con tu jefe.   *I insist that you talk with your boss.*

3. Used after expressions of doubt and uncertainty.

Dudo que apruebe el examen.   *I doubt that he'll pass the exam.*

4. Used to express ambivalence or future uncertainty.

Empezamos **cuando llegue**   *We'll begin when Donato arrives.*
   Donato.
Empezamos **cuando sea**.   *We'll begin whenever.*

5. Used to express wishes, wants, and desire. This includes wanting, wishing, hoping, requesting, suggesting, commanding, ordering, and insisting.

Espero que llame.   *I hope she calls.*
¡Que empiecen los juegos!   *Let the games begin!*
Ojalá que sobrevivan.   *Let's hope they survive.*

6. Used with **es... que** impersonal expressions, to express (a) doubt and uncertainty, (b) wishes, wants, and desires, and (c) emotions and opinions.

Es una lástima que no venga   *It's a shame that Mario isn't coming.*
   Mario.

7. Used with other expressions of (a) doubt and uncertainty, (b) wishes, wants, and desires, and (c) emotions and opinions.

Qué pena que no les **guste**   *What a shame that they don't like the*
   el restaurante.   *restaurant.*
Me extraña mucho que no haya   *It seems strange that no one is at*
   nadie en el trabajo hoy.   *work today.*

8. To talk about things that may or may not exist.

Busco una tienda **que venda** pan.   *I'm looking for a store that sells*
                                               bread.

The subjunctive is *not* used with expressions of certainty and objectivity. These take the *indicative*.

Está claro que están enamorados.   *It's clear that they're in love.*
Jorge **piensa que somos** hermanos.   *Jorge thinks we're siblings.*
Hay una tienda **que vende** pan   *There's a store that sells bread on*
   en la calle Séptima.   *Seventh Street.*

Written Practice 3

▶ Track 62

Complete the sentences with the present subjunctive or present indicative of the verbs in parentheses.

1. No necesito que tú me _____ (hacer) más favores. *I don't need you to do me any more favors.*

2. Es evidente que los niños no _____ (entender). *It's evident that the children don't understand.*

3. Ojalá que todo _____ (salir) bien. *Let's hope (that) everything turns out ok.*

4. Sospecho que me _____ (estar) engañando Carlos. *I suspect (that) Carlos is cheating on me.*

5. ¡Que (ustedes) _____ (llamar) a la policía! *(I want you to) call the police!*

6. Te recomiendo que _____ (hacer) el viaje a Guatemala. *I recommend that you make the trip to Guatemala.*

7. ¿Conoces alguien que me _____ (poder) ayudar? *Do you know anyone who can help me?*

8. Yo sé que él _____ (estar) mintiendo, porque no me mira a la cara. *I know that he's lying, because he doesn't look me in the face.*

9. Toma el autobús que te _____ (convenir). *Take whichever bus is most convenient for you.*

10. Conozco a tres médicos que _____ (trabajar) cerca. *I know three doctors who work nearby.*

11. Hace falta que ustedes _____ (hacer) copias de las llaves. *It's necessary that you make copies of the keys.*

12. Te doy este folleto para que lo _____ (leer). *I'm giving you this pamphlet so that you read it.*

13. Es cierto que la ruptura todavía me _____ (doler). *It's true that the breakup still hurts.*

14. No me gusta que me _____ (gritar) los niños. *I don't like it when the kids scream at me.*

Written Practice 4

Complete the following personal ad with the present subjunctive or present indicative of the verbs in parentheses.

Mujer inteligente, atleta e internacional busca un hombre que _____
(1. tener) un buen sentido de humor. Quiero conocer alguien que _____
(2. querer) comer en buenos restaurantes, ir a la playa, y salir en bicicleta por
las mañanas. No hace falta que _____ (3. ser) ni rico ni guapo, pero
es importante que _____ (4. tener) un buen corazón, que
_____ (5. apreciar) las cosas buenas de la vida, y que _____
(6. ser) apasionado. Quiero un compromiso serio, y me gustaría encontrar
alguien que _____ (7. buscar) lo mismo.

Yo soy periodista internacional. Viajo mucho para el trabajo y me gustaría
estar con alguien a quien le _____ (8. gustar) viajar también. No es
necesario que _____ (9. ser) profesional ni que _____
(10. tener) trabajo… ¡mientras _____ (11. tener) dinero! Ja ja.
En serio, en el fondo, lo más importante es que los dos _____
(12. tener) los mismos valores.

No quiero el hombre perfecto, pero me gustaría conocer a alguien sano,
física y mentalmente. Pienso que el verdadero amor _____ (13. ser)
posible, y creo que se _____ (14. poder) encontrar por Internet.
¿Por qué no? Estoy segura de que _____ (15. existir).

QUIZ

Circle the letter of the word or phrase that best completes each sentence.

1. **Insisto en que tú _____ al evento.**
   A. vas
   B. fuiste
   C. vayas
   D. irá

2. **Raúl y Julia no quieren que nadie les _____ regalos de boda.**
   A. da
   B. dé
   C. dan
   D. den

3. **Hace falta que _____ su número de seguridad social.**
   A. pones
   B. pongas
   C. pone
   D. ponga

4. **Ojalá que te _____ la cena.**
   A. gusta
   B. guste
   C. gustas
   D. gustes

5. **Eduardo está seguro de que _____ a Guadalajara.**
   A. se muda
   B. se mude
   C. se mudo
   D. se mudamos

6. **Quiero salir con alguien que _____ bien.**
   A. bailo
   B. bailar
   C. baila
   D. baile

7. **Los niños dudan que _____ Papá Noel.**

   A. existe

   B. exista

   C. existan

   D. existen

8. **¿Hay una farmacia que esté abierta?**

   —Sí, hay una en la calle Mayor que _____ abierta hasta la medianoche.

   A. estoy

   B. estés

   C. esté

   D. está

9. **¿Conoces a alguien que me pueda prestar una bicicleta?**

   —No, no conozco a nadie que _____ bicicleta.

   A. tenga

   B. tengo

   C. tiene

   D. tienes

10. **Es una pena que no _____ a nadie.**

    A. conoces

    B. conozcas

    C. conocerás

    D. conocieron

chapter **18**

Using the Past Participle

In this chapter you will learn how to make the past participle and how to use it in a variety of ways: in the present perfect, past perfect, passive voice, and as an adjective.

CHAPTER OBJECTIVES

In this chapter you will learn

- How to make the past participle
- How to use the past participle as an adjective
- The passive voice
- The present perfect tense
- The past perfect tense

The Past Participle

For those of you who don't recognize it in English, the past participle is a verb form that ends in *-ed* for regular verbs, such as *walked*, *closed*, or *robbed*. For irregular verbs you can think of it as the third most "removed" form in the past:

know, knew, known. The past participle of *to know* is *known*. Similarly, the past participle of *sleep* is *slept*, and *eat* is *eaten*.

The past participle in Spanish can be used in a number of ways. It is used to form *perfect tenses*, such as **Yo he ido** (*I have gone*) or **Yo había sabido** (*I had known*). It is used as an *adjective*, to say, for example, **la tienda está cerrada** (*the store is closed*), and with the *passive voice*, **la tienda fue robada** (*the store was robbed*). First you will learn how to form the past participle, and then how to use it.

Forming the Past Participle

Forming the past participle in Spanish is relatively easy, and you won't have to memorize more than ten or twelve irregular forms.

To form the past participle, drop the ending **-ar**, **-er**, or **-ir** from the infinitive, and add **-ado** for **-ar** verbs and **-ido** for **-er** and **-ir** verbs.

Infinitive		Past Participle	
hablar	*to speak*	hablado	*spoken*
beber	*to drink*	bebido	*drunk*
vivir	*to live*	vivido	*lived*

Even some Spanish verbs that are often irregular when conjugated follow these rules for the past participle. For example:

Infinitive		Past Participle	
ir	*to go*	ido	*gone*
ser	*to be*	sido	*been*
estar	*to be*	estado	*been*
saber	*to know*	sabido	*known*

NOTE *The past participles of **caer**, **creer**, **leer**, and **traer** all have an accent mark over the **i**: **caído**, **creído**, **leído**, and **traído**.*

Past Participle of Irregular Verbs

Here are some of the most common irregular past participles. It is important to remember these because they come up often. Using them will help you sound more fluent. Of course, even if you get them wrong, Spanish speakers will likely know what you're trying to say. However, while incorrect usage of the irregular past participle in Spanish can sometimes sound "cute," as when a child says, *I breaked it*, it may prevent you from being taken seriously in conversation.

Infinitive		Past Participle	
abrir	*to open*	abierto	*opened*
cubrir	*to cover*	cubierto	*covered*
decir	*to say*	dicho	*said*
escribir	*to write*	escrito	*written*
freír	*to fry*	frito	*fried*
hacer	*to do*	hecho	*done*
morir	*to die*	muerto	*died*
poner	*to put*	puesto	*put*
resolver	*to resolve*	resuelto	*resolved*
romper	*to break*	roto	*broken*
ver	*to see*	visto	*seen*
volver	*to return*	vuelto	*returned*

Verbs based on the previous irregular verbs follow the same rules.

descubrir	*to discover*	descubierto	*discovered*
imponer	*to impose*	impuesto	*imposed*
devolver	*to return*	devuelto	*returned*
satisfacer	*to satisfy*	satisfecho	*satisfied*

Written Practice 1

Practice forming the past participle of the following verbs.

1. pensar _____   6. rehacer _____

2. dormir _____   7. mudar _____

3. revolver _____   8. comer _____

4. querer _____   9. repetir _____

5. dar _____   10. inscribir _____

Using the Past Participle as an Adjective

The past participle can be used as a descriptive adjective, often with the verb **estar**. Like most adjectives, it agrees in number and gender with the noun it modifies.

La puerta **está abierta**.	*The door is open.*
Mario **está deprimido**.	*Mario is depressed.*
Las ventanas **están cerradas**.	*The windows are closed.*
Los huevos **estaban rotos**.	*The eggs were broken.*

You'll notice that a multitude of common expressions and vocabulary are derived from the past participle. Here are just a few:

estar bien visto	*to be considered acceptable*
estar mal visto	*to be frowned upon*
por lo visto	*apparently*
bien hecho	*well done (as in a task, or as in cooked meat)*
poco hecho	*rare (as in cooked meat)*
trato hecho	*it's a deal*
estar hecho polvo	*to be exhausted (literally: made of dust)*
ida y vuelta	*round trip*
dar la vuelta	*to turn over*
estar de vuelta	*to be back*
dar una vuelta	*to go for a walk*

Voy a dar una vuelta por el barrio.	*I'm going to go for a walk around the neighborhood.*
En algunas culturas, está mal visto andar con manga corta.	*In some cultures, wearing short sleeves is frowned upon.*

Written Practice 2

Complete the following sentences using the past participle of the verb in parentheses as an adjective or in a fixed expression. Make sure it agrees in number and gender with the noun it modifies.

1. La niña está _____ (dormir). *The girl is asleep.*

2. ¿Los huevos están _____ (freír) o _____ (revolver)? *Are the eggs fried or scrambled?*

3. El rojo es mi color _____ (preferir). *Red is my favorite color.*

4. Sergio está muy _____ (deprimir). *Sergio is really depressed.*

5. Carlos y yo estamos _____ (estresar) con el trabajo. *Carlos and I are stressed with work.*

6. Este trabajo está bien _____ (hacer). *This work is well done.*

7. La tienda está a la _____ (volver) de la esquina. *The store is around the corner.*

8. ¿Ustedes están _____ (cansar)? *Are you tired?*

9. Su cabeza está _____ (cubrir) con un velo. *Her head is covered with a veil.*

The Passive Voice

The past participle can also be used to make the passive voice. (**El libro** fue publicado **en Argentina.** *The book was published in Argentina.*) The passive voice is less common in Spanish than in English, and Spanish speakers often prefer to use the active voice. Furthermore, the passive voice can actually be expressed—or avoided—several ways in Spanish. You will learn two of them here.

As you probably know, the passive voice is the grammatical construction in which the agent or person performing an action is "excused" from the action, and the emphasis is placed on what was done, not on who did it. The passive voice is usually used when the agent of the action is unimportant or doesn't want to be identified, when the action itself is important and should be highlighted, or in news headlines.

In English the passive is expressed with *to be* + the past participle. In Spanish it is expressed with **ser** + the past participle. Note that in Spanish the past participle agrees with the *subject* of the sentence when used in the passive voice construction.

El décimo planeta **fue descubierto** en 2005.

The tenth planet was discovered in 2005.

If you want to introduce the agent of the action, use **por** (*by*).

El décimo planeta fue descubierto **por** el Dr. Mike Brown en 2005.

The tenth planet was discovered by Dr. Mike Brown in 2005.

To make this sentence active, change the verb in the past participle to an active verb. Notice how the agent becomes the subject of the sentence.

El Dr. Mike Brown descubrió el décimo planeta en 2005.

Dr. Mike Brown discovered the tenth planet in 2005.

Here are more examples. Notice how the past participle agrees in number and gender with the subject.

Los edificios **fueron construidos** el año pasado.

The buildings were built last year.

La cena **fue preparada** por mi hermana.

The dinner was prepared by my sister.

Written Practice 3

Put the active sentences in the passive voice and the passive sentences in the active voice.

1. Todo el mundo admiraba a la Princesa Diana. *Everyone admired Princess Diana.*

   _____ *Princess Diana was admired by everyone.*

2. El paquete fue entregado por el mensajero. *The package was delivered by the messenger.*

   _____ *The messenger delivered the package.*

3. Un carro atropelló al perro. *A car hit the dog.*

   _____ *The dog was hit by a car.*

4. El secreto fue descubierto por la policía. *The secret was discovered by the police.*

   _____ *The police discovered the secret.*

5. La galería vendió cinco cuadros. *The gallery sold five paintings.*

   _____ *Five paintings were sold by the gallery.*

6. Los murales fueron pintados por la comunidad. *The murals were painted by the community.*

   _____ *The community painted the murals.*

Using the Impersonal *Se*

A more economical—and fun—way to express the passive in Spanish is with the impersonal se. This type of passive is used when the agent is unimportant, unknown, or indefinite. You will often see this usage on signs advertising services.

Se abre a las ocho.	*Open at eight.*
Se vende.	*For sale.*
Se compra oro y plata.	*Silver and gold are bought.*
Se alquila.	*For rent.*
En España **se come** muy bien.	*In Spain one eats very well.*
No **se ven** los toros desde aquí.	*The bulls can't be seen from here.*
¿Cómo **se dice** «passive» en español?	*How do you say "passive" in Spanish? (How is "passive" said in Spanish?)*

NOTE *The third person singular or plural of the verb is used depending on the subject it agrees with.*

*Se **vende** vino.*	*Wine is sold (here).*
*Se **venden** dulces.*	*Sweets are sold (here).*

For those of you who don't like to take the blame for anything, Spanish is the perfect language. If you add indirect object pronouns to the passive voice with **se**, you can excuse yourself from almost any blooper or blunder! The loose translation in English might be the colloquial *on me*, as in *She just disappeared on me.*

Se me cayó el vaso.	*The glass fell (from my hand).*
Se me fue la hora.	*The time just disappeared (on me).*
Se le fue la mano.	*He overdid it (Literally: He lost control of his hand).*

Written Practice 4

Complete the following sentences in the passive voice in the present using the impersonal **se** and the verbs in parentheses. Note that the English translations are loose translations.

1. _____ (oír) que aquí _____ (comer) muy bien. *I hear that the food is really good here.*

2. Aquí _____ (encontrar) todo lo necesario. *Here you can find everything you need.*

3. _____ (servir) el desayuno a las ocho. *Breakfast is served at eight.*

4. ¿A qué hora _____ (abrir) la oficina de correos? *What time does the post office open?*

5. Esto no _____ (hacer) aquí. *That is not done here.*

6. ¿A qué hora _____ (cerrar) las tiendas por la tarde? *At what time do the shops close in the afternoon?*

7. En China, no _____ (usar) cubiertos. _____ (usar) palillos. *In China, they don't use silverware. They use chopsticks.*

8. _____ (hablar) español. *Spanish spoken (here).*

The Present Perfect Tense

Now that you know the past participle, you are ready to construct and use the *perfect* tenses. The first one you will learn is the *present perfect*.

Forming the Present Perfect

In English, the present perfect is expressed with the auxiliary verb *to have* in the present tense + the past participle: *I have gone; She has slept.* In Spanish the present perfect is formed with the verb **haber** in the present tense + the past participle. Here is a review of **haber** in the present:

Present of *Haber*

yo	he	nosotros	hemos
tú	has	vosotros	habéis
él/ella/usted	ha	ellos/ellas/ustedes	han

Here is an example of the verb **estar** in the present perfect:

Present Perfect of *Estar*

yo	he estado	*I have been*
tú	has estado	*you have been* (singular, informal)
él/ella/usted	ha estado	*he, she, it has been; you have been* (singular, formal)
nosotros	hemos estado	*we have been*
vosotros	habéis estado	*you have been* (plural, informal)
ellos/ellas/ustedes	han estado	*they, you have been* (plural)

When the past participle is used in the present perfect, it *never agrees* with the subject. It always ends in **-o**.

María no ha ido a clase.	*María hasn't gone to class.*
Ellos han decidido.	*They have decided.*

NOTE *The conjugated form of **haber** + the past participle are never separated. This is true even in the negative, in questions, or with pronouns.*

¿Ustedes **han pedido**?	*Have you ordered?*
Tú nunca **has estado** en Bolivia.	*You have never been to Bolivia.*
¿**Ha llamado** Silvia?	*Has Silvia called?*
Se le **ha ido** la mano.	*He overdid it.*

Oral Practice 1

▶ Track 63

Practice forming the present perfect and saying it aloud with each subject and verb provided. Listen to the CD to check your answers and pronunciation.

1. Tú...   (terminar)
2. Nosotras...   (sentir)
3. ¿Usted...?   (vender)
4. Yo...   (nunca ir)

5. Ellas...   (no decir)

6. Él...   (romper)

7. Tú...   (no poner)

8. ¿Ella... ?   (llamar)

9. Ustedes...   (seguir)

10. Yo...   (no almorzar)

Use of the Present Perfect Tense

To many, the name *present perfect* seems like a misnomer, since the tense actually talks about the past. (In Spanish, it's actually called the **pretérito perfecto** or *preterit perfect*.) However, the implication is that this tense describes a past action that is related to the present. This can include an action that starts in the past and continues into the present; an action that is somehow associated with the present; or an action or situation, often continuing into the present, that has no reference to a particular time and therefore has no clear beginning or end.

Mi madre **ha estado** enferma.	*My mother has been sick. (Implies that she is still sick.)*
No **han llegado**.	*They haven't arrived. (They're still not here.)*
¿**Has comido**?	*Have you eaten? (Have you eaten recently/yet? Are you hungry now?)*
Hemos estado en París.	*We have been to Paris. (At an unknown point in time.)*

The present perfect is often used with the adverbs **ya** (*already/yet*) and **todavía** (*still/yet*).

¿Han comido **ya**?	*Have you already eaten?*
—No hemos comido **todavía**.	*—We haven't eaten yet. / We still haven't eaten.*

In contrast, the *preterit* is used to refer to a completed action in the past with no connection to the present.

Comí a las dos.	*I ate at two o'clock.*
Fueron a París el año pasado.	*They went to Paris last year.*

You may notice that, depending on context, the preterit and present perfect can be interchangeable. This is handy when an irregular form of the preterit doesn't come to mind, or you just can't remember an irregular past participle. Just choose the one you know! Look at the following example where the preterit and present perfect have very similar meanings.

Ha muerto su padre.	*Her father has died.*
Murió su padre.	*Her father died.*

Learning to use the present perfect shouldn't be too difficult, as the use is almost exactly the same as in English. There are a couple of exceptions, however. As you have learned, with time expressions using **hacer**, the *present tense* is used to talk about an action continuing into the present.

Vive aquí **desde hace tres años.**	*He's lived here for three years.*
Hace media hora que **estoy esperando.**	*I've been waiting for half an hour.*

Also, to say you *have just* done something, the verb **acabar de** + infinitive is used in the present tense.

Acabo de terminar.	*I've just finished.*
Alberto **acaba de llegar** de Paraguay.	*Alberto has just arrived from Paraguay.*

Finally, the verb **llevar** in the present can also be used idiomatically to talk about how long something has been happening.

Estoy cansada. **Llevo** tres horas estudiando.	*I'm tired. I've been studying for three hours.*
¿Ustedes **llevan** cuánto tiempo aquí?	*How long have you been here?*

Written Practice 5

Complete the following sentences with the present perfect.

1. Yo no _____ (hacer) los deberes. *I haven't done my homework.*

2. ¿Ellos ya _____ (recibir) las noticias? *Have they already received the news?*

3. Adán nunca _____ (viajar) fuera del país. *Adán has never traveled abroad.*

4. Nosotros no _____ (pagar) el alquiler todavía. *We haven't paid the rent yet.*

5. ¿(Tú) _____ (ver) a Manuel? *Have you seen Manuel?*

6. Nos _____ (escribir) tu madre. *Your mother has written us.*

7. Su perro _____ (morir). *His dog has died.*

8. Los niños no _____ (volver) todavía. *The children haven't gotten back yet.*

Oral Practice 2

Answer the following questions about yourself in complete sentences using the present perfect.

1. ¿Con quién has hablado hoy? *With whom have you spoken today?*

2. ¿Has aprendido mucho español? *Have you learned a lot of Spanish?*

3. ¿Has viajado fuera del país alguna vez? ¿Dónde has ido? *Have you ever traveled outside the country? Where have you been?*

4. ¿Has leído tu email hoy? ¿Quién te ha escrito? ¿Qué te han contado? *Have you read your e-mail today? Who has written you? What have they told you?*

5. ¿Alguna vez has hablado español con alguien de Latinoamérica? ¿De España? *Have you ever spoken Spanish with someone from Latin America? From Spain?*

6. ¿A quién has visto hoy? *Who have you seen today?*

The Past Perfect Tense

The *past perfect tense* is used to talk about an action that happened prior to another action in the past. This is similar to its use in English: *she had gone, they hadn't eaten.*

Forming the Past Perfect

The past perfect is formed by using the imperfect forms of **haber** + the past participle. All rules regarding agreement and placement of verbs are the same as with the present perfect.

Here is a review of the forms of **haber** in the imperfect:

Imperfect of *Haber*

yo	había
tú	habías
él/ella/usted	había
nosotros	habíamos
vosotros	habíais
ellos/ellas/ustedes	habían

Here is an example of the verb **estar** in the past perfect:

Past Perfect of *Estar*

yo	había estado	*I had been*
tú	habías estado	*you had been* (singular, informal)
él/ella/usted	había estado	*he, she, it had been, you had been* (singular, formal)
nosotros	habíamos estado	*we had been*
vosotros	habíais estado	*you had been* (plural, informal)
ellos/ellas/ustedes	habían estado	*they, you had been* (plural)

Oral Practice 3

 Track 64

Practice forming the past perfect and saying it aloud with each subject and verb provided. Listen to the CD to check your answers and pronunciation.

1. Tú...   (terminar)
2. Nosotras...   (sentir)
3. ¿Usted... ?   (vender)
4. Yo...   (nunca ir)
5. Ellas...   (no decir)
6. Él...   (romper)
7. Tú...   (no poner)
8. ¿Ella... ?   (llamado)
9. Ustedes...   (seguir)
10. Yo...   (no almorzar)

Use of the Past Perfect

The past perfect is used to talk about an action that happened before another action in the past, usually in the preterit, took place.

Silvia dijo que **había llegado** a las cinco.	*Silvia said that she had arrived at five o'clock.*
El ladrón entró porque Julio **no había cerrado** la puerta con llave.	*The burglar entered because Julio hadn't locked the door.*
Los niños ya se **habían dormido** cuando llegaron los abuelos.	*The kids had already gone to sleep when their grandparents arrived.*

The comparison with the past action can be stated or implied.

Todavía **no había recibido** una respuesta ayer cuando hablé con ella.	*She still hadn't received an answer when I spoke to her yesterday.*
Todavía **no había recibido** una respuesta.	*She still hadn't received an answer.*

You will often see the past perfect used with the expressions **ya** (*already/yet*), **todavía** (*still/yet*), **antes (de)** (*before*), **después (de)** (*after*), and **cuando** (*when*).

No habíamos comido antes de salir.	*We hadn't eaten before going out.*
¿Ya habían ido al museo **antes?**	*Had you been to the museum before?*
Todavía no habían terminado cuando me fui.	*They still hadn't finished when I left.*

Written Practice 6

Join the following pairs of sentences by putting one sentence in the preterit and one in the past perfect and using **ya** and **cuando** when possible. Follow the example given.

Yo salí. Después me llamó Javi para cancelar. *I went out. Then Javi called me to cancel.*

Ya había salido cuando me llamó Javi para cancelar. *I'd already gone out when Javi called me to cancel.*

1. Empezó la música. Después entraron los bailarines. *The music began. Then the dancers entered.*

    _____ *The music had already begun when the dancers entered.*

2. Gema se fue. Después su jefe la buscó. *Gema left. Then her boss looked for her.*

    _____ *Gema had already left when her boss looked for her.*

3. Compré el boleto de avión. Después el hotel canceló la reserva. *I bought the plane ticket. Then the hotel canceled the reservation.*

    _____ *I had already bought the plane ticket when the hotel canceled the reservation.*

4. Mozart escribió dos piezas musicales. Después cumplió cuatro años. *Mozart wrote two musical pieces. Then he turned four (years old).*

    _____ *Mozart had already written two musical pieces when he turned four (years old).*

5. Nadie terminó el examen. La hora se acabó. *No one finished the exam. The time was up.*

    _____ *No one had finished the exam when the time was up.*

Written Practice 7

 Track 65

Listen to the following telephone conversation. Then put the sentences in the order that they occurred from a–h. You can listen to the conversation in the correct order on the CD recording.

Eva: ¿Sí? *Yes?*

María: ¿Eva? Soy María. *Eva? It's María.*

Eva: Hola María, ¿Qué tal? *Hey María. How are you?*

María: Ay, pues muy mal. *Ugh. Horrible.*

Eva: ¿Por qué? ¿Qué pasó? *Why? What happened?*

María: ¿Pues te acuerdas que te había dicho que iba a escribirle a Rafa
          para decirle que no podía verlo más? *Well, do you remember that
          I had told you that I was going to write Rafa and tell him that it
          was over, that I couldn't see him any more?*

Eva: Sí... *Yeah . . .*

María: Pues escribí un email muy bueno, creo, en que le dije que
          tenía novio, que nos vamos a casar, y que no podríamos seguir
          viéndonos. *Well, I wrote him a really good email, I think, in which
          I said I had a boyfriend, that we were going to get married, and
          that we (he and I) couldn't continue seeing each other.*

Eva: Pues me parece muy bien. ¿Cuál es el problema? *So that sounds
          good. What's the problem?*

María: El problema es que después de pulsar «enviar», ¡me di cuenta
          de que se lo había enviado a Ramón! *The problem is that after
          pressing "send" I realized that I had sent the email to Ramón!*

Eva: ¡Noooooooo!

María: ¡Síííííííí! Además, cuando le llamé a Ramón para pedirle que lo
          borrara, ya lo había leído. *Yeeeeeeees! And not only that, when I
          called Ramón to ask him to erase it, he had already read it.*

Eva: ¡Qué lío! ¿Y qué pasó entonces? *What a mess! So what
          happened then?*

María: Pues terminó conmigo y ahora estoy sola. *Well, he broke up with
          me and now I'm alone.*

1. Ramón termina con María. _____

2. María llama a Eva para contarle la historia del email. _____

3. María habla con Eva sobre su plan de terminar con Rafa. _____

4. María manda el email a Ramón. _____

5. María llama a Ramón para pedirle que borre el email. _____

6. María empieza a salir con Rafa. _____

7. Ramón lee el email de María. _____

8. María le escribe un email a Rafa. _____

QUIZ

Circle the letter of the word or phrase that best completes each sentence.

1. **Los huevos están _____.**
   A. roto
   B. rota
   C. rotos
   D. rotas

2. **Me gusta la carne _____.**
   A. bien hecho
   B. poco hecha
   C. trato hecho
   D. mal vista

3. **El castillo fue _____ por los franceses en 1804.**
   A. construido
   B. construyendo
   C. construida
   D. construyeron

4. **Los cuadros _____ pintados por Vermeer.**
   A. fue
   B. fui
   C. fuimos
   D. fueron

5. **No _____ el mar desde este cuarto.**
   A. se ve
   B. está ve
   C. ve
   D. ve se

6. **Nosotros _____ ido a ver "Titanic" veintitrés veces.**
   A. he
   B. ha
   C. hemos
   D. han

7. **Mis padres nunca _____ del país.**

   A. ha salido

   B. han salido

   C. ha salidos

   D. han salidos

8. **Yo _____ en Manhattan desde hace quince años.**

   A. vivo

   B. he vivido

   C. estaba viviendo

   D. viví

9. **Las tiendas ya _____.**

   A. había cerrado

   B. habían cerrados

   C. habían cerrado

   D. había cerrados

10. **El vuelo ya _____ cuando ellos _____ al aeropuerto.**

    A. había salido; habían llegado

    B. salió; llegaron

    C. salió; habían llegado

    D. había salido; llegaron

19

Using the Imperfect Subjunctive

In this chapter you will learn how use the subjunctive in the past (imperfect subjunctive). You will learn how to choose between the imperfect subjunctive and the conditional, and how to make a variety of **si** (*if*) clauses.

CHAPTER OBJECTIVES

In this chapter you will learn

- The imperfect subjunctive
- How to choose between the imperfect subjunctive and the conditional
- Conditional sentences with *si* clauses

The Imperfect Subjunctive

Just when you thought you were safe with the present subjunctive, the imperfect subjunctive appears! Luckily, the imperfect subjunctive is used in the same situations as the present subjunctive, except that it expresses the past. The basic rule is that the imperfect subjunctive is used when *the main clause trig-*

gering the subjunctive is in the past or in the conditional. Compare the following sentences.

Present	Present Subjunctive
Yo **quiero que vayas** a la tienda.	*I want you to go to the store.*

Past	Imperfect Subjunctive
Yo **quería que fueras** a la tienda.	*I wanted you to go to the store.*

The following chart may help you know when to use the imperfect subjunctive.

Main Clause	Dependent Clause
present future	present subjunctive
imperfect preterit conditional	imperfect subjunctive

Formation of the Imperfect Subjunctive

To make the imperfect subjunctive, first take the **ellos/ellas** (third-person plural) form of the preterit tense of the verb and drop the **-ron**.

Infinitive	Ellos/Ellas form	Drop the -ron
hablar	hablaron	habla-
decir	dijeron	dije-
comer	comieron	comie-

Then add the following endings:

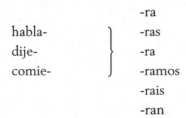

habla- dije- comie-	-ra -ras -ra -ramos -rais -ran

NOTE *The **nosotros** (first-person plural) form always carries an accent mark over the third-to-last syllable (i.e., **habláramos**).*

Here are some examples.

Subject	hablar	decir	comer
yo	hablara	dijera	comiera
tú	hablaras	dijeras	comieras
él/ella/usted	hablara	dijera	comiera
nosotros	habláramos	dijéramos	comiéramos
vosotros	hablarais	dijerais	comierais
ellos/ellas/ustedes	hablaran	dijeran	comieran

NOTE *The third-person plural **ellos/ellas** form in the preterit always ends in -**ron**. In the imperfect subjunctive it always ends in -**ran**.*

Written Practice 1

Practice writing the **yo** and **nosotros** forms of the following verbs in the imperfect subjunctive according to the example.

Infinitive	Yo form	Nosotros form
beber	*bebiera*	*bebiéramos*
1. cantar		
2. dormir		
3. contribuir		
4. andar		
5. hacer		
6. poder		
7. ir		
8. ser		
9. estar		
10. saber		
11. poner		
12. leer		

You may occasionally hear or see an alternate form of the imperfect subjunctive, ending in **-se, -ses, -se, -semos, -seis, -sen**. For example, **hablase** or fuésemos. This form is uncommon, but it is sometimes heard in spoken language, especially in Spain.

Uses of the Imperfect Subjunctive

The verbs and expressions that cue the present subjunctive also cue the imperfect subjunctive. In the main clause, however, they always appear in the *past* or the *conditional*. As with the present, these cues often express subjective feelings such as doubt, uncertainty, wishes, wants, and desires, as well as feelings and emotions. The imperfect subjunctive is translated in a number of ways in English—as the past, as the conditional, etc.—so it will be easier for you to approach its use directly in Spanish rather than trying to find parallel meaning in English.

Expressing Doubt and Uncertainty in the Past

When doubt or uncertainty is expressed in the past or conditional, it is followed by a subordinate clause in the imperfect subjunctive. (For a more complete list of expressions of doubt and uncertainty, see Chapter 16.)

El profesor **dudaba que** los estudiantes **aprobaran** el examen.	*The professor doubted that the students passed the exam.*
Es imposible que fuera a la India.	*It's impossible that she went to India.*
No sé donde está. **Quizás saliera** un rato.	*I don't know where he is. Maybe he went out for a minute.*

Expressing Wishes, Wants, and Desires in the Past

The imperfect also follows cues in the main clause in the past or conditional that express wanting, wishing, hoping, requesting, and suggesting. (For a more complete list of expressions of wishes, wants, and desires, see Chapter 17.)

Quería que me **llamara** antes de irse.	*I wanted him to call me before he left.*
Elena **esperaba que fuéramos** a su concierto.	*Elena hoped that we would go to her concert.*
Fue imposible que llegara a tiempo.	*It was impossible for her to arrive on time.*

Ojalá (or **Ojalá que**) can also be used with the imperfect subjunctive to say *I wish . . .* or *If only. . . .* When used this way, the speaker is implying that is unlikely or impossible that the wish will come true.

Ojalá pudieras venir esta noche.	*I wish you could come tonight.*
Ojalá tuviera dinero para comprar una casa.	*If only I had the money to buy a house.*

Compare this to **Ojalá** used with the present subjunctive to say *I hope . . . ,* which expresses something that is more likely to happen.

Ojalá que vengas a mi casa esta noche.	*I hope you come to my house tonight.*

With Impersonal Expressions in the Past

There are a wide variety of impersonal expressions that cue the subjunctive from the main clause. (For a list of these expressions see Chapter 17.) These cues express subjective ideas of wanting or doubting, as well as feelings, emotions, or opinions.

Fue tan **triste que muriera** así.	*It was so sad that she died like that.*
Sería mejor que tomaras un taxi.	*It would be better if you took a taxi.*
Fue importantísimo que aprendiera usted español.	*It was very important that you learn Spanish.*

With Other Expressions that Cue the Subjunctive

The same expressions that cue the subjunctive in the present also can be used in the past.

¡Qué pena que se acabara así!	*What a shame that it ended like that.*
Sentí mucho **que no nos acordáramos de** su cumpleaños.	*I was sorry that we didn't remember her birthday.*

Written Practice 2

Complete the following sentences with the imperfect subjunctive of the verbs in parentheses.

1. Los padres querían que sus hijos _____ (estudiar) más.
   The parents wanted their children to study more.

2. Fue necesario que (tú) _____ (estar) en la reunión. *It was necessary for you to be at the meeting.*

3. Cuando vi a Isabel con el pelo corto, no creía que _____ (ser) ella. *When I saw Isabel with short hair, I didn't believe it was her.*

4. Mis amigos insistían en que (yo) _____ (salir). *My friends insisted I go out.*

5. Dudaba que Pablo _____ (poder) conducir un carro con marchas. *I doubted that Pablo could drive a standard shift car.*

6. Me pareció muy curioso que Sergio _____ (decidir) mudarse a Alaska. *It seemed really strange to me that Sergio decided to move to Alaska.*

7. Sería más fácil que (nosotros) _____ (pagar) juntos. *It would be easier for us to pay all together.*

8. Qué pena que tus padres no _____ (saber) de la exposición. *Too bad that your parents didn't know about the exhibit.*

9. Es imposible que ella no _____ (contribuir) a la cena. *It's impossible that she didn't contribute to the dinner.*

10. ¿Tenías miedo de que se _____ (caer) la niña? *Were you afraid that the girl would fall?*

To Talk About Something That May or May not Exist

You learned in Chapter 17 that the present subjunctive could be used to talk or ask about something that may or may not exist. The subjunctive is used because the outcome of the situation is unknown or uncertain. For example:

Busco una tienda **que venda** pan.   *I'm looking for a store that sells bread.*
   (present subjunctive)

The same applies if the main clause is in the past tense or in the conditional. Look at the previous example again, but this time changed to the past.

Buscaba una tienda **que vendiera**
pan. (imperfect subjunctive)

I was looking for a store that sold bread.

Remember that once the idea, event, or thing is confirmed to exist, the indicative (not the subjunctive) is used.

Encontré una tienda **que vendía**
pan. (imperfect indicative)

I found a store that sold bread.

When Future Uncertainty Becomes Past Certainty

You may remember from Chapter 16 that the present subjunctive is used to express future uncertainty with expressions such as **cuando** and **hasta que**. This is because the actions have not yet occurred, and hence are uncertain. For example:

Te llamo **cuando llegue**.
(present subjunctive)

I'll call you when I arrive.

In the past, however, expressions of time such as **cuando**, **hasta que**, **en cuanto**, **tan pronto como**, and **después de que** *always take the indicative* (not the subjunctive), since the action has already taken place.

Te llamé **cuando llegué**.
(preterit indicative)

I called you when I arrived.

Ellos me reconocieron **tan
pronto como me vieron**.
(preterit indicative)

They recognized me as soon as they saw me.

However, conjunctions that do not express time often *do* take the imperfect subjunctive when used in the past. These include **sin que**, **a menos que**, **a pesar de que**, and **para que**.

La chica salió **sin que** sus padres
lo **supieran**.

The girl went out without her parents knowing.

Mi hermana no comería los callos
a menos que los **comiera** yo.

My sister wouldn't eat the tripe unless I ate it.

These conjunctions use the indicative, however, when stating facts, especially in past time.

Salí a pesar de que llovía.

I went out even though it was raining.

Written Practice 3

Complete the following sentences with the imperfect subjunctive or preterit or imperfect indicative of the verb, according to the situation.

1. Necesitábamos un taxi que nos _____ (llevar) a las afueras. *We needed a taxi that would take us to the suburbs.*

2. La mujer hablaba lento para que yo la _____ (entender). *The woman spoke slowly so that I would understand her.*

3. Fui a un médico que _____ (ser) especialista en cardiología. *I went to a doctor who was a specialist in cardiology.*

4. Julia empezó a sonreír cuando me _____ (ver). *Julia started to smile when she saw me.*

5. Pedro quería una novia que _____ (saber) bailar salsa. *Pedro wanted a girlfriend who knew how to dance salsa.*

6. Por tentadora que _____ (ser) la oferta, ella no lo quería. *As tempting as the offer was, she didn't want it.*

7. Había cinco personas que no _____ (hablar) inglés en mi clase. *There were five people who didn't speak English in my class.*

8. ¿Tendría usted el periódico que _____ (salir) ayer? *Do you have a newspaper that came out yesterday?*

9. No quería usar el vaso a pesar de que _____ (estar) limpio. *I didn't want to use the glass even though it was clean.*

10. Juan Manuel se marchó en cuanto tú _____ (aparecer). *Juan Manuel took off as soon as you appeared.*

Choosing Between the Subjunctive and the Conditional

You may have noticed that many of the English translations of the Spanish imperfect subjunctive are in the conditional, or *would* form in English. For example:

No pensaba que **fuéramos** a su casa. (imperfect subjunctive)   *He didn't think we would go to his house.*

When the idea being expressed in Spanish is *not* a subjective idea (which signals the subjunctive), the Spanish conditional is, in fact, used. These are usually declarations of certainty or fact.

Sabía que iríamos a su casa.   *He knew that we would go to his house.*
(conditional)

Written Practice 4

Complete the following sentences with the *conditional* or the *imperfect subjunctive*, depending on the situation.

1. Sarita dudaba que Eduardo la _____ (llamar). *Sarita doubted that Eduardo would call her.*

2. Pero Lidia sabía que Ernesto la _____ (llamar). *But Lidia knew that Ernesto would call her.*

3. Parecía imposible que el equipo _____ (perder) el partido. *It seemed impossible that the team would lose the match.*

4. Pero el entrenador estaba seguro de que ellos no _____ (ganar). *But the coach was sure that they wouldn't win.*

5. Yo pensaba que tú _____ (ir) con tu familia de vacaciones. *I thought you would go with your family on vacation.*

6. Mis padres estaban tristes que nosotros no _____ (pasar) las Navidades con ellos. *My parents were sad that we didn't spend Christmas with them.*

Conditional Sentences with *Si* Clauses

Si (*if*) clauses, also known as conditionals, are used to talk about conditions, real, unreal, or past, and their actual or hypothetical results. There are three main types of sentences that use a main clause and a **si** clause to express conditions. They are:

Main clause	Si clause	Usage
Present or Future	si + Present	Real or possible situations
Conditional	si + Imperfect subjunctive	Hypothetical situations
Conditional perfect	si + Past perfect subjunctive	Impossible past situations

The order of the two clauses is unimportant, but the formation of each clause should follow the above chart.

To Express Possible or Real Conditions

Conditional sentences can be used to express something that is likely to happen—a condition that is real, as opposed to hypothetical. In this case, the sentences take the following form:

Main clause	Si clause
Present or Future	si + Present

For example:

Te **ayudaré**...   *I will help you . . .*
... si **termino** mis deberes.   *. . . if I finish my homework.*

Remember that in this case, **si** is always paired with the present, and the main clause takes the future (or the present).

Written Practice 5

 Track 66

Complete the following sentences with the present or the future of the verb in parentheses.

1. Si estudias, _____ (aprobar) el examen. *If you study, you'll pass the exam.*

2. Nosotros no _____ (trabajar) si llueve. *We won't work if it rains.*

3. ¿Ellos _____ (venir) al concierto si nosotros los _____ (invitar)? *Will they come to the concert if we invite them?*

4. Pilar no _____ (hacer) la maestría si _____ (costar) demasiado. *Pilar won't do her master's if it is too expensive.*

5. Xavier nunca _____ (recibir) un aumento de sueldo si _____ (seguir) así. *Xavier will never get a raise if he goes on like this.*

6. Si tú _____ (escuchar) el CD te _____ (gustar). *If you listen to the CD you'll like it.*

To Express Hypothetical or Unlikely Situations

One of the most important uses of the imperfect subjunctive is to express a hypothetical or unlikely result of a situation. In this case, the main clause takes the conditional, and the **si** clause takes the imperfect subjunctive.

Main clause	Si clause
Conditional	**si** + Imperfect subjunctive

For example:

| **Iría** contigo… | *I would go with you . . .* |
| … si no **tuviera** clase ahora. | *. . . if I didn't have class now.* |

Hypothetical **si** clauses can be used to express a number of ideas.

1. To talk about a situation that is untrue or contrary to fact.

| Si **supiera** francés **hablaría** con ella. | *If I knew French, I would talk to her. (But I don't know French.)* |

2. To talk about a hypothetical condition.

| **Ganarías** más dinero si **trabajaras** más. | *You would earn more money if you worked more. (But at the moment you're not working more.)* |

3. To talk about something that is unlikely to happen.

| Si **ganara** la lotería, me **compraría** una casa en la playa. | *If I won the lottery, I'd buy a house on the beach. (Alas, this is but a dream.)* |

Written Practice 6

▶ Track 67

Complete the following sentences with the conditional and the imperfect subjunctive of the verbs in parentheses.

1. Si (tú) _____ (venir) a Lima, saldríamos mucho. *If you came to Lima, we would go out a lot.*

2. Yo no _____ (ir) a correr si lloviera. *I wouldn't go jogging if it rained.*

3. ¿Qué _____ (hacer) Santiago si _____ (perder) su trabajo? *What would Santiago do if he were to lose his job?*

4. Si José _____ (tener) razón, le _____ (pagar) mil pesos. *If José were right, I would pay him a thousand pesos.*

5. Si yo le _____ (dar) una semana más, usted _____ (poder) terminar el trabajo? *If I gave you one more week, would you be able to finish the job?*

6. María nos _____ (ayudar) si nosotros se lo _____ (pedir). *María would help us if we asked her.*

To Express Impossible Past Situations

Si clauses can also be used to express impossible past situations. The situations are, of course, impossible because they are in the past, and didn't happen. For instance: *If you had told me about Miguel, I wouldn't have gone out with him.* Unfortunately (so it seems) she did go out with him, so the condition of telling can never take place. Feelings of regret are also expressed with these clauses: *If I had been a better friend she wouldn't have left.* Alas, it's too late. She's already gone. The condition of being a better friend can never take place.

In Spanish, this type of conditional sentence uses two verb tenses that you have not yet learned, but for which you already have all the tools: the *conditional perfect* and the *past perfect subjunctive*. As you have already learned with the present and past perfect, the "perfect" forms are made by using the verb **haber** as an auxiliary, followed by the past participle.

Main clause	Si clause
Conditional perfect	si + Past perfect subjunctive

For example:

| No lo **habría hecho**... | *I wouldn't have done it . . .* |
| ... si lo **hubiera sabido**. | *. . . if I had known.* |

The conditional perfect is used to say *would have* or *would not have*. To make the conditional perfect, use the conditional of **haber** followed by the past participle of the verb. Here is an example with the verb **estar** (**estado**):

Conditional perfect

	Conditional of *haber*		**Past participle**
yo	habría	+	estado
tú	habrías	+	estado
él/ella/usted	habría	+	estado
nosotros	habríamos	I	estado
vosotros	habríais	+	estado
ellos/ellas/ustedes	habrían	+	estado

To make the past perfect subjunctive, use the imperfect subjunctive of **haber** followed by the past participle of the verb. Here is an example with the verb **hacer** (**hecho**):

Past perfect subjunctive

	Imperfect subjunctive of *haber*		**Past participle**
yo	hubiera	+	hecho
tú	hubieras	+	hecho
él/ella/usted	hubiera	+	hecho
nosotros	hubiéramos	+	hecho
vosotros	hubierais	+	hecho
ellos/ellas/ustedes	hubieran	+	hecho

Here are some more examples of this type of conditional sentence:

| Si te **hubiera visto** te **habría** saludado. | *If I had seen you I would have said hello.* |
| ¿Me **habrías invitado** si te **hubieras acordado**? | *Would you have invited me if you had remembered?* |

You will often hear Spanish speakers using the imperfect subjunctive for *both* the **si** clause and the resultant clause. For example: **Si te hubiera visto, te hubiera saludado.** This usage is quite common and the meaning is the same.

Written Practice 7

Complete the following sentences with either the conditional perfect or the past perfect subjunctive.

1. Nosotros _____ (ir) a Lituania si hubiéramos tenido el dinero. *We would have gone to Lithuania if we'd had the money.*

2. El avión hubiera llegado a tiempo si no _____ (hacer) mal tiempo. *The plane would have arrived on time if there hadn't been bad weather.*

3. Yo no _____ (terminar) el trabajo si Alicia no me hubiera ayudado. *I wouldn't have finished the job if Alicia hadn't helped me.*

4. Los turistas no habrían pagado tanto si _____ (saber) que los cuadros eran falsificados. *The tourists wouldn't have paid so much if they had known the paintings were fakes.*

5. ¿Tú me _____ (llamar) si _____ (saber) que era mi cumpleaños? *Would you have called me if you had known it was my birthday?*

6. ¿Julie _____ (aprender) tan bien el español si no _____ (vivir) en México? *Would Julie have learned Spanish as well if she hadn't lived in Mexico?*

Sentences with *Como Si*

Similar to the **si** clauses, the phrase **como si** (*as if*) followed by the imperfect subjunctive or the past perfect subjunctive can be used to convey something that is contrary to fact or hypothetical. This is similar to saying something like *As if it were the end of the world* in English. Here are some examples:

Ella habla **como si lo supiera** todo.	*She talks as if she knew everything.*
Como si fuera el fin del mundo.	*As if it were the end of the world.*
Él actúa **como si hubiera ganado** el premio Nobel.	*He acts as if he had won the Nobel prize.*

QUIZ

Circle the letter of the word or phrase that best completes each sentence.

1. **Yo estaría triste si ella _____.**

    A. pierde

    B. pierda

    C. perdiera

    D. perdió

2. **Mi madre no quería que yo _____ azúcar.**

    A. como

    B. come

    C. comiera

    D. comieras

3. **Ese día, vi un perro que _____ un hogar.**

    A. necesita

    B. necesitaba

    C. necesitara

    D. necesitará

4. **Celia llamó a su marido tan pronto como _____ del trabajo.**

    A. sale

    B. saliera

    C. salió

    D. salga

5. **Juan se rió mucho cuando _____ el chiste.**

    A. oye

    B. oyera

    C. oiga

    D. oyó

6. **Hablé alto para que mi abuelo me _____ mejor.**

    A. escuchó

    B. escucha

    C. escuchara

    D. había escuchado

7. **Si ganaras la lotería, ¿_____ el dinero conmigo?**

    A. compartes

    B. compartieras

    C. compartirías

    D. compartirás

8. **Elio me dijo que si se muda a Argentina, yo _____ con él.**

    A. iré

    B. fui

    C. fuera

    D. hubiera ido

9. **Si _____ del accidente, habría ido al hospital.**

    A. habría sabido

    B. hubiera sabido

    C. supiera

    D. sé

10. **Estaba segura de que _____ el examen.**

    A. aprobaría

    B. aprobara

    C. apruebe

    D. aprueba

chapter **20**

Using Para *and* Por

In this chapter you will learn how to distinguish between **para** and **por** and some common expressions with **por**. You will learn how to talk about money and currency as well as how to express a number of simple concepts that require complex Spanish.

CHAPTER OBJECTIVES

In this chapter you will learn

- The prepositions *para* and *por*
- Expressions with *por*
- How to talk about money and currency
- Not-so-simple expressions for simple concepts

The Prepositions *Para* and *Por*

Spanish learners often have difficulty knowing when to use **por** and when to use **para** because they can both mean *for* in Spanish.

Compré un regalo **para** mi mamá.	*I bought a gift for my mother.*
Compré un regalo **por** cincuenta pesos.	*I bought a gift for fifty pesos.*

These two words are probably more different than they are similar, however. It helps to think of **por** and **para** as distant relatives with distinct personalities. In general, **para** is associated with purpose, intention, or destination.

Here are examples of the most common uses of **para**:

Para

1. To talk about a recipient or beneficiary of something (*for*):

Compré el regalo **para mi mamá**.	*I bought the gift for my mother.*
¿Hay algo **para mí**?	*Is there something for me?*
Trabajo **para el ministerio de finanzas**.	*I work for the Ministry of Finance.*

2. To talk about a destination or direction toward a place (for):

Salieron **para el monte**.	*They left for the mountains.*

3. To express the purpose of something (*for; in order to*):

Este tenedor es **para ensalada**.	*This fork is for salad.*
¿Tienes ingredientes **para hacer tortilla**?	*Do you have ingredients for making an omelet?*
Necesito los anteojos **para leer**.	*I need the glasses in order to read.*

4. To refer to a time deadline (*for; by*):

Mi jefa quiere la presentación **para el lunes**.	*My boss wants the presentation for Monday.*
Alan no llegará **para mañana**.	*Alan won't be here by tomorrow.*

5. To make a "one-sided" comparison (*for*):

Para ser inglés no habla mal español.	*For an Englishman he doesn't speak bad Spanish.*
Javier es muy maduro **para su edad**.	*Javier is very mature for his age.*

Por

Por, the more versatile and complicated of the two, has many uses, the most common related to exchange (things, money), motive, or general location. **Por** can have many meanings beyond *for*, such as *through*, *along*, *by*, and *around*. In addition to *for*, **para** often takes the meaning of *in order to*. While memorizing the following lists and getting a feel for the examples will help you, understanding **por** and **para** will also come with time and familiarity with the language.

Here are examples of the most common uses of **por**:

1. To talk about exchange or monetary transactions (*for; in exchange for*):

Compré un regalo **por cincuenta pesos**.	*I bought a gift for fifty pesos.*
Cambié el suéter **por uno más grande**.	*I exchanged the sweater for a bigger one.*

2. To express thanks for something (*for*):

Gracias **por el regalo**.	*Thanks for the present.*

3. To express "why" or "how" (*because of; for; for the sake of; by*):

Mandé las direcciones **por email**.	*I sent the directions by email.*
Andrés fue **por dinero**.	*Andrés went for (to get) money.*
Lo hizo **por amor**.	*She did it for love.*
No llores **por mí**.	*Don't cry because of me (on my account).*

4. To talk about direction, or a general location or time (*by; along; through; around*):

Viajamos **por toda Europa**.	*We traveled all through Europe.*
¿Pasamos **por la casa**?	*Can we pass by the house?*
Sara trabaja **por la noche**.	*Sara works at night.*
Los niños están **por aquí**.	*The kids are around here (somewhere).*

5. To talk about a specific period of time (*for*):

No dormí **por tres días**.	*I didn't sleep for three days.*

6. To talk about speed or frequency (per):

Voy al médico dos veces **por semana**.

I go to the doctor twice per/a week.

Este carro corre a cien millas **por hora**.

This car goes a hundred miles per/ an hour.

7. To talk about mistaken identity or a misjudgment (*for*):

Lo tomé **por español**.

I took him for a Spaniard (but he's not).

David pasa **por estudiante**.

David passes for a student.

8. Between **estar** and the infinitive to mean *to be in the mood to; to feel like:*

Estoy **por salir**.

I'm in the mood to go out.

Written Practice 1

Complete each sentence with **para** or **por** and then write the number of the explanation above (1–6 for **para** and 1–8 for **por**) for why you chose that word.

1. Uso este libro _____ aprender español. _____ *I use this book in order to learn Spanish.*

2. ¿Compramos comida _____ el bebé? _____ *Shall we buy food for the baby?*

3. Andábamos _____ el río. _____ *We walked along the river.*

4. Vendía la cámara digital _____ doscientos cincuenta dólares. _____ *He was selling the digital camera for two hundred and fifty dollars.*

5. _____ una comedia, no es muy chistosa. _____ *For a comedy, it's not very funny.*

6. Fuimos a la playa _____ una semana. _____ *We went to the beach for a week.*

7. Lo hizo _____ venganza. _____ *He did it for revenge.*

8. ¿Puedes terminar el artículo _____ el martes? _____ *Can you finish the article by Tuesday?*

9. El tren rápido viaja a una velocidad de **220** kilómetros _____ hora. _____ *The fast train gets up to a speed of* **220** *kilometers per hour.*

10. Mil gracias _____ llevarme al trabajo _____ *Thank you so much for driving me to work.*

11. Juan es tan guapo que siempre lo toman _____ una estrella de cine. _____ *Juan is so handsome that people always take him for a movie star.*

Expressions with *Por*

Por is commonly used in a number of fixed expressions.

por allí	*over there; that way*	por fuera	*outside*
por casualidad	*by chance*	por el momento	*for the moment*
por cierto	*by the way*	por lo menos	*at least*
por ejemplo	*for example*	por mi parte	*as for me*
por eso	*that's why*	por supucsto	*of course*
por favor	*please*	por lo tanto	*consequently*
por fin	*finally*	por lo visto	*apparently*
por todos lados/ por todas partes	*everywhere*		

Oral Practice

 Track 68

Read the following conversation aloud, filling in the spaces with the correct **por** expression from the following list. Expressions may be used more than once. When you're finished, listen to the CD and follow along to check your answers and pronunciation.

por favor	por lo visto	por supuesto	por mí
por lo menos	por fin	por cierto	

Raquel: Buenos días. Quiero hablar con Camila Reyes 1. _____. *Good morning. I'd like to speak to Camila Reyes please.*

Recepcionista:	2. _____. Un momento,
	3. _____. *Of course. One minute, please.*
Camila:	¿Aló? *Hello?*
Raquel:	Hola, Camila, soy Raquel. *Hi Camila, this is Raquel.*
Camila:	Anda, Raquel, qué buena sorpresa. ¿Qué tal? *Hey, Raquel What a nice surprise. How are you?*
Raquel:	Muy bien, gracias. ¿Tienes un momento para hablar? *Great, thanks. Do you have a minute to talk?*
Camila:	4. _____. Dime. *Of course. What's up?*
Raquel:	Te acuerdas cuando me dijiste que estabas buscando un nuevo empleo? Pues, 5. _____ se va a abrir un puesto aquí en la agencia. *Remember when you told me you were looking for a new job? Well, apparently there's a position opening up here at the agency.*
Camila:	¿Ah, sí? Qué bien, porque estoy harta de este trabajo. ¿Qué tipo de trabajo es? *Really? How great, because I'm fed up with this job. What type of job is it?*
Raquel:	Agente de ventas. Perfecto para ti. 6. _____ ¿cuánto esperas ganar? *Sales agent. Perfect for you. By the way, how much do you expect to earn?*
Camila:	Pues aquí gano unos treinta y cinco mil, así que 7. _____ eso. *Well, here I earn thirty-five thousand, so at least that.*
Raquel:	Creo que pagaría 8. _____ cuarenta mil por año. *I believe it pays at least forty thousand a year.*
Camila:	Ah, pues bien. Te mando mi currículo ahora mismo. *Oh, good. I'll send you my CV right away.*
Raquel:	Perfecto. 9. _____ sería estupendo. Me gustaría tener más gente joven aquí en la agencia. *Perfect. It would be great for me. I'd like to have more young people at the agency.*
Camila:	Y tal vez yo puedo salir de aquí 10. ¡_____! *And maybe I can finally get out of here!*

Talking About Money

When talking about units of currency, it's important to know if the noun is masculine or feminine, and how to form the plural. Remember that any number ending in **ciento** (*hundred*) or **millones** (*millions*) will have plural and feminine forms.

el dólar   trescien**tos** dólares
el peso   dos millo**nes** de pesos
la peseta   trescien**tas** pesetas

Here is a list of Spanish and Latin American currencies:

Estados Unidos	el dólar	Argentina	el peso argentino
España	el euro	Chile	el peso chileno
México	el peso	Colombia	el peso colombiano
Guatemala	el quetzal	Venezuela	el bolívar
El Salvador	el dólar	Perú	el nuevo sol
Honduras	el lempira	Ecuador	el dólar
Nicaragua	el córdoba	Bolivia	el boliviano
Costa Rica	el colón	República Dominicana	el peso dominicano
Panamá	el balboa	Cuba	el peso cubano
Paraguay	el guaraní	Uruguay	el peso

Written Practice 2

Complete each sentence by writing out the number in parentheses with the proper currency depending on the country described.

1. Pagué _____ (**50**) por esta mola en Panamá. *I paid fifty balboas for this mola in Panama.*

2. Un viaje a Tikal desde la ciudad de Guatemala cuesta más de _____ (**700**). *A trip to Tikal from the capital costs more than seven hundred quetzals.*

3. En Managua, Nicaragua, el apartamento más caro cuesta _____ (**500**) por mes. *In Managua, Nicaragua, the most expensive apartment costs five hundred córdobas per month.*

4. En Argentina no pago más de _____ (200) por unas botas de cuero. *In Argentina I don't pay more than* **200** *Argentine pesos for a pair of leather boots.*

5. El sueldo mínimo en Honduras es de sólo _____ (5500). *The minimum wage in Honduras is only* **5500** *lempiras.*

6. En Bolivia, cien dólares valen _____ (700). *In Bolivia, a hundred dollars are worth* **700** *bolivianos.*

Money Talk

Spain officially made the switch to the **euro** from the **peseta** in 2000. For many, the transition was a difficult one—don't be surprised if you still hear people calculating sums in **pesetas**. This is especially true for large amounts. So next time you hear someone say that real estate prices have plummeted, and that they couldn't sell their house for more than **cincuenta millones** (*fifty million*), remember, they don't mean euros! At the old exchange rate, fifty million **pesetas** equaled about $330,000.

You may be wondering why **el dólar** is included in the list of currencies. Spanish speakers in the U.S. and **Puerto Rico** are not the only ones to use this term. Some countries tie their currency to the U.S. dollar, and in **El Salvador** (which formerly used **el colón**), **Ecuador** (which formerly used **el sucre**), and Panamá the economy has become **dolarizado** (*converted to the dollar*). This means that the U.S. dollar has become the official local currency. Finally, in many countries in Latin America, the U.S. dollar is accepted as a parallel currency.

Due to severe inflation, **Peru** changed its currency from **el sol** to **el inti** in 1985. By 1991 **el inti** had become so inflated it was rendered useless. It was then converted to **el nuevo sol** at the rate of 1,000,000 **intis** to 1 **nuevo sol**. The names of both currencies are related, as **sol** means *sun* and **Inti** is the Inca sun god.

Not-So-Simple Expressions for Simple Concepts

There are some straightforward concepts that are not always easy to express in Spanish. Following is a list of simple ideas, and a number of ways to express them in Spanish.

To Have Fun

The most common way to talk about having fun is to use the reflexive verb **divertirse**.

¿Te divertiste anoche?	*Did you have fun last night?*
—**Me divertí** mucho en la fiesta.	*—I had a lot of fun at the party.*

Another more informal way to talk about having fun or having a good time is to use the expression **pasárselo bien**. Remember, you will have to use the reflexive pronoun and the pronoun **lo** when conjugating this verbal expression.

¿Te lo pasaste bien anoche?	*Did you have a good time last night?*
—Sí, **me lo pasé** muy bien.	*—Yes, I had a great time.*

These expressions can also be used with commands.

¡Pásatelo bien!	*Have a good time!*
¡Que te lo pases bien!	*Have a good time!*
¡Diviértanse!	*Have fun!*

To Become

To become is one of the more troublesome concepts for Spanish learners. In English it can have many meanings: *to get, to turn, to turn into*. In Spanish, there is no one word that expresses the concept of *becoming*.

Hacerse is used to talk about *becoming*, usually with long-lasting results.

Se hicieron amigos.	*They became friends.*
Susana **se hizo** monja.	*Susana became a nun.*
Mi abuela **se está haciendo** vieja.	*My grandmother is getting old.*
Hazte socio del gimnasio.	*Become a member of the gym.*

Ponerse can also be used for *to become*, usually to talk about changes in state of mind or condition we express with *to get* in English. Some of the most common expressions with **ponerse** include **ponerse malo** (*to get sick*), **ponerse nervioso/-a** (*to get upset*), and **ponerse de moda** (*to become fashionable*).

Después de comer en el restaurante, **se puso mala**.	*After eating in the restaurant, she got sick.*
Me puse furioso.	*I got angry.*

Volverse is another reflexive verb meaning *to become* and is mostly used with the phrase **volverse loco** (*to go crazy*). **Volverse** is often used to describe transformations that happen suddenly.

Cecilia **se ha vuelto** loca.	*Cecilia has gone crazy.*
Bruno **se ha vuelto** muy agresivo.	*Bruno has become very aggressive.*

Llegar a ser often refers to a long process of becoming.

Después de muchos años, ella **llegó a ser** directora del departamento.	*After many years, she became director of the department.*

The verbs **convertirse en** and **transformarse en** are often used with the meaning *to turn into*.

La piedra **se convierte en** polvo.	*The rock turns into dust.*
La oruga **se transforma en** mariposa.	*The caterpillar turns into a butterfly.*

Quedarse can also be used to say *to become* in the sense of *to end up*; for instance, **quedarse embarazada** (*to get pregnant*). You already learned this use of **quedarse** in Chapter 9.

Many of the previously used expressions can be interchanged, with subtle distinctions. For example, **hacerse rico** (*to become rich*) may imply a longer process of accumulating wealth than **volverse rico** (*to get rich*), which sounds more sudden—as in *to get rich quick*.

A final way to talk about *becoming* or "*getting*" is to use reflexive verbs, such as **mojarse** (*to get wet*) or **cansarse** (*to get tired*). Reflexive verbs often describe processes of becoming, often with the prefixes **en-** or **a-**; for instance, **enloquecerse** (*to go crazy*), **entristecerse** (*to get sad*), or **arrinconarse** (*to get cornered*). These verbs are often derived from adjectives or nouns. Take a look at just a few:

loco	*crazy*	enloquecerse	*to go crazy*
triste	*sad*	entristecerse	*to become sad*
mojado	*wet*	mojarse	*to get wet*
rincón	*corner*	arrinconarse	*to become/get cornered*
cansado	*tired*	cansarse	*to get tired*
caliente	*hot*	calentarse	*to get hot*
enojado	*angry*	enojarse	*to become angry*

To Happen

The easiest and most common way to say *to happen* is **pasar**. This can be used in almost any situation.

¿Qué **está pasando** aquí?	*What's happening here?*

Spanish also has a few other synonyms that mean *to happen*: **ocurrir**, **acontecer**, and **suceder**. You will recognize these when they are spoken or written, but use them only in more formal situations.

¿Qué **ocurre**?	*What's happening?*
Eso nunca **acontece**.	*That never happens.*
No sé qué **sucedía**.	*I don't know what was happening*

To Take

Expressing the concept of *to take* is problematic in Spanish due to regional variations in usage. In Spain, it is extremely common and totally acceptable to say **coger** for all manner of *taking*, such as **coger el autobús** (*to take the bus*) or **coger la mano** (*to take someone's hand*). However, in much of Latin America, **coger** is totally *unacceptable* because it is a vulgar way of saying *to have sex* (I'm sure you can come up with an equivalent in English). As a result, you need to know other ways of saying *to take*. The most common are **tomar** and **agarrar**. **Llevar** is also used in the sense of *to take (along) with*.

No **tomes** el autobús. Es muy lento.	*Don't take the bus. It's very slow.*
Toma este dinero.	*Take this money.*
Agarra ese taxi.	*Grab that taxi.*

To Miss

To miss has many meanings in English, which are all expressed differently in Spanish. When talking about missing someone, **extrañar** is used in Latin America, and **echar de menos** in Spain.

Extraño mucho a mi gato.	*I really miss my cat.*
¿Me **echas de menos**?	*Do you miss me?*

The verb **perder** is used when talking about missing a train, plane, class, etc.

Perdí la clase ayer.	*I missed class yesterday.*
Rodrigo **perdió** su avión.	*Rodrigo missed his plane.*

Faltar a can also be used to talk about missing something you were supposed to go to.

¿**Faltaste a** clase ayer?   *Did you miss class yesterday?*

The trickiest form of *to miss* is to express ideas such as *You just missed her* or *The car just missed me.* Usually the best solution is to come up with another way of expressing the idea.

Acaba de salir.   *She just left. (You just missed her).*

El carro **casi** me atropella.   *The car almost hit me. (The car just missed me.)*

Written Practice 3

Circle the letter of the word or phrase that best completes each sentence.

1. ¿Por qué _____ a la boda?

    (a) perdiste

    (b) faltaste

2. No me grites. _____.

    (a) Me pone nerviosa

    (b) Me echa de menos

3. Cristina _____ mala después de la cena.

    (a) se volvió

    (b) se puso

4. No me gusta correr. _____ mucho.

    (a) Me canso

    (b) Me enojo

5. En Buenos Aire puedes _____ un taxi en cualquier esquina.

    (a) coger

    (b) tomar

6. Carla y Carlos se _____ amigos.

    (a) pusieron

    (b) hicieron

QUIZ

Circle the letter of the word or phrase that best completes each sentence.

1. **Caminamos _____ las calles.**
   A. para
   B. por

2. **¿Me prestas cien pesos _____ la factura?**
   A. para
   B. por

3. **Compré el anillo _____ ochocientos dólares.**
   A. para
   B. por

4. **Gracias _____ no decir nada.**
   A. para
   B. por

5. **¿_____ quién trabajas?**
   A. Para
   B. Por

6. **Lo siento, pero el restaurante no admite perros. Para tu entrevista, ponte un traje y no lleves la camisa _____.**
   A. por fuera
   B. por dentro

7. **Compré el bolso en Guatemala por cincuenta _____.**
   A. lempiras
   B. quetzales

8. **En ecuador se usan _____.**
   A. pesos ecuatorianos
   B. dólares

9. ¡_____ bien en la fiesta!

   A. Pásatelo

   B. Hazte

10. ¿Has visto a Ángela?

    —Ay, _____.

    A. acaba de salir

    B. la echaste de menos

PART FOUR TEST

Circle the letter of the word or phrase that best completes each sentence.

1. **No parece que Mario _____ alcohol.**
   A. bebe
   B. beba
   C. beban
   D. bebes

2. **No estoy segura de que el grupo _____ esta noche.**
   A. toca
   B. tocan
   C. toque
   D. toquen

3. **Creo que el bebé _____.**
   A. sonría
   B. sonríe
   C. sonrío
   D. sonreí

4. **Cuando _____ con Julio, ¿le preguntas si va a clase mañana?**
   A. habla
   B. hablas
   C. hable
   D. hables

5. **Cuando _____ al gimnasio, siempre llevo una toalla.**
   A. va
   B. vaya
   C. voy
   D. vayas

6. **Es tu cumpleaños. Vamos adonde tú _____.**
   A. quieres
   B. quieras
   C. gustas
   D. gustes

7. **El hotel recomienda que los huéspedes no _____ de las instalaciones turísticas.**

   A. salen

   B. salgan

   C. saldrán

   D. salieron

8. **Los niños quieren _____.**

   A. jugar

   B. juegan

   C. jueguen

   D. jugaron

9. **¿Quién quieres que gane el partido de fútbol?**

   —Que _____ los Magos.

   A. gana

   B. gane

   C. ganan

   D. ganen

10. **¿Hay un teléfono público donde _____ hacer una llamada?**

    A. puedo

    B. puede

    C. pueda

    D. puedes

11. **La ventana _____.**

    A. es cerrado

    B. está cerrado

    C. es cerrada

    D. está cerrada

12. **La Ciudad de las Artes y las Ciencias _____ por Santiago Calatrava y Félix Candela.**

    A. fue diseñado

    B. fue diseñada

    C. fueron diseñados

    D. fueron diseñadas

13. **Aquí _____ piedras preciosas.**
    A. se vende
    B. se venden
    C. está vendido
    D. es vendido

14. **¿Tú _____ a tus padres?**
    —No todavía.
    A. ha llamado
    B. has llamado
    C. ha llamados
    D. has llamados

15. **El ladrón ya _____ cuando los detectives _____.**
    A. ha salido; llegaron
    B. había salido; han llegado
    C. salió; habían llegado
    D. había salido; llegaron

16. **Fue extraño que Lidia no _____ en la fiesta.**
    A. aparezca
    B. aparece
    C. apareciera
    D. apareció

17. **_____ tienda que vendiera chorizo.**
    A. Buscaba una
    B. Conozco una
    C. Hay una
    D. Encontré

18. **Si Ernesto te _____ matrimonio, ¿lo aceptarás?**
    A. pide
    B. pedirá
    C. pida
    D. pidiera

19. **Si yo tuviera vacaciones, _____ contigo a la República Dominicana.**
    A. voy
    B. iré
    C. iría
    D. habría ido

20. **Si Pablo hubiera ido a la fiesta, _____ a Regina.**

    A. hubiera visto

    B. habría visto

    C. vería

    D. verá

21. **_____ ser español habla muy bien inglés.**

    A. Por lo

    B. Por

    C. Para

    D. Para él

22. **Adán está enfadado conmigo.**

    —Ah, _____ no te habla.

    A. por supuesto

    B. por eso

    C. por fuera

    D. por casualidad

23. **Compré este tejido en _____ por cien mil guaraníes.**

    A. Nicaragua

    B. Bolivia

    C. Perú

    D. Paraguay

24. **Salí durante una tormenta de lluvia y _____.**

    A. me enojé

    B. me arrinconé

    C. me mojé

    D. me calenté

25. **Espero que no hayamos _____ el último tren.**

    A. perdido

    B. convertido

    C. acabado

    D. faltado

Final Exam

Circle the letter of the word or phrase that best completes each sentence.

1. The sound of the g in the word gente sounds closest to the _____ sound in English.

   A. *g*   B. *th*   C. *h*   D. *j*

2. The sound of the v in the word vaso is closest to the _____ sound in English.

   A. *v*   B. *b*   C. *z*   D. *zh*

3. El Dr. Hernández es _____ médico.

   A. un   B. una   C. el   D. —

4. _____ casa es grande.

   A. El   B. La   C. Un   D. —

5. The stress in the word peluquería falls on _____.

   A. pe-   B. -lu-   C. -que-   D. -rí-

6. _____ eres de Chicago.

   A. Yo   B. Tú   C. Ella   D. Usted

7. Silvia y Pedro _____. Son estudiantes.

   A. trabajan no   B. no trabajan   C. no trabajas   D. no trabajamos

8. ¿Es tu cartera?

—Sí, es _____ cartera.

A. mi   B. tu   C. su   D. nuestra

9. Jorge es un hombre _____.

A. simpática   B. optimista   C. delgada   D. tímida

10. ¿_____ es?

—Es mi primo, Quique.

A. Qué   B. Cuál   C. Dónde   D. Quién

11. Ahora ustedes _____ en Atascadero.

A. vive   B. vivan   C. viven   D. vivo

12. ¿Cómo _____ David?

—Alto, moreno y muy guapo.

A. es   B. está   C. eres   D. estoy

13. La tienda no_____ hasta las diez.

A. abra   B. abren   C. abre   D. abro

14. ¿Cómo vas tú a trabajar?

—Yo _____ a pie.

A. va   B. ve   C. voy   D. van

15. Un año tiene _____ días.

A. cincuenta y dos   B. trescientos sesenta y cinco   C. siete   D. treinta

16. _____ una menos cuarto. Vamos a almorzar.

A. Son las   B. Son el   C. Es la   D. Es el

17. ¿_____ mucho tráfico en la ciudad?

A. Hay   B. Tiene   C. Hace   D. Haber

18. Hace mucho sol. ¿Usted no_____?

A. tiene miedo   B. tiene calor   C. tiene frío   D. tiene sed

19. **El camarero sirve _____ cliente.**

    A. a   B. el   C. al   D. —

20. **_____ regalo es para ti.**

    A. Este   B. Éste   C. Esto   D. Esta

21. **A Mónica y Alicia _____ la paella.**

    A. le gusta   B. le gustan   C. les gusta   D. les gustan

22. **En la clase de español nosotros _____ *Don Quijote*.**

    A. somos leyendo   B. estamos leyendo   C. somos leído   D. estamos leído

23. **_____ está llamando.**

    A. Alguien   B. Nadie   C. Ninguna   D. A, B, o C

24. **La bufanda es de Nicolás. Es _____.**

    A. suya   B. tuya   C. suyo   D. nuestro

25. **El restaurante _____ cerrado el domingo.**

    A. voy a estar   B. va a estar   C. van a estar   D. va estar

26. **¿A qué hora _____ por la noche?**

    A. te acuestas   B. te levantas   C. te despiertas   D. te sientas

27. **Los niños están _____ mucho en Disneylandia.**

    A. divirtiéndose   B. se divirtiendo   C. diviertan   D. divirtiéndole

28. **São Paulo, Brasil es la ciudad _____ de Sudamérica.**

    A. que más grande   B. más grande   C. mayor   D. grande

29. **Jenny no habla _____ rápido como su hermana.**

    A. tan   B. tanto   C. igual   D. A, B, o C

30. **_____ listos. ¿Nos vamos?**

    A. Estoy   B. Soy   C. Están   D. Son

31. **No _____ con tu hermano. Quédate aquí.**

    A. Vas   B. Va   C. Vaya   D. Vayas

32. Sra. Moreno, _____ mañana, por favor.

    A. llámame   B. me llama   C. llámeme   D. llame me

33. Me gusta tanto la película *El Señor de los Anillos* que _____ he visto siete veces.

    A. el   B. lo   C. le   D. la

34. ¿_____ usted a Chile el año que viene?

    A. viajará   B. viajarás   C. viajaré   D. viajara

35. Yo _____ envié unas flores a mi madre.

    A. le   B. la   C. lo   D. las

36. ¿Fuiste a clase el lunes?
    —No, no _____ ir.

    A. puse   B. pude   C. cupe   D. supe

37. ¿Me diste la llave de la casa?
    —Sí, _____ di ayer.

    A. se lo   B. se la   C. te lo   D. te la

38. Cuando yo era pequeño, _____ dos perros.

    A. tengo   B. tenía   C. tuve   D. tendría

39. Pedro _____ música cuando lo llamé.

    A. está escuchando   B. estaba escuchando   C. está escuchado   D. estaba escuchado

40. Hace cuatro años que _____ sola. Ahora vivo con mi marido.

    A. vivo   B. vivía   C. viví   D. viviría

41. ¿_____ cuando _____ a casa?

    A. Llovió; llegaste   B. Llovía; llegaste   C. Llovió; llegabas   D. Llovía; llegabas

42. Mi profesor no es muy exigente.
    —¿De verdad? _____ nos enseña a nosotros es muy difícil.

    A. El que   B. Él que   C. La que   D. Lo que

43. No quiero que él se _____ esa camisa.

    A. pone   B. pon   C. ponga   D. puse

44. Temo que nosotros _____ perdidos.

    A. estamos B. estemos C. estaremos D. estuvimos

45. Insisto en que ustedes _____ conmigo. Será interesante.

    A. viene B. vienes C. venga D. vengan

46. ¿Entiendes a los cubanos cuando _____?

    A. hablaron B. hablaran C. hablan D. hablen

47. Quiero comprar un boleto de ida y _____.

    A. hecha B. vuelta C. vista D. llegada

48. Cuando miré el celular, vi que _____ Héctor.

    A. llama B. habría llamado C. había llamado D. había llamando

49. Yo no esperaba que ellos _____ tan bien.

    A. cantaron B. cantaran C. cantarían D. habían cantado

50. Necesito la presentación _____ mañana.

    A. para B. por C. en D. a

English-Spanish Glossary

A

a, an un, una
a lot mucho
above arriba, encima de, sobre
across (from) enfrente, frente a
actor actor (*m.*)
actress actriz (*f.*)
address dirección (*f.*)
after después
afternoon tarde (*f.*)
airplane avión (*m.*)
airport aeropuerto (*m.*)
alcohol alcohol (*m.*)
all todo, todos
alone solo
along por
already ya
always siempre
ancient antiguo
and y
angry enojado, enfadado

anyone, anybody alguien, cualquier persona, nadie
anything algo, cualquier cosa, nada
answer respuesta (*f.*), responder, contestar
apartment apartamento (*m.*)
apple manzana (*f.*)
argue discutir
around alrededor
arrive llegar
art arte (*m.*)
artist artista (*m., f.*)
as como, tan
as much cuanto, tanto
ask preguntar
ask for pedir
attend asistir
attractive atractivo, guapo
aunt tía (*f.*)
author autor (*m.*), autora (*f.*)

autumn otoño (*m.*)
avenue avenida (*f.*)

B

bad malo
badly mal
balcony terraza (*f.*), balcón (*m.*)
bank banco (*m.*)
bark ladrar
bath baño (*m.*)
bathe bañar(se)
bathroom cuarto de baño (*m.*),
   baño (*m.*)
be ser, estar
be able to poder
be afraid tener miedo
be left quedar
be located estar, quedar
be obliged to tener que
be worth valer
beach playa (*f.*)
beautiful hermoso, bello, guapo
because porque
bed cama (*f.*)
bedroom dormitorio (*m.*),
   cuarto (*m.*), habitación (*f.*)
beer cerveza (*f.*)
before antes
beg rogar
begin comenzar, empezar
behind atrás, detrás
believe creer
besides además
better mejor
between entre
big grande
bigger mayor

birthday cumpleaños (*m.*)
black negro
block cuadra (*f.*)
blond rubio
blue azul
boardwalk malecón (*m.*)
book libro (*m.*)
bookstore librería (*f.*)
boss jefe (*m.*), jefa (*f.*)
bottle botella (*f.*)
boy niño (*m.*), chico (*m.*),
   muchacho (*m.*)
boyfriend novio (*m.*)
bread pan (*m.*)
breakfast desayuno (*m.*)
bring traer
broken roto
brother hermano (*m.*)
building edificio (*m.*)
bus autobús (*m.*)
but pero
but rather sino
buy comprar
by por

C

café cafetería (*f.*)
call llamar, llamada (*f.*)
cap gorro (*m.*)
car carro (*m.*)
card tarjeta (*f.*)
cat gato (*m.*)
center centro (*m.*)
certain cierto
change cambiar,
   cambio (*m.*)
chat platicar

cheap barato

check (at restaurant) cuenta (f.)

cheese queso (m.)

chewing gum chicle (m.)

chicken pollo (m.)

child niño (m.), niña (f.)

Christmas Navidad (f.)

church iglesia (f.)

cinema cine (m.)

city ciudad (f.)

class clase (f.)

clean limpio

client cliente (m., f.)

climb subir

clock reloj (m.)

close cerrar

clothing ropa (f.)

coffee café (m.)

cold frío

come venir

comfortable cómodo

company empresa (f.)

computer computadora (f.),
   ordenador (m.)

cook cocinar, cocinero (m.),
   cocinera (f.)

cool fresco

corner rincón (m.)

cost costar

count contar

country país (m.)

countryside campo (m.)

couple par (m.), pareja (f.)

cousin primo (m.), prima (f.)

crazy loco

current actual

customer cliente (m., f.)

D

dance bailar

dark oscuro

dark (-haired, -skinned) moreno

daughter hija (f.)

day día (m.)

day before yesterday anteayer

dead muerto

decide decidir

delete borrar

delicious delicioso, rico

demonstration manifestación (f.)

deny negar

dessert postre (m.)

die morir

difficult difícil

dinner cena (f.)

dirty sucio

discuss discutir

do hacer

doctor doctor (m.), doctora (f.), médico
   (m.), médica (f.)

dog perro (m.)

door puerta (f.)

double doble

doubt dudar

dream sueño (m.), soñar

dress vestir(se), vestido (m.)

drink beber, tomar

drinking glass vaso (m.)

during mientras

E

each cada

earn ganar

earring arete (m.), pendiente (m.)

easy fácil

eat comer
eat breakfast desayunar
eat dinner cenar
eat lunch almorzar
egg huevo (*m.*)
either tampoco
English inglés (*m.*)
enormous enorme
equal igual
erase borrar
essay ensayo (*m.*)
every todo, cada
exactly efectivamente
exam examen (*m.*)
exercise ejercicio (*m.*)
exhibit exposición (*f.*)
expense gasto (*m.*)
expensive caro
eye ojo (*m.*)

F

face cara (*f.*)
facing enfrente
fall caer
fall otoño (*m.*)
fan (sports) hincha (*m., f.*)
far (from) lejos (de)
fat gordo
father padre (*m.*)
fear miedo (*m.*), temer, tener
  miedo
feel sentir(se), encontrarse
fiancé novio (*m.*)
fiancée novia (*f.*)
film película (*f.*)
find encontrar
finger dedo (*m.*)

fire (from a job) despedir
first primero
fish pez (*m.*), pescado (*m.*)
flee huir
fly volar
follow seguir
food comida (*f.*)
for para, por
forget olvidar(se)
frequently frecuentemente,
  a menudo
Friday viernes (*m.*)
friend amigo (*m.*), amiga (*f.*)
friendly simpático, amable
front: in front of delante de
fruit fruta (*f.*)
fun divertido
furthermore además

G

game partido (*m.*), juego (*m.*)
garden jardín (*m.*)
generous generoso
gentleman señor (*m.*)
get conseguir
girl niña (*f.*), chica (*f.*), muchacha (*f.*)
girlfriend novia (*f.*)
give dar
give back devolver
glass: drinking glass vaso (*m.*)
go ir
go out salir
go up subir
gold oro (*m.*)
good bueno
grab agarrar
grandchild nieto (*m.*)

granddaughter nieta (*f.*)
grandfather abuelo (*m.*)
grandmother abuela (*f.*)
grandson nieto (*m.*)
gratuity propina (*f.*)
green verde
gym gimnasio (*m.*)

H

hair cabello (*m.*)
hairdresser peluquero (*m.*),
  peluquera (*f.*)
half medio, mitad (*f.*)
hand mano (*f.*)
handsome guapo, hermoso
happen pasar, ocurrir, suceder
happy alegre, feliz, contento
have tener, haber, tomar
have to deber, tener que
he él
health salud (*f.*)
heat calor (*m.*)
hello hola
help ayudar
her su, sus
here aquí, acá
highway carretera (*f.*)
his su, sus
homework deberes (*m. pl.*), tarea (*f.*)
hope esperar, esperanza (*f.*)
hope: let's hope ojalá
horse caballo (*m.*)
hot caliente
hotel hotel (*m.*)
hour hora (*f.*)
how cómo, como
how much cuánto

however sin embargo
huge enorme
hundred cien, ciento
hunger hambre (*m.*)
husband esposo (*m.*), marido (*m.*)

I

I yo
ice cream helado (*m.*)
ice hielo (*m.*)
idea idea (*f.*)
identification identificación (*f.*)
if si
ill enfermo
impossible imposible
in en
in front of delante de
in order to para
incredible increíble
inexpensive barato
intelligent inteligente, listo
invite invitar

J

journalist periodista (*m., f.*)

K

key llave (*f.*)
kiss beso (*m.*)
kitchen cocina (*f.*)
know saber, conocer

L

lack faltar
lady señora (*f.*)
language idioma (*m.*),
  lenguaje (*m.*)

last último, pasado
last night anoche
later luego, más tarde
laugh reír
lawyer abogado (*m.*), abogada (*f.*)
learn aprender
leave irse, salir, marcharse
left: be left quedar
let's hope ojalá
letter carta (*f.*)
library biblioteca (*f.*)
lie mentir
life vida (*f.*)
lift levantar
light encender
like gustar
listen (to) escuchar
little poco
located: be located estar, quedar
long largo
look at mirar
look for buscar
lose perder
lot: a lot mucho
lottery lotería (*f.*)
love amor (*m.*), encantar, querer, amar
lover amante (*m., f.*)
low bajo
luck suerte (*f.*)
lunch almuerzo (*m.*), comida (*f.*), almorzar

M

madam señora (*f.*)
magazine revista (*f.*)
make hacer
man hombre (*m.*), señor (*m.*)
manage to conseguir

map mapa (*m.*)
market mercado (*m.*)
match partido (*m.*)
matter asunto (*m.*), importar
maybe quizás, tal vez, a lo mejor
mayor alcalde (*m.*), alcaldesa (*f.*)
me mí
measure medir
meat carne (*f.*)
menu carta (*f.*)
midnight medianoche (*f.*)
milk leche (*f.*)
minus menos
miss perder, echar de menos,
   hacer falta
moment momento (*m.*)
Monday lunes (*m.*)
money dinero (*m.*)
month mes (*m.*)
more más
morning mañana (*f.*)
mother madre (*f.*)
mountain montaña (*f.*)
mouth boca (*f.*)
move mover, mudarse (de casa)
movie película (*f.*)
movies cine (*m.*)
mural mural (*m.*)
museum museo (*m.*)
music música (*f.*)
musician músico (*m.*), música (*f.*)
my mi
myself mí

N

name nombre (*m.*)
named: be named llamarse

near cerca
need necesitar, hacer falta
neighborhood barrio (*m.*)
neither tampoco, ni
never jamás, nunca
new nuevo
news noticias (*f. pl.*)
newspaper periódico (*m.*)
night noche (*f.*)
no no
no one nadie
noisy ruidoso
noon mediodía (*m.*)
nor ni
normal normal
nothing nada
now ahora
nurse enfermero (*m.*),
  enfermera (*f.*)

O

obtain conseguir
obvious obvio
ocean mar (*m., f.*), océano (*m.*)
of de
of course claro, por supuesto
office oficina (*f.*)
often frecuentemente,
  a menudo
old viejo, antiguo
older mayor
on en, sobre, encima de
only solamente, sólo, único
open abrir, abierto
or o
orange naranja (*f.*)
organize organizar

our nuestro
owe deber

P

pair par (*m.*)
park parque (*m.*)
party fiesta (*f.*)
pass aprobar, pasar
path camino (*m.*)
pay pagar
pen bolígrafo (*m.*)
pencil lápiz (*m.*)
people gente (*f.*)
person persona (*f.*)
pharmacy farmacia (*f.*)
photograph foto (*f.*)
pity lástima (*f.*)
place sitio (*m.*), lugar (*m.*)
play jugar
please por favor, gustar
police (department, force) policía (*f.*)
police officer policía (*m., f.*)
poor pobre
possible posible
prefer preferir
pregnant embarazada
prepare preparar
prepared preparado
president presidente (*m.*),
  presidenta (*f.*)
pretty bonito, lindo
probable probable
problem problema (*m.*)
profession profesión (*f.*)
prove probar
public público
put meter, poner

Q

quarter cuarto (*m.*)
question pregunta (*f.*)
quite bastante

R

rain lluvia (*f.*)
raise subir, levantar
rare raro
read leer
ready listo, preparado
reason razón (*f.*)
red rojo
refrigerator frigorífico (*m.*)
relative pariente (*m., f.*)
remember acordarse de, recordar
repeat repetir
rest descansar
restaurant restaurante (*m.*)
return regresar, volver, devolver
rich rico
river río (*m.*)
road carretera (*f.*), camino (*m.*), calle (*f.*)
rock piedra (*f.*)
room cuarto (*m.*), habitación (*f.*), lugar (*m.*)
run correr

S

sad triste
salary sueldo (*m.*)
salt sal (*f.*)
same mismo
same: the same igual
Saturday sábado (*m.*)
say decir
say good-bye despedir(se)
school escuela (*f.*), colegio (*m.*)

sea mar (*m., f.*)
second segundo
see ver
seem parecer
selfish egoísta
sell vender
send enviar, mandar
sensitive sensible
serve servir
server camarero (*m.*), camarera (*f.*)
shame vergüenza (*f.*) lástima (*f.*), pena (*f.*)
shave afeitar(se)
she ella
shirt camisa (*f.*)
shoe zapato (*m.*)
short bajo, corto
show mostrar, enseñar
shower duchar(se), ducha (*f.*)
shy tímido
sick enfermo
side lado (*m.*)
silver plata (*f.*)
silverware cubiertos (*m. pl.*)
since desde, como
sing cantar
singer cantante (*m., f.*)
sir señor (*m.*)
sister hermana (*f.*)
sit (down) sentar(se)
skinny flaco, delgado
skirt falda (*f.*)
sleep sueño (*m.*), dormir
sleepiness sueño (*m.*)
small pequeño
smaller menor
smile sonreír

smoke humo (*m.*), fumar
snack bar cafetería (*f.*)
snow nieve (*f.*)
so tanto
so many, so much tanto,
   tantos(as)
soccer fútbol (*m.*)
some unos, unas
someone alguien
something algo
son hijo (*m.*)
song canción (*f.*)
space espacio (*m.*), lugar (*m.*)
Spanish español (*m.*)
speak hablar
special especial
spend gastar
spend (time) pasar
spring primavera (*f.*)
stadium estadio (*m.*)
start comenzar, empezar
station estación (*f.*)
stay quedarse
still todavía
stone piedra (*f.*)
store tienda (*f.*)
strange raro, extraño
street calle (*f.*)
strong fuerte
student alumno (*m.*), alumna (*f.*),
   estudiante (*m., f.*)
study estudiar
stupid estúpido
subject asunto (*m.*)
success éxito (*m.*)
suffer sufrir
sugar azúcar (*m.*)

suggest sugerir
suitcase maleta (*f.*)
summer verano (*m.*)
sun sol (*m.*)
Sunday domingo (*m.*)
supermarket supermercado (*m.*)
sure claro, por supuesto, seguro
sweet dulce
swim nadar
swimming pool piscina (*f.*)

T

table mesa (*f.*)
take tomar, coger, agarrar
take off quitar
take (to) traer
tall alto
taxi taxi (*m.*)
teach enseñar
teacher maestro (*m.*), maestra (*f.*),
   profesor (*m.*), profesora (*f.*)
telephone teléfono (*m.*)
television televisión (*f.*), televisor (*m.*)
tell decir
test probar
that que, eso
that one eso
the el (*m.*), la (*f.*), los (*m. pl.*),
   las (*f. pl.*)
theater teatro (*m.*)
then luego, entonces, pues
there allí, ahí, allá
there is, there are hay
thin delgado, flaco
thing cosa (*f.*)
think pensar
third tercero

thirst sed (*f.*)
this este, esta
this one éste, ésta, esto
thousand mil
through por
Thursday jueves (*m.*)
ticket boleto (*m.*)
time tiempo (*m.*), rato (*m.*), vez (*f.*)
tip propina (*f.*)
today hoy
together junto
tomorrow mañana
too demasiado
town pueblo (*m.*), ciudad (*f.*)
town square plaza (*f.*)
train tren (*m.*)
travel viajar
trip viaje (*m.*)
true cierto, verdad (*f.*)
try probar, intentar
Tuesday martes (*m.*)

U

ugly feo
uncle tío (*m.*)
under debajo, abajo
understand comprender, entender
university universidad (*f.*)
unless a menos
until hasta
up arriba
us nosotros

V

very muy
view vista (*f.*)
visit visitar
voice voz (*f.*)

W

wait for esperar
waiter camarero (*m.*), camarera (*f.*)
wake up despertar(se)
walk andar, caminar
wallet cartera (*f.*)
want querer
warn advertir
wash lavar, lavarse
watch reloj (*m.*), ver, mirar
water agua (*f.*)
wedding boda (*f.*)
way camino (*m.*)
Wednesday miércoles (*m.*)
week semana (*f.*)
weekend fin de semana (*m.*)
well bien, pues
what qué
when cuando, cuándo
where donde, dónde
which qué, que, cual
while mientras, rato (*m.*)
white blanco
who que, quien, el (la, los, las) que, quién
whom que, quien, el (la, los, las) que, quién
why por qué
wife esposa (*f.*), mujer (*f.*)
win ganar
wind viento (*m.*)
wine vino (*m.*)
winter invierno (*m.*)
with con
without sin
woman mujer (*f.*), señora (*f.*)

word palabra (*f.*)
work trabajo (*m.*),
   trabajar
work of art obra (*f.*)
worse peor
worth: be worth valer
write escribir

Y

yard jardín (*m.*)
year año (*m.*)

yellow amarillo
yes sí
yesterday ayer
you tú, ti, usted(es),
   le(s)
young joven
younger menor
your tu, su, vuestro
yourself ti, se

Spanish-English Glossary

A

a lo mejor maybe
a menos unless
a menudo frequently, often
abajo under
abierto open
abogado, -a (*m.*, *f.*) lawyer
abrir to open
abuela (*f.*) grandmother
abuelo (*m.*) grandfather
acá here
acordarse to remember
actor (*m.*) actor
actriz (*f.*) actress
actual current
además furthermore, besides
advertir to warn
aeropuerto (*m.*) airport
afeitar(se) to shave
agarrar to take, grab
agua (*f.*) water

ahí there
ahora now
alcalde (*m.*) mayor
alcaldesa (*f.*) mayor
alcohol (*m.*) alcohol
alegre happy
algo something
alguien someone
allá there
allí there
almorzar to eat lunch
almuerzo (*m.*) lunch
alrededor around
alto tall
alumno, -a (*m.*, *f.*) student, pupil
amable friendly
amante (*m.*, *f.*) lover
amar to love
amarillo yellow
amigo, -a (*m.*, *f.*) friend
amor (*m.*) love

andar to walk
anoche last night
anteayer day before yesterday
antes before
antiguo old, ancient
año (*m.*) year
apartamento (*m.*) apartment
aprender to learn
aprobar to pass, approve
aquí here
arete (*m.*) earring
arriba above, up
arte (*m.*) art
artista (*m., f.*) artist
asistir to attend
asunto (*m.*) subject, matter
atractivo attractive
atrás behind
autobús (*m.*) bus
autor, -a (*m., f.*) author
avenida (*f.*) avenue
avión (*m.*) airplane
ayer yesterday
ayudar to help
azúcar (*m.*) sugar
azul blue

B

bailar to dance
bajo short, low
balcón (*m.*) balcony
banco (*m.*) bank
bañar(se) to bathe
baño (*m.*) bath, bathroom
barato cheap, inexpensive
barrio (*m.*) neighborhood
bastante quite

beber to drink
bello beautiful
beso (*m.*) kiss
biblioteca (*f.*) library
bien well
blanco white
boca (*f.*) mouth
boda (*f.*) wedding
boleto (*m.*) ticket
bolígrafo (*m.*) pen
bonito pretty
borrar to erase, delete
botella (*f.*) bottle
bueno good
buscar to look for

C

caballo (*m.*) horse
cabello (*m.*) hair
cada each, every
caer to fall
café (*m.*) coffee
cafetería (*f.*) snack bar, café
caliente hot
calle (*f.*) street, road
calor (*m.*) heat
cama (*f.*) bed
camarero, -a (*m., f.*) server, waiter
cambiar to change
caminar to walk
camino (*m.*) road, way, path
camisa (*f.*) shirt
campo (*m.*) countryside
canción (*f.*) song
cantante (*m., f.*) singer
cantar to sing
cara (*f.*) face

carne (*f.*) meat

caro expensive

carretera (*f.*) road, highway

carro (*m.*) car

carta (*f.*) letter, menu

cartera (*f.*) wallet

cena (*f.*) dinner

cenar to eat dinner

centro (*m.*) center

cerca near

cerrar to close

cerveza (*f.*) beer

chica (*f.*) girl

chicle (*m.*) chewing gum

chico (*m.*) boy

cien hundred

cierto certain, true

cine (*m.*) cinema, movies

ciudad (*f.*) city, town

claro of course, sure, clear

clase (*f.*) class

cliente (*m., f.*) client, customer

cocina (*f.*) kitchen

cocinar to cook

coger to take

colegio (*m.*) school

comenzar to begin, start

comer to eat

comida (*f.*) food

como as, since, how

cómo how

cómodo comfortable

comprar to buy

comprender to understand

computadora (*f.*) computer

con with

conocer to know

conseguir to get, obtain, manage to

contar to count

contento happy

contestar to answer

correr to run

corto short

cosa (*f.*) thing

costar to cost

creer to believe

cuadra (*f.*) block, street

cual which

cuando, cuándo when

cuanto all, as much

cuánto how much

cuarto (*m.*) room, bedroom, quarter

cuarto de baño (*m.*) bathroom

cubiertos (*m. pl.*) silverware

cuenta (*f.*) check (at restaurant)

cumpleaños (*m.*) birthday

D

dar to give

de of

debajo under

deber to owe, have to

deberes (*m. pl.*) homework

decidir to decide

decir to say, tell

dedo (*m.*) finger

delante de in front of

delgado thin, skinny

delicioso delicious

demasiado too, too much

desayunar to eat breakfast

desayuno (*m.*) breakfast

descansar to rest

desde since

despedir to fire (from a job)
despedir(se) to say good-bye to
despertar(se) to wake up
después after
detrás behind
devolver to return, give back
día (*m.*) day
difícil difficult
dinero (*m.*) money
dirección (*f.*) address
discutir to discuss, argue
divertido fun
doble double
doctor, -a (*m., f.*) doctor
domingo (*m.*) Sunday
donde where
dónde where
dormir to sleep
dormitorio (*m.*) bedroom
ducha (*f.*) shower
duchar(se) to shower
dudar to doubt
dulce sweet

E

echar de menos to miss
edificio (*m.*) building
efectivamente exactly
egoísta selfish
ejercicio (*m.*) exercise
el the
él he
ella she
embarazada pregnant
empezar to begin, start
empresa (*f.*) company
en in, on

encantar to love
encender to light
encima de above, on
encontrar to find
encontrarse to feel
enfadado angry
enfermero, -a (*m., f.*) nurse
enfermo sick, ill
enfrente across (from), facing
enojado angry
enorme enormous, huge
ensayo (*m.*) essay
enseñar to teach, show
entender to understand
entonces then
entre between
enviar to send
escribir to write
escuchar to listen (to)
escuela (*f.*) school
eso that, that one
espacio (*m.*) space
español (*m.*) Spanish
especial special
esperar to wait (for), hope
esposa (*f.*) wife
esposo (*m.*) husband
estación (*f.*) station
estadio (*m.*) stadium
estar to be
esto this, this one
estudiante (*m., f.*) student
estudiar to study
estúpido stupid
examen (*m.*) exam
éxito (*m.*) success

exposición (*f.*) exhibit
extraño strange

F

fácil easy
falda (*f.*) skirt
faltar to lack
farmacia (*f.*) pharmacy
feliz happy
feo ugly
fiesta (*f.*) party
fin de semana (*m.*) weekend
flaco skinny, thin
foto (*f.*) photo, photograph
frecuentemente frequently
frente a across from, facing
fresco cool
frigorífico (*m.*) refrigerator
frío cold
fruta (*f.*) fruit
fuerte strong
fumar to smoke
fútbol (*m.*) soccer

G

ganar to win, earn
gastar to spend
gasto (*m.*) expense
gato (*m.*) cat
generoso generous
gente (*f.*) people
gimnasio (*m.*) gym
gordo fat
gorro (*m.*) cap
grande big
guapo attractive, handsome, beautiful
gustar to like, please

H

haber to have
habitación (*f.*) bedroom, room
hablar to speak
hacer to do, make
hacer falta to miss
hambre (*m.*) hunger
hasta until
hay there is, there are
helado (*m.*) ice cream
hermana (*f.*) sister
hermano (*m.*) brother
hermoso beautiful, handsome
hielo (*m.*) ice
hija (*f.*) daughter
hijo (*m.*) son
hincha (*m., f.*) fan, supporter
hola hello
hombre (*m.*) man
hora (*f.*) hour
hotel (*m.*) hotel
hoy today
huevo (*m.*) egg
huir to flee
humo (*m.*) smoke

I

idea (*f.*) idea
identificación (*f.*) identification
idioma (*m.*) language
iglesia (*f.*) church
igual equal, the same
importar to matter
imposible impossible
increíble incredible
inglés (*m.*) English
inteligente intelligent

invierno (*m.*) winter
invitar to invite
ir to go
irse to leave

J

jamás never
jardín (*m.*) garden, yard
jefa (*f.*) boss
jefe (*m.*) boss
joven young
juego game
jueves (*m.*) Thursday
jugar to play
junto together

L

la (*f.*) the
lado (*m.*) side
ladrar to bark
lápiz (*m.*) pencil
largo long
las (*f. pl.*) the
lástima (*f.*) shame, pity
lavar(se) to wash
le to you, to her, to him
les to you, to them
leche (*f.*) milk
leer to read
lejos (de) far (from)
lenguaje (*m.*) language
levantar to lift, raise
librería (*f.*) bookstore
libro (*m.*) book
limpio clean
lindo pretty
listo ready, intelligent

llamar to call
llamarse to be named
llave (*f.*) key
llegar to arrive
llevar to take
lluvia (*f.*) rain
loco crazy
los (*m. pl.*) the
lotería (*f.*) lottery
luego later, then
lugar (*m.*) room, space, place
lunes (*m.*) Monday

M

madre (*f.*) mother
maestro, -a (*m., f.*) teacher
mal badly
malecón (*m.*) boardwalk
maleta (*f.*) suitcase
malo bad
mandar to send
manifestación (*f.*) demonstration
mano (*f.*) hand
manzana (*f.*) apple
mañana (*f.*) morning, tomorrow
mapa (*m.*) map
mar (*m., f.*) sea, ocean
marcharse to leave
marido (*m.*) husband
martes (*m.*) Tuesday
más more
mayor bigger, older
medianoche (*f.*) midnight
médico, -a (*m., f.*) doctor
medio half
mediodía (*m.*) noon
medir to measure

mejor better

mejor: a lo mejor maybe

menor smaller, younger

menos minus

menos: a menos unless

mentir to lie

menudo: a menudo frequently, often

mercado (*m.*) market

mes (*m.*) month

mesa (*f.*) table

meter to put

mi my, me, myself

miedo (*m.*) fear

mientras while, during

miércoles (*m.*) Wednesday

mil thousand

mirar to look at, watch

mismo same

momento (*m.*) moment

montaña (*f.*) mountain

moreno dark-haired, dark-skinned

morir to die

mostrar to show

mover to move

muchacha (*f.*) girl

muchacho (*m.*) boy

mucho a lot

mudarse to move (residence)

muerto dead

mujer (*f.*) woman, wife

mural (*m.*) mural

museo (*m.*) museum

música (*f.*) music

músico, -a (*m., f.*) musician

muy very

N

nada nothing, anything

nadar to swim

nadie no one, anyone

naranja (*f.*) orange

Navidad (*f.*) Christmas

necesitar to need

negar to deny

negro black

ni neither, nor

nieta (*f.*) granddaughter

nieto (*m.*) grandson, grandchild

nieve (*f.*) snow

niña (*f.*) girl (child)

niño (*m.*) child; boy

no no

noche (*f.*) night

nombre (*m.*) name

normal normal

nosotros us

noticias (*f. pl.*) news

novia (*f.*) girlfriend, fiancée

novio (*m.*) boyfriend, fiancé

nuestro our

nuevo new

nunca never

O

o or

obra (*f.*) play, work of art

obvio obvious

océano (*m.*) ocean, sea

ocurrir to happen

oficina (*f.*) office

ojalá let's hope, in only

ojo (*m.*) eye

olvidar(se) to forget

ordenador (*m.*) computer
organizar to organize
oro (*m.*) gold
otoño (*m.*) autumn, fall

P

padre (*m.*) father
pagar to pay
país (*m.*) country
palabra (*f.*) word
pan (*m.*) bread
par (*m.*) pair, couple
para for, in order to
parecer to seem
pariente (*m.*, *f.*) relative, relation
parque (*m.*) park
partido (*m.*) match, game, party
  (political)
pasado past, last
pasar to happen, spend (time), pass
pedir to ask for
película (*f.*) **movie, film**
peluquería (*f.*) hairdresser
pena (*f.*) shame
pendiente (*m.*) **earring**
pensar to think
peor worse
pequeño small
perder to lose, miss
periódico (*m.*) newspaper
periodista (*m.*, *f.*) journalist
pero but
perro (*m.*) dog
persona (*f.*) person
pescado (*m.*) fish (to eat)
pez (*m.*) fish (to catch)
piedra (*f.*) rock, stone

piscina (*f.*) swimming pool
plata (*f.*) silver
platicar to chat
playa (*f.*) beach
plaza (*f.*) (town) square
pobre poor
poco little
poder to be able to
policía (*f.*) police department,
  police force
policía (*m.*, *f.*) police officer
pollo (*m.*) chicken
poner to put
por by, through, for, along
por favor please
por qué why
por supuesto of course, sure
porque because
posible possible
postre (*m.*) dessert
preferir to prefer
pregunta (*f.*) question
preguntar to ask
preparado prepared, ready
preparar to prepare
presidente, -a (*m.*, *f.*) president
primavera (*f.*) spring
primero first
primo, -a (*m.*, *f.*) cousin
probable probable
probar to prove, try, test
problema (*m.*) problem
profesión (*f.*) profession
profesor, -a (*m.*, *f.*) teacher,
  professor
propina (*f.*) tip, gratuity
público public

pueblo (*m.*) town
puerta (*f.*) door
pues well, as, then

Q

que that, which, who, whom
qué what, which
quedar to be left, be located
quedarse to stay
querer to want, love
queso (*m.*) cheese
quitar to take off
quizás maybe

R

raro strange, rare
rato (*m.*) while, time
razón (*f.*) reason
recordar to remember
regresar to return
reír to laugh
reloj (*m.*) watch, clock
repetir to repeat
responder to answer
respuesta (*f.*) answer
restaurante (*m.*) restaurant
revista (*f.*) magazine
rico rich, delicious
rincón (*m.*) corner
río (*m.*) river
rogar to beg, pray
rojo red
ropa (*f.*) clothing
roto broken

rubio blond
ruidoso noisy

S

sábado (*m.*) Saturday
saber to know
sal (*f.*) salt
salir to leave, go out
salud (*f.*) health
sed (*f.*) thirst
seguir to follow
segundo second
semana (*f.*) week
semana: fin de semana (*m.*) weekend
sensible sensitive
sentar(se) to sit (down)
sentir(se) to feel
señor (*m.*) man, gentleman, sir
señora (*f.*) woman, lady, madam
ser to be
servir to serve
si if
sí yes
siempre always
simpático friendly
sin without
sin embargo however
sino but rather
sitio (*m.*) place
sobre on, above
sol (*m.*) sun
solamente only
solo alone
sólo only

sonreír to smile
soñar to dream
su his, her, your
suceder to happen
subir to go up, climb, raise
sucio dirty
sueldo (*m.*) salary
sueño (*m.*) sleep, sleepiness, dream
suerte (*f.*) luck
sufrir to suffer
sugerir to suggest
supermercado (*m.*) supermarket
supuesto: por supuesto of course, sure

T

tal vez maybe
tampoco neither, either
tan so, such, such a, as
tanto as much, so much
tantos, tantas as many, so many
tarde (*f.*) afternoon
tarea (*f.*) homework
tarjeta (*f.*) card
taxi (*m.*) taxi
teatro (*m.*) theater
teléfono (*m.*) telephone
televisión (*f.*) television
televisor (*m.*) television (set)
temer to fear
tener to have
tener miedo to fear, be afraid
tener que to have to, be obliged to
tercero third

terraza (*f.*) balcony
ti you, yourself
tía (*f.*) aunt
tiempo (*m.*) time
tienda (*f.*) store
tímido shy
tío (*m.*) uncle
todavía still
todo all, every
tomar to take, have, drink
trabajar to work
trabajo (*m.*) work
traer to take (to)
tren (*m.*) train
triste sad
tu your
tú you

U

último last
un, una a, an
único only
universidad (*f.*) university
unos, unas (*m., f. pl.*) some
usted, ustedes you

V

valer to be worth
vaso (*m.*) drinking glass
vender to sell
venir to come
ver to see, watch
verano (*m.*) summer
verdad (*f.*) true, truth
verde green
vergüenza (*f.*) shame

vestido (*m.*) dress
vestir(se) to dress, get
  dressed
vez (*f.*) time
viajar to travel
viaje (*m.*) trip
vida (*f.*) life
viejo old
viento (*m.*) wind
viernes (*m.*) Friday
vino (*m.*) wine
visitar to visit
vista (*f.*) view

volar to fly
volver to return
voz (*f.*) voice
vuestro your

Y

y and
ya already
yo I

Z

zapato (*m.*) shoe

Answer Key

PART ONE: CHAPTER 1

Written Practice 1

1. Juan eats tacos in a restaurant.   2. The tequila is horrible.   3. The actor is special.   4. The chocolate is delicious.   5. Carla and David adopt a child.   6. Emilia organizes the party.   7. Julia is pregnant.   8. Jorge attends class.

Oral Practice 1

1. 3 syllables (moo-*seh*-oh)   2. 2 syllables (soo*ehr*-teh)   3. 2 syllables (nee*eh*-toh)   4. 3 syllables (kooee-*dah*-doh)   5. 2 syllables (*meh*-deeoh)   6. 4 syllables (ehoo-roh-*peh*-oh)   7. 2 syllables (re-*ahl*)   8. 4 syllables (nee-kah-*rah* gooah)

QUIZ

1. C   2. A   3. C   4. A   5. A   6. A   7. C   8. A   9. A
10. B

CHAPTER 2

Written Practice 1

1. m   2. f   3. f   4. f   5. m   6. f   7. m   8. f   9. m   10. m
11. m   12. m   13. f   14. f   15. m   16. f   17. f   18. f
19. m   20. f

Written Practice 2

1. María tiene un perro.   2. David quiere los mapas.   3. Un libro está encima de una televisión.   4. Una vaca da leche.   5. Los hombres están en una cocina.   6. Gonzalo vive en la ciudad.   7. Marta bebe la botella de agua.   8. Marco es un fundador de una empresa.

Written Practice 3

1. una   2. un   3. un   4. un   5. unos   6. unas   7. una   8. un
9. —   10. una

Written Practice 4

1. La   2. Las   3. —   4. El   5. La   6. —   7. El   8. Los   9. —   10. el

Written Practice 5

1. los árboles   2. los meses   3. unas ranas   4. las televisiones   5. los maníes
6. los aviones   7. las armas   8. unas montañas   9. los peces   10. los huéspedes
11. las calles   12. unos mapas

Oral Practice

1. jo-ye-**rí**-a (hhoh-yeh-*ree*-ah)   2. **hé**-ro-e (*eh*-roh-eh)   3. lla-**ma**-da (yah-*mah*-dah)
4. cir-**ue**-la (seer-oo*eh*-lah)   5. al-go-**dón** (ahl-goh-*dohn*)   6. al-**muer**-zo (ahl-moo*ehr*-soh)
7. **hí**-ga-do (*ee*-gah-doh)   8. **miér**-co-les   (mee*ehr*-coh-lehs)   9. al-re-de-**dor** (ahl-reh-deh-*dohr*)   10. ve-**hí**-cu-lo (veh-*ee*-coo-loh)   11. **vier**-nes (bee*ehr*-nehs)   12. pre-gun-**tar** (preh-goon-*tahr*)   13. pan-ta-**lo**-nes (pahn-tah-*loh*-nehs)   14. di-**fí**-cil (dee-*fee*-seel)
15. **o**-jo (*oh*-hhoh)   16. **lá**-piz (*lah*-pees)   17. bo-**lí**-gra-fo (boh-*lee*-grah-foh)   18. pas-**tel** (pahs-*tehl*)   19. ce-re-**a**-les (seh-reh-*ah*-lehs)   20. res-tau-**ran**-te (reh-stahoo-*rahn*-teh)

QUIZ

1. B   2. D   3. A   4. B   5. C   6. D   7. A   8. A   9. B   10. A

CHAPTER 3

Written Practice 1

1. Tú eres de Brasil. Eres brasileña.   2. Ella es de Canadá. Es canadiense.   3. Ustedes son de Japón. Son japoneses.   4. Nosotros somos de Rusia. Somos rusos.   5. Usted es de Austria. Es austriaca.   6. Él es de Senegal. Es senegalés.   7. Yo soy de Grecia. Soy griego.

Written Practice 2

1. descansamos   2. trabaja   3. cambian   4. llevamos   5. enseña   6. estudia
7. necesitan   8. llego; llego   9. bailas   10. bailo

Oral Practice 2

1. yo llamo   2. tú cocinas   3. ellos cantan   4. usted organiza   5. ella busca
6. nosotros miramos   7. él gana   8. ustedes ayudan   9. tú hablas   10. yo gasto

Oral Practice 3

1. Sí, soy de Paraguay.   2. No, no somos amigos.   3. Sí, es una bicicleta.   4. No, no
son hermanas.   5. Sí, (Elena) es psicóloga.   6. No, (Santos y Marisol) no son de Buenos
Aires.

Written Practice 3

1. mi hija   2. su hijo   3. tu madre   4. nuestro padre   5. sus padres   6. sus hijas
7. tu padre   8. nuestras hijas   9. mis hijos   10. sus madres   11. Mi casa es tu casa.
12. Mi casa es su casa.   13. Nuestra casa es su casa.

Written Practice 4

A: 1. Los exámenes del profesor. The professor's exams.   2. Los monumentos de Europa.
The monuments of Europe. *or* Europe's monuments.   3. El perro de las niñas. The girls'
dog.   4. El sueño de ella. Her dream.   5. Las canciones de Shakira. Shakira's songs.
B: 1. Sus exámenes.   2. Sus monumentos.   3. Su perro.   4. Su sueño.   5. Sus
canciones.

QUIZ

1. D   2. D   3. C   4. A   5. B   6. B   7. D   8. C   9. B   10. C

CHAPTER 4

Written Practice 1

1. joven   2. vieja   3. hondureña   4. azules, bonitos   5. materialistas   6. difícil
7. amables   8. cara, cómoda   9. francesa, deliciosa   10. felices

Written Practice 2

1. The young boy is my son.   2. The old bicycle is my mother's.   3. Tegucigalpa is the
Honduran capital.   4. The blue shoes are pretty.   5. My friends are quite materialistic.
6. The physics class is difficult.   7. Camilo's parents are friendly.   8. The chair is
expensive, but it's comfortable.   9. French food is delicious.   10. These are some happy
children.

Oral Practice 1

1. Miguel trabaja en un edificio enorme. 2. Saskia es una vieja amiga. 3. El señor Márquez es un gran hombre. 4. No gasto mucho dinero. 5. Adán vive en el tercer piso. 6. La mujer rubia es mi esposa.

Oral Practice 2

1. El carro es viejísimo. El carro es muy viejo. El carro es bastante viejo. El carro es demasiado viejo. 2. La caja es fuertísima. La caja es muy fuerte. La caja es bastante fuerte. 3. El español es facilísimo. El español es muy fácil. El español es bastante fácil. El español es demasiado fácil. El español es bien fácil. 4. Las joyas son carísimas. Las joyas son muy caras. Las joyas son bastante caras. Las joyas son demasiado caras. 5. Es una película violentísima. Es una película bastante violenta. Es una película demasiado violenta. Es una película bien violenta.

Written Practice 3

1. Quién 2. Quiénes 3. Qué 4. Por qué 5. Quién 6. Quién 7. Quién 8. Qué

Written Practice 4

1. Cuál 2. Qué 3. Qué 4. Cuáles 5. Qué 6. Cuál 7. Qué 8. Qué/Cuál 9. Cuál 10. Qué

Written Practice 5

1. crees 2. comprendo 3. corre 4. ve 5. vende 6. prometemos 7. deben 8. meto 9. aprenden 10. lee

Written Practice 6

1. bebo 2. ve 3. venden 4. come 5. lee 6. corren

Written Practice 7

1. vive 2. abro 3. escribimos 4. sube 5. asisten 6. admite 7. sufres 8. cubre 9. discuten 10. recibe

Oral Practice 3

1. vivimos 2. escribes 3. sube 4. admiten 5. abro

QUIZ

1. C 2. B 3. C 4. A 5. B 6. B 7. D 8. A 9. A 10. D

CHAPTER 5

Written Practice 1

1. Dónde   2. Cuánto   3. Cuándo   4. Cómo   5. Cuántas   6. Cómo   7. Dónde

Written Practice 2

1. está   2. están   3. Estás   4. estamos   5. está   6. están   7. está   8. Estoy

Oral Practice 1

1. Estoy.   2. Trabajo.   3. Vivo.   4. Soy.

Oral Practice 2

Possible answers: 1. ¿Dónde está la playa? Está allí.   2. ¿Dónde queda la parada de autobús? Está delante del hotel.   3. ¿Dónde están el palacio y la catedral? Están al final de la calle.   4. ¿Dónde queda la calle Juan Bravo? Queda en el centro, cerca de la estación de tren.   5. ¿Dónde está el restaurante La Limeña? Está aquí/acá a la derecha encima del Hotel Excelsior.

Written Practice 3

1. vamos   2. va   3. van; van   4. Voy   5. van   6. va   7. Vamos   8. vas, vas   9. van   10. vas

Oral Practice 3

1. cinco   2. trece   3. veintiséis   4. cuarenta y uno   5. cincuenta y ocho   6. ochenta y cinco   7. noventa y nueve   8. ciento dos   9. ciento treinta y siete   10. cuatrocientos cincuenta   11. quinientos cinco   12. seiscientos cincuenta y siete   13. ochocientos veintinueve   14. mil tres   15. mil cuatrocientos noventa y dos   16. mil ochocientos cuarenta   17. cinco mil   18. siete mil ochocientos treinta y cuatro   19. cuatro millones   20. dos mil millones   21. dos millones de dólares   22. ciento una mujeres   23. quinientas cosas   24. treinta y un libros   25. doscientos cincuenta y una muchachas

Oral Practice 4

1. es la una menos cuarto; son las doce (y) cuarenta y cinco   2. es la una y media; es la una (y) treinta   3. son las tres (y) cincuenta; son las cuatro menos diez   4. son las siete y cuarto; son las siete (y) quince   5. son las ocho cuarenta y cinco; son las nueve menos cuarto

Oral Practice 5

1. Voy a clase al mediodía.   2. El supermercado abre a las seis de la mañana.   3. Vamos a la playa a las dos de la tarde.   4. Llego a casa a las nueve menos cuarto/ocho (y) cuarenta y cinco de la noche.   5. La obra termina a las diez de la noche.   6. Es la una y cuarto/una y quince de la tarde.   7. Cenamos a las siete y cuarto/siete y quince de la noche.

QUIZ

1. C   2. D   3. D   4. A   5. A   6. B   7. D   8. B   9. D   10. B

PART ONE TEST

1. B   2. B   3. D   4. B   5. A   6. B   7. B   8. A   9. D   10. D   11. A
12. D   13. D   14. B   15. A   16. B   17. D   18. B   19. C   20. A   21. A
22. D   23. D   24. C   25. A

PART TWO: CHAPTER 6

Written Practice 1

1. Hay una silla en la sala de estar.   2. Hay tres parques en la ciudad.   3. ¿Hay un restaurante cerca?   4. ¿Hay montañas en Venezuela?   5. No, no hay un restaurante cerca.   6. Sí, hay montañas en Venezuela.   7. Hay un teléfono en el cuarto.   8. Hay quince bares en el barrio.

Written Practice 2

1. F   2. T   3. F   4. T   5. F   6. F   7. T   8. F   9. F   10. T   11. T
12. F   13. F

Written Practice 3

1. Hace   2. Hago   3. hace   4. hacemos   5. hacen   6. hacen   7. hacen
8. hace   9. hago   10. haces

Written Practice 4

Possible answers: 1. hace frío, hace viento, hace fresco, hace mal tiempo, hace buen tiempo, hay granizo, hay neblina, hay niebla, nieva, está nublado   2. hace calor, hace sol, hace buen tiempo, hay humedad, llueve, hay llovizna   3. hace fresco, hace fresquito, hace buen tiempo, hace mal tiempo, hace sol, hay niebla, hay neblina, hay viento, hay llovizna, llueve   4. hace fresco, hace fresquito, hace buen tiempo, hace mal tiempo, hay niebla, hay neblina, hay viento, hay llovizna, llueve, está nublado

Written Practice 5

1. Tienes 2. viene 3. tengo 4. vienen 5. Tiene 6. Vengo 7. tienen
8. vengo 9. Tenemos 10. Venimos

Written Practice 6

1. Tengo calor 2. Tiene trece años 3. Tengo prisa 4. Tienes suerte 5. tienen
sueño 6. tenemos frío 7. tiene ganas de 8. Tiene sed 9. años tiene 10. Tienes
razón

Written Practice 7

1. Tenemos que vender la casa. 2. Hay que hacer cola. 3. Tengo que limpiar el cuarto
de baño. 4. Sin embargo, no tenemos que hacer nada. 5. Hace sol. Hay que hacer una
fiesta. 6. ¿Tiene(s) que fumar? 7. ¿Hay que hacer el almuerzo? 8. Tenemos que
llegar a las ocho. 9. Hay que hacer la cama por la mañana. 10. Ustedes no tienen que
venir a clase mañana.

QUIZ

1. A 2. B 3. B 4. C 5. D 6. A 7. B 8. B 9. A 10. C

CHAPTER 7

Written Practice 1

1. Almorzamos 2. Duermo 3. Empiezan 4. quiero; Prefiero 5. Puedes
6. miente 7. sirve 8. cuesta 9. piensa 10. sonríe 11. volvemos; vuelve
12. frío; hiervo

Written Practice 2

1. a 2. — 3. — 4. al 5. a 6. a

Written Practice 3

1. Esta 2. Aquella 3. estas 4. ese 5. Esos 6. aquel 7. Este 8. Esos

Written Practice 4

1. ésta; ésa 2. aquéllos 3. aquélla 4. ésos 5. Éste

Written Practice 5

1. gusta 2. gustan 3. gusta 4. gusta 5. gustan 6. gustan 7. gusta; gustan
8. gusta

Written Practice 6

1. A mí   2. a Eduardo   3. a ustedes   4. A Emilio   5. a nosotros   6. A mi tío
7. A ti   8. A tu padre

Written Practice 7

1. me cae   2. le caen   3. me molesta   4. le molestan   5. les encanta   6. me encantan   7. te quedan   8. me queda   9. le parece   10. les parece   11. le falta
12. nos faltan

QUIZ

1. C   2. D   3. C   4. C   5. B   6. D   7. B   8. C   9. C   10. A

CHAPTER 8

Written Practice 1

1. estás hablando   2. Estamos construyendo   3. están durmiendo   4. está leyendo
5. están comiendo   6. están haciendo   7. está mintiendo   8. Estás usando   9. está esperando   10. estamos buscando

Written Practice 2

1. a   2. a   3. b   4. a   5. a   6. b

Oral Practice

Possible answers: Estoy estudiando español.   Estoy aprendiendo español.   Estoy hablando en español.   Estoy leyendo un libro.   Estoy escribiendo ejercicios de español.
Estoy haciendo mis deberes.

Written Practice 3

1. b   2. a   3. a   4. b.   5. b   6. a   7. b   8. b   9. b   10. b   11. a
12. b

Written Practice 4

1. Está comprando los nuestros.   2. ¿Tienen los suyos?   3. La mía no es cómoda.
4. ¿Dónde está la suya?   5. El mío sale a las ocho. El tuyo sale a las nueve y cuarenta.
6. Ésta es la nuestra. La próxima es la suya.   7. El de ella es caro, pero el de ustedes es carísimo.   8. Éstas son (las) de ella. ¿Dónde están las de ustedes?

Written Practice 5

1. conozco   2. sé   3. Conoce   4. sabes   5. Conocemos   6. conoce; sabe
7. conociendo   8. saben   9. conozco   10. sé; conozco

QUIZ

1. C   2. D   3. D   4. A   5. A   6. A   7. C   8. D   9. B   10. C

CHAPTER 9

Written Practice 1

1. ¿Vamos a hacer algo esta noche?   2. Van a hablar con tus padres.   3. ¿No vas a poder venir?   4. Voy a vivir en las afueras de Madrid.   5. Vamos a tener tres hijos.   6. ¿Van a hacer la cama?   7. Voy a conocer a los padres de mi novio.   8. Va a haber mucha gente en mi fiesta.

Oral Practice

Possible answers: 1. Hoy voy a comer con mis amigos.   2. Esta noche voy a bailar.
3. Mañana voy a visitar Mendoza.   4. El año que viene voy a trabajar en la oficina central.
5. Esta semana voy a dormir poco.   6. Después de aprender español voy a viajar por Suramérica.

Written Practice 2

1. Sales   2. vale   3. Traigo   4. pongo   5. valen   6. pones   7. hago   8. sale

Written Practice 3

1. traes; traigo   2. llevas; llevo   3. llevo   4. llevar; llevo

Written Practice 4

1. se   2. te   3. Nos   4. se   5. Me   6. te   7. te   8. se   9. se   10. Nos; nos

Written Practice 5

1. Me pienso quedar hasta el final.   2. Luis se tiene que despertar a las seis.   3. Vamos a sentarnos aquí.   4. Silvia está duchándose.   5. Manolo se está engañando con esta relación.   6. ¿Te vas a poner un vestido o una falda?

Written Practice 6

1. te vienes   2. me divierto   3. te quejas   4. te alegras   5. ducharme   6. vestirme
7. te vienes   8. se / enojar   9. se queda   10. se fija
11. me interesa   12. divertirnos

Written Practice 7

1. b   2. c   3. a   5. a   5. b   6. a   7. b   8. c   9. c   10. a

QUIZ

1. D   2. C   3. C   4. A   5. B   6. C   7. B   8. A   9. B   10. B

CHAPTER 10

Written Practice 1

1. más complicada que   2. mejores que   3. más miedo que   4. más limpio que
5. más de dos mil dólares   6. peor que   7. más horas que   8. más
que ciento cincuenta dólares   9. más estudiosa que   10. más paciencia que
11. menor que; mayor   12. más de seis

Oral Practice 1

Answers may vary.   1. El metro en Nueva York es más grande que el metro en Boston. El
metro en Boston es más pequeño.   2. El metro en Nueva York es más sucio que el metro
en Boston.   3. Nueva York es tan cara como Boston.   4. Nueva York tiene más tráfico
que Boston.   5. En Nueva York hay más diversiones que en Boston.   6. Hace tanto frío
en Nueva York como en Boston.   7. Los restaurantes en Nueva York son mejores que los
restaurantes en Boston.

Written Practice 2

1. la; más; de   2. la; más; de   3. el; más; de   4. las; más; de   5. el; más; de   6. es;
el; del   7. la; más; de   8. las; más; de

Written Practice 3

1. David es el que menos lee.   2. Este carro es el que más corre.   3. Nosotros somos los
que más pagamos.   4. Este perro es el que más ladra.   5. Mi hija es la que más habla.
6. Mi diamante es el que más brilla.

Oral Practice 2

Answers will vary. 1. ¡Qué pena! ¡Qué lástima! ¡Qué malas noticias! ¡Qué noticias más
malas!   2. ¡Qué rico! ¡Qué bueno! ¡Qué delicioso!   3. ¡Qué barbaridad! ¡Qué idiota!
¡Qué vergüenza! ¡Qué triste! ¡Qué hombre más malo!   4. ¡Qué película más buena! ¡Qué
buena película! ¡Qué divertido!   5. ¡Qué idea más buena! ¡Qué divertido! ¡Qué idea más
estupenda!

Written Practice 4

1. están   2. está   3. estoy   4. son   5. está   6. es   7. estás   8. es   9. es
10. están   11. estamos   12. son

QUIZ

1. B   2. B   3. A   4. D   5. A   6. A   7. B   8. D   9. B   10. C

PART TWO TEST

1. B   2. B   3. C   4. B   5. C   6. B   7. A   8. C   9. B   10. A   11. C
12. A   13. D   14. C   15. B   16. B   17. A   18. B   19. A   20. B   21. B
22. C   23. C   24. B   25. C

PART THREE: CHAPTER 11

Written Practice 1

1. abra; abran   2. doble; doblen   3. corra; corran   4. suba; suban   5. prometa;
prometan   6. busque; busquen   7. haga; hagan   8. salga; salgan   9. diga; digan
10. tome; tomen   11. vuelva; vuelvan   12. ponga; pongan   13. oiga; oigan
14. ande; anden   15. cuente; cuenten   16. huya; huyan

Written Practice 2

1. salgan ahora.   2. no tome la medicina.   3. vuelva en seguida.   4. vayan a comer.
5. pida la cuenta.   6. no traigan a los hijos.   7. venga con nosotros.   8. no hable con
su jefe.

Written Practice 3

1. abre; no abras   2. dobla; no dobles   3. corre; no corras   4. sube; no subas   5. ten;
no tengas   6. busca; no busques   7. sal; no salgas   8. di; no digas   9. toma; no tomes
10. vuelve; no vuelvas   11. trae; no traigas   12. oye; no oigas   13. anda; no andes
14. cuenta; no cuentes   15. huye; no huyas

Written Practice 4

1. sal ahora.   2. no comas una manzana.   3. vuelve mañana.   4. no vayas a cenar.
5. no hagas eso.   6. trae dinero.   7. ven con Emilio.   8. no hables con tu jefe.

Written Practice 5

1. Volvamos a casa.   2. Hagamos algo.   3. Comamos fuera.   4. Sigamos adelante.
5. Vamos a la playa.   6. Traigamos algo de comer.

Oral Practice 1

1. Fíjate. No te fijes.   2. Cállense. No se callen.   3. Acuéstese. No se acueste.
4. Olvidémonos del asunto. No nos olvidemos del asunto.   5. Siéntate aquí. No te sientes
aquí.   6. Vístase. No se vista.   7. Parémonos allí. No nos paremos allí.   8. Quédense.

No se queden.   9. Ponte al teléfono. No te pongas al teléfono.   10. Vaya a hablar con nosotros. No vaya a hablar con nosotros.

Written Practice 6

1. no   2. sí; tomates   3. sí, galletas   4. no   5. sí; azúcar   6. no

Oral Practice 2

1. Los pongo encima de la mesa.   2. La quiero usar *or* Quiero usarla.   3. ¿Lo podrías pagar mañana? *or* ¿Podrías pagarlo mañana?   4. Voy a verlo esta tarde. *or* Lo voy a ver esta tarde.   5. No los compres.   6. Llévela.   7. Lo bebemos todos los días.   8. ¿La vamos a ver esta noche? *or* ¿Vamos a verla esta noche?

Written Practice 7

1. e   2. b   3. h   4. c   5. f   6. a   7. d   8. j   9. i   10. g

QUIZ

1. B   2. D   3. D   4. B   5. A   6. C   7. B   8. B   9. C   10. D

CHAPTER 12

Written Practice 1

1. (Nosotros) no cabremos todos en el carro.   2. ¿Qué dirán sobre el examen?   3. Un día iré a México.   4. ¿Volverás en avión?   5. Malena verá los murales de Diego Rivera.   6. ¿Cuánto valdrá un diamante?   7. Nunca haré ningún viaje.   8. ¿Quién estará llamándome?

Oral Practice 1

1. dirás   2. creará   3. querrán   4. dejarán   5. Será   6. habrá   7. Se pondrán   8. esconderás   9. usaré   10. darán   11. darán

Written Practice 2

1. No le mandes el paquete a ella.   2. Diles a tus hermanos que vengan.   3. ¿El cantante me está hablando a mí?   4. La profesora le habla a su alumno.   5. Penélope les dio un beso a ustedes.   6. No les des la espalda a tus amigas.   7. Les mando una tarjeta de navidad a mis parientes.

Written Practice 3

1. Lo   2. la   3. Le   4. Le   5. los   6. nos   7. la   8. los

Written Practice 4

1. gustaría   2. viajarías   3. sabríamos   4. podría   5. vendría   6. viviría   7. diría
8. iría; tendría

Oral Practice 4

Answers will vary. 1. haría la maleta; renovaría el pasaporte; compraría un boleto de avión;
leería una guía turística   2. llamaría a 911; agarraría la cartera; saldría despacio por la
escalera   3. haría un cursillo de español en Antigua, Guatemala; escalaría los Andes;
visitaría las playas de Panamá

Written Practice 5

1. besote; besazo   2. mujerona   3. padrote   4. llorón; llorona   5. mandona
6. cajón   7. ratón   8. cinturón   9. flechazo

QUIZ

1. C   2. D   3. A   4. B   5. C   6. B   7. C   8. D   9. A   10. C

CHAPTER 13

Written Practice 1

nadar: nadé, nadaste, nadó, nadamos, nadaron   **tocar:** toqué, tocaste, tocó, tocamos, tocaron
creer: creí, creíste, creyó, creímos, creyeron   **jugar:** jugué, jugaste, jugó, jugamos, jugaron
vender: vendí, vendiste, vendió, vendimos, vendieron   **escribir:** escribí, escribiste, escribió,
escribimos, escribieron   **huir:** huí, huiste, huyó, huimos, huyeron   **repetir:** repetí,
repetiste, repitió, repetimos, repitieron   **almorzar:** almorcé, almorzaste, almorzó,
almorzamos, almorzaron   **sentir:** sentí, sentiste, sintió, sentimos, sintieron

Written Practice 2

1. Yo pagué cien dólares por esta camisa.   2. Nosotros comenzamos a estudiar.
3. Selena y su hermana duermieron hasta el mediodía.   4. María estudió mucho.   5. ¿Tú
compraste los remedios?   6. El bebé casi no lloró.   7. Mis padres no me creyeron.
8. ¿Ustedes pidieron arroz con leche?

Oral Practice 1

Answers will vary.

Written Practice 3

1. e   2. b   3. h   4. f   5. a   6. c   7. d   8. g

Written Practice 4

1. Laurita me lo presta.   2. Se las estamos comprando. *or* Estamos comprándoselas.
3. El profesor se las explica.   4. Explícamelo, por favor.   5. ¿Quieren prestárselo? *or* ¿Se lo quieren prestar?   6. Mercedes se las da.   7. No te los confiaré.   8. Mi jefe me lo invitó.

Written Practice 5

1. Los jóvenes   2. Las bellas   3. La rubia   4. El pequeño   5. La verde   6. Los grandes   7. Las altas   8. Las serias

Written Practice 6

1. fuiste   2. dijeron   3. atrajo   4. hizo   5. pude   6. fuimos; cupimos
7. estuviste   8. tuvieron

Written Practice 7

Answers may vary.   1. Oscar conoció a Anabel la conoció en línea.   2. Porque Patricia quiere conocer a alguien. Porque Patricia nunca conoce a nadie.   3. Piensa que no es normal.   4. No, Anabel no fue la primera chica que Oscar conoció por Internet.
5. Fueron a tomar un café.   6. Fue amor a primera vista/un flechazo. La vio y casi no pudo hablar.   7. Anabel llamó a Oscar llamo al día siguiente.   8. Creo que sí.

Oral Practice 2

Answers will vary.

QUIZ

1. D   2. C   3. A   4. C   5. C   6. B   7. B   8. A   9. B   10. A

CHAPTER 14

Written Practice 1

1. encontrabas   2. veían   3. salía   4. cerraba   5. manteníamos   6. decías   7. se iban   8. platicábamos   9. hacía   10. éramos

Written Practice 2

1. era   2. vivía   3. gustaba   4. Jugaba   5. tiraban   6. compraban   7. tenían
8. volvía   9. trabajaban   10. iba   11. sabía   12. se metía   13. tomaba
14. comía   15. bebía   16. encantaba

Oral Practice 1

Answers will vary.

Written Practice 3

1. La chica estaba platicando con sus amigas.   2. ¿Qué estabas diciendo?   3. Los niños estaban jugando baloncesto.   4. Mercedes no estaba comiendo nada.   5. Los vecinos estaban chismeando.   6. ¿Usted estaba viendo el reportaje?

Written Practice 4

1. Acababan de ir   2. Acabo de ver   3. Vuelvo a verte *or* Te vuelvo a ver *or* Te volveré a ver *or* Volveré a verte   4. Ibas a decir   5. Iban a visitarme *or* Me iban a visitar.
6. Volvieron a mentir.

Written Practice 5

1. Francamente   2. Afortunadamente   3. divinamente   4. difícilmente
5. perfectamente   6. completamente

Oral Practice 2

Answers will vary. 1. Hace tres meses que no veo a mis padres.   2. Vivo en mi casa actual desde hace cinco años.   3. Hace diez años que estudio español.   4. Uso este libro desde hace cuatro meses.   5. Hace muchos años que me interesa la cultura latina.   6. ¿Hace cuántos días que no abres el libro de español?   7. ¿Hace cuánto tiempo que estás en la universidad?   8. ¿Desde hace cuando que no hablas español?   9. ¿Hace cuánto tiempo que usted viaja por Centroamérica?   10. ¿Hace cuánto tiempo que tu tía nada todas las mañanas?

Written Practice 6

1. estudió   2. hace   3. conoció; hace   4. tuvo; hace   5. Hace   6. Hace cuánto tiempo/cuántos años que   7. tuvo; siete   8. Hace; se jubiló

Oral Practice 3

Answers may vary. 1. Me levanté hace tres horas.   2. Empecé a estudiar español hace tres años.   3. Hablé con mi amigo hace un rato.   4. Compré estos zapatos hace un par de meses.

QUIZ

1. B   2. A   3. C   4. A   5. A   6. B   7. A   8. C   9. C   10. C

CHAPTER 15

Written Practice 1
1. El dueño del apartamento estaba aquí a menudo.   2. Caminaba al trabajo a menudo.
3. Ellos me lo decían a menudo.   4. Veía a Elmer a menudo.   5. Gorky recibía los emails que mandaba a menudo.   6. Pedíamos el pollo con arroz a menudo.

Written Practice 2
1. Fui a clase de yoga hace dos días.   2. ¿Tú hiciste la comida hace dos días?   3. Ellos vieron a los vecinos hace dos días.   4. Nosotros la visitamos hace dos días.   5. Comí carne hace dos días.   6. Sarita vino a mi casa hace dos días.

Written Practice 3
1. me acostaba; sonó   2. se encontraba; juró   3. Eran; nos levantamos   4. quería; se fue   5. sabías; contó   6. dormía; sonó

Written Practice 4
1. terminó   2. decidió   3. Escogió   4. interesaba   5. Quería   6. se metió
7. eligió   8. se matriculó   9. Decidió   10. compró   11. Iba   12. se sentía/se sintió
13. hablaba   14. llegó   15. se dio   16. estaba   17. hablaba   18. hablaban
19. entendía   20. llevaban   21. Había   22. destacaba   23. pensaba   24. miraba
25. veía   26. empezó   27. apareció   28. decía   29. dio   30. Se fue   31. se llamaba   32. empezó

Written Practice 5
1. a   2. c   3. b   4. c   5. a

Written Practice 6
1. El huipil que veo es de Guatemala.   2. La película de la que hablo es de Luis Buñuel.
3. El chavo que me gusta es mexicano.   4. El bebé que llora está cansado.   5. El anillo que tienes es de plata peruana.   6. El hombre que edita el libro es super inteligente.
7. El restaurante en que pienso es muy caro.   8. Los volcanes que están alrededor del lago Atitlán no son activos.

Written Practice 7
1. quien   2. que   3. quienes   4. quien   5. que   6. que   7. quien   8. que

Written Practice 8
1. a   2. b   3. a, b   4. b   5. a, b, c   6. a, b

Written Practice 9

1. cuyo   2. cuya   3. cuyos   4. cuya   5. cuyas   6. cuyo

QUIZ

1. A   2. B   3. D   4. C   5. B   6. C   7. D   8. A   9. D   10. D

PART THREE TEST

1. A   2. B   3. D   4. B   5. D   6. B   7. B   8. C   9. B   10. A   11. C
12. A   13. B   14. C   15. C   16. B   17. A   18. C   19. B   20. B   21. B
22. C   23. B   24. B   25. C

PART FOUR: CHAPTER 16

Written Practice 1

1. beba   2. viajes   3. abramos   4. mande   5. corran   6. escriba   7. hable
8. sonrías

Written Practice 2

1. midamos   2. cuentes   3. pida   4. perdamos   5. muestren   6. vuelva
7. rindan   8. muramos

Written Practice 3

1. quieras   2. empiece   3. seamos   4. venga   5. valga   6. pongas   7. salga
8. traguemos   9. vayan   10. estén

Written Practice 4

1. lleguemos   2. sea   3. ame   4. pierda   5. trabajen   6. estén   7. quiera
8. estés

Written Practice 5

1. gustan   2. hagan   3. vayamos   4. ama   5. sepa   6. quiere   7. conozcan
8. cabemos

Written Practice 6

1. quiera   2. viajo   3. puedas   4. digas   5. sepan   6. sea   7. como   8. haya

QUIZ

1. B   2. C   3. B   4. A   5. B   6. B   7. A   8. B   9. A   10. A

CHAPTER 17

Written Practice 1
1. hagan   2. se laven   3. digan   4. tengas   5. hable   6. utilice   7. corran
8. hablen

Written Practice 2
1. tenga   2. lleguen   3. es   4. vayamos   5. estés   6. cante   7. estudian
8. haya

Oral Practice
1. tengan   2. trabaje   3. sepa   4. paga   5. viva   6. tiene   7. tiene

Written Practice 3
1. hagas   2. entienden   3. salga   4. esté   5. llamen   6. hagas   7. pueda
8. está   9. convenga   10. trabajan   11. hagan   12. leas   13. duele   14. griten

Written Practice 4
1. tenga   2. quiera   3. sea   4. tenga   5. aprecie   6. sea   7. busque   8. guste
9. sea   10. tenga   11. tenga   12. tengamos   13. es   14. puede   15. existe

QUIZ
1. C   2. B   3. D   4. B   5. A   6. D   7. B   8. D   9. A   10. B

CHAPTER 18

Written Practice 1
1. pensado   2. dormido   3. revuelto   4. querido   5. dado   6. rehecho
7. mudado   8. comido   9. repetido   10. inscrito

Written Practice 2
1. dormida   2. fritos; revueltos   3. preferido   4. deprimido
5. estresados   6. hecho   7. vuelta   8. cansados   9. cubierta

Written Practice 3
1. La Princesa Diana fue admirada por todo el mundo.   2. El mensajero entregó el
paquete.   3. El perro fue atropellado por un carro.   4. La policía descubrió el secreto.
5. Cinco cuadros fueron vendidos por la galería.   6. La comunidad pintó los murales.

Written Practice 4

1. Se oye; se come   2. se encuentra   3. Se sirve   4. se abre   5. se hace   6. se cierran   7. se usan; se usan   8. Se habla

Oral Practice 1

1. has terminado   2. hemos sentido   3. ha vendido   4. nunca he ido   5. no han dicho   6. ha roto   7. no has puesto   8. ha llamado   9. han seguido   10. no he almorzado

Written Practice 5

1. he hecho   2. han recibido   3. ha viajado   4. hemos pagado   5. has visto   6. ha escrito   7. ha muerto   8. han vuelto

Oral Practice 2

Answers will vary.   1. He hablado con...   2. He aprendido...   3. He viajado a...   4. He leído...   5. He hablado con...   6. He visto a...

Oral Practice 3

1. habías terminado   2. habíamos sentido   3. había vendido   4. nunca había ido   5. no habían dicho   6. había roto   7. no habías puesto   8. había llamado   9. habían seguido   10. no había almorzado

Written Practice 6

1. Ya había empezado la música cuando entraron los bailarines.   2. Gema ya se había ido cuando su jefe la buscó.   3. Ya había comprado el boleto de avión cuando el hotel canceló la reserva.   4. Mozart ya había escrito dos piezas musicales cuando cumplió cuatro años.   5. Nadie había terminado el examen cuando la hora se acabó.

Written Practice 7

1. f   2. g   3. h   4. c   5. e   6. a   7. d   8. b

QUIZ

1. C   2. B   3. A   4. D   5. A   6. C   7. B   8. A   9. C   10. D

CHAPTER 19

Written Practice 1

1. cantara; cantáramos   2. durmiera; durmiéramos   3. contribuyera; contribuyéramos   4. anduviera; anduviéramos   5. hiciera; hiciéramos   6. pudiera; pudiéramos   7. fuera;

fuéramos   8. fuera; fuéramos   9. estuviera; estuviéramos   10. supiera; supiéramos
11. pusiera; pusiéramos   12. leyera; leyéramos

Written Practice 2
1. estudiaran   2. estuvieras   3. fuera   4. saliera   5. pudiera   6. decidiera
7. pagáramos   8. supieran   9. contribuyera   10. cayera

Written Practice 3
1. llevara   2. entendiera   3. es *or* era   4. vio   5. supiera   6. fuera   7. hablaban
8. salió   9. estaba *or* estuviera   10. apareciste

Written Practice 4
1. llamara   2. llamaría   3. perdiera   4. ganarían   5. irías   6. pasáramos

Written Practice 5
1. aprobarás   2. trabajaremos   3. vendrán; invitamos   4. hará; cuesta   5. recibirá;
sigue   6. escuchas; gustará

Written Practice 6
1. vinieras   2. iría   3. haría; perdiera   4. tuviera; pagaría   5. diera; podría
6. ayudaría; pidiéramos

Written Practice 7
1. habríamos ido   2. hubiera hecho   3. habría terminado   4. hubieran sabido
5. habrías llamado; hubieras sabido   6. habría aprendido; hubiera vivido

QUIZ
1. C   2. C   3. B   4. C   5. D   6. C   7. C   8. A   9. B   10. A

CHAPTER 20

Written Practice 1
1. para; #3   2. para; #1   3. por; #4   4. por; #1   5. Para; #5   6. por; #5   7. por;
#3   8. para; #4   9. por; #6   10. por; #2   11. por; #7

Oral Practice
1. por favor   2. Por supuesto   3. por favor   4. Por supuesto   5. por lo visto
6. Por cierto   7. por lo menos   8. por lo menos   9. Por mí   10. Por fin

Written Practice 2

1. cincuenta balboas   2. setecientos quetzales   3. quinientos córdobas   4. doscientos pesos argentinos   5. cinco mil quinientos   6. setecientos bolivianos

Written Practice 3

1. a   2. a   3. b   4. a   5. b   6. b

QUIZ

1. B   2. A   3. B   4. B   5. A   6. A   7. B   8. B   9. A   10. A

PART FOUR TEST

1. B   2. C   3. B   4. D   5. C   6. B   7. B   8. A   9. D   10. C   11. D
12. B   13. B   14. B   15. D   16. C   17. A   18. A   19. C   20. B   21. C
22. B   23. D   24. C   25. A

FINAL EXAM

1. C   2. B   3. D   4. B   5. D   6. B   7. B   8. A   9. B   10. D   11. C
12. A   13. C 14. C   15. B   16. C   17. A   18. B   19. C   20. A   21. C
22. B   23. D   24. A   25. B   26. A   27. A   28. B   29. A   30. C   31. D
32. C   33. D   34. A   35. A   36. B   37. D   38. B   39. B   40. C   41. B
42. A   43. C   44. B   45. D   46. C   47. B   48. C   49. B   50. A

Index

About the Author

Jenny Petrow is a developer of Spanish-language, bilingual, and ESL curricula for such publishers as McGraw-Hill, Oxford University Press, and the language website Parlo.com. She has lived in Madrid, Guatemala, and Peru, and she has worked as a Spanish instructor in Brazil. When not writing and editing language textbooks, Jenny consults on education issues in international development and plays the cello.